Computer Supported Cooperative Work

T0139971

Computer Supported Cooperative Work's synergistic combination of computing science/software engineering with a range of theoretical and applied human sciences has made it one of the most exciting areas of everyday computer use. The Computer Supported Cooperative Work (CSCW) series provides an overview of current knowledge, research and debate for designers, users and students. Each volume in the series provides detailed coverage of a specific topic within CSCW and groupware.

Dave Randall, Richard Harper and
Mark Rouncefield

Fieldwork for Design

Theory and Practice

 Springer

Dave Randall
Manchester Metropolitan University, UK

Mark Rouncefield
Lancaster University, UK

Richard Harper
Socio-Digital Systems
Microsoft Research Cambridge
Cambridge, UK

British Library Cataloguing in Publication Data
A catalogue record for this book is available from the British Library

Computer Supported Cooperative Work ISSN 1431-1496
ISBN-13: 978-1-84996-647-4   e-ISBN-13: 978-1-84628-768-8

Printed on acid-free paper

© Springer-Verlag London Limited 2010

9 8 7 6 5 4 3 2 1

Springer Science+Business Media
springer.com

*To John Hughes (again) . . . as Wes Sharrock says, though there may well be
less of him that doesn't mean we think any the less of him. . . .*

Acknowledgements

First, and most important, much of the discussion in this book has been iterated through any number of tutorial versions dating back to 1992, when Dik Bentley and Dave Randall had the temerity to first produce a version for the CSCW conference in Toronto. Dik Bentley produced a large part of the argument and just as important, many of the diagrams and schedules we use here. These are still being used, often unacknowledged, by ourselves and – we note – by others. All the diagrams we use in Chapter 6 originate with him. He is a better analyst of ethnographic work than he is of test-match cricket. Mike Twidale subsequently took over the role of taming the beast and again made a significant contribution to our thoughts, notably on matters relating to evaluation.

We have to thank a huge number of people in addition to family and close friends. These people, over many years, have been instrumental in helping us refine our thoughts, challenge our own assumptions, and in teaching us how to argue politely.

They include, in no particular order:

Christine Halverson, Jonathon Grudin, Kjeld Schmidt, Peter Carstenson, Carsten Sorenson, Elihu Gerson, Liam Bannon, Bo Helgeson, Morten Peterssen, Jon O'Brien, Hans Tap, Andreas and Tobias Larsson, Yvonne Rogers, Maria Normark, Wes Sharrock, Richard Hamilton, Tom Rodden, John Hughes, Andy Crabtree, Alex Voss, Roger Slack, Jo Mackie, Karen Clarke, Terry Hemmings, Abigail Sellen, Peter Tolmie, Rob Procter, Mark Hartswood, Dave Martin, John Rooksby, Ian Sommerville, Caroline Warbrick, Simon Kelly, Marian Iszatt-White, Connor Graham, Keith Cheverst, Dan Fitton, Alan Dix, Dave Francis, Jeanette Blomberg, Alex Taylor, and Guy Dewsbury.

On a better day, we might even find time to thank each other. On the other hand, that might spoil it.

Contents

Ethnography, Fieldwork, and Design: Preliminary Remarks

1.1 Preamble

Something has gone seriously wrong. According to one estimate (quoted in 'The Business,' 31 August, 2003), as much as £75 billion may be wasted annually on IT projects in the United Kingdom (and we have no reason to believe the situation is markedly better in the United States or the rest of Europe). At the same time a number of well-publicised 'disasters'[1] have suggested that traditional methods of requirements elicitation are inadequate, or in need of supplementation, by methods better designed to bring out the socially organised character of work settings. There has been a growing (unfortunately belated) realisation that the success of design has much to do, though in complex ways, with the social context of system use. This has included the recognition that so-called 'structured design' methodologies (at least in some design contexts) carried with them some pretty naive assumptions about requirements gathering, that systems often did not confer the benefits anticipated (Grudin, 1991,1994), that, in the worst case, much design work did not result in usable products; and that the optimism of the 'new paradigm' economic view was perhaps unjustified in the light of our difficulties in identifying and measuring the productivity gains associated with some computing developments relating to white-collar work (office work and 'knowledge work' are two of the most contentious areas). Explanations for these apparent failures have included: the separation of the technical from organisation- and work-related strategies, such that technological development (and spending) became a 'black box' to other organisational interests; the confusion of 'ideal' conceptions of process with real-world activity; the belated recognition of the cooperative nature of much work, and the absence

---

[1]For example, the London Ambulance System, the Taurus System for the Stock Exchange.

of a 'user-centred' perspective on design; the research focus on small and limited work groups engaged in artificial tasks; and so on.

Attempts to rectify this situation have come from many different perspectives, including in some cases business-led strategies such as total quality management, business process re-engineering, and workflow management. Nevertheless, in the context of HCI, IS, and CSCW, it is ethnography (and its presumed merits) that has occupied most attention. Indeed, if we might be forgiven a cynical observation about the role and status of ethnography in CSCW today, it seems as if going out and doing some observational work, attaching some theoretical framework to it, and making some broad design claims is a panacea for everything that has gone wrong. Of course, no one really believes this – there is no silver bullet – but it remains the case that market penetration and user acceptance of the CSCW system has not been as high as researchers expected (Grudin, 1988; Markus and Connolly, 1990). It seems that the promise held out by the ethnography and design partnership has not yet been fully realised. If true, this merits some questioning of the relationship of ethnography to design. That is what we undertake here. What we have to say orients to a number of unresolved questions concerning some of the major themes and discussions surrounding ethnography. Answers to the questions, insofar as they are possible at all, come later.

Within sociology, ethnography has been deployed to study an array of topics. In CSCW, unsurprisingly, it has primarily focused upon the study of work and work settings for which new technology is being designed. The intention, apparently, has been to inform that design (Hughes et al., 1992; Heath and Luff, 1991,1992; Suchman, 1993). Ethnography, has gained some distinction as a fieldwork method that could contribute both to a general understanding of systems in use in a variety of contexts and to the design of distributed and shared systems (Hughes and King, 1993).

This 'turn to the social' in design, the interest in the role of social science theories and approaches in informing design, under the banner 'ethnography', arose out of dissatisfaction with existing methods of informing design as offering overly abstract and simplistic analyses of social life. If design, as a 'satisficing activity' is more of an art than a science, dealing with messy indeterminate situations and 'wicked problems' (Rittel and Webber, 1973), then before designers can solve a design problem they need to understand some basics such as what they are designing, what it should do, and who should use it and in what circumstances. It was argued that ethnography was the method attuned to gathering relevant data in real-world environments, that is, settings in which systems were likely to be used rather than in laboratories or other artificial and remote environments. The 'turn to the social' recognised a new kind of end-user, a 'realtime, real-world' human being and consequently designers turned to the social sciences to provide them with some insights, some sensitivities, to inform design. Ethnography with its emphasis on the in situ observation of interactions within their natural settings seemed eminently suited to bringing a social perspective to bear on system design.

With its emphasis on the real-world character of work settings, ethnography is often contrasted with what are commonly regarded as unrealistic and unsatisfactory notions about both systems and the users of systems that tend to be proffered by more traditional methods. Traditional methods of system design perhaps owe far too much to the traditions of engineering and, as a consequence, important aspects of the real world of work are obscured, misrepresented, or ignored. It is in this respect that approaches such as task analysis, or the assumptions of office automation, for example, were and are found wanting (Shapiro, 1994; Suchman, 1983) representing an intrusion of the engineering mentality into areas where it is inappropriate. This complaint also attacks the individualistic slant that underlies some analytic approaches by acknowledging the implications of the observation that, as already suggested, work is, typically, collaborative. Although performed by individuals, the various activities that constitute work are performed within an organised environment composed of other individuals and it is this that gives shape to the activities as real-world activities.

Just as prior methods were seen to be inadequate thus changes in the real world made the ethnographic turn seem more appealing, meshing with the now ubiquitous use of information technologies within everyday life. As computers increasingly, and seemingly inexorably, are adopted and diffused into the world of work and organisation – and equally into domestic and public arenas – there is a growing awareness that the ubiquitous nature of networked and distributed computing poses new problems for design, requiring the development and deployment of methods that analyse the collaborative social character of work. Systems are used within populated environments that are, whatever technological characteristics they may have, social in character and thus the intent to design distributed and shared systems means that this social dimension has to be taken into account. Requirements elicitation has to be informed by an analysis of the real-world circumstances of work and its organisation (Goguen, 1993). The virtue of ethnographic approaches then, comes from this recognition that computers are enmeshed into a system of working as instruments incorporated in highly particular ways (used, misused, modified, circumvented, rejected) into the flow of work. One of the virtues of ethnography lies in revealing these myriad usages in the context of real-world work settings; furthermore being (Button and King, 1992).

> ... more capable than most methods of highlighting those 'human factors' which most closely pertain to system usage, factors which are not always just about good interface design but include training, ease of use in work, contexts full of contingencies which are not the remit of system design ... even though design may be concerned with developing a completely

new system, understanding the context, the people, the skills they possess are all important matters for designers to reflect upon.

The advantages of using ethnographic methods in CSCW for studying work, lie in the way it promotes the real-world character and context of work; in the opportunity it provides to ensure system design resonates with the circumstances of its use. In attempting not only to document or describe activities but also in accounting for them ethnography seeks to answer what might be regarded as an essential CSCW question as to what to automate and what to leave to human skill and experience. Ethnographic methods thereby assist in the delineation of work design 'problems' through providing greater knowledge of the social organisation of work, the recognition that 'problems' need to be placed (and resolved) within the context of the work setting and not some abstract model of the work process.

At the same time, ethnography is not, and, indeed, does not claim to be, a methodological panacea, although (perhaps fortunately) many of the critiques applied to it are directed at sociological, as opposed to ethnomethodological, variants of ethnography. In practical terms, and historically, ethnography has generally been limited to small-scale, well-defined, and usually quite confined contexts (the 'village', the 'cockfight', the 'racetrack', the 'control room') well suited to the observational techniques employed. Similarly, in small-scale settings there tends to be a clear focus of attention for the participants, who are typically few in number, and for whom there is a relatively clearly visible differentiation of tasks at a single work site.

Scaling such inquiries up to the organisational level or to processes distributed in time and space is a much more daunting prospect. Consequently, problems can arise with the method's application to large-scale, highly distributed organisations (but see Harper et al. (2000)). In a similar vein, historically ethnography has been a prolonged activity and whilst 'quick and dirty' approaches have been developed, the timescales involved in ethnographic research are often unrealistic in a commercial setting where the pressure is typically for 'results yesterday'. Moving out of the research setting into a more commercial one also raises different sets of ethical responsibilities as well as making access to sites more vulnerable to the contingencies of the commercial and industrial world. Ethnography insists that its enquiries should be conducted in a nondisruptive and non-interventionist manner, principles that can be compromised given that much of the motivation for IT is to reorganise work and, as part of this, often seek to displace labour. These kinds of 'problems' are real practical problems and as such range in their importance from massive obstructions to the business of doing fieldwork down to the petty irritation involved in having to write more than one letter in order to gain access.

The ethnographic turn, then, has had a strong recent influence on system design. Some commentators, indeed, have described this way of looking at design problems as a new paradigm, in which the analysis and description of cooperative behaviour becomes a central plank for design. (See, for instance, Hughes et al. (1992), Schmidt (1991)). If so, then methods for acquiring knowledge about cooperative behaviour become important. A central presumption has indeed been that the methods in question must be qualitatively distinct from those which preceded the ethnographic 'turn'. That is, of course, why ethnography has become a sine qua non for the design of so-called cooperative systems and indeed for many other design-related activities. Ethnography had what appeared to be a number of merits, including that it was associated with disciplines – sociology and anthropology – which had not previously been given a chance to fail in the design context. Thus they were worth a try. Not for the first time, the hype surrounding a new 'method' in the early 1990s was such that people were tempted to forget Brooks' (1987) injunction that there is 'No Silver Bullet.'

As with all radical changes in perspective, the initial rush to adopt is often followed by more critical reflection. It became clear that some fundamental issues needed addressing. CSCW and its cognates have arguably been effective in providing a critique of systems design, in raising a series of difficult to answer questions, but less adept at producing solutions. It has brought to centre stage the notion that the design, use, and evaluation of computer systems cannot be done without serious attention being given to organisational and work context but has been less successful in explaining exactly how that translates into firstly good investigative and secondly good design practice. The recognition of a new problematic, in other words, is not the same thing as agreement about how to solve its problems.

While CSCW research was drawing heavily on fieldwork data, it was at exactly the same time marshalling perspectives from a range of different disciplines in its examination of groups and computer support for group working. These include sociology, psychology, anthropology, and organisational studies, in addition to the traditional complement of disciplines informing HCI. Furthermore, as with so many areas in which the social sciences are implicated, it contains any number of competing candidate approaches, theories, perspectives, and analytic strategies within each discipline. For CSCW practitioners, there seems little doubt that the successful and directed interchange and development of ideas across these different disciplines will be essential to the future of both CSCW and IT development in general.

In light of the above, it is obvious that there is as yet no basic agreement about how that is to be done. Several questions remain, questions which this book seeks to address. These include general questions about analytic relevance, the mechanics of data capture, and the relationship between ethnography and other 'methods'. We orient to this by seeking throughout the book to answer five more specific questions:

1.1.1 What Is Fieldwork, and Is Ethnography a Special Kind of Fieldwork?

Here, we have in mind some obvious differences of 'sensibility' between researchers brought up in a variety of analytic traditions. In some traditions, such as anthropology and sociology, we are led to believe that ethnography is a skilled enterprise requiring substantial training and a sophisticated pre-existing conceptual grasp. It carries, in short, methodological rather than merely methodical commitments. In a second version it is a simpler and more natural form of data collection which acts as a corrective to omissions in other data collection methods. Put simply, it is just a method with some technical problems. In a third version, and one which we try to promote, the important problems ethnographers have to deal with are problems pertaining to sensibility. That is, they have to do with elusive issues of how we (as ethnographers) tend to see things and how we, in turn, relate them to how other people tend to see things.

All three versions point to some interesting and important issues. Some, however, are more important than others. We suggest that overemphasis on the first version can lead to a somewhat fetishistic relationship between theory and data collection, one that is neither necessary nor particularly useful in the interdisciplinary context. Furthermore, we hold to the view that data collection itself is a relatively straightforward matter and that most technical issues are easily resolved. We do, however, hold strongly to the view that the sensibilities associated with various kinds of analysis might be critical to the ethnographic project, and that these sensibilities ultimately derive from a combination of our disciplinary origins and our interdisciplinary interests. The difficulty lies in marrying the two. How do we pursue the enquiries which we undertake – enquiries which depend heavily on our disciplinary sensibilities – in such a way that they are design-relevant? We further argue in this vein that design relevance has no determinate form but is something that itself must evolve in and through disciplinary cooperation.

1.1.2 Where Does One Start or Is a View from Nowhere Acceptable?

This is a way of asking about the nature and importance of fieldwork 'descriptions'. Here, we have in mind another path-steering exercise, in this instance between an insistence on starting afresh with each enquiry, letting the data 'speak for themselves' on each occasion with an indifference to organised concepts and formal theories, and an alternative that uses concepts and theories in a highly organised and deterministic way. Of course, CSCW (influenced by ethnomethodological work) has made much of 'context' and one way of reading context is to assert and celebrate the uniqueness of every event. There is, of course, a sense in which every event is unique, just as there is a sense in which each event is pretty much like others. It seems clear that, for design purposes, understanding the richness of the situation and the contingencies that make it what it is has added value. At the same time, it sometimes seems as if this kind of empirical/analytic orientation might replace more theoretically driven work.

In the end, in our view, this comes down to a different emphasis on the importance of similarities and differences. The battleground has been the 'concept' and its relationship to data (or evidence) and theory. For some, theoretical relationships define concepts that in turn drive enquiry. In contrast, we suggest, in line with some classic sociologies (associated with, for instance, Glaser and Strauss (1967)) that concepts should be used as 'illuminating' devices and that the process of building concepts is linked to empirical enquiry in some complex ways. Here, the critical issue is one of generalisation and generalisation, moreover, to design-relevant purposes. Our perspective is that much of the argument concerning the relevance or otherwise of theory is based on entrenched positions associated with disciplines. Thus and for instance, much of ethnomethodology's argument about theory is predicated on its own difficult relationship with many forms of sociological theorising.

We argue that taking interdisciplinarity seriously means forgetting entrenched disciplinary positions (much easier said than done, as the authors guiltily acknowledge). There is nothing in ethnomethodology, for example, that is opposed to the principle of generalisation. Everything, we feel, hangs on what kinds of generalisation and for what purpose. Much of what we do later in the book is geared towards 'illuminating' categories that we hope do some rather tentative generalising work. Forgetting disciplinary wars does not, however, mean forgetting the sensibilities acquired through disciplinary study, for they are what allow sociologists, psychologists, and even ethnomethodologists to claim to be providing a unique insight. We expand on this theme at various points because we feel it is central to our interests.

1.1.3 What Is Done When One Does 'Fieldwork'?

This has to do with the degree to which problems of ethnographic enquiry are technical problems and hence whether it makes sense to think of ethnography as a 'method'. Here, we discuss some of the practical issues that surround ethnographic enquiry and try to demystify many of them. As we have already implied, the discussion of method can be a tiresome business. What to us appear to be largely commonsense matters are treated in textbooks as methodological injunctions. Again, we should be clear on the difference between 'method' and 'methodology'. Only the latter contains all the analytic and possibly theoretical choices we might make (and thus is what makes ethnography something distinct from the more generic category of fieldwork). The former simply concerns the practical steps we take. We suggest that dealing with the 'methodical' elements of fieldwork is not particularly difficult. For the most part, agonies concerning the 'right' or 'wrong' way to do fieldwork are confined to those who are new to the business. Old hands, for the most part, just get on with it. Much of what we discuss later, then, has to do with reassurance.

1.1.4 How Does One Decide What and Who Might Be the Appropriate Subjects of an Enquiry?

When designers speak of a design space there must be a corollary in terms of choices about which human beings might be relevant to the design problems under consideration, and in which contexts. This is associated, in some admittedly vague ways, with the problems of culture and organisation alluded to above. Our point is that real and difficult choices have to be made about the relevance of different contexts when ethnographers (or their bosses) decide who and what they intend to study. Where in the past this was a largely simple matter when ethnographic enquiries were limited to control room settings (and may still be a simple matter in some forms of enquiry such as, for instance, those pertaining to domestic life), it is much less so today when the remit is larger and more complex.

It may include, for instance, work in complex organisational settings, where one might find a wide range of professional skills, competencies, relevant rules and procedures, parallel hierarchies, and so on. Medical work would be an example of this. Sometimes we might be engaged in studies which encompass more than one organisation, as with coordination work across supply chains. We might be embarking on studies which are supposed to relate to applications for vaguely understood and barely existing technologies such as 3G telephony, and so on. That is, we might be in a situation where not only is an application searching for a use, it might even be searching for a domain in which it might be used. This kind of problem raises a whole set of issues which relate to the size, scope, and intensity of any given enquiry, along with the degree of comparison required, evaluative function, critical function, and so on. It ought to be apparent that such matters as the level of detail required of ethnographic enquiry also depend on the kind of relationship it has with a proposed design space. It is surprising to find that, apart from Hughes et al.'s (1994) seminal paper on 'Moving Out of the Control Room' (which we discuss later), which posited four basic modes of ethnographic work, little has been said on this subject.

1.1.5 How Do We Orient to Ethnographic Data Either During Feedback Processes or Subsequent to the Fieldwork?

Again, this covers a range of somewhat intractable problems. This includes whether fieldwork is a sole individual's (or small group's) unique task within a complex division of labour where others do the design work. If so, how data are represented to others and equally crucially, when data are of major importance. How, for instance, are design insights based on field-work data agreed, tested, and iterated? Do they need to be? We argue that the answers to these kinds of question are themselves contextual: there are no general solutions to the problem of relating ethnographic enquiry to design. It will depend on the many and varied possible uses to which ethnography can be put, the kinds of design team in which the data are to be examined and used, the scale of the project in question, the relationship of ethnography to other methodologies which might be in use, and so on.

Part of this has to do with what is usually held to be a (somewhat vexed) problem of representation. We argue that it may be helpful to think of it in other ways. In other words, we feel there is a tendency to think of the prob-lem of representation as being a product of incommensurability between different kinds of research paradigm. Although there may be some truth in this, it may be more useful to treat these problems as more prosaic problems of timeliness and relevance.

1.2 Overview of the Book

This book attempts to provide some answers to these and other questions. We discuss the various perspectives on work and organisational context that are commonplace in CSCW research with the specific intention of relating them to the practice of fieldwork, and especially the kind of field-work normally glossed as 'ethnography'. The aim is to provide a working knowledge of the use of ethnography and its relationship with the theories that inform systems development. The book is organised into three broad and interrelated sections.

In 'Part 1: Theoretical and Analytic Issues' we try to flesh out the nature of the sociological sensibility and how it relates to the conduct of ethno-graphy – to answer, that is, the first of our questions – 'what is fieldwork?' We follow this with brief descriptions of some of the most influential perspectives and theories associated with ethnography. The point here is to identify what it is that people mean when they talk about the 'social'. What is often understated is the way in which theoretical and analytic choices link in with the way we collect and 'see' data. Data, as sociolo-gists are wont to argue, ad nauseam, are 'theoretically laden'. Therefore, in principle, the theoretical devices chosen to formulate research questions, and to organise results, matter. Exactly how they matter, however, has evident consequences for the 'view from nowhere' or 'innocent enquiry' or 'indifference' associated with ethnomethodological stances.

Of course, along with theoretical choice, actually deciding how to go about the business of conducting fieldwork, the practical business, is equally important. In 'Part 2: The State of Play' we point to some known problems and some ways of dealing with them. We should stress here that we are not trying to provide a programmatic account. We do not believe in the 'one best way', but we perhaps believe that there are some very bad ways. Problems to be dealt with and techniques for performing 'good' ethnography, then, are highlighted, but not with a view to proselytising. We should stress that the very fact that there can be such a thing as 'good' and 'bad' work means that there are pitfalls to be overcome, but these pitfalls pose no intellectual difficulty. They are not, in other words, especially technical. For the most part, they are dealt with by the confidence that comes from experience.

We draw heavily on the practical experiences of the authors in ethnographic work undertaken in commercial and academic contexts, outlining lessons learned from that experience. In particular, several examples are given from data which have been collected under the auspices of a range of projects conducted at Lancaster University, the University of Surrey, Manchester Metropolitan University, and from various consultancy and business exercises.

The main theme of this book can be summed up as, 'all the issues are analytic issues.' In the first two sections, we discuss a range of problems which, although real, are considerably less important than those of trying to work out what data mean, how they are relevant to a set of design problems, and so on. It complicates matters that the issues in question have hardly been resolved and remain highly contested. They have to do with the questions we have raised above and with one other question in particular. What exactly is it that ethnography can contribute to design? It is always possible to find both similarities and differences between one environment and another. Much of the debate between competing theoretical perspectives and those, like ethnomethodology, that are (incorrectly) viewed as antitheoretical comes down to the appropriateness of particular categories for the kind of research question or investigative problem with which one is confronted.

In 'Part 3: Some Perspectives,' we continue to emphasise the point that, rather than generalisation being the issue, the question is, and always should be, that of what kinds of generalisation and for what purpose. In this section we use data from a variety of studies of organisations to indicate the possible role of general and illuminating categories in helping the enquirer formulate a research direction. The value or otherwise of these categories, however, we assert, depends on what the ethnographer is trying to do in relation to what kind of design problem. For some kinds of work, we attempt to show, they might not in the first instance be very useful at all. Some of the areas we deal with were, until recently, less familiar to CSCW researchers. They include various public and domestic environments. We argue that the kinds of generalisation that prove to be informative here are what Schutz (1972) called commonsense typifications. They are a valuable resource for subsequent analytic work. Our aim, in any event, is to provide some nuance. Our point here is that one can provide some kind of picture of the local order of work as well as provide broadbrush analytic work for comparison purposes, if that is what is sought. It is all a question of purpose. The value of each, it seems to us, is to be determined by interdisciplinary outcomes not disciplinary squabbles. It is not about what theoretical prejudice is being pandered to but about what kind of design outcome is sought.

Part 1
Theoretical and Analytic Issues

The State of Play

2

Progress is marked less by a perfection of consensus than by a refinement of debate.

Clifford Geertz (1973)

Much of what is sailing under the name of sociology is a swindle.

(Reputedly said by Max Weber)

Given that the central theme of this book is the application of ethnographic stances to design problems, it might appear that the quintessentially sociological issues that trouble social scientists in standard texts on ethnography and, indeed, elsewhere are not worthy of consideration here. For the most part, we are in agreement with this sentiment insofar as we are impatient, sometimes downright rude, about this tendency towards *'nombrilisme'*[2] in sociology. Having said that, Kenneth Burke (1935) pointed many years ago to 'occupational psychosis' (borrowing from Dewey): that tendency to see and understand everything through the occupational or intellectual concerns of one's own chosen professional and disciplinary viewpoint, and there may be some truth in the idea that some of the problems involved in interdisciplinary working stem from occupational psychosis. If so, it would seem to have a direct relationship with problems of 'communication' and 'understanding'. It may well turn out to be what occludes the 'sensibility' of which we speak. In any event, our interests in this chapter lie in the origins of this sociological sensibility and its relationship, in outline, to design issues.

We are, of course, merely setting out a stall as to what ethnography, as a fieldwork method, might offer CSCW. Fieldwork of one kind or another has been around for almost a century now, and has been a key component of

---

[2]This is the French for 'navel-gazing'. Because we do, in fact, discuss some of these inward-looking issues of reflexivity and other sociological issues here, we thought a certain pretension would set the right tone.

design-related research for longer than we imagine; certainly some kind of fieldwork has been endemic in Scandinavian work science, German industrial sociology, Tavistock school social psychology in the United Kingdom, the francophone 'cognitive ergonomics' tradition,[3] and so on at least since the 1960s and in some instances earlier. Not least, of course, cognitive science has always had some tradition of fieldwork and this has been consistently present, if not always to the fore, in areas such as human factors research and its cognate, HCI. If so, we need to ask ourselves what our version of fieldwork (as typically practiced in CSCW) has to offer that was not already there. It would be bizarre, to say the least, in a context where new technology (often of a radical kind) is our main interest, if we were to reinvent the wheel. This point exemplifies our main concern, which is the analytic auspices of the fieldwork we do, a form of fieldwork that we, and others down the years, have called 'ethnography'. These auspices pertain not to sociology but to design.

Whatever our view, ethnography remains contested. This is firstly on the basis of its theoretical auspices, where proponents of ethnomethodologically informed ethnography grapple with those who prefer distributed cognition, who in turn attempt to establish the value of their perspective as against, say, activity theory and vice versa. In the meantime, various other theoretical commitments are inserted while no one is looking, such as actor-network theory (Callon, 1986a; Latour, 1987; Law and Hassard, 1999) and structuration theory (Giddens, 1984), arguably long after they have reached the limits of their fashionability in sociology. The functions of ethnography, or what it can be expected to achieve in practice, are equally contested. Not only has it been hyped to such a degree at times that one (nonsensically) might almost consider it a fully fledged replacement for requirements analysis, it has also been promoted as a solution to all the moral ills of the design process and a means for 'critical' reflection on the theory and politics of design. It has been, conversely, critically received because it takes too long, offers only snapshots (and of 'current practice' at that), and it seems is so bereft of theory that we are in desperate need of some general theoretical concepts which will allow us to make sense of more than one immediate context. Above all, in the light of what has already been stated, its relationship to more formal, idealised, or 'businesslike' models has also been puzzled over. In sum, why it has becoming increasingly promoted in systems design in the past decade or so requires some elaboration.

---

[3]Vicente (1999) notes that although the use of fieldwork is sometimes thought to be new, in fact it is old within the ergonomics community, and indeed the descriptive approach has a long history in what is called francophone 'cognitive ergonomics', where phenomenological descriptions have long been a stock in trade. (For an overview in English see De Keyser (1991).)

2.1 Disciplinary Assumptions, Fieldwork, and Ethnography

Here then, we want to sketch out the range of perspectives on fieldwork and the set of historical transformations that have led to the version of it which we call ethnography. We do so by caricaturing two stances at extreme ends of a continuum. One we call antianthropology (or antisociology), and this would be the stance that would typically concern fieldwork rather than ethnography. On this side, we have a position which holds that fieldwork is merely the observation of people in their natural contexts, and requires no particular analytical acumen or expertise. It is, for the most part, just a case of watching and gathering data and thus can be done by anyone. This same position is somewhat more concerned with the tools that enable observational materials to be transformed into theoretical or design insight by, for instance, providing models, and with the tools that enable teams of individuals with different skills – interface designers being one group for example, work process people another – to agree on design and systems implementation choices to be driven by fieldwork data. In this position, then, fieldwork is easy and requires little training; transforming data into design is hard and does require tools, theoretical expertise, and practice.

The other end of the scale is exemplified in the anthropological (and to a lesser extent, sociological) tradition, where being able to do fieldwork equals being able to do ethnography. Here, doing ethnographic fieldwork depends upon years of prior training into the mechanics of data gathering and into forms of exposition and 'account telling' (or 'narrative' as it is more often put). Key to the nature of ethnographic fieldwork, and the processes of documenting that work, are how the topics and themes of generations of prior ethnographers are referred to and invoked. That fieldworkers needed to be familiar with prior work and understand the cargo of knowledge that ethnographic practice had built up in that tradition went without saying.[4] From this view, ethnographers do what they do, are interested in the things that interest them, and communicate with designers as required to establish a design relevance, but design work itself would be separate from the business of narrative construction.

Obviously, we see ourselves as being situated at the ethnographic end of this rhetorically convenient continuum, but with some major reservations which have to do with the intellectual history of anthropology and sociology. Our reservations are twofold. Firstly, we are uncomfortable with the professional status given to 'method', by which we mean issues of notetaking, indexing, and interviews against observation. Secondly, we are uncomfortable with the status of theoretical or perspectival claims which

---

[4]Epistemic revisions mean the themes invoked may be, as with some postmodern reportage, in a rather mocking way.

emanate from specific social and human sciences but are applied, largely unchanged, in interdisciplinary contexts.

The perspectival or paradigmatic issues raised by interdisciplinary working are important. They are key to understanding, for instance, the power of Suchman's (1987) work. The persuasiveness of the various theoretical positions we sketch below depends on an understanding of the distinction between approaches which stress some notion of human conduct as being inescapably bound up in context, locality, situation, and sensemaking (and which imply methods founded variously on a hermeneutic, on interpretation, or on just plain common sense)[5] and those which are founded on rationalistic, calculative, or computational models of human conduct and which carry with them 'scientific' assumptions about appropriate method. For this reason, we emphasise, at least to an extent, a third variant: the so-called ethnomethodological tradition. This position, for some, puts us at the ethnography end of this scale. In fact, although we believe in something called ethnography rather than simply fieldwork, we are impatient with much of the sociologising of method and theory that we see around us. We want to treat fieldwork as an ordinary and mundane business which requires neither sophisticated skills nor years of training. We suggest, indeed state openly, on several occasions that 'going out and looking' is easy.

> The important skills are mobilised back in the office (although not only there). They are analytic skills and are predicated on a sensibility or way of looking.

Sensibility can sometimes seem in short supply. We believe we learn much from a sociological sensibility, but much less from sociology's specific interests. The view that we develop in this book entails building on and expanding our perspective so that broadly ethnomethodological insights might be used in conjunction with models, processes, tools, and ideas from other traditions and perspectives, as one of many tools in the toolkit. Of course, and as stated, these positions are caricatures. There has arguably always been far too much posturing about positions taken in opposition to one's own and we do not wish to be accused of that. We have pointed out that there is a tradition of fieldwork which owes nothing to sociology at all and it is worth examining, briefly, what kinds of assumption are entailed in this work. We can illustrate this by briefly referring to Vicente's (1999) book, *Cognitive Work Analysis*.

---

[5] Again, interdiscipliary practitioners will have had to suffer, at some point, the ethnomethodologist who insists that what is going on in a particular setting is not a matter of interpretation either for the people working in that setting, or for the person observing it. This is because the term 'interpretation' carries with it, at least when being used in a technical sense, the implication that cognitive work has to be done in order to understand any social setting. This is a strong paradigmatic claim, unlike one which says that cognitive work may sometimes be done in settings that are in some way problematic.

2.1.1 Cognitive Work Analysis

Vicente represents the human factors perspective in a way that highlights a particular view of the need for fieldwork, the nature of doing fieldwork, and the role fieldwork plays in a larger scheme of design. He describes a method specifically suited for highly complex sociotechnical systems where the nature of design solutions might not be easily iterated and where there is a need, because of the task being supported, to get the solution right first time round. Not all human factors and ergonomics research incorporating a perspective on fieldwork entails this method, of course. Nevertheless, cognitive work analysis is a good example of how these disciplines characterise different levels of description and evidence gathered in fieldwork, distinguishing, for example, between normative and descriptive (the kinds of thing that an ethnographer would think of as his or her normal forms of evidence), and on the other hand, what Vicente calls formative or predictive models. These are the things that human factors and ergonomists want to turn data into and in which ethnographers have seemed reluctant at times to get involved.

This work seeks to develop techniques and methods that could enable the design of truly failsafe systems in extraordinarily complex environments. The concern here, as we have alluded to already, is that these complex sociotechnical systems have to be designed to work from the outset, and cannot be gradually iterated and improved. Any failure of any element in the system could be catastrophic. Therefore, there is a need, in these situations, to develop methods that could enable the specification of sociotechnical systems that are well in advance of current systems and practices. These are based on abstraction and modelling of the constraints of a sociotechnical system. The modelling captures both the human and the technical in an abstract schema that the designers can use to determine, assess, and evaluate design solutions before any eventual system is built. This preference for modelling may be taken to its extreme in cognitive work analysis but is the norm in ergonomics and human factors.

Although this preference may seem alien to those trained in ethnographic traditions, it forces us to deal with the question of prediction. If, as we show, contextual inquiry (Beyer and Holzblatt, 1998) claims that one can design new systems through close reference to the current processes and technologies used in any context, then Vicente takes a quite different view. He believes that this approach, which he calls descriptive, can only lead to incremental design improvements and although this is satisfactory for some types of settings and technologies, it is not adequate for all. In highly complex sociotechnical systems, Vicente argues that there is a need for tools which enable designers to specify sociotechnical systems that go well beyond current systems, and thus fieldwork and description of current practice can only be a part of the tools necessary.

Vicente's main goal, his mantra if you like, is summed up by Rasmussen's (in Vincente, IX) observation that,

> the pace of change has become so fast. And the need for high reliability of new systems so high, that the design of new work tools and systems cannot be based solely on empirical incremental evolution based on studies of existing work conditions. Predictive models of work behaviour become necessary, models that can serve to predict work behaviour by explicitly identifying the behaviour-shaping features of a new work environment ... we need to replace the normative and descriptive models of work analysis by formative analysis.

In sum, the approach requires understanding of the constraints that shape an environment, and these constraints are both human and technical. To get to these requires a mixture of data gathering, one of which is the task of fieldwork. Fieldwork is useful according to Vicente, because it provides evidence about how workers actually do their work and the skills that are necessary in that real work. Fieldwork data may be contrasted with data produced by studies that tend to overidealise work, especially those which use laboratory data-gathering tools alone. These Vicente calls normative.

This in turn has implications for work analysis, or, put another way, uncovering these issues enables work analysis to do the following. First, the information that workers require when dealing with the unfamiliar and unanticipated will be specified. Vicente calls these work domain skills. Then the more limited set of information required to get the right work done, irrespective of contingencies, will also be specified. These are called control tasks. The strategies used by workers to learn and adopt their work practices to the context will also be captured. These strategies can be used to design mechanisms that can replace current ones in future systems.

However, this is only part of what designers need to do their work. Vicente claims that these topics only describe or capture what he calls the current 'workaround processes' designed to achieve certain functional ends. These functional ends are also captured by the descriptive analysis. But, to consider what alternative ways of doing the work might be requires a leap beyond what these descriptive resources allow.

There are a number of reasons for these limits, and he seeks to prove the existence of these limits by showing how ways of dealing with them fail. First he explains how rapid or iterative prototyping or scenario-based design invalidates descriptive analysis. He explains this by referring to what he calls the 'artifact task cycle'. According to Vicente, if one introduces a new artefact into a domain (an artefact could be a new computer system), this automatically alters the way work is done and thus invalidates any prior descriptions of the work. Thus the use of rapid prototyping and design iteration, or even a scenario-based approach to exploring what the future might hold is not a solution to peeling away what the future might be, he contends,

inasmuch as these techniques serve only to invalidate the description used to produce the scenarios or prototypes in the first place. Introducing these things, that is to say, results in the description always being one step behind itself.

A second problem has to do with what he calls incompleteness in rapid prototyping. Iterative design prototypes never offer complete solutions, he says, instead offering only partial solutions for bits of the overall process. This means that the overall ecology of the desired sociotechnical system is never prototyped. By not looking at the overall ecology the designer not only fails to understand the full interrelatedness of the ecology but might even be distracted by the specifics of a prototype at the expense of the totality. It leads to a piecemeal approach to design.

The solution to these limits and problems, he argues, is to model all of the constraints on a system, be they human, informational, cultural, or technical. By model is meant an abstract representation of the functions of various elements which in turn allow designers to assess and explore the interrelationship among these different elements and among different solutions to satisfying the needs within each element. These elements he has already defined, and they are the classes above: starting with domain skills, then control tasks, strategies, social, organizational, and so on.

Each of these can be represented as a list of requirements and then possible solutions to satisficing them. Each is placed within a frame provided by the subsequent stage. This reflects what he calls a move from the ecological, related to the work domain and its local features, through to the cognitive, which relate to worker competencies, what an individual can be realistically (cognitively) expected to do. The important point is that the data from the descriptive analysis is to be used to populate these elements or stages, but the stages themselves are universally applicable, and the ways in which they interrelate and are subject to one another in hierarchical order is also universal. By placing the descriptive data within this framing the analyst can transcend the limits of that data and do predictive design.

But to do this, Vicente argues, the descriptive analysis should be used as a resource for the greater task of 'peeling away' current practices to specify 'intrinsic work constraints.' These are the things that are fundamental to the work and have to be treated as given in the design of any new sociotechnical system. Unfortunately, descriptive analysis is not capable of doing this alone.

Now, as should be clear, Vicente represents a perspective that is very sympathetic to the descriptive approaches exemplified by ethnographic inquiry. At the same time he is clear that there are limits to this form of analysis, and these mainly have to do with the gap between descriptions of current practice and the design of new systems which may alter those practices. There are a number of issues that we could raise, but what we want to take from his discussions at the moment, however, primarily has to do with the role and function and auspices of fieldwork.

Cognitive work analysis has, we think, three main threads:

- It sees fieldwork as a descriptive rather than analytic process, and thus in need of remedy (e.g., through modelling).
- It offers fieldwork as an element in a systematic process that leads to generic design.
- It attempts to overcome the gap between descriptions of current events and design for the future.

This approach has one deeply serious challenge to the ethnographic community, particular those who insist on description above all else. It states unequivocally that description is not enough, and that it must be supplemented with some systematic analytic work. It thus incorporates 'work' in the way that various CSCW practitioners have been advocating, but argues that the problem in systems design is not to gather data or to understand and describe work practice. It is to reduce the work practice descriptions to abstract models that can then enable, in turn, even more abstract models of the sociotechnical systems. Leaving aside the question of modelling for the moment, actually undertaking fieldwork, getting to understand the relevant aspects of human action and relatedly the role of technology in that setting, is neglected in the discussion. Now of course it could be that Vicente chooses to neglect the issue of how to do fieldwork as an editorial necessity; after all his book is about more than fieldwork. But we pick up on this because we think that this is rather more typical of the attitude of human factors and ergonomics to fieldwork as against a more sociological treatment.

Our reason for discussing this work is specifically to show that cognitive work can indeed show the same sensitivity to context, contingency, complexity, and skill that we advocate, and without any of the specifically sociological training demanded at the other extreme. Cognitive ergonomics, human factors, and so on are not deluded as to the nature of work practice and may well seek to avoid overidealising it. What is curious, however, is the treatment of 'description'. It is as though description were an undemanding, self-evident set of procedures in which the world 'out there' simply has to be represented on a canvas. Our point is that this is true only if one accepts certain kinds of analytic commitment, and in particular a commitment to seeing the world through the eyes of those who inhabit it. The objectivist view avoids the very questions about what one might look for to which we have alluded. After all is it certain or clear what, say, a work skill or a control task might be? Can a fieldworker simply go and gather data about them and if so, where should he go? How are these to be distinguished, described, and clarified? All of these questions, it seems to us, need to be dealt with before the modelling starts.

2.2 Sociological Method, Sensibility, and Analytic Stance

One central theme that has exercised and continues to exercise the social scientific ethnographer is its status as a method. Some flavour of this is gleaned from the vast literature available (for those interested, one can trace various kinds of methodological reflection and the evolution of 'how to do it' manuals by looking at any number of texts, for example, Adams and Preiss (1960), McCall and Simmons (1969), Filstead (1970), Habenstein (1970), Wax (1971), Lofland (1976), Burgess (1982), Hammersley and Atkinson (1983), Bryman (1988), Ackroyd and Hughes (1992), Brewer (2000), Silverman (2000,2001), Schensul and Schensul (1999), Schensul et al., (1999), and Hine (2000). This emphasis can be traced back almost a century.

When Sir James Fraser's (1993) huge work, *The Golden Bough*, was first published, in 1922 it was in twelve volumes. It purported to be a theoretical examination of the roles of myth, magic, and religion throughout human society. Unfortunately, Fraser's grand anthropological scheme foundered on the simple fact that he, like Emile Durkheim (who was also interested in religion), had not actually investigated empirically any of the cultures from which he drew his conclusions. Ethnography was thus a remedy for the failings of this theoretical approach. During the first half of the twentieth century immensely influential ethnographies were published which detailed a number of 'strange tales of faraway places', including Malinowski (1922,1929,1935; see also Malinowski (1967)). From the 1920s onwards, a second motivating force for ethnographic research was also being established.

The Chicago School, as it was known, (because it was based mainly in the department of sociology at the University of Chicago), became famous for its use of fieldwork methods. This was to be found notably in the work of Park and Burgess (1921), Park et al. (1925), and Park (1952) on the social ecology of the city, Thomas and Znaniecki[6] (1927) on immigration and social disorganization, and Shaw (1930,1931) on delinquency. We need not concern ourselves too much with the themes of these studies, because they are quintessentially sociological. We can and should, however, point to some of their methodological implications. First, Chicago school theorists were fundamentally concerned with the problematic relationship between the subjective and the objective. Thomas, famous for his deliberations on the 'definition of the situation,' was engaged in challenging dominant psychological views of the nature of motivation at that time. More specifically, he was concerned with distinguishing 'values', which he thought were objectively and institutionally given from 'attitudes', which he thought were subjective. This, of course, carried with it the implication that sociology had to be concerned with both the analysis of causal relations and of subjective experience.

---

[6]We should not exaggerate the commitment to ethnography here. Chicago school sociologists were eclectic in their methods. Thomas and Znaniecki, for example, were heavily reliant on diary material.

Even at this early stage, then, ethnography entailed no 'purist' commitments and could go hand in hand with general theoretical laws. Robert Park, in a similar vein, made much of the distinction between nomothetic and ideographic study. The former is basically study which aims to generalise and the latter is more straightforwardly historical and concrete. Ideographic study is what we associate with ethnography, of course, and Park's by now well-known and much reported injunction to 'go and get the seat of your pants dirty' reinforces that idea (quoted in Hammersley and Atkinson (1983)). Park was recommending a 'social ecology', whereby ways of exploring urban sites could be found which were analogous to the psychologist's laboratory. He suggested that our task is primarily the analysis of experience and argued in effect that individual experiences could be collected and compared in a way that had much in common with biological classification. We pick up on the notion of 'ecology' at a later stage.

It was really with the work of Herbert Blumer that naturalistic enquiry became more rigorously counterposed to other methods. Blumer's famous (1940,1954,1956) 'critique of variable analysis' was a savage attack on the hypothetico-deductive model in sociology. In other words, Blumer was an early critic of the notion of sociology as a science. In his 1940 paper he makes the case against variable analysis by comparing sociology/social psychology with science. He points out that the scientific approach to quantitative analysis is not statistical, and that consequent scientific laws are universal, not probabilistic. Furthermore, the statistical methods associated with social psychology give us no adequate measures for how things change.

Lastly, he suggests that such statistical relationships presume a behaviouristic model of human conduct (i.e. leave no room for the analysis of human experience). Blumer subsequently extended his critique (1954,1956) by arguing that variable analytic sociology does not succeed in its objectives because it fails to provide precise, unambiguous, and clear concepts.[7] Indeed, he rejects the idea that there can be any definitive concepts in sociology at all. That is, Blumer is the first to point out that social science concepts involve an inevitable element of judgement.

This argument has had a profound effect. It has led critical sociology, for instance, to explicitly embrace its values, the feminist epistemologists to consider how being a woman can affect one's knowledge of the world, and the ethnomethodologists to argue that sociology's project should be limited

---

[7]Basically, his argument is that variable analysis cannot do what it sets out to do because it is predicated on the view that we can safely ignore any ordinary or 'pre-scientific' interpretations of the world on which our more rigorous concepts may be based. That is, variable analysis trades on the assumption that any 'interpretation' that goes on has no relationship to the construction of rigourous concepts. Blumer in contrast believes that commonsense interpretation is fundamental to our procedures and that the concepts we habitually use in sociology are saturated with commonsense usage. In other words, Blumer is denying the existence of a neutral descriptive language for sociological purposes.

to careful description and, at best, commonsense generalisation. Even contemporary 'realist' sociologists (who believe that the causal nature of the world is independent of our perceptions of it) have accepted that cause and effect in sociology has a moral component (see Sayer (1992)).

'Naturalistic sociology', for Blumer, must 'respect the world' rather than lurching into explanation long before it has adequate description. In other words, it involves the world as it actually is, rather than substituting a shorthand for it. As Matza (1969) later pointed out, such a commitment requires methods which can maintain loyalty to the world but does not, in itself, presuppose any particular methodological procedures. This is important, for it suggests that one of the problems with sociology is that it is too obsessed with method, and raises the possibility that interdisciplinary research can be the victim of the same overmethodical approach. What looks like a set of tools for doing research might be replaced by a simple recommendation to go out and look at the world, and then think carefully about what you've seen in order to represent it in a way that reflects how ordinary people experience it. We have a certain sympathy for this viewpoint in that our own view of method is an impatient one.

Of course, for interdisciplinary working the problem lies in the terms under which this apparently simple business of going out and looking should take place. Blumer insists (1969) that through processes of 'exploration' and 'inspection', one can provide detailed descriptions of events and patterns of activity, and thus speak from fact rather than speculation. The point here, to reiterate, is that any technique, including observation, interviews, life histories, the study of official and personal documents, and even 'counting' might turn out to be appropriate.

It is as well to remember this, for it forestalls naive questions concerning whether one is 'allowed' to do certain things when undertaking ethnographic work. It, for instance, opens a space for 'inspection'. Inspection, or thinking about what you've got, requires us to develop sensitizing or illuminating concepts. This is an important, if underused, notion in sociology. It refers to the difference between concepts which identify those things that classes of object have in common (definitive concepts) and those that just give the user a general sense of reference, a way of helping decide what to look for and organising your thoughts. The important thing about sensitising concepts is that they can develop and change as the course of study is refined.

Thus, two themes begin to emerge from this tradition. First, ethnography can be viewed as a method that remedies the faults of other methods, and hence training of some kind is critical to the success of the ethnographer. Second, ethnography is analytically distinctive; the task of the ethnographer is akin to a cataloguing of experience. These two emphases are variously present in work on the role of ethnography today and we can discern the first, in particular, in well-known treatments such as that of contextual design (Beyer and Holzblatt, 1998).

2.2.1 Contextual Design

Beyer and Holzblatt report on the development of a practice that has much to do with a need to ensure the usefulness of systems as it does with usability, and has been developed on the basis of considerable familiarity with academic discourse about ethnography (particularly the ethnomethodologically informed variety), although the intellectual auspices of their work are not always apparent, presumably because of their intended audience. Their book is clearly intended as a hands-on practical guide to integrating ethnographic work into the system design problematic. It is intended to be used as a reference guide, a book of rules of thumb and maxims of conduct for practitioners in many industrial settings. In part the success of the book on both counts has to do with how it lays out some of the practical tools and techniques that need to be used in any design process in ways that can be easily understood by students. For industrial settings, it offers guidance for how individual workers might do their own tasks as well as how they might cooperate with fellow workers, making numerous suggestions about how to enable the data gathered by individuals to be made sense of by the group as a whole, and this includes the use of Post-it notes, whiteboard diagrams, and so on.

Contextual design makes it clear that fieldwork is nearly always only an element of a larger process that entails multiple individuals and, moreover, that fieldwork in design itself is nearly always a multiperson activity. This has consequences on how data are gathered, shared, and analysed. In more traditional approaches to ethnography, the task of fieldwork is typically a solitary one, and fieldworkers have sole responsibility for writing up their data (which might go some way towards explaining the postmodern obsession with narrative). In contrast, the multiperson data gathering mechanisms of contextual inquiry are largely oriented to producing a coherent and demonstratively evidence-based perspective on the actions and needs of users that anyone on the project would recognise and to which they would agree. Indeed, ensuring this shared view is one of the sought-after goals of the methods of contextual inquiry. It is also something that we believe is a prerequisite of good practice in fieldwork for design.

Contextual inquiry treats fieldwork as only one part, the first, in a three-step set of actions: fieldwork, design, and implementation. And as a consequence of this, what fieldwork entails, how it is organized and documented, is always construed in reference to the larger purpose at hand. There is no sense in which fieldwork can be done by, let us say, one individual or team and then handed over to the next team who undertake subsequent tasks. Although there is a clear distinction between the skills used at different points in a contextual inquiry – interface design in particular having an especial role – the process of undertaking fieldwork is structured from the outset around the needs of design and the practical process of implementation.

Focusing more particularly on fieldwork, contextual inquiry treats it as a task that can be done without reference to any particular body of theory or narrative of fieldwork reportage. What we are thinking of here is to contrast contextual design with the idea that ethnography, as one take on fieldwork, exists as part of a tradition that has built up certain ideas, theories, and concepts which in turn have some value when referred to and invoked in any new study. This is what makes ethnography distinct from fieldwork.

At first glance, straightforward fieldwork would seem to be the sole concern of contextual design, in that the main emphasis is certainly on the practical skills necessary in the field. Nevertheless, in our opinion, there are certain assumptions about the nature of fieldwork that underscore the use of the practical skills built into their work, and which Beyer and Holtzblatt are keen to justify. These, we would suggest, are the output of the ethnographic tradition and in particular ethnomethodological inquiries. But Beyer and Holzblatt do not dress up these assumptions in histories of their use and importance in prior research, nor do they consider what competing assumptions could be deployed, and what is good and bad about each. Instead, they present these assumptions 'as is' and simply justify them, admittedly in a very disarming way.

For example, they point out that one of the problems fieldworkers have is to try to get their minds around the huge amount of data that can be gathered. Beyer and Holzblatt say that this begs the question of what is relevant, what is useful, what is too much, and what is too little. Certainly, they note that everyone is easily persuaded that having a look at the context in which a system is to be introduced is necessary, but the trouble is, they ask, what is it that one is to look for and what is it that one should take away? They claim (Beyer and Holzblatt, 1998, p. 4):

> The trick is to give (fieldworkers) tools that let them see the breadth of the data with out being overwhelmed; to see the common structure and pattern with out losing variation, and to understand the wealth of details with out losing track of its meaning.

So far so good, but Beyer and Holtzblatt then start bringing in some lessons from prior research, particularly so-called work practice research in the ethnomethodological tradition. They explain that the central problems of knowing what to look for and what to disregard, what is too much detail and too little, what is the patterning that needs to be sought, and what is too broad and varied, has to do with two things: the first has to do with the nature of descriptions; the second has to do with the skills, most especially the tacit skills, used in real everyday contexts. They explain that there is a subtle relationship between descriptions of work and the work as it is done in situ. This has to do with a variation on the old argument about situated action and descriptions of that action.

According to this view, descriptions are always reductive in one way or another. Having users describe their work, getting those who live in the context in question to account for what they do, is not sufficient for good design inasmuch as something might be left out by those descriptions. In this view, ethnography is clearly remedial. Beyer and Holtzblatt draw attention to the potentially limited, somehow incomplete, descriptions offered by subjects and treat the firsthand knowledge of the fieldworker as a compensation for that failure. The prospect that ethnographic data might in some way, for some purposes, be incomplete, does not seem to occur.

Beyer and Holtzblatt think, secondly, that the fieldworker should take on board the 'tacit' nature of many workplace skills. Skill deployed in the work being observed often becomes, Beyer and Holtzblatt note, invisible to the subjects themselves. These tacit invisible skills have to do with the things that people have to undertake to get to the work tasks on which they consciously focus. Oftentimes when a clerk, for instance, is asked to describe his work, even if he could more or less provide a good description, he may well fail to mention parts of his work, judging them to be irrelevant or related to a routine trouble that no one needs to know about especially if solving these troubles means breaches of the rules. Beyer and Holtzblatt see the failure of certain methods, notably interviews, as endemic in certain approaches to understanding users. Instead, they want the fieldworker to assume that part of work – any work, whatever it is that is being investigated for the purposes of design – is not easily articulated, even by those who are deeply experienced in it. There is a need, therefore, for a different approach, one that makes direct observation more important, one where watching is as necessary as listening, where mixtures of accounts and descriptions are used alongside other evidence to construct an understanding of the work itself that is greater than the indexical expressions used when the work is done. It is thus that Beyer and Holtzblatt get to the need for fieldwork. So, and in sum, the purpose of fieldwork, then, is as follows.

- To be able to articulate the unarticulated and tacit knowledge used in that work
- To make low-level details that have become invisible and habitual into visible materials that can be considered in design decision making
- To get to the work structure

We do not mean to imply here Beyer and Holzblatt underspecify analysis, for that is evidently not the case. They speak explicitly of a 'language of description'. Watching, occasionally listening, making notes, and so forth are not sufficient, they insist, to do good fieldwork. They argue that this 'language' is necessary so that the actions under observation can be coherently and systematically structured. This language, for them, combines textual descriptions and diagrammatic representations along five different

dimensions. These have been selected, we are told, on the basis of what has turned out to be important over years of fieldwork and design. They are

- The flow of work
- The sequencing of work
- The role of artefacts in the work
- The nature of culture in the workplace
- The physical space in which work occurs

For the most part, these seem eminently sensible ways of thinking about some issues that arise in working life, hardly surprising inasmuch as suggestions about tacit knowledge, artefacts, the flow of work, and so on have variously been on the table for anything between ten and fifty years- and we use similar constructions ourselves later, albeit with a slightly different emphasis. We do, however, want to point to one or two rather problematic usages because they reflect precisely the absence of a sociological sensibility of the kind with which we are dealing.

Firstly, this has to do with the term 'culture'. Culture is perhaps the most ambiguously articulated concept in Beyer and Holtzblatt's exposition, and it is described as consisting in attitudes towards customers, hierarchy, and decision making. Culture here means how organisations who are in the same business might nonetheless undertake their work in a distinct manner. This is, we might note, a somewhat superficial take, and moreover one which is hardly in keeping with a rigorously observational stance, because attitudes and values can be seen as mental constructs. The point here is that 'culture' itself is a highly contested term and one which has been subjected to a wide range of definitions. Indeed, the distinctiveness of say, ethnomethodological work, can be seen, ultimately, as a particular take on culture in much the way, as we show, that Peter Winch recommends. Culture, in this view, is no more or less than what people knowingly do.

Secondly, and similarly, other concepts could be unpacked further, particularly some of those that ethnomethodologists have highlighted. Within the flow of work concept, for example, one of the topics that Beyer and Holtzblatt identify has to do with individual responsibilities. Anderson et al. (1989) have made much in their work of the importance of the individual and his or her relationship to others within a working division of labour. They coin the term 'egological' as a label for how one might analyse work processes in terms of the intersection of the perspectives of individuals constituted by their knowledge of a particular division of labour. This concept is valuable for drawing attention precisely to the way in which individual tasks are melded with orientations to, understandings of, noticings of, and so on, the work that other people have done or are doing.

Nevertheless, our words are not meant to be critical. Beyer and Holzblatt make a significant contribution, predicated on a huge amount of empirical work both on their part and on the part of others, and from which they draw their arguments. Moreover, they are perhaps the first to take the problem of 'design teams' seriously. They very sensibly concern themselves with how, having gathered data, the next step is data consolidation. They note that many of the detailed ways in which people get their work done, details that enable them to get their work done in particular and often rather unique circumstances, are not necessarily required for design. There is a fundamental difference they suggest, between designing what are called point solutions for the specific ways in which a particular individual works, and designing a generic system that can be useful in a set of users across an organisation.

Consolidation occurs in step-by-step fashion as follows. First, once a large number of interviews and observations have been completed, each researcher presents her data to her colleagues in what are called interpretation sessions. Here, the common properties of the work start being teased out and topics clarified. Sometimes the need for further interviews and observations also becomes clear when a researcher begins to see that her understanding of the work does not seem as complete as some of her colleagues'. Once this entire cycle of researching is done, the next step is to use graphical tools to create models of the systemic properties of work across the subject set. This is called an *affinity analysis*. Here, the key stages and elements in the observed work are labelled and presented as Post-it notes on a large wall. Those stages and elements that seem similar or even identical are physically placed near one another and gradually a map of the main features of the work emerges. An affinity analysis is done for all five dimensions of work: flow, sequence, artefact, culture, and space.

The outputs of these sessions are then used in design sessions. Here the goal is to develop designs that can deal with the complexity conveyed in the affinity analysis: a complexity that cannot be modelled as if it were merely a workflow representational task. Instead it is better thought of as a case of designing processes and supporting tools that can enable anyone to comprehend the task at hand given all the ways in which those tasks are typically completed. Necessarily, of course, part of evolving and developing a design solution will entail mapping the balance between human action and technological support, between space and artefact, between workflow and sequencing of work, and so on. It may also mean identifying areas of work that seem unnecessary and redundant. When contentious issues arise, such as apparent redundancy in a work task, the possibility of that redundancy is considered carefully and this often involves revisiting observed subjects and even getting subjects to participate in design iteration sessions.

In other words, Beyer and Holtzblatt argue that a design team will always consist of various specialities and experts, but that the work of design is not a serially organised event with fieldwork being task one and, let us say, interface design task two. It is rather that the data from the fieldwork, the insights they provide, become the basis for all activities, referred to at an early stage in the work but then not forgotten, being referred to again and again and indeed sometimes even being revisited.

In contextual inquiry, fieldwork is then partly iterative and deeply bound to the overall process of design. It is thus also endemically bound up with the goals and purposes of design and is not a separate task or skill that produces a freestanding object, a description of work practices that is handed over to designers and then forgotten. Fieldwork data, or rather the analysis and consolidated representations of fieldwork observations, the descriptions of the work in question, the ways it is sequenced, flows, is supported by space and artefacts; all these concerns are specifically oriented with the purpose and needs of design in mind. Even when the researcher starts to interview, his goals, the concepts that he has at hand, the tools he will use to transform fieldnotes and other materials such as transcripts into usable evidence, all are driven by and bound up with the purposes of design. For Beyer and Holtzblatt there is then no separation between looking at the work, observing the work, describing and analysing the work, and designing that work.

We want to highlight four important aspects of contextual enquiry and try to clarify our own reactions to them. The first has to do with the assumption that fieldwork can be done without a sociological sensibility, as long as the fieldworker is aware of certain key assumptions about the limits of description, the need to observe work in situ, and the need to ensure that analysis captures the ways in which the complexity of any work task is handled in a day-by-day, routine way. We, in our turn, and as already stated, do not believe that collecting data requires anything more than the most mundane of skills, and agree wholeheartedly with their implicit conclusion that analysis is fundamental to the ethnographic project.

In the ethnographic tradition as practiced by sociologists and anthropologists, researchers are expected to be familiar with prior research and indeed are expected to invoke this research in their own work, even if it is by way of pointing out the contrasts. Whether ethnography can be done without reference to previous traditions, practices, concepts, and so on, it would seem to matter whether the ethnographer-to-be has some sense of what to look for and how to look at it.

At root, the problem is what sociologists refer to as 'reification', which has to do with making concepts 'thinglike'. We can treat concepts as 'things' which we can more or less take from the shelf and apply to the specific circumstances of our enquiry (and we see many examples of people doing so), or we can make use of concepts in the way that Blumer (ibid.) suggests. We unequivocally take the side of the latter. Good ethnographies, we think, are those in which the way of looking and its results, however represented, will show not only the use of a set of concepts but will also demonstrate the existence of an ethnographic imagination at work. If not, the business of doing good ethnography can be reduced to that of following some rules. We have reviewed too many papers, shaken our heads, and sighed too many times at too many conferences to believe that for one second.

The second distinct element of contextual inquiry that we want to mark out has to do with how it entails teamwork both in the field and thereafter in the design process. According to Beyer and Holtzblatt, this means that interview and observational data gathered by individuals need to be reconciled against data gathered by others. This distinguishes contextual inquiry from traditional ethnography, where there is very little if any research addressing this particular problem. For mainstream ethnographers, fieldwork is essentially a task of solitary individuals. Now, these are clearly proposals. They are suggestions concerning how good design might be done where generic software properties are to be uncovered by ethnographic research. The proposals in question seem solid, if largely unremarkable. However, in our view, this is to significantly limit the remit of ethnographic enquiry in relation to design and we have a lot to say about this later. The assumption that ethnography and design can and should be closely linked at all is a somewhat problematic one and we want to point out that even if it were the case that ethnographic insights seldom resulted in clear design requirements this would not invalidate the ethnographic project because the results of ethnographic enquiry can, in principle, be used in a large number of different ways.

A third issue has to do with the insistence within contextual inquiry on being data-driven. This may seem to be an odd issue to highlight. After all, what fieldwork does not produce evidence and what is it for if not to produce evidence-based insights? But what contextual inquiry highlights is how evidence needs to be shared, tested, and reconsidered by everyone in the design team. That is, the assumption in contextual design is that the fieldwork data the contextual inquiry produces intrinsically address design issues. As we have seen, design is constantly present in the task of gathering fieldwork data in contextual inquiry, as it is also in data analysis and in considerations of design options once fieldwork has been completed. This is, we think, an important and contentious claim. It is rarely dealt with adequately, in our minds at least, in many other perspectives and contrasts directly with the 'over the wall' approach which lays out some more or less rigid demarcations between ethnographer and designer, thus preserving professional expertise and implying strict limits to responsibility in either camp. For a variety of reasons we are not entirely happy with either position and once again we return to the issue at various points.

In sum, contextual design is important in at least three ways:

- It sees ethnography in the interdisciplinary process as being saturated with design problems from the outset.

- It sees the advantages of ethnography as being to do with its status as a method and form of analysis.
- It lays out a programme for working with designers.

2.3 The Third Variant: Ethnomethodological Indifference

In 1958, Peter Winch's seminal book, *The Idea of a Social Science*, was published. Winch's book was enormously influential in sociology, and prompted an ongoing debate concerning 'reflexivity'. Winch followed Wittgenstein, and applied his arguments concerning the nature of philosophy to the problem of sociological theory and method. Winch's concerns are the degree to which an empirical investigation of the social world is possible, and what it means to analyse and understand a society. He is adamant that the natural sciences do not constitute a model for the social sciences because aping the former relies on confusions between empirical and conceptual issues. That is, mere data collection in the social sciences is not and cannot be the objective, neutral, fact-gathering it purports to be because our very reality is constructed out of the way we think of facts, and the words we use to describe them. In particular, he argues that 'To ask whether reality is intelligible is to ask about the relation between thought and reality.'

Because thinking, in this view, arises out of language use, we cannot consider the nature of thought without considering the nature of language. In turn, to use language is to act in the world and because we speak in different ways in different contexts, then we must analyse 'understanding' contextually. The problems of philosophy and the social sciences, if they arise out of language, must therefore involve what counts as being in the world. Whatever aspect of a culture we investigate, and indeed whatever culture we investigate, understanding how meaning is arrived at must be our method. Understanding, for instance, what scientists do or what religious belief consists in is, in both instances, a matter of understanding how they make sense to each other. Winch suggests, borrowing from Wittgenstein, that to make sense of social relations is to understand social behaviour as rule-following behaviour.

This argument, of course, is of profound importance because it has a close relationship with ethnomethodology and with Suchman's (1987) argument about plans. This is because arguments about 'plans' or 'situatedness' depend on what we mean when we talk about rules. Winch argues that understanding how someone is following a rule firstly requires us to understand not only how the individual takes action in a sensible way, but also to take into consideration what the reactions of others are. In other words, the rules are achieved out of the sense of the meanings individuals attach to their actions and the way in which others come to understand what is being done as meaningful. They are bound up with cultures, traditions, plans and procedures, and so on, and thus we sociologists understand them only in and through our familiarity with what is typically done in certain contexts. Understanding what the rules of conduct are, then, must be a matter of understanding how these rules are exhibited in a social setting.

A second feature of rules as they apply to social life is that they exist only in the sense that we act typically. One cannot separate the rule from its application. Hence, as Wittgenstein put it, 'What has to be accepted, the given is – so one could say – forms of life.' We do not do what we do because there are rules (in a causal sense), rather there are rules because we do what we do. All behaviour which we can call rule-governed must by definition be meaningful behaviour. We cannot say someone is following a rule unless they know what counts as behaving in accordance with a rule.

What this means is that rules cannot be applied independently of judgements about their applicability. Activities are things about which we could sensibly say they have a meaning. This has to do with inferring motive and purpose. This is a subtle point and needs analysis; motives and purposes cannot be presumed from mental states, nor can they be equivalent to causes. What goes on in the head is not observable. Neither can we derive the rule which is apparently in operation just by introspection (i.e. thinking about it); we must derive it at least in part from our experience of the world in which the rules apply. Rule following and meaningful activity are, then, the same thing. It would be a mistake to think that this means we cannot break a rule, or make a mistake about a rule, because of course we can. Activities cannot be summed up by precepts (rules about rules). Rules are not recipes which we follow slavishly; neither are they 'rationalist' principles. They cannot be causal in the social world, for they are in their nature normative. (Searle (1995) makes a similar point about institutional 'facts'.)[8]

The importance of all this for CSCW-related work has to do with the kind of analytic procedure it recommends. Sociology's task, in this variant, is to elucidate the concepts which actors use: how actors define the contexts in which they find themselves. Sociology, in a nutshell, can map activities and concepts, or as Wittgenstein put it, identify and explore the 'language games' which are being played. Understanding motive and purpose is the relevant business of sociology, but motive and purpose cannot exist independently of our knowledge of social context. The task of the ethnographer, then, is to understand context in such a way that we can identify the rules which are in place and how people decide on their applicability; understand why people do what they do, and identify the social contexts which make them meaningful things to do. The ethnographer cannot do any of these things without familiarity with cultural activity. This is why we referred

---

[8]Winch allows that we do, of course, use a vocabulary of cause when we speak of motives. For example, 'I wonder why he did that?' (see also Burke (1945)) but denies the causal status of 'motives' in any strict scientific sense.

above to the problem of 'culture', because for Winch there is no thing as culture; there are only activities.[9]

Winch's argument, difficult and contested though it is, has a relevance to fieldwork in design communities, for it has implications for our understanding of regularities. Regularities are constant recurrences of the same thing, and as such would appear to be evidence of structures or institutions in a culture. There is nothing wrong in principle with identifying regularities, but Winch makes the point that ethnographers who simply describe various activities as being 'examples' of a particular thing are missing the point. The problem is precisely what counts as the same thing and what warrant we might have for so deciding. This position informs ethnographic work of the kind exemplified by, for instance, Andy Crabtree's (2003), *Designing Collaborative Systems*.

2.3.1 Designing Collaborative Systems

Crabtree's book is distinguished by its resolute insistence on an ethnomethodological stance in ethnographic work, a view common in the CSCW literature but underrepresented elsewhere. Such work often, implicitly and explicitly, criticises cognitive science both for the 'scientistic' errors Winch (and Wittgenstein) accuses it of and for the conceptual confusions inherent in the rush to generalisation about regularity. Broadly speaking, *Designing Collaborative Systems* consists of a set of fieldwork-based investigations of how people in workplaces deal with the endemic contingencies of working routines, contingencies, and incidents which result in people 'working at' and 'achieving' what they construe as the goals of that work. According to this view, the purpose of fieldwork is to capture what these contingencies might be and to document the ways in which they are solved.

Ethnomethodological studies of work would seem primarily empirical rather than theoretical, and thus at first glance well suited to delivering materials for design. Indeed, this very claim – albeit oversimplified here – is made often in the CSCW literature, by ourselves amongst others. But it should not, we feel, be made uncritically nor should the empirical focus of ethnomethodological studies mislead CSCW practitioners into thinking that studies of work are merely empirical. Ethnomethodological studies of work are empirical in a specific and contrastive sense. They deal in the 'facts' of the social world in a way that is quite distinct from what sociology has typically done, and do not produce theories of the type that sociology

---

[9]Note also that, for Winch, motive and purpose are legitimate problems for sociology to deal with, but they have to be dealt with through our reasoning about social context. By and large, ethnomethodologists agree with Winch about this. It is simply not the case, as Nardi (1996b) has suggested, that ethnomethodology (or 'situated action theory' to use her neologism) has no account of motive.

normally does. Put simply, for good or ill, ethnomethodology has often been measured against sociology at large. Of course, in design-related contexts, ethnomethodology's relationship to sociology is wholly irrelevant. Designers would be quite entitled to ask, 'Who cares?'

The problem here is, as postmodern sociologists like to emphasise ad nauseam, descriptions are potentially infinite. One can choose to describe any event or situation in any number of ways. We need, in other words, to figure out how our work can be made empirically relevant in the sense of what may be understood as such from the perspective of designers and system engineers, and not from the interests of sociology, whilst retaining whatever it is that makes sociological ways of thinking interesting. The ethnomethodological solution is to insist on the description of members' meaningful actions, their 'lived experience,' to the exclusion of the more constructive kind of analysis to be found in sociology at large. Hence, when we read the condemnations of the 'cognitivism' and 'scientism' (that obscure the 'actualities of work') that characterise Crabtree's book we need to decide whether such critiques are relevant only to ethnomethodology's unremittingly hostile relationship to both sociology and psychology, or to the specific problems of design work.

Now, we have made similar claims ourselves at various times and can hardly complain about this partisan line. At the same time, there is something very important at stake here. This is that those of us who practice something like ethnomethodological work in an interdisciplinary context need to justify the particular advantage involved in doing our work ethnomethodologically. In other words, we need to be able to state, and state reasonably clearly, what we get from our ethnomethodological commitments that we cannot get elsewhere, and which enriches and refreshes design. It is worth reminding ourselves that the likes of Vicente (ibid.), who come from a cognitive tradition, can be equally critical of studies that idealise or overly schematise work, that overly emphasise the formal over the informal, that focus on the standard procedures rather than the more flexible, and fail to capture the skills, techniques, and processes that are actually entailed.

Crabtree recommends, in line with standard ethnomethodological positions, quite finely detailed descriptions of particular aspects of work. These aspects to be focused on, he argues, are not to be selected by the researcher who might wish to simply look or record and thus capture what she thinks is relevant; it is rather that the practical concerns of the participants in the setting should be used to guide what the researcher should look at. This sounds fairly straightforward, and for the most part, it is.

Where Beyer and Holtszblatt make specific, and strong, suggestions about analytic themes, Crabtree does not. In taking a resolutely ethnomethodological view, he wants to emphasise the way in which any analyst can see what is out there in respect of the fact that a commitment to understanding the members' world as they understand it is what is primarily required. This is done by a number of devices familiar to ethnomethodo-logists, and includes notions of 'vulgar competence', '*lebenswelt* pairs', 'unique adequacy', and so on. This sounds rather opaque, and for the individual unfamiliar with ethnomethodological language, rather intimidating, but Crabtree tries to show how this pans out in terms of three kinds of explanatory materials that need to be presented when doing design.

The first has to do with the ordinary meaning of what is said by those studied, those 'endogenous' formulations as he puts it. The researcher should trap these or in some other way capture them.

The second is to describe the relevant nonverbal actions of those persons, particularly those material resources used in work. Little guidance is given as to what these might be, although presumably whatever the members treat as relevant and as an important resource in their work, should be captured or at least described by the fieldworker.

The third is to describe the work in terms of its sequential organisation and 'component events'. By this he means the moment-by-moment series of actions that are linked to each other as in a chain. The most obvious example of this is turn-taking in conversation, but as Crabtree points out, quite rightly, we should remember that this is only one form of sequential organisation.

Fieldwork, then, consists of assembled instances of work. Any material could be gathered to do this, whether it be tape recordings or video, fieldwork notebooks, articles, or objects from the field. The ordering, cataloguing, and analysis of the material has to be determined by the context itself. To do otherwise, Crabtree warns, is to produce a version of 'constructivist' explanation. What needs to be done instead, is to look at how the 'vague descriptions' of the subjects are transformed into 'tailored descriptions' (p. 73). This is a kind of filtering work and how it is done needs to be understood. Doing so will lead to what he calls, following Ryle, a thick description of 'members formulations as they are hear-ably produced and recognised *in situ* by the parties to their production' (p. 73).

The relevance of the assembled data to design has to be established in some way. Crabtree argues (pp. 94–95),

> It might be said that those who contested ownership of the problem were right to do so only in the sense that ethnographers rarely possess the necessary technical competence to formulate design solutions on their own....This does not rule out a constructive role for ethnography in the formulation of design solutions. Adopting any such role will require that ethnographers move beyond 'imparting knowledge' to directly inform the construction of design solutions in collaboration with the other parties to systems development....If ethnography cannot actively and constructively support system development in the reorganization of work through technology design rather than run for cover, then it has no business in the field. While rightly leaving the actual production of design solutions to designers, ethnographers are nevertheless obliged to assume a constructive role

if their craft is to be of any lasting utility. This means that the ethnographer will have to rid themself of disciplinary baggage and become a bricoleur in design practice.

He goes on to discuss some methods by which this might be done, including using viewpoints analysis (Kotonya and Sommerville, 1992) and subsequently, the coherence model (Viller and Sommerville, 1997) and argues that these models sidestep the problem of communication in the design process. He also rehearses air traffic control material in order to demonstrate the way in which designers could misunderstand the import of, for instance, analysis of the functionalities of flight strips as 'found' data. He is kinder to pattern languages (Alexander, 1977,1979), admittedly in an adapted form. This analytic device might, at some stage, provide a lingua franca for design, through analysis of 'commonsense typifications'. He further discusses aspects of scenario-based design, use case modeling, and so on in terms of how workplace study can contribute to design as a form of co-construction. Similarly, ethnography has an evaluative role to play through its emphasis on situated evaluation or through a relationship with participatory design.

From this perspective:

- Ethnography is a descriptive and analytic process that needs no remedy.
- The appropriate analytic stance is rigorously ethnomethodological, emphasising finely detailed, processual/sequential analysis.
- The ethnographer has the role of *bricoleur* in relation to design.

There is a danger here, although not one specific to ethnomethodological enquiry. It is that readers can presume that there are relevant empirical facts simply waiting to be uncovered. Where Crabtree suggests that ethnomethodological fieldwork produces free-standing objects – the descriptions – that are handed over to the design community, this can be read (mistakenly) as suggesting that there is no particular issue with what kind of description is at stake as long as it is in keeping with the above ethnomethodological injunctions. This will work fine, we feel, in known settings with known technological relevance. Quite how it is to be applied in situations where we have only the sketchiest understanding of technological possibility and of the domains in which innovation might apply, we do not know. Deciding on a programme of ethnographic work, in this situation, will require rather more than an ethnomethodological determination to render the phenomenon for the simple reason that figuring out which phenomena will be relevant phenomena will be far from straightforward.

Given our own research record, we might be expected to be sympathetic to Crabtree's formulations, and of course we are. Nevertheless, we want during the course of our own exegesis to ask a few questions about the relationship between ethnomethodological studies of work and the design problem. That is, we are interested in the specific context of design-related work, and in interrogating some of ethnomethodology's assumptions in this area. No one would assert, we assume, that ethnomethodology has all the answers. At the same time, it does seem to us to be important to discuss which answers, and to which questions, ethnomethodology might provide. Moreover, we feel that it is equally important to try to understand what relationship ethnomethodology might have with other perspectives. This is because there are a host of as yet unresolved questions about what ethnomethodology can do in relation to the design of what kinds of thing and in what kinds of design community.

Where, for instance, Beyer and Holzblatt suggest that organisational culture is a relevant matter for designers, ethnomethodologists tend in the design context to be quiet about matters of culture, wider organisational context, and so on. There are good reasons for this: ethnomethodology has been (for good reason) negative about anthropological conceptions of culture and about formal and informal conceptions of the organisation. We need, then, to discuss whether ethnography and the ethnographer need concepts of culture and organisation and, if so, what kinds of conceptions they might be. We also, in our opinion, need a much more nuanced view of ethnography's relationship to design. Crabtree uses, as do many others, Hughes et al.'s (1994) 'Moving Out of the Control Room' paper as a basis for his discussions. So do we. We, however, argue that the four functions of ethnographic enquiry they suggest are nowhere near adequate for describing the range of possible inputs into the design process, for it will depend ultimately on what kind of design process we are talking about, and it is increasingly evident that there may be many different kinds.

2.4 Morals and Metaphors

A further turn in the ethnographic project dates from the publication of Howard Becker's famous paper, 'Whose Side Are We On?' (1967) Becker's work was very much associated with an ethnographic approach to the study of crime and deviance, and he was one of the first sociologists to identify the way in which deviance can be a 'social construction'. That is, that what is deviant is to some extent at least a matter of definitions by more powerful people such as the police, social workers, and the courts. This became known as labelling theory and within it the task of an ethnographic sociology in this context, then, was to explain what it is like for the people so labelled. Crucially, for Becker, this entailed an ethnographic stance where one knew where one's sympathies lay.

This can be argued in two ways. For Becker, sympathy for the underdog was a necessary result of ethnographic enquiry because, failing completely cynical use of the groups in question, it would be impossible to fit in without the required empathy/sympathy. Becker was not suggesting that we should explicitly take sides before we undertake investigations, rather that when one adopts the ethnographic stance one inevitably gets involves in a sympathetic consideration of their viewpoint. One could not, in Becker's view, understand their world unless one did this. In a nutshell, ethnography involves seeing things from the point of view of the participants through a moral/political lens.

'Seeing things from the point of view of participants' takes on a rather different cast yet again, however, when we take a brief look at explicitly 'standpoint' epistemologies. In these, Becker's inevitability is embraced from the outset. Readers will be quick to see a relationship between this initial position and the subsequent stances rehearsed by Marxists, feminists, and, in the design community, participatory design.[10] If we may characterise this move in a rather broadbrush way, we might call it standpointism, after standpoint feminism. Standpoint ethnography by definition refutes any possibility of neutral or objective stance in ethnography. Hence (Edles, 2002, p. 145):

> "The questions were political, epistemological and methodological"; who gets to say what about whom, and why? What are the interests and motivations behind alleged ethnographic "realism".

Some feminists have defended the idea that there can be and is a distinctive feminist methodology, characterized in part by its commitments. It must be recognised that there are a number of different versions of feminist epistemology, and indeed some doubts have been expressed whether a distinctively feminist method is possible at all. Sandra Harding (1986,1987,1991; Harding and Merrill 1983), for one, believes that the methods feminists adopt are not to any degree distinct, but their methodology is. There is, she argues, something distinctive going on, in that feminism implies rather more than 'adding women' to an orthodox analysis. Standpointism, then, rejects the possibility of a neutral description and analysis and embraces political purpose. For interdisciplinary work, this raises the prospect that ethnographies should recognise such matters as power, interest, and commitment. It places the enquirer 'in the same critical plane' as the subject. Rather than the

---

[10]In passing, one obvious problem with this basic view is that it makes a presumption about the nature of the relationship between the 'underdog/class' and those who label them. For some, Becker is confusing 'understanding all' with 'forgiving all', suggesting they are indeed the same thing whereas they are not. For others, the problem is that Becker misses the point about why there are underdogs. In other words, his interactionist viewpoint tells us nothing about the structure of power relations in society, which in turn might explain why the police, courts, and so on do the labelling that they do. A third, and rather more incidental argument for sociology, which has seldom troubled itself with such problems, is that sometimes it is rather difficult to judge who the underdog is. Hunter Thompson's classic book (1966), *Hells Angels*, for instance, shows considerable sympathetic understanding of a community of people the rest of us might not view as underdogs at all.

researcher being faceless, researchers place themselves alongside the subject by identifying their own class/race/gender position.[11]

Now, not for the first time we suspect, HCI and CSCW practitioners at this point will be wondering what, if anything, this excursion into standpoint epistemology has to do with design. The simple answer is to invite the reader to substitute the word, 'users' for the word 'women' at every point. When we do so, we see that standpoint epistemologies are pretty much what underpin approaches to design such as participatory design, and this is our reason for raising the issue. Nevertheless, there are some difficulties with such an analysis. As we show, developments in Participative Design (PD) are very much concerned with how we answer such questions when we apply standpointism to the user.[12]

This debate opens up a space, as we soon show, for the most radical of the intellectual positions that can be associated with ethnography, and the one that is most distinguished from the view that ethnography is just about collecting the facts, for in this (postmodern) view, facticity itself is under scrutiny. Postmodern ethnographies are often described as relativistic (whether strongly so or not) because they challenge the idea of the ethnographer's authority, and particularly the view that the ethnographer is involved in truth telling. In other words, ethnographic work is to be regarded as just telling a story, and only one among many possible stories; notions of truth are fundamentally problematised for there is no cultural 'whole' behind the ethnographic story.

James Clifford (1988), a proponent of this view, argues that the ethnographic narrative which sought to convince an audience that data were 'objectively acquired' has been overtaken by a new formulation, one which at least in part, takes cultural relativism seriously (see also Clifford and Marcus, (1986). Part of this, says Clifford, involved the play between the value of experience and of interpretation and, he says, increasing emphasis was placed on the second of these two because experience is difficult to articulate and our claims in respect of it naive (at its worst it is dishonest;

---

[11]In contrast, Clifford Geertz (1973) questions whether, 'seeing things from the point of view of the actor' needs to be seen as a moral commitment at all. Geertz makes reference to a famous incident in the history of anthropology – the publication of Malinowski's (1967) diaries. With Malinowski, what became clear was that despite his sympathy/empathy for the native in his published work on the Trobriand Islanders, he was in fact a rather nasty individual who disliked the natives he was studying, thought them 'primitive', and generally wished he were somewhere else. The point is that a cornerstone of the ethnographic imagination has always been the notion that we put ourselves 'in the place of the native,' suspending our critical views, biases, and what have you. Malinowski clearly did not do that. Geertz asks whether this means that Malinowski's general conclusions are unjustified, and for him the answer is unequivocally, not at all. Ethnographers can and must be capable of transcending experience. They do this in and through reflexivity.

[12]Standpointism has subsequently widened its remit. Ethnography has, for instance, been accused of promoting a colonialist attitude (Said, 1978), telling us more about the researchers, and their (usually his) attitudes, than the cultures they purport to describe.

see Freeman (1999) for a discussion of Margaret Mead's anthropology. See also Cote (1994) and Murray (1990)).

The claim to interpretation is equally suspect. In entering a foreign culture precisely what is missing is the commonness of cultural background that is the foundation of Weber's '*Verstehen*' and hence that became what had to be recovered. In other words, the ethnographic task became, in part, that of discovering a common language in its widest sense. It suggests a cumulative and deepening knowledge of the culture in question. Clifford doubts whether any such claim can be maintained. This attack has been influential in the production of postmodern ethnography, in which the role of, and status of, the ethnographer becomes part of the topic of the ethnographer. Put simply, the dialogue between ethnographer and subject is scrutinised.

Again, nonsociological readers must be in a state of some agony at this point, and for once we can only sympathise with their pain, for it is hard to see what it is exactly that matters in postmodern accounts, other than the prospect of intellectual *nombrillisme*. One consequence, however, has been a growth of 'insider' ethnographies, whereby familiarity with a culture is a given, providing ethnographies which are empowered and restricted in unique ways and this does have some significant ramifications. The choice between insiders who have prior knowledge of the field in question and outsiders who claim some neutrality is not a trivial one. One small caution that results from the postmodern perspective, and worth remembering, is that we should not represent our findings in too complete a way, for our results may not be as reliable as we would like to think, especially when we seek to generalise them precipitately.[13] In exploring the relationship between purpose and method, Marcus also explores the issue of the ethnographer as solitary individual, as a sole researcher on a voyage of observation. These voyages, like Sinbad's, produce stories. Like John Barth's (1991) postmodern version of Sinbad, however, this begs all sorts of questions about fact versus fiction in storytelling, about narrative structure and the problem of evidence in those same stories, and much more besides. By 1999, however, the crisis in anthropology led Marcus to consider new forms of ethnography which explicitly addressed the need for interdisciplinary enquiry.

---

[13]We do no justice to the subtleties of postmodern argument here. The textuality debate, for instance, has historical roots in philosophy and critical theory but has recently culminated in the 'ethnographies as texts' movement. See, for instance, Marcus and Fischer (1986) and Hammersley (1990). In one view, ethnographic writing is determined contextually, rhetorically, institutionally, generically, and historically. Moreover, these features govern how 'ethnographic fictions' are produced. In this view the notion of a naturalist ethnography that merely describes the facts of the matter should instead be regarded as, 'An insidious discursive strategy whose underlying purpose is to assert authority, dominate and maintain privilege' (Edles, 2002, p. 151). Dicks and Mason (1998) identify two aspects of postparadigm ethnographic enquiry in particular – the demarcation of ethnography's object of study and its mode of presentation – as areas of vociferous debate.

In case any interdisciplinary practitioners should find themselves seduced by postmodernism, they should be aware that it too has come under attack (see, for instance, Sharrock (1995) and Slack (2000)) and justifiably so. Nevertheless, the postmodern turn, especially in George Marcus's *Ethnography Through Thick and Thin* (1998) does point to at least one other relevant matter. Marcus insists that ethnography needs to be understood as always driven by particular analytic foci. Traditionally these have been construed by the anthropological and sociological disciplines but latterly they have been developed and imposed by other disciplines and concerns (he does not mention design). At this point, we should perhaps acknowledge that the nature of interdisciplinarity is all too seldom discussed and might be a great deal more problematic than is normally acknowledged (see Fish (1994)). 'Multisited' ethnography, for Marcus (1998) is a way forward. The erosion of anthropology's traditional interests in primitive societies and the close investigation of their particularities has been replaced, he suggests, by the need for an ethnography which recognises globalising tendencies. Marcus (ibid) suggests that multisited ethnography represents a return to comparative ethnography, but in a different way:

> ... comparison emerges from putting questions to an emergent object of study whose contours, sites and relationships are not known beforehand, but are themselves a contribution of making an account which has different, complexly connected real-world sites of investigation ....In the form of juxtapositions of phenomena that have conventionally appeared to be "worlds apart".

The crux of the matter lies in the degree to which we can think of ethnographic research for CSCW purposes as an 'emergent object of study' and the degree to which this informs what questions we are to ask, and what answers we are to seek. Marcus' notion of interdisciplarity is worlds removed from the kinds of interest we have, but we can legitimately ask what contribution multisitedness – or new forms of comparison – can make in contexts where the primary analytic concern might be (but not exclusively) the use rather than the effect of new technology, and the purposes of the kind of ethnographic analysis we provide might be the design rather than the critique of technology. Regardless, the multisited view of interdisciplinarity might at least give us pause to reflect on problems of empirical relevance, of conceptual orientation, and of the role of comparison.[14]

The questions that are entailed have not gone away: what kind of site constitutes an appropriate site for investigation? To what extent can the detailed and local results typically resulting from ethnographic enquiry produce results which are generalisable, and for what relevant purpose? Who decides, in this context, what an appropriate analytic framework looks

---

[14]See Randall et al. (2005) for an extended discussion of these themes.

like, and what should our ambitions be? The questions thus entail some engagement with the relationship between data and theory, or at least with the possibilities for relevant analytic purpose and relevant generalisation. The failure to answer these questions adequately might account for the hitherto rather disappointing set of achievements in the fields we are interested in and address the problems inherent in ethnography's move away from the co-located, 'shared goal' work associated with control rooms, professional work, office work, and even domestic life.

In other words, by looking at the problem of empirical adequacy in anthropological ethnography, Marcus highlights (and we strongly agree) that the first and primary question in fieldwork, whether it be for anthropology or any other discipline, is what the purpose behind that fieldwork might be. If one follows the line of argument then the thesis in respect of design might state:

- That design should produce its own set of concerns that will drive the fieldwork-for-design enterprise
- That it should result in certain types of styles of reporting, with particular tropes at its heart
- That it should deliver a corpus of reasoning that constitutes its essential framework

If all this holds true, then, fieldwork-for-design or ethnography-for-design will be distinct from what we find elsewhere. This takes us back to the beginning of the chapter, to the question of what is done when fieldwork is undertaken, what is looked for and ultimately how these 'seeings' and 'tellings' are rendered.

2.4.1 Issues Arising

We have tried, above, to say something about the social scientific tradition and the way it imparts a sensibility (of one kind or another) to ethnographers. We have used particular texts to demonstrate the variety of takes on the descriptive, analytic, and theoretical roles of ethnography there might be within a broad tradition. Of course, we could have chosen other texts to encompass the range of views we have in mind, but these were chosen for particular reasons. They are precisely that they broadly represent some of the differences we have outlined above, holding positions along the continuum we outlined. Thus and for instance, Vicente holds that data from the field are insufficient to design the future and Crabtree that fieldworkers should produce 'whatever it is' they find as materials for designers to use. Beyer and Holzblatt, in contrast, have a strong commitment to the idea that ethnographic output should strongly orient to design at the outset.

We suggest that all these convictions can, in some circumstances, be wrong and in others perfectly reasonable. In large part, this is for the same reasons in both cases, and they have to do with the purposes of the ethnographic enquiry, which can be many and varied.

It is our view that descriptions of any sort are always a function of the questions that have necessitated those descriptions in the first place, and really what is at stake here is who has the professional right, and at what time, to define what those purposes might be. It is quite wrong, we feel, to suggest that results can stand independent of the purposes behind them. It is not so wrong to argue that these purposes, and rights over them, may themselves be a matter of ongoing controversy.

In many ways, and perhaps here is an example of the sociological imagination at work, the situation is akin to Max Weber's discussion of values in sociology. Weber was much concerned with how, if at all, sociology might intervene to make a difference in social change. He was at pains to point out all of the problems that ensue when enquiry is 'value laden' and nonetheless argued strongly for a sociology which was 'value relevant'. We find this a useful analogy. We do not believe that ethnographers in CSCW and other design-related contexts can and should produce enquiries that stand in no relevant relationship to design: we strongly believe that ethnographic enquiry should be 'design relevant'. We would at the same time strongly resist the notion that our enquiries should be 'design laden'. Ethnographers cannot serve an underlabourer role here. They cannot ply their trade in an environment where they are pointed at a predetermined 'context', and told what to look for and how to organise the results. We argue, rather, that in being concerned with seeking out aspects of work practice with a design-relevant intent, the descriptions that result are naturally design resources; although to be really useful, or better, evocative, they require imagination.

Tacit Knowledge and Ethnographic Analysis

At this point, we want to emphasise the main issues that, for us, seem to arise from these different viewpoints. All, we feel, are important and during the course of the book we hope to establish our position vis-à-vis each of them. Beyer and Holtzblatt make much of the 'incompleteness' of interviews as data-gathering techniques. Now of course some might say that the failure of a person to describe all aspects of his work is a failure on the part of the interviewer to ensure all that is necessary is elicited, but they disagree. They say that such a failure, if that is what one wants to so label it, is endemic and a typical feature of interview-based approaches to understanding users and is thus a methodological problem.

In some respects, and although in others we are in wholesale agreement with these authors, we find this distinction mystifying. We have no doubt at all that work has its 'tacit' dimensions, but find it very hard to understand why this should be a problem of articulation for the worker. In our experience, people at work have few if any difficulties articulating their work when asked the right questions and we can see no reason why we as ethnographers should not talk to our subjects. If not, the kind of ethnography that seems to result is the 'fly on the wall', 'point a video camera at it' kind where some type of (rather spurious) objectivity is conferred on the data in virtue of the fact that they have been recorded.

We, in contrast, are of the 'when in doubt, ask a question' school of enquiry and doubt whether problems of either completeness or objectivity are of quite the kind that are implicated in contextual design. The importance of this, in our view, lies in the emphasis on method as against analysis. We, we hope, consistently argue throughout this book that issues of method turn out for the most part to be much less problematic than one might assume. That they are issues at all, we feel, comes largely from that long sociological and anthropological tradition of using a language ridden with jargon, and in particular the illusion that some sort of precise technical language will distinguish sociology from the commonsense equivalents of the layperson. Issues of sensibility, in contrast, we believe to be vitally important.

An example of the consequences of this kind of methodological/analytic discussion might be how we go about talking about the notion of 'skill', for instance, and how it might relate to an emphasis on tacit knowledge. We have to decide, for design-related purposes, whether categories such as skill are relevant, and this is a nontrivial exercise. Experienced ethnographers will know, for instance, that in pretty well all jobs of work, operators will know that, and talk about the way in which some people are better than others at what they do. In principle, of course, such matters are observable/reportable in the way that ethnomethodologists say they are.

What these skills are and how best to describe them is by no means simple, however, and a domain such as air traffic control illustrates this as well as any other. 'Skill' used in this way is, without question, an analytic construct. Put simply, our experience of working in a domain such as air traffic control was one of studying the processual character of interaction, understanding the sequential character of what they do, and the artefacts which they use in much the way that Crabtree recommends.

At the same time, however, we became interested in the way in which 'good' air traffic controllers could be distinguished from others and how we might characterise this. Now, air traffic controllers are perfectly willing to talk about matters such as what makes a good air traffic controller and did so for us on many occasions. The general picture of skill that resulted – one that we would defend as being deeply relevant to the allocation of function problem – is not, however, one that depends on an ethnomethodological form of enquiry. Any decent ethnographer, from any sociological or psychological background could, on the assumption that they take the business of doing ethnography seriously, come up with similar results. This leads us on to what we consider an absolutely central theme.

Why Ethnomethodology?

One of the things that we, as ethnographers plying our trade in CSCW surely have to do is explain why, if it is indeed the case, ethnomethodological ethnographies are in some way superior to others in a design context and justify exactly why it might be that these specific analytic choices confer an analytic advantage. In our view, critique of the idealised conceptions to be found in other perspectives is a little past its sell-by date now and ethnomethodologists working in design-related arenas still have questions to answer. All of these questions relate, in one way or another, to the relationship between what sociologists call case studies (of which ethnographies are an example and which are often criticised within sociology for having very little generalisable consequence) and the existence of generic systems. That is, we need to take generalisation seriously.

We have no particular view on the kinds of generalisation endemic in versions of pattern languages, as advanced by Crabtree, for it seems to us that 'patterns' as used by ethnomethodologists and others are nothing more than a convenient coathanger for doing some kind of generalising work. An alternative we mention later is meta-ethnography (Noblit and Hare, 1988). The existence of a framework called a 'pattern language', however, does nothing for us in terms of deciding which patterns, typifications, general features, call them what you will, might turn out to be useful and relevant.

Equally, appeals to the commonsense nature of these typifications by ethnomethodologists rather begs questions in the design context of whose commonsense typifications might be relevant given that, in any other context but the classic control room study, this might turn out to be a nontrivial stakeholder problem. Of course, we can argue as ethnomethodologists that this is the kind of question we are not equipped to answer, or that answers to questions of this kind require us to remove our ethnomethodological hats and answer in another capacity. Neither response, once we take design relevance to be our primary problem, seems entirely satisfactory. There is, it seems to us, a more fundamental issue and that has to do with the idea that fieldwork consists of a natural task, that of describing actions and contexts as they are, or whether an analytic sensibility towards fieldwork-informed design is desirable at the right moment. It seems to us that the materials that fieldwork produces need, by definition, to be sifted somehow to become relevant to design thinking and that the progress of fieldwork itself, at some stage, must orient to design interests. These are issues of responsibility and much of what we argue below is about the responsibilities that ethnographers – ethnomethodological or otherwise – can and should take on.

The Variety of Relationships Between Ethnography and Design

Most of the authors under discussion above refer in different ways to the relationship between ethnography and design and make suggestions as to how ethnographers might help in design projects. We feel they are under-nuanced. This has to do with the ordinary practical problem that the ethnographer has when going to do her work for the first time. This problem, depending on experience and orientation, manifests itself in worries about what one is likely to see and how to determine what to look for, whether one will understand it when one sees it, how long it is likely to take, what one might miss if one is not extremely careful, and lastly how exactly can one talk about it in such a way that someone, somewhere, can draw some design conclusions from it? All of these problems, of course, take place in a variety of design and observation contexts.

Although Beyer and Holzblatt (op. cit.) make clear recommendations about how ethnographic data might be represented to others, they are less clear on the sheer variety of practices that one might find when ethnographers and ethnographies get used. They are, in effect, proposing ways to use ethnographic results in focused commercially based projects. In contrast, Crabtree, for instance, makes no distinction between the uses that ethnographic data might be put to according to what kind of project might be in question.

In turn, this matters a great deal because the purposes of the ethnography in question are, in practice, often up for grabs. We want to say a great deal about this, because in our view the scale, auspices, and timeframe of design projects are hugely consequential for the way ethnography might be used. Much more important, we find the argument that design is a technical matter tiresome. There are, of course, stages in design processes that look rather technical, and programming would be one of them.

The idea that figuring out what a technology is for (high-level requirements analysis in some views) or even decompositional strategies aimed at meeting completeness and consistency requirements are technical in nature is, in our view, absurd. Moreover, some aspects of design can be thought of as 'scoping'. That is, design might be viewed sometimes as what might be possible in environments where relatively little (computer) technology has been historically applied, such as the home or the public space. Design might equally be to do with look and feel, with aesthetic properties, with fun, and with sheer creativity. It might, more prosaically, be closely associated with issues of cost and benefit, with, if you will, accountancy. Now, we are not suggesting that ethnographers can be involved in all these things, for some aspects of design have no discernable relationship with the concerns of ethnographers. Other aspects, however, might well be susceptible to an ethnographers-as-designers treatment that is some way removed from the fairly orthodox views expressed in the literature we address.

Current Practice and the Future

Vicente (op. cit.) assumes that descriptive data (his name for fieldwork data) are about the present and therefore cannot be sufficient for design of the future. This is because any attempt to design necessarily goes beyond the evidence provided by those descriptive data. Such arguments have been around in HCI and CSCW, as well as in other fields, for a long period of time and it is perhaps time to dispose of them. Ethnographic insights cannot, on their own, replace the modeling work associated with design endeavours. Design, by definition, is formalization. Ethnography's analytic interests offer something different in addition to, not something which replaces, other and more methodical approaches to the design of the future.

Whilst accepting the view that analyses of current practices cannot on their own provide future system states, there has been a casual assumption that current and future are two quantumlike states between which there is no movement. One of the things that ethnographers and others in the CSCW community have pointed to is the long-term contingent outcomes of technological interventions. That is, we might envisage a solution whereby, at some future point, everyone is now working in an entirely different fashion as a result of some new and sophisticated computer system, but there are real questions about how we arrive at this point. There are, in the ordinary reality of human experience, and unlike the quantum universe, a whole series of potential transitions to go through before we arrive at our ideal state.

These issues of transition, for instance, were what informed the Lancaster Air Traffic Control project. Thus and for instance, when the functionalities of flight strips were considered in some detail in this work, the argument was never, 'This work is so rich and complex that technological solutions will never be found to replace it,' but that we need a close and careful analysis of what these functionalities actually are in order to begin to make judgements about both the advantages and disadvantages that might be implicated in our redesigned work environment (see Shapiro et al. (1994)). To put it another way, where Vicente emphasises the constraints endemic in current work practices, he is curiously silent on their affordances. Both, it seems to us, might matter.

By way of concluding, it should be obvious that no toolkit, method, or fully fledged methodology can possibly produce a guaranteed successful outcome in design. Designing the future is by definition designing for the unknown. Nevertheless, and as we all know, educated guesses are better than uneducated guesses. In each instance, our tools, methods, and procedures are intended to reduce the uncertainties associated with design. These uncertainties might have a number of sources, some of which ethnography was never intended to address. There might be others, however, which only it can address.

Concepts and Common Sense

One of the authors found himself in a position recently where, upon asserting that he wasn't particularly interested in theory, but he was interested in concepts, got the reply, 'Nonsense, you can't have concepts without a theory.' To which we must answer, 'Yes, you can.' Above, we have presented some of the ways in which concepts might work. For ethnomethodologists like Crabtree, they are of no interest beyond members' typifications (see also Sharrock and Randall (2004)). They work for others in an illuminating way. For the likes of Vicente, they have a more determining quality, albeit in a relatively narrowly defined set of circumstances. For Marcus, they can be thought of as part of an evolving canon of tropes. Ethnographers in this view, do not simply gather data but, in contrast, what they look for, what they invoke as relevant matters, and how they explicate those materials that they find interesting, and because this is what they are speaking about and dealing with, are driven in part by their familiarity with the ethnographic canon. They are dealing with matters internal to the discipline and not producing empirical evidence that would make sense elsewhere. It is precisely Marcus' point that a multisited ethnography, dependent on interdisciplinary objectives, will need to develop tropes all of its own.

One way through all this is to recall, as the anthropologist Clifford Geertz (1973) does, the distinction between -emic and -etic concepts. Geertz (ibid.) is probably best known for providing a semiotic view of culture through which local partial practices (which can only be inadequately described according to postmodernists but which ethnomethodologists see as their task to describe) and more general cultural features can be reconciled. The '-emic' and '-etic' refer to 'experience near' and 'experience distant' concepts. Compare, for instance, notions like 'beggar' or 'unemployed' with notions such as 'underclass' or '*lumpenproletariat*'. Experience distant concepts allow us to generalise and abstract. For Geertz there are two problems:

- First, experience near concepts leave us with nothing but experience, and tangled up in the vernacular.
- Second, experience distant concepts leave us with vague generalisations.

Here we can see something of the same general issue examined by Glaser and Strauss (1967), to whit the relationship between the general and the specific. Geertz is in no doubt that the task is to generalise, but for him the general is visible in the specific. The micro and the macro are, in other words, aspects of the same thing, linked by the symbolic universe. One of the points Geertz is strongly making is that 'the point of view of the native' is not about empathy, or indeed any other emotional position (and again we see a relevance for those interested in the moral/political aspects of design). It is an argument about whether we can understand and/or interpret the concepts others use. Put another way, we do not experience what others experience, but we can make sense of the way they make sense of their experience. He is primarily concerned with the symbolic forms, the words used, institutional regularities, rituals, and so on to be found in a society.

We are then concerned with what he usually terms 'thick description' (borrowing, somewhat inaccurately, from Ryle (1963)), and with the most global or general themes as well. The two modes of description require and articulate each other. Geertz' position is unusual in that he seeks to dissolve the debate between the relativists and the rationalists, at least in part, by suggesting it is miscast. Whether particular cultural features are 'really' science, religion, ideology, or what have you is not the point. Rather the point is how and in what ways are they systematic representations. In particular, Geertz is famous for treating common sense as a systematic phenomenon. That is, within any particular culture we should be able to identify the properties of common sense.

Such matters clearly relate to the role of theory in CSCW for they have to do with the kinds of concept that allow us to relate situations to generalities.[15] Certainly, in the work we discuss, there do appear to be, glimpsed vaguely, a set of tropes that might help us build towards a heartland of fieldwork-for-design. Thus, in contextual design we found the flow of work, the sequencing of work, the role of artefacts, and the role of space as some of the tropes on which the fieldworker should focus. In Vicente, we found a set of further tools, the most dominant of which is the idea of constraints. These have various forms and levels, and each can be analysed in distinct ways, even with distinct methods.

Thus work domain skills and work strategies are tropes for the things that workers need to apply when dealing with everyday contingency and when focusing on the specifics of work. We also suggested that some tropes were rather weak, and notions of skill, culture, and constraint seem to us to be examples. Our purpose is to try to find some way between concepts or tropes that are so high level as to be useless or, in contrast, so deterministic that enquiry becomes nothing more than slavishly following a method. At very least, later, we try to negotiate a passage.

---

[15]Ethnomethodologists typically dislike constructive sociological concepts because they trade in unacknowledged fashion on commonsense knowledge. For the most part, we share this distate for sociologising ordinary matters, but of course the point here is whether generalisations are legitimate and necessary for design purposes. We should point out here that we have nothing to say about the semiotic conceptions of culture that lie behind Geertz' argument (see Chalmers (2003) for a defence of semiotic conceptions in design-related work).

2.5 Conclusion

We finish by identifying some important features of ethnographic practice (as it pertains to design) that are not always well understood by new practitioners, and often seriously misunderstood.

2.5.1 Ethnography Is Part of a Social Science Tradition

Ethnography clearly does form part of the traditions of both sociology and anthropology. At the same time, the term disguises a wide range of analytic and practical commitments. If writings on ethnography up to the 1950s were largely to do with its relationship to science, and the possibility of a rationalistic model of human conduct, then what followed was a progressive break with any conception of science at all. This can be seen in our rehearsal of Becker's work, through standpointism and latterly through what is usually termed postmodern ethnography as well as our treatment of ethnomethodological *trahison*. We have discussed these only because they sometimes have a tangential relationship to fieldwork-for-design, and because they are useful for building sensibility. Readers may even see some relevance to design insofar as case studies and general conclusions seem to be as important in design-related activities as they are in social science.

In briefly ranging through some of the human sciences' obsessions in respect to ethnography, then, we did not intend to give them a dignity they do not deserve but have tried to give a flavour of what it is that concerns sociologists so much and suggest what aspects of sociological obsession we can safely ignore and which might have some relevance to our interests. In so doing, we have given some weight to an ethnomethodologically informed approach to ethnography.[16] This might be seen as a claim to a superior method for addressing some design questions, one which is distinct from, and perhaps runs counter to, the kind of fieldwork that goes on when done within other theoretical perspectives.

It does not have to be seen that way. That ethnomethodology is distinct from social science, and runs counter to many social scientific assumptions, is largely recognised in the social sciences (although there have been

---

[16]This somewhat dubious term has a provenance both in ethnomethodological studies themselves (Dingwall, 1981; Silverman, 1985) and subsequently in design-related work (see Hughes et al. (1992)). In the latter work, it was never intended to carry the weight it sometimes appears to, and serves as a useful term of art for distinguishing the issues of method associated with ethnography from analytic choices associated with ethnomethodology. It further, and given ethnomethodology's insistence on indifference to 'versions', was intended as a signal that design should be taken seriously.

various attempts to integrate ethnomethodology into the wider concerns of sociology, for instance, Giddens (1984)). The idea that the same antithetical relationship exists between ethnomethodology and generalising tendencies when fieldwork is being done in relation to design is much more doubtful. The foundation of this putative hostility lies in the assumption that ethnomethodology is rigorously opposed to the principle of generalisation, or theory construction and thus that theories which use general concepts must be inimical to ethnomethodological work. We suggest that neither of these things is true. We expand on this at a later stage, but suffice it to say that many of the claims made about ethnomethodology are founded on misunderstandings of what is actually said, and moreover that ethnomethodology's undoubted hostility to some sociology and psychology is precisely a hostility to sociological and psychological theorising of a particular kind. It has no necessary relationship with any other kind of theorising. The point is that theories should be treated according to the degree to which they make the wheels turn. It is these sorts of subtleties that need to be understood and appreciated.

We contend that the kind of ethnographic fieldwork we propose is based on knowledge of a great tradition, but is at the same time geared towards establishing a distinct design-oriented fieldwork tradition, with its own tropes and themes. We say that fieldwork is much more effectively done with an analytic sensibility which orients to design but which does not accept design problems as given. Familiarity with prior design-oriented fieldwork as much as with the social sciences can help produce this. Part of this sensibility has to do with a recognition that when fieldwork-for-design is undertaken, the evidence it produces may be of a number of quite particular kinds. The way the fieldworker in design looks, what he looks for, what he captures, all this and more is wrapped up, at least at some point in enquiry, with his design motivation. As we suggest (and reiterate throughout later chapters),

> if all design can be thought of as the relevant and timely reduction of uncertainty, then ethnography can be thought of in the first instance as a means to identify the relevant uncertainties.

This has implications as to what uses that evidence can be put, and it distinguishes this kind of evidence from what would be produced if the purpose of the fieldwork were different from, for instance, an ethnomethodological inquiry working contrastively against orthodox sociological interests.

One further consequence of this view on data or evidence is that the kind of materials produced enable or help create a space for design thinking. This space is created in part through the material itself and in part through the ways it is conveyed. By way of contrast, in traditional ethnography, to take its role in anthropology and sociology (and thus ethnomethodology too), fieldwork leads to the production of long, detailed, written texts, often if not exclusively book length. In design, we show that there is a variety of ways in which descriptions of the setting can be conveyed and presented, and the long written monograph is only one of these. Other ways, as Beyer and Holzblatt have shown, may include graphical representations of elements of the work in question, arranged through the themes and topics we pursue. Another is to undertake design workshops where the fieldworker or fieldwork team acts as surrogate users, offering stories about how they do the work.

If the kind of data that are captured and rendered in design fieldwork are distinct, and so too are the many ways they might be used to create a space for design thinking, then another distinguishing characteristic of design-oriented fieldwork is the possibility that it can be undertaken by teams. This is rare in the ethnographic approaches exemplified in the anthropological and sociological traditions. Multiperson fieldwork requires its own tools and processes, and part of the motivation for these is to enable evaluation and testing of fieldwork understanding. We suggest that doing fieldwork collaboratively alters the mechanisms used to assess when it is complete or sufficiently thorough for design thinking to commence, and for the management of the team itself.

In short, we are proposing that fieldwork-in-design is a new practice, however much it builds on a fieldwork tradition in the social sciences. It is one that has slowly begun to build a corpus of research materials in CSCW and other related disciplines in the past decade or so, but one which is, we believe, of growing importance and use.

2.5.2 Ethnography Is Naturalistic

That is, it predicates its inquiries on the principle that studies should be studies of real people and their activities, operating in their natural environment, whatever that may be. An important justification of the approach is that it is not known in advance of inquiry just what the relevant features of some settings are, let alone how they might be relevant to system design. Thus, and distinct from some approaches derived from cognitive science, it refuses to deal with artificial environments and controlled versions of work but argues that only by studying the natural environment of work and its activities can system design be adequately informed. As Michael Lynch (1993) has put it, in another context,

> Stop talking about science. Go to a laboratory – any laboratory will do – hang around a while, listen to conversations, watch the technicians at work, ask them to explain what they are doing, read their notes, observe what they say when they examine the data, and watch how they move equipment around ....

However, and as already suggested, this naturalism might involve any number of analytic commitments and any range of substantive interests. It may entail a variety of approaches to the notion of context and a great deal of (largely unnecessary) agonising about the nature of the context in question. It could be predicated on more or less behaviourist stances on social action or a concern for meaningfulness. It may find meaning in accounts of motive or treat meaning as an intersubjective phenomenon. At the early stage of deciding what needs to be looked at, however, none of these issues needs to matter much. A simple rule of thumb is that context is exhibited by people in the place being observed.

2.5.3 Ethnography Is Prolonged

This background assumption comes largely from the fact that anthropological studies of other cultures have usually implicated enculturation. That is, the post-Fraser (1993) view has been that to understand another culture means having to learn its language, mores, practices, and values. In virtue of the fact that it is another culture that is under investigation, it is reasonable to assume this will take some time. However, we should perhaps point out here that there is no logical reason why an ethnography should take so long, and it has been argued that, for CSCW purposes at least, there are times when it need not do so (see Hughes et al. (1994)), because the point must be that duration relates to the size of the task.

To elaborate the point, the ethnography of cashier work undertaken by Randall and Hughes (1995) lasted approximately three weeks, and that because it was undertaken in three different settings to ensure some kind of validity. Here, the task was quite specific: to understand and assess the kind of problems that cashiers had working with technology when dealing with the public. The problem, that is, was tightly bounded by those who had commissioned the work. (Nevertheless, the ethnography subsequently opened up and more work was done, lasting another six weeks.) The main reason for prolongation is that in advance, for the most part, ethnographers have no clear idea what they will find. Because there are in principle any number of aspects which may turn out to be interesting, and any number of things which may be mystifying, it will take time to form a coherent view of what is going on. Nevertheless, ethnographic enculturation over time and a range of domains does rather suggest, on a commonsense basis, that experienced ethnographers will have some notion of what they are likely to see next time out. Again, Marcus is relevant here, insofar as multisitedness at least reminds us that ethnographies can be done with varying degrees of intensity, over different periods of time, with the need for comparison, or otherwise, being one thing that underpins choices.

2.5.4 Ethnographic Enquiries Seek to Elicit the Social World from the Point of View of Those Who Inhabit It

It should be obvious, given much of what has been said above, that ethnographic enquiries can, in principle, be into an enormous range of matters which might be of interest, depending on analytic purpose. They might, for instance, be enquiries into beliefs and attitudes, the symbolic universe of a culture, customs, law, gender relations, power relations, discursive formations, and so on. They do not, that is, have to provide detailed pictures of patterns of interaction and collaboration. As a result ethnography is too diverse a set of practices to be described as a method.

At a minimum, however, we would argue that ethnography is (should be) about uncovering the world from the point of view of the social actors within it. For this reason, although it is behavioural (interested in the detail of the behaviour to a greater or lesser extent) it is not behaviourist because it does not consider the behaviour itself as the appropriate or only level of analysis. The appropriate level is the meaningful behaviour of those who undertake it. Moreover, we are not necessarily referring to a commitment to the beliefs of social actors. This is true regardless of whether these beliefs are reality claims or value judgements. As an ethnographer, we do not have to accept that what people believe is true, is true. As an ethnographer, one does not have to accept that what people believe is right, is right. Equally, one does not have to be indifferent to these matters, and something which looked like an ethnography undertaken under the auspices of, for instance, participatory design, might have a very different orientation to it than one undertaken by an ethnomethodologist.

The different commitments entailed in doing an ethnographic study are discussed at a later stage. In the context of the design of CSCW systems, however, the kind of ethnomethodologically informed ethnography we have referred to entails some minimum commitments that in our view are inescapably part of fieldwork-for-design. Firstly, such ethnographies have primarily focused on the social organisation of work activities. There has been considerable discussion of the nature of cooperation in work settings and one stance on this has been that the phenomenon of interest must be limited to a fairly narrow sense of cooperation which implies attention to the kinds of dependency that are necessary for the completion of work tasks (Schmidt, 1991).

We prefer the initial and foundational assumption of ethnomethodology that work is anything done in order that a social activity is accomplished, and moreover that such work has a processual character. That is, that it is sequentially organised. We believe, regardless of the theoretical auspices under which investigation takes place, that the processual character of work should be one central research topic for interdisciplinary work of this kind even if other possibilities are opened up as well by theoretical commitments. We remain wedded to this conception of ethnography-for-design.

The task of ethnography is to take the obvious fact of the social organisation of human life and describe and analyse how this social organisation is accomplished, understood, and achieved by social actors. In the context of HCI and CSCW, its purpose is to relate such descriptions and analysis to the concerns of system design.

Under the auspices of the ethnomethodologically informed version, the issue of generalisation also changes. The ethnomethodological conception of social research presumes the immense orderliness of the social world from the outset and seeks to understand how this is accomplished. This orderliness, its regularity, is there in advance of, and independent of, any social scientific accounts, theoretical or otherwise, that we might produce of it. Generalisation here will draw on ordinary and widely held understandings about the social organisation of the world. They will, that is, treat typicalities as the culturally recognisable kinds of activity we are already, and unavoidably, trading on in our understandings of the social organisation of the world. As Sharrock and Anderson (1991) argue, as with so many of the conventional dichotomies that characterise sociology, ethnomethodology does not acknowledge the separation of the particular and the general. Instead, ethnomethodology suggests that it is impossible to assemble a collection of observable occurrences, instances, without already having introduced some element of generality that identifies the actions – right down to mundanities such as organising the family for breakfast before the kids go off to school – as what they so observably and obviously are.

2.5.5 Ethnographic Data Resist Formalisation

Ethnographies of work, then, have been widely undertaken since the late 1980s. Because the ethnographic stance stresses the importance of context or setting, and thus that there can be no theoretical perspective which can explain in advance what one is likely to see in a new setting (*pace* BPR), nor any data which constitute the 'right' data to be collecting, this raises a data collection and organisation issue. Put simply, ethnographic data take a variety of forms and can include general descriptions of behaviours, descriptions of physical layouts, close descriptions of conversation, thoughts and feelings about what is going on, tentative hypotheses, examples, repeated occurences, and so on. Inevitably, this makes it rather difficult to distil data down to an essential and structured form, and particularly difficult to do so for system design purposes. In the commonplace usage, ethnographic data is messy or unstructured. This has, at times, been used as a stick with which to beat ethnographers inasmuch as systems designers, quite rightly, point to the necessity of structured, not to say formalised data for design purposes. It is important, therefore, to make an obvious point. There is no reason whatsoever why ethnographic data has to be messy and unstructured.

Let us go further:

> The commonplace attitude that ethnographic data are necessarily messy and unstructured needs to be challenged, for there is no reason in principle why it should be this way. Instead, we argue that this sometime messiness is actually a result of hesitancy about analytic relevance. That is, it is a question of deciding what data are needed, for what purposes, and especially when.

Once these things are decided ethnographic data can be as structured as any other form. Of course, a world of pain is hidden in that simple formulation. In our view, many of the by-now celebrated system disasters that exemplify what is wrong with traditional approaches to system development are often if not always a result of precipitate decisions about what our problem is.

The whole business of structuring data, no matter how it has been collected, and as Glaser and Strauss (1967) point out, is an analytic matter. In much the same way, ethnography-for-design may be a collaborative task and not a solitary one, which raises the issue of responsibility. If fieldwork is the recounting of the view from someone in some particular position, as Marcus (op. cit.) puts it, then this begs the question as to what other views and perspectives might be gathered and listened to. For fieldwork-in-design, this perspectivalism may be avoided by treating the task as essentially a collaborative one. Thereby the evidence gathered, the iterations of research into the setting in question, will not produce a 'view from here' but a view that anyone within the team agree is a reasonable and adequate description. In other words, by making fieldwork-in-design essentially collaborative, the problems that ensue, and the materials that are produced, are all subject to different possibilities and constraints. By treating it as collaborative, many of the problems that beguiled anthropological ethnography are eliminated.

3

Some Perspectives

CSCW, as many have suggested, represents an outward move from existing approaches towards a range of technical and organisational issues. These include a move from human factors work as practiced in early versions of HCI and from similar varieties of organisational science and change management (see Harper et al. (2000) for a brief overview). One consequence has been the development of interest in a range of theoretical and analytic perspectives in CSCW which, to a greater or lesser extent, challenge the dominant model of the 'rational person'. These perspectives often compete and certainly cover a broadly similar terrain, insofar as all have some commitment to a notion of situatedness. As a result, all share as well some interest in the methods that might help us understand situations, and hence some approach to going out and looking.

These perspectives represent a move away from theory as embodying the logico-deductive method. This basically means the kind of hypothesis testing or deductive approach that is often associated with natural science and which by definition involves the formulation of hypotheses and their testing.[17] None of our candidates meets any orthodox test of scientific theory, not least in respect of the fact that they would not be associated with any predictive claims. Their proponents would almost certainly agree that they are theories only in a weak sense. Nevertheless, they are pursuing the theme of generalisation in some way, often through the idea that building a set of related and structured concepts might provide us with reusable tools for all our investigations in CSCW and elsewhere. We make no attempt to judge

---

[17]The philosophy of science has shown that there are major difficulties with this model of scientific conduct. See Popper (1968), Kuhn (1970), Feyerabend (1975), Lakatos (1970), Latour and Woolgar (1986), and Barnes and Bloor (1982). See especially Williams (2000). What is striking is the resilience of scientific practice against persistent attack, indicating perhaps that scientists have few or no difficulties in continuing to work in the way in which they work, regardless of what philosophers and sociologists want to say about their procedures.

among these contributions here, for our purpose is to understand how they might relate to fieldwork and whether they have any consequences for it.

Hence we aim in this chapter to briefly provide a fairly superficial overview of each of these candidates such that readers can decide for themselves whether a more sophisticated and nuanced reading might repay the effort.

All the candidate theories and perspectives we discuss over the next two chapters have been deployed to some effect in the CSCW and HCI communities. All stand in some positive relation to the business of ethnography and most, at various points, make claims concerning generalisation. Candidates continue to multiply. There seems to be a general 'wish to theory' on the part of academic practitioners, one perhaps not shared by commercial researchers. In turn, this associates with the presumption that what distinguishes academic work from the commercial context is the need to provide generalisable results. Theory, of course, is conventionally held to be the device by which generalisation becomes possible. Be that as it may, the term 'theory' covers an enormous amount of ground. Work that is described as theoretical can meet an enormous range of standards, starting with those we expect of the natural sciences through to some fairly loose conceptual frameworks aimed at illuminating.

Of course if we are not in the business of generating a hypothesis, testing it, and then constructing theories with general and predictive qualities, then it remains to be seen in what kind of business we are. Suffice it to say at this moment that the ethnographic approach is generally held in sociology at least to sit uneasily, to say the least, with anything that looks like hypothesis testing.

Without detailing all the objections, we can at least point to the problem of context in the social world. Put simply, if social behaviour is context bounded, then it is not possible to suppose in advance what all the relevant concepts might be when it comes to analysing any given context. This is not to say that we cannot make judgements in advance about what we are going to see because we can and do. The point, however, is that these judgements are common sense, and founded on what we conventionally assume is true about the context under investigation. Thus and for instance, there are several things that we might assume about a job of work, including that to some degree at least it will entail some fixed hours, a place of work, payment, some co-workers who relate to each other in various ways, and so on. Like all commonsense judgements, however, occasions will arise when they turn out to be wrong.

Our aim, then, is to provide a relatively brief explanation of the underpinnings of some popular and well-known (at least by name) approaches applied to the study of work, technology, and organisations, and which in principle can be extended to other contexts as they arise. We have selected these approaches because they all entail some orientation to fieldwork, although what they mean by fieldwork may vary. We do not attempt to choose among them, and hope that our portrayal of them is principled and objective. Equally, we cannot provide, for reasons of space, the same degree of thoroughness for all perspectives and indeed all the issues we examine.

We begin, then, by examining what it means to see social scientific enquiry as emergent rather than as hypothetico-deductive. We do so by focusing in particular on grounded theory as discussed by Glaser and Strauss. Their grounded theory is only occasionally used by CSCW practitioners, certainly less commonly than one sees references to activity theory or distributed cognition, for instance. Nevertheless, we consider it an important starting point. This is not because we think there are major procedural insights to be gained from it (although reading their work on the constant comparative method produces the reflection that it says just as much as Alexander's pattern languages about the process of typification and categorization) but because it is an ideal starting point for those who are puzzled by the unscientific relationship between theory and method that seems to be implicated in ethnographic study. It will certainly help those who struggle with the refusal of ethnographers to address issues of verification and validity.

3.1 Grounded Theory – Glaser and Strauss

> *. . . in generating theory it is not the fact upon which we stand, but the conceptual category . . . that was generated from it.*
>
> *(Glaser and Strauss, 1967, p. 23)*

It is as well to bear in mind a number of points about grounded theory. First, Glaser and Strauss, who first formulated the notion, were part of the Chicago school tradition that we have already briefly described. We are not the first to observe that the Chicago school was not simply an enterprise for churning out ethnographic studies, nor even a tradition which emphasised fieldwork at the expense of other methods (see Hammersley and Atkinson (1983)). Indeed, Glaser and Strauss themselves (and Glaser in later work even more so; see Glaser (1998)) are adamant that the principles of grounded theory apply as much to so-called quantitative research as to qualitative research. Although they seldom make it explicit, this is because the distinction between qualitative and quantitative method is not a distinction based on method at all, but based on analytic stance. The real distinction is between inductive and deductive analysis, and numbers can be made to serve either.

This may seem blindingly obvious, but it carries with it some lessons for CSCW and HCI researchers. As Glaser and Strauss point out (in *The Discovery of Grounded Theory* (1967, p. 67)):

> This book is intended to underscore the basic sociological activity that only sociologists can do: generating sociological theory. Description, ethnography, fact-finding, verification (call them what you will) are all done well by professionals in other fields and by laymen in various investigatory

agencies. But these people cannot generate sociological theory from their work. Only sociologists are trained to want it, to look for it and to generate it.

This argument, which many working in interdisciplinary collaborations might find controversial, is in many ways central to the whole problem of fieldwork-for-design, because it turns on who should do it and how it should be done. Firstly, however, we should note that it is generalisation (of whatever appropriate kind) that they insist is the province of the sociologist, not data collection. This bears repeating, for it is easily missed. It is central to some of the different perspectives on ethnography previously discussed. The point of fieldwork, for them, is to generate theories. Data collection is for the most part, once a series of quite prosaic and mundane problems are dealt with, easy. Its results will be uninteresting if they consist in nothing more than lengthy descriptions. Decisions concerning what data to collect, from where, and for what purpose, go to the heart of the fieldwork task and interdisciplinary collaboration. Allied to this is the concept of 'theoretical sensitivity' (1967, p. 46), which might equally well be described as a 'way of thinking'. Where, and as we argue throughout, we have some reservations about sociological generalisation, we have none at all about theoretical sensitivity.

Most sociologists who also teach will recall without much difficulty students who ask, 'But am I allowed to do that?' or 'What should I look for?' or look puzzled when it is suggested that there might be, for instance, something to learn from avoidance behaviour by adults in the context of noisy and vexatious schoolchildren or beggars when they have already decided that their topic is 'strategies for avoiding street crime.' Such students, at that point in time, evidently lack this somewhat nebulous sensitivity which has to do with an imaginative capacity to decide what might be a useful insight.

Grounded theory was a reaction to the tendency to grand theory in American sociology during the 1950s and 60s and, perhaps more importantly, to the logico-deductive theorists. These were the people like Paul Lazarsfeld who at that time, through their statistical procedures for operationalising deductive enquiry, dominated American sociology. Glaser and Strauss, then, were advocating some variety of inductive analysis whereby theory is generated from data collected, rather than data being collected to test existing theories. They were insistent, as we have suggested, that (1967, p. 17), '. . . there is no fundamental clash between the purposes and capacities of qualitative and quantitative methods or data. What clash there is concerns the primacy of emphasis on verification or generation of theory.'

The importance of this apparently surprising assertion cannot be overemphasised because it returns us to the issue of data collection as against data analysis. Their point, and we can only agree once again, is that far too much is made of the costs and benefits of particular methods and far too little of the analytic purposes to which those methods can be put.

Anyone, as they point out, can do fact-finding, whether we choose to dignify it with terms such as fieldwork or ethnography. The issue is what to do with the data we collect and most of the (largely subterranean) arguments within HCI and CSCW about the value or otherwise of ethnography in the end must turn on this. Glaser and Strauss are offering analytic procedures for a certain kind of generalisation, and below we discuss the extent to which this can usefully be applied to interdisciplinary problems.

Glaser and Strauss provide an approach that is essentially comparative. There is some truth in the notion that all sociology is in the business of comparison, and it is especially true, as grounded theory recognizes, that the unit to be subject to comparative analysis can be of any size. This is of particular importance because it implies that concepts generated can be of any size too. We can in principle compare societies, ethnic communities, or pick-up strategies in a nightclub. Their work uses the constant comparative method, as they term it, for instance to analyse 'loss rationales', 'dying trajectories', and 'professional strategies' in hospital wards where dying is commonplace (Glaser and Strauss, 1965,1968). There is no reason to explore this work except to note that they were insistent that their study of patients, staff, and institutional structures had policy implications. That is, there were design implications, although the design in question had to do with training and planning rather than technological aspects.

Regardless, comparison can be done for many different reasons and at many different levels. It can be done, they say, to:

1. Establish the validity of facts.
2. Establish the generality of a fact.
3. Specify the unit of analysis for a one-case study.
4. Verify a theory.
5. Generate a theory.

As a consequence, the kinds of conceptual work going on may also vary considerably in type and precision. They are insistent that (1967, p. 30) 'Since accurate evidence is not so crucial for generating theory, the kind of evidence, as well as the number of cases, is also not so crucial.'

Equally (1967, p. 30),

> Generation by comparative analysis requires a multitude of carefully selected cases, but the pressure is not on the sociologists to "know the whole field" or to have all the facts from a "careful random sample." His job is not to provide a perfect description of an area, but to develop a theory that accounts for much of the relevant behaviour.

At first glance some might find this hard to take for they appear to be suggesting that issues of coverage, sampling, and thoroughgoing description are not that important for theory generation. However, and with some reservations, there are reasons to support this kind of view. One of the issues, of course, is whether the kind of theory to be generated in interdisciplinary work is in any way like the kinds of theory generated in sociology. Insofar as the ethnographic topic, as we have seen, is always (in some sense) to do with the work that people do, then the kinds of generalisation that might result are sociological. The task is to figure out whether there might be ways of turning generalisations of a sociological kind into design generalisations. The variation in analytic levels also means that the kinds of theory generated may be different. Their distinction between formal and substantive theories and their insistence that the former should not be used to structure research questions is still vital, and flies in the face of much sociological and psychological convention. It also has ramifications for the way concepts in HCI and CSCW are deployed, 'For it indicates that, if grounded theory is to be useful in design then we should never have concepts strongly in mind when we investigate a domain for design purposes.'

We believe that for fieldwork purposes this is more or less correct. The issue is, nevertheless, made a great deal more complex in the matter of interdisciplinary working because the fault-line would have to be described in terms of whether (a) it is appropriate for ethnographers to set out to do data collection and analysis with particular analytic categories in mind at all, and (b) whether these categories should include assumptions such as the type of system envisaged for use in a domain.

By way of example, there has been some discussion of the role of awareness as a category in CSCW research. It is evident that the concept has some importance, for it is used by a large number of researchers (see Schmidt et al. (2002)) and there is no reason why it should not. However, there are good reasons why ethnographers should not go into domains imagining that awareness is their problem, and the problem of those who inhabit the domain before it has ever been examined.

Again, this is at the crux of much of the confusion about the role of ethnography in design-related work. If the model to be employed is along the lines of:

a. Technology of interest is determined by designers;
b. Designers employ ethnographers to investigate a domain;
c. Ethnographers identify modifications to the technology which will enable it to work in the domain;
d. Designers iterate design solution;

then of course Glaser and Strauss' argument is largely irrelevant because the model being employed is one which restricts ethnography to a service role and one which involves little serious analytic work. The problem is, of course, that the neat technology school of ethnographic research provides us with no means of identifying whether the technology in question is what is needed and how that will be judged.[18] We think that, ideally, ethnography should not have merely a service role but should somehow evolve a combination of service and critical role (and here we are not referring to moral or political critique).

In the context of awareness the dangers are obvious. If the concept drives the research, then the risks are firstly that researchers with an interest in placing their own research in a competitive market stretch concepts to fit existing frameworks and stretch them in such a way that the concept becomes largely incoherent, vague, and ambiguous (Schmidt, ibid.). Secondly and relatedly, the concept can become progressively reified as a core disciplinary assumption as when awareness is treated as a mental attribute. Thirdly, treating any one concept in a more or less obsessive way can lead to other relevant material being excluded from the research (Petersson et al., 2002). As Schmidt implies, such choices are to some extent at least led by the choice of computing machinery under development but, as we have been at pains to suggest, this only begs the question.

The question is, if pre-existing concepts and theories are not to determine either the focus of what to study or how to study it, how exactly do we decide what an appropriate research problem might be. Questions that have to do with the right of any parties to interdisciplinary research to decide a research focus are not Glaser and Strauss' concern, but they are ours. Our attitude is very much like theirs, however, insofar as we too believe that not only concepts and theories, but also specific and detailed choices about what to study (rather than a general choice of domain), cannot be determined by any particular interest in an interdisciplinary community and cannot be determined early. Their inherently sociological argument (that we share) is as follows (1967, pp. 45–46):

> The sociologist may begin the research with a partial framework of "local" concepts, designating a few principal or gross features of the structure and processes in the situations that he will study. For example, he knows before studying a hospital that there will be doctors, nurses, and aides, and wards and admission procedures. These concepts give him a beginning foothold on his research. Of course, he does not know the relevancy of these concepts to his problem – this problem must emerge – nor are they likely to become part of the core explanatory categories of his theory. His categories are more likely to be concepts about the problem itself, not its situation. Also, he discovers that some anticipated "local" concepts may remain unused in the situations relevant to his problem – doctors may, for the problem, be called therapists.

---

[18]It will work fine, however, for purposes of market research and selling in both commercial and academic contexts.

It is in this way that grounded theory combines description with discovery, the commonsensical with the theoretical. The problem is the movement between these in any particular case. As Glaser and Strauss (1967, p. 47) say in their discussion of theoretical sampling, the essential question to be answered is, '*What* groups or subgroups does one turn to *next* in data collection? And for what theoretical purpose? [their italics].' 'Theoretical sampling' refers, then, to a particular kind of comparative work. Glaser says (1998) that it is the 'where next' in collecting data, the 'for what' according to the codes, and the 'why' from the analysis in memos. It is further (1998, p. 157),

> . . . the conscious, grounded deductive aspect of the inductive coding, collecting and analyzing. It is grounded deductions, feeding into data for more induction as the growing theory leads the researcher on. It constantly focuses and delimits the collection and analysis of data, so that the researcher is not collecting the same data over and over based on the same questions which ignore the interchangeability of indices.

Comparison under grounded theory can be done without worrying too much, if at all, what underlying similarities or differences exist (to begin with) from group to group. All that matters is that the data pertain to a similar category or property. Hence, analysis of reactions to dying, as they suggest, can be done by looking at what goes on in hospitals, at home, on the street, and so on. No strict control is in place and nor need it be. No pre-planning of which groups can be compared and in which similar settings need be done. As they accept, the kind of choices made about what to study affect the generality of the theory being developed. In very large part, of course, that is the point. What to study is selected in an ongoing way to reflect the theoretical interests that are developing, and these interests can be very modest and local, or more ambitious, general, and ultimately formal.

The scope of any theoretical apparatus can be changed by choices about widening parameters for comparison. The selection of groups for comparison, then, can be done along several different axes. They can be done in accordance with the level of generality of the concepts being developed, in accordance with a desired population scope, and in accordance with decisions about similarity and difference, depending on what kind of theoretical relevance is required. Minimising differences has, of course, a number of advantages including that a great deal of very similar data can be collected around one category and thus used for verification purposes.

At the same time the opposite choice also has advantages, including that a range of data will be found which may aid considerably in finding what they term 'strategic' similarities. In effect, Glaser and Strauss broadly advocate a strategy whereby one moves from the first strategy towards the second. Initial work can be done on a relatively narrow comparative basis so as to produce well-organised, reliable, and consistent data. However, and as theoretical ambition increases, so differences will have to be understood

and emphasised, requiring the selection of groups for study which are increasingly divergent. Eventually, theoretical saturation is reached. This is the stage at which no further properties for any given category can be developed. In other words, all the data seem to fit nicely into the categories and typologies one has developed and additional data never seem to generate any further reflection.

3.1.1 The Constant Comparative Method

Perhaps the most significant part of Glaser and Strauss' approach is their notion of the constant comparative method. They argue that typically one finds one of two strategies in human science research. In the first, data are coded first and then analysed. This is the method by which 'proofs' are arrived at in response to some initial hypothesis. In the second, coding is done afterwards. That is, data are collected with no particular regard to what they mean and are used to generate concepts and categories which can then be systematically organised into a theoretical apparatus. Glaser and Strauss actually argue not for the second, but for a combination of the two and in fact this is where they can in effect claim that their methods are more than simply a version of analytic inductivism. Thus, 'The purpose of the constant comparative method of joint coding and analysis is to generate theory more systematically than allowed by the second approach, *by using explicit coding and analytic procedures* [their emphasis].'

This is a method for generating categories, or concepts. Categories in turn have properties. They use their studies of nursing care for the dying to illustrate this. They give two categories of nursing care: 'professional composure' and 'perception of social loss' (meaning their perception of what the loss of a loved one will mean to relatives and friends). A property of the latter is 'loss rationales', whereby nurses decide how to explain the death of a patient to others when the death involves a high social loss (and hence matters to people). These loss rationales help them maintain their professional composure.

In effect, what is being suggested is that the analyst can look at a number of events, situations, and facts, and identify those that seem to be similar. Thus, in the case of nursing care, the analyst may collect a number of examples of nurses dealing with the death of patients, and derive some categories which make sense of what they see. The point is that at some point in the research the categories one has developed can act as a guide to what to look for. Analysis should continue only so far as it helps develop new categories or properties.

This argument has been very influential in sociology, and we can see its relevance to CSCW. Firstly, it clearly implies that fieldwork is an evolving affair, and that categories should not be imposed on the domain prior to investigation. Secondly, it clearly sees the value of data collection in terms of some kind of generalisation. The aim, then, is to allow the analyst to produce reasonable categories at some level of generality with which to describe what is going on.

Their 'constant comparative method' (as they call this approach) can be described in terms of four stages.

1. Comparing incidents applicable to each category. Here, the analyst takes each segment of data and determines an appropriate category with which to describe it. The basic stance should be a promiscuous one: as many categories as possible. On a practical level, this coding may be as formal as embedding concepts in computer software or as informal as making a note in the margin of fieldwork data. As this takes place, it should prompt reflections concerning how similar and different each instance of the category in question is from other instances, and thus properties begin to emerge.

2. Integrating categories and their properties. As coding continues, the units of analysis being used will undergo a transformation. Early on, incidents are being compared with incidents. As the analytic process gets underway, however, it is the properties of the category that become comparable. In other words, they take on a more theoretical character as relationships become evident.

3. Delimiting theory. As the process continues, two things happen. Firstly the theory solidifies, which means that categories and properties are less and less likely to be changed. One implication of this is that the promiscuously generated categories we referred to earlier will progressively lessen as it becomes obvious that some work better than others, and offer more coverage.

4. Writing the theory. Although this may seem an obvious phase, it carries more importance than one might imagine because the key feature of writing the theory is that it depends on certain assumptions, which are (1967, p. 113), 'When the researcher is convinced that his analytic framework forms a systematic substantive theory, that it is a reasonably accurate statement of the matters studied, and that it is couched in a form that others going into the same field could use.'

Their position means that the standards of evidence need to be relaxed. Their standard is plausibility. In this respect, their conclusions have something in common with ethnomethodological presuppositions, as we show below. Grounded theory, then, offers at very least a plausible reasoned way for social scientists to do research if they are assailed with doubts concerning the 'scientism' of some approaches and on the other hand the vague inductivism that merely going out and looking seems to entail. Certainly, it contains elements with which not only social scientists but other practitioners ought to be comfortable. They are explicit about the ease with which data can be collected, and insistent that anyone can do it, whilst at the same time reserving a theoretical space for professional sociologists.

Applied to interdisciplinary enquiry, then, we might infer that from a grounded theory perspective, anyone can collect data and any legitimate participant can generate relevant theory (or relevantly generalise). We are not so sure. To deal with the problem of data collection first, we are mostly in agreement with the general assertion that data collection is a largely trivial exercise. It is a continuing theme in our own analysis of fieldwork that collecting data is for the most part unproblematic.[19] Anyone, that is, can indeed do it. As ethnomethodologists never tire of pointing out, it would have to be this way because members of a society are by definition experts in their own culture and hence are in the business of collecting data (in a loose sense) from around them all the time. What is much less straightforward is the analysis of data, and we have much to say about this as we proceed.

The second issue, which has to do with the status of generalisation and who has the right to do it is altogether more problematic. Broadly, if it is the case that some kind of theoretical work has to be done on fieldwork data, the important question is whether useful theory will look like the kinds of theory we associate with sociology. Another way of putting this would be: if a sociological sensibility is required to generate useful generalisations in HCI and CSCW then perhaps we sociologists ought to do it, but if not, then there is no particular reason to make way for professional ethnographers.

Grounded theory has become something of an industry, and readers who wish can find out more, especially about coding procedures, from Strauss and Corbin (1998). Equally, if looking for practical examples of how to put grounded theory into practice, Strauss and Corbin (1990) is a handy source book. Specific applications of grounded theory are to be found in, for instance, management research (see Locke (2000)). Examples of Glaser and Strauss' influence in CSCW include the work of Fitzpatrick et al. (1996) in their study of the work of system administrators, and Grinter (1997), who has used insights from Glaser and Strauss in her study of the development of a workflow system. Indeed, Fitzpatrick (2003) makes interesting observations about the merits of what she calls the 'Locales Framework', drawing heavily on both grounded theory and Strauss' theory of action. In so doing she sideswipes ethnomethodology, with some justification, for its typical strategy of putting an 'implications for design' section at the end of each paper. Her theoretical approach is designed to rectify this rather vague relationship with design and its problems. We are not here interested in any critique of the locales framework or indeed any other approach inspired by

---

[19]Not entirely so, and the second part of our book deals with some of the practical exigencies associated with this kind of enquiry.

grounded theory. Instead, we want to address the real issue of generalisation, at least in outline, for what such a framework attempts to do is provide a conceptual organisation.

Grounded theory can be said to have the following important elements for design-related work:

- It insists that the relevance of fieldwork is unfolding.
- It insists on constant comparison, and thus takes generalisation seriously.
- It dismisses the need for deductive, or natural scientific, standards.

3.2 Participative Design (PD)

As we have seen, participatory design, if it is to have a relationship with ethnography at all, is likely to have a relationship which involves some kind of standpointism. To reiterate, standpoint theories have it that moral or political commitments are inevitable in research, and should be embraced. We feel there are very strong grounds for treating PD as a standpoint epistemology. Nevertheless, it would be entirely unfair to describe participatory design as a theory in anything but the very weakest sense. Rather, it can be described in terms of a set of analytic and constructive commitments, predicated in turn on some general beliefs about the state of the world. These commitments can be understood as either moral/political or as methodological, depending on which version of PD is under review. For good or ill, PD has always been associated with Scandinavia, and is sometimes called the Scandinavian movement. As Nielson and Relsted (1993) argue, 'Participation is expected in Scandinavia. Far from being an ideology, it has become the normal way of doing development and implementation work . . . in many cases actual participation exceeds formal rights.'

This is a gloss in that it ignores the considerable spread of PD methodology into a great range of contexts. Indeed, as Blomberg and Kensing (1998) point out, PD projects can be found in many, often unpromising, contexts. They go on to discuss what the conditions might be for successful PD work. These include, in their view, a perspective on the politics of design; on participation; and on methods, tools, and techniques. We follow this framework below. We suggest, however, that the spread of methodological commitments has not been accompanied by the spread of unifying ideological commitments, and without the ideology it is hard to see what is so unique about PD. Related to this, as has often been recognised, there is no single PD movement, insofar as the term covers a range of political and moral commitments as well as many different practises. Bansler (1989), for instance, writes,

> I would like to stress that there is no such thing as the Scandinavian approach. There is not one, but several Scandinavian approaches to system

development, including the Collective Resources approach and various Socio-technical approaches. These approaches differ with regard to their basic goals and ideological foundations as well as their development strategies and design methods.

For our purposes, it is enough to point out that increasingly one of these practises is ethnography.

3.2.1 The Politics of Design

PD, despite its many-faceted nature, can be said to have some foundational commitments. First, it has a broad concern with the politics of design. It has been remarked in several studies that one of the fundamental problems with systems implementation is resistance to change. That is, users confronted with new and potentially invasive systems find ways of preventing them from working. Resistance, in other words, is not futile. It is seen as a political problem that can be overcome through involvement. Thus, researchers like Sandberg (1975) distinguished between conflict- and harmony-based approaches to design, and the latter was taken up as a means to resolve conflicts. As we show, the harmony-based approach is fundamentally social democratic in its ideology, and works on the basis that organisational improvements, like social improvements, are best arrived at through consensus.

The consensus-led version of PD owes much to sociotechnical systems theory. There have been many proponents of this kind of theoretical approach, but perhaps the best known are Mumford (1983) and the Tavistock school (e.g. Emery and Trist (1960), Trist and Bamforth (1951), and Emery and Thorsrud (1976)). Mumford, for instance, showed how concepts such as knowledge fit, psychological fit, efficiency fit, task structure fit, and ethical fit (ibid.) related closely to the effectiveness of technical systems. Similarly, Trist and Bamforth, in their study of 'long-wall' mining, showed how the organisation and motivation of teams had an impact on the effectiveness of new technology. That is, the culture and work practices of people have been seen as deeply relevant to design for quite some time in a number of countries, including Germany (Jenkins, 1978), the United States (Work in America, 1973), and the United Kingdom (Wilson, 1973). Robertson (1998) points out that the same can be said of Australia. In Sweden, there has been a longstanding 'human work science' tradition that, even in the 1950s, was committed to the observation of, for instance, domestic life.

In turn, this broad sociotechnical approach created an interest in the HCI community which became known as 'job design' (see e.g. Hertzberg (1966), Hackman and Oldham (1975)). Much of the resulting research has centred on a multifaceted concern for the explication and decomposition of the sources of skill and workload in work, the nature of teams, a concomitant interest in the potential sources of inefficiency and error (see e.g.

Rasmussen (1988)), and the identification of problems and solutions for working with computer equipment through, for instance, the analysis of tasks. (see e.g. Schlager et al. (1990)).

It would be entirely wrong to see this kind of work as being central, or even necessarily sympathetic, to the concerns of PD in that it lacks both the political and methodological concerns of some varieties of PD. It is, however, a springboard for these concerns. Nevertheless, through the extraordinary process of forgetting that sometimes passes for academic life in the social sciences, these honourable programmes are seldom cited in CSCW and its cognates today. Thus, issues such as how to design jobs, using notions of job satisfaction or skill, in the job design movement, were not merely analytic problems but were predicated on a vision of humanity, much as the participatory design framework. Equally, they showed in their different ways that concern for the nature of work had to be a concern for the role of technology and its design.

PD takes the obvious extra step, however, in moving from this to a conception of the user as a participant both in organisational life and to any design process that may associate with it. These prior approaches, in other words, tended to see users both individualistically, and to treat them only as sources of information for the analyst or designer. That is, although we may regard job design as a step forward in the treatment of the user, it was still designers who designed jobs. The PD movement sought to rectify that.

The consensus view soon became subject to considerable criticism, and more radical alternatives were posited. Thus and for instance, the Florence project (Bjerknes and Bratteteig, 1987,1988), which took place between 1984 and 1987, and was a project aimed towards the work of nurses, reported on some of these tensions. It was predicated on the principle that medical support systems tended to be supply-led, and that knowledge of nurses' work might rectify this. Florence was intended to be a system to support nurses' daily work, based on their language and skills. Other groups, notably doctors, were included in the design team as well. They concluded that the main benefit of the research was its emphasis on mutual learning. That is, it emphasised communication between professionals and designers as a critical factor, and analysed the pathways by which knowledge of each other's concerns was established. The researchers acknowledged very considerable tensions between the harmony perspective and a more conflict- based one, and suggested that one ignores these conflicts at one's peril.[20]

In particular, sociotechnical systems research was held to be merely a means to integrate behavioural aspects (i.e. work) into the design process,

---

[20]In fact, Utopia moved from some fairly traditional approaches to requirements capture towards a mock-up approach. This approach became called 'design by doing' and traded on the idea that watching workers doing work, even in simulation, was better than orthodox knowledge elicitation. A 'tool perspective' was developed during the course of this project, which is predicated on the view that the computer is a tool for the skilled worker. It has an obvious relationship to ethnographic practice.

and it was argued that it did not take into account other aspects of the organisation, not least the existence of power structures Conflict-based approaches, obviously, involve taking sides on the grounds that design can and should serve certain interests over others. These collective resources approaches in PD derive from Marxist insights into social and industrial conflict and are very much a 'who's side are we on?' clarion call.

They owe much, in particular, to Braverman's (1974) labour process work, and arguably inherit much of Braverman's naivete. In this view, of course, conflict is inevitable because the interests of workers and the owners of capital are fundamentally opposed, and it is workers' interests that need better protection. Furthermore, one of the principal ways in which capitalism furthers its own interests is a relentless attack on the skilfulness of the worker. Braverman, among many other faults in his work, never documented through empirical work exactly what the skills in question might be. Indeed, in selecting a car assembly line to document the de-skilling process he could be accused of selecting his case to prove his argument and ignoring all those cases which run counter to it. Much of the debate about de-skilling has been empirical, in which cases of de-skilling can be found in some locations but are absent in others. It is beyond the remit of this work to discuss the conceptual confusions inherent in Braverman's work (see Thompson (1989) for a flavour of the debates).[21]

The basic commitment to designing tools for skilled work remains a strong current in CSCW research and we can have no objection to it. There is a large literature on the success and failure of projects which to a greater or lesser extent can be said to associate with the collective resources approach. It includes, for instance, the well-known Utopia project (Ehn, 1988) and Due (Kyng and Mattiessen, 1975). Versions of its commitments can be found in Bjerknes et al. (1987), and in Greenbaum (1988,1996). Politically founded design work is also sometimes called work-oriented design, or critical design (e.g. Ehn, 1988,1993). Although there are clearly many different versions of collective resources perspectives, all share some vision of preserving skill, whatever that might be, and providing a countervailing political locus in and through participation.

3.2.2 Participation

Similarly, PD is (obviously) driven by some commitment to user participation. This may seem axiomatic, but the fact is that much of the debate about PD, inside and outside that community, is a debate about what kinds of

---

[21]Not least, in case it should be thought that we are criticising the moral commitments of collective resources research, labour process theory has been criticised from within a Marxist tradition for ignoring the 'full circuit of capital': i.e. for emphasising one aspect of the relations of capital at the expense of others.

participation might be entailed. That is, PD was in part a reaction to technical analysis in the form of structured design or what have you. This reaction took the form of a less theoretical and more action-based research programme. It is not too unrealistic to say that one of the things that characterises the PD rhetoric is a reflective style, in which the relationship between researcher and subject is in the foreground, and used to account for what was achieved and what was not. PD in this version often refers to mutual learning as being constitutive of the design process. (see for instance Bjerknes and Bratteteig (1987,1988)). In this respect, it is not dissimilar to some postmodern versions of ethnography.

Later versions of PD, then, were heavily based on some of the above work, but developed new methodological commitments which had to do with working with users rather than merely studying them. Various benefits, it was suggested, accrued from this including:

- That it improves the knowledge base on which systems design is based
- That it enables people (users) to develop realistic expectations, and thus reduces resistance to change
- That it increases workplace democracy by giving individuals the right to participate

These purposes and more are encapsulated in the following (Greenbaum and Kyng, 1991).

> By viewing the people who use computers as competent in their field of work, we find that the workplace takes on the appearance of a rich tapestry, deeply woven with much intricacy and skill ... [there is a need to] ... take work practice seriously [recognise] ... we are dealing with human actors, not cut and dried human factors. [recognise] ... work tasks must be seen in their context, and are therefore situated actions. [recognise] ... work is fundamentally social, involving extensive co-operation and communication.

This is to raise a host of issues concerning users. Whether PD has been successful in providing the answers is a different matter. Blomberg and Kensing (1998, p. 173) suggest:

> In many P.D. projects it is not possible for all those affected by the design effort to fully participate. In these cases the choice of user participants and the form of participation must be carefully considered and negotiated with relevant organizational members, including management and the workers themselves. At times researchers or design professionals suggest the type of workers needed for the project (e.g. representatives of various occupational groups, workers with particular skills). Alternatively existing worker organizations may identify project participants.

This also rather begs some questions, most notably concerning quite how one identifies workers with particular skills or the range of occupations in advance of any enquiry concerning the organisation. Equally, the idea that worker organisations will offer the necessary democratic involvement would occasion a bitter laugh in some quarters.[22] Certainly, one cannot help feeling, when reading some of the more crass versions of management and worker scenarios put forward in the collective resources tradition, that the sociology of stratification has escaped many otherwise well-intentioned people.

Marx, for instance, at no time reduced the complexities of the class structure of industrial society down to management and worker, aware as he always was that reality is much more complex than analysis can ever allow. Edith Mumford was at pains to point out that in real organisational life, problems of worker–worker relations impinge as much on organisational change as management–worker relations. Segregation by status, by geography, by type of work done, and by knowledge deployed have all created organisational difficulties, difficulties of which CSCW researchers are well aware. Indeed, concepts such as articulation work reflect exactly that kind of problem.

As a result, the issue of participation can turn out to be extraordinarily complex. We might term this first question the 'what users?' problem. It might include questions concerning how many and drawn from where. Bjerknes and Bratteteig (op. cit.), for instance have argued that not only the immediate workplace is important in terms of users' input, but also much wider communities of users might be relevant, including the organisation as a whole, interorganisational features, and even a societal level. True though this undoubtedly is, it does raise some difficult issues of population mobilisation.

The second question is 'when?' There seems to be a natural fit between PD and some version of rapid prototyping. Indeed, more recently, PD has been related to agile processes (see Hanssen et al. (2004)). Several studies have reported on the problem of maintaining user involvement at various points of a more traditional system lifecycle, especially at the point where work becomes extremely technical. (See Hales (1993) for a review of some of these issues as they occurred in one case study.)

Thirdly, there is the question of 'to do what?' Users might variously be involved in specifying the interface, specifying the system, or designing primary work functions or wider organisational features. The jobs of users are often task-specific and they may have difficulty relating the system requirements to other people's functions.

Implicated in these three questions is the relationship presumed among users, management, and developers. Some studies, for instance, have raised

---

[22]Marge Piercy's fine novel, *Vida* (1980), indicates some of the tensions on the Left around participation and involvement, particularly for women. It is dedicated to 'street and alley soldiers', not to researchers or union bureaucrats.

a problem in that developers may stick to old practices, and even when there is sensitivity to user involvement, management can intervene at any stage. Blomberg and Kensing go as far as to say that the participation of management is more or less necessary if PD projects are to be successful, and other studies have certainly shown that results can be disappointing, at least in some respects, when management views alter. We might also point out that there are few, if any, examples of PD projects which have ranged over a whole organisation and where there are significant variations in occupational role and which implicate a large-scale technological system.

3.2.3 Methods, Tools, and Techniques

PD has become more sophisticated than it once was in its deployment of a range of methods and tools. A number of methodologies now exist which can be placed under its broad umbrella. They include Cooperative Experimental Systems Development (CESD; Groenbaek et al. (1997)), Soft Systems Methodology (SSM; Checkland (1981), Checkland and Scholes (1989), and Patching (1990)) and MUST (Kensing et al., 1998b) We should perhaps indicate here that not all of these methodologies would be naturally thought of as PD. Soft systems methods, for instance, have too strong a systems thinking element to be termed PD. Nevertheless, it involves strong elements of participation. Methods used by PD researchers include visualisation tools, mock-ups, future workshops, cooperative prototyping, case-based prototyping, and so on.

PD relates to the practice of fieldwork in some interesting ways. As Blomberg and Kensing (1998, p. 176) say, 'Increasingly, ethnographically inspired fieldwork techniques . . . are being integrated with more traditional PD techniques.'

If so then we need to ask why, because early work rather implied that fieldwork of the type associated with ethnography would not be necessary, in that evolving 'good practice' would appear to obviate the need for rigourous observation. Latterly, however, various PD projects have moved to incorporate some element of fieldwork. Simonsen and Kensing (1997; see also Kensing et al. (1998a)) for instance, suggest that their motivation in taking an ethnographic stance along with more orthodox PD strategies in their study of a film board was based on two relevant features of the design process: users often don't get what (they thought) they asked for and there is a need for a more flexible approach to system design.

They further imply that one source of complication, and one which ethnography may be well suited to deal with was organisational complexity. This is much in line with what we have argued above.

The above project is one where one gets a sense that PD interests have moved towards real-world issues. Blomberg and Kensing (1998, p. 175)

point to some of the difficulties entailed in the separation of any given project from its real world context:

> Equally important to the principles of organization are the issues of resource and time allocation. PD projects often take place in "greenhouse" settings where projects are shielded from the harsher realities of organizational life ... to be effective in the long run, PD practices must survive in "realworld" settings with their limited resources, conflict and serious time constraints.

Other work has also stressed the way in which some orthodox ethnographic assumptions and some PD assumptions might need to be challenged if they are, together, to be made useful for design. Karasti (2001), for instance, following Blomberg (2000), insists on the process of co-construction among ethnographer, practitioner, and designer as central to the design process.

This is as good a starting point as any for discussing PD's relationship with ethnography. Our position goes something like this: in small-scale studies, with tightly knit groups who are strongly motivated, and where there are few problems of complexity, PD practices will suffice and no additional knowledge furnished by ethnographers is likely to prove especially useful. Few real-world contexts are like that. Problems of coordination, cooperation, and so on, as CSCW practitioners know, are difficult to get to grips with in large-scale organisations because they involve issues of timing, of the social distribution of expertise and of local knowledge. It is unlikely in the extreme that any set of users, especially if drawn from a narrow subset of all possible users, could provide adequate knowledge or information for the design of such systems without appreciable guidance. In turn, however, the problem is, what knowledge is held by 'experts' such that adequate guidance can be given to users?

A related problem is methodological in respect of the ordinary techniques used in PD and elsewhere to elicit information. That is, if PD can be thought of as a kind of extended, and two-way, set of interviews then there are some well-known methodological issues to be dealt with in respect of asking and answering questions (see Crabtree (1998)). These include firstly that the answers to questions very much depend on the context in which they are asked. Answers are, as ethnomethodologists term it, recipient-designed which means that answers are given on the basis of assumptions made about the person asking the question.

The vexed problem of what is sometimes termed tacit knowledge, which is knowledge not articulated at least at a given moment, is in our view a subset of this problem. What is tacit is likely to be what is not considered worth saying in that context, for those purposes.

Compounding these issues is the further, and nontrivial, problem of whom to ask questions. Anyone with a knowledge of organisational politics will recognise that some people are more ready to put themselves forward than others, or indeed to be put forward by others. Whilst not wanting to be overly cynical, many with an experience of left-wing or trade union politics will know that there is no guarantee of equal representation inherent in left-leaning political institutions. This raises the question of the 'superuser', or to put it more conventionally, the problem of representativeness. In turn, this problem takes on a knowledge dimension in respect of the fact that no one in a large-scale organisation is likely to have an overall picture of the organisation and its work. Indeed, the invisibility of work owes much to the fact that management is frequently unaware of how things are done.

None of this is to challenge the credibility of PD. Rather, it is to establish reasons why PD and ethnography can fit together quite naturally. Of course, a great deal of PD work, as with CSCW, has concerned the work of easily identified, often co-located, small teams or groups. In such contexts, many of the issues we have discussed simply do not occur. As CSCW's ambitions extend, however, into more complex technologies and organisations, they will arise more frequently. Ethnography provides organisational knowledge of one kind or another.

Having said that, the kind of organisational knowledge at stake is not predetermined. Analytic choices have to be made. Even so, at the very least it would seem intuitively obvious that the ethnographer with sophisticated domain knowledge is likely to be something of a 'bridge' between domain experts who may have problems articulating their work to experts, and experts who have problems all of their own. (see Twidale et al. (1994) for experiences of this kind). In principle, whilst acknowledging that practicalities place restrictions on the extent of the organisational knowledge that they can have, ethnographers, in virtue of their nonspecific location in the organisation can know more about its workings than anyone else. In summary, PD might have the following characteristics in relation to fieldwork.

- It suggests that ethnography can provide analytic complementarity and can provide a knowledge base for designers' work with users.
- It insists that design is political, and hence draws attention to the different stakeholders in the design process.
- It pushes ethnographers towards a more 'active subject' stance in ways which are analogous to sociological interests in standpoint theory.

3.3 Conversation Analysis and Interaction Analysis

The fact that we turn independently to what are called Conversation Analysis (CA) and Interaction Analysis (IA), having already talked at points about ethnomethodology, will strike many as odd. Most casual observers would assume that these movements are simply subsets of ethnomethodology involved in pretty much the same thing. We suggest that they are not.

There is a degree of irony attached to the fact that as CA and ethnomethodology have awakened to the fact that they are not quite the fellow travellers they have always been assumed to be, so CA and its derivatives have begun to attract more adherents and from a wide variety of disciplinary interests.

CA has been a major enterprise within, or parallel to, ethnomethodology for many years. There are many examples, including the work of, for brief mention, Schegloff (1972), Schegloff et al. (1977), Schegloff and Sacks (1973), Pollner (1974), Drew and Heritage (1992), Sacks, 1992, and many others. It has taken a number of directions in this time, including for instance attempts to formulate conversation as manifesting power structures (Drew and Heritage, op. cit.). It is not the place here to enter into debates about whether these attempts make sense, but we suggest, following Harvey Sacks, that the focus on the formal properties of conversation and in particular on the turn-taking mechanism, although it may be useful in some design-related enterprises, may equally well be irrelevant to others.

Sacks observed that his interest in conversation was not because conversation had any unique properties or was somehow more important in the social world than other phenomena, but because conversation was *replicable* data. In other words, the fact that anyone can inspect the data in question (through transcripts or latterly video) and draw whatever conclusions they consider warranted, and whether they coincide with the original analysis, is a powerful empirical weapon. Such inspection of raw data is not normally available in the sociological community.

We take Sacks at his word here and suggest that conversation, and for that matter interaction, should be seen as perspicuous examples of data: they have the characteristics that Sacks (1984a) wanted to see in a 'natural, observational science.' Ethnomethodology's project has been, as Button (1991) has argued, the 'respecification' of sociology and for that matter the other human sciences. In keeping with this desire for analysis based on replicable, commonly available data, CA imposed a strict 'warrantability' clause for its enquiries. Ethnomethodologists of whatever stripe have always insisted that the foundation for any argument concerning 'what is going on here' must be the data, and in the spirit of Sacks' work have argued that the warrant for any given assertion should be visible in the data. Of course, such a position is unexceptional to ethnomethodologists, especially in respect of their relationship with sociology. We argue, however, that it does elide some possible differences in what our understanding of relevant data might be when we are confronted with interdisciplinary requirements.

These remarks about conversation analysis are relevant inasmuch as it provides an analytic foundation for what today is called interaction analysis and its cognate discipline, interaction design. We suggest that the distinction between CA and IA seen as methods for uncovering the formal properties of conversation or of interaction and as fellow-travellers of an ethnomethodological program which emphasises the situatedness of behaviour is what opens up the space for Nardi's critique of 'situated action theory' (Nardi, 1996b) wherein the latter approach is accused of a 'mild' behaviourism and one, moreover, which is incapable of recovering 'motive'.

In our view, although Nardi's general critique is highly selective and unwarranted, it is applicable to a subset of interaction analytic problems. That is, at the point where the problem space of interaction analysis is given by the latter's interest in the formal properties of interactional sequences, and by those matters alone, then we cannot presuppose any relevance to design problems in general. There may nevertheless be a plausible relevance to some specific design problems. Our suspicion is that the relevance of conversation analytic and cognate frameworks is most likely to be found in studies of computer-mediated communication precisely because the sequencing, design, and repair of conversation is evidently relevant to technologies which primarily support communication. Interaction analysis, whilst obviously casting its net wider, may nevertheless fall victim to the same problem of relevance. That is, where the technologies in question are self-evidently proposed as solutions to certain kinds of interactional problem then analysis of interaction is likely to prove deeply relevant. To assume that this is the limit of CSCW's legitimate interest in design, however, is to define CSCW very narrowly. These issues drive our own analytic interests and are why, in due course, we argue for an analytic interest in work rather than interaction.

In suggesting this, we take our inspiration from another of Sacks' (1984b, p. 414) papers, 'On Doing "Being Ordinary"' in which he argues, 'Whatever you may think about what it is to be an ordinary person, an initial shift is not to think of "an ordinary person" as some person, but as somebody having as one's job, as one's constant preoccupation, doing "being ordinary".'

'Work' then, in this sense, is to do with the 'constant preoccupation' of individuals and groups as they engage in whatever they are engaged in. Our point here would be that the analysis of conversation and interaction generally should serve the purpose of illuminating the preoccupations of the people doing these things. Now we do not need to go into any great detail here in order to cover the basic elements of conversation analysis. Many readers will already be familiar with elements of the 'simplest systematics', such matters as the way one person talks at a time, that any overlaps will not persist, the structuring of utterances in terms of adjacency pairs, and turn-allocation (Sacks et al., 1978) Of course, the field has developed considerably from there.

We can do much worse than adopt Paul Ten Have's suggestion that conversation analysis can be thought of as being concerned with four types of interactional organisation, which he suggests are 'analytically distinguished but interlocking . . .' (1999, p. 110) and which constitute an 'exploratory analytic shopping list' (ibid., p. 119). These consist in the analysis of turn-taking (see e.g. Sacks et al. 1978), of sequence organisation (Sacks, 1992), of repair organisation (see e.g. Schegloff et al. (1977)), and of the organisation of turn-construction and design. The last covers a range of possible topics, but includes the notion of recipient design (Sacks et al., 1984b) in which talk is analysed according to the way in which utterances are designed by one speaker with knowledge of another speaker in mind; and preference organisation, in which, given alternative courses of action, one may be visibly preferred over another (see e.g. Pomerantz (1984).[23]

We see basic issues with CA and IA in design. Firstly we would point out here that, in the context of relevant analysis for HCI and CSCW purposes, it should be obvious that not all of Ten Have's analytic choices will prove equally valuable in all circumstances. After all, and associated with the very nature of interdisciplinarity across this analytic/synthetic design terrain is the degree to which 'informing' design will depend in no little part on what is being designed. Thus, where the focus on turn-taking might prove extremely useful for the analysis of problems of computer-mediated communication, and sequence organisation might prove fruitful in understanding the way people mutually organise tasks, a focus on 'repair' might prove more useful in understanding the way in which, for instance, customers in a queue are dealt with (see e.g. Randall and Hughes (1995)). This, we think, is likely to hold whether one is dealing narrowly with conversation or more broadly with interaction.

There is an important issue buried here, which has to do with the difference between treating CA or IA as a method or as an analytic choice. Ten Have's 'shopping list' rather disguises a possible faultline: whether CA and IA are to be treated as methods which can be used to uncover data about almost anything, or as analytic choices which restrict themselves to uncovering the formal (and thus noncontextual) properties of conversation or interaction. In a third option we might consider them to be forms of analysis predicated on some foundational assumptions about human interaction, such as that utterances are recipient-designed and in so doing retain a clear sense of the importance of contextuality.

In any event, there is a second (although related) issue to contend with here, which has to do with appropriate granularity. Even those with the most cursory interest in CA will recognise its close attention to the details of turn-taking, sequencing, and the like. In design terms, however, we surely need to ask the question concerning the circumstances in which such very close analysis of sequence is either necessary or desirable. There is a major difference between insisting on work as a sequentially organised phenomenon, which it surely is, and presuming that the description of those sequences should therefore take place at a certain level of detail (or that every possible description of working life should be provided in terms which describe sequential organisation).

---

[23]For those who want a more detailed but nevertheless introductory text on CA, we recommend Ten Have's, *Doing Conversation Analysis* (1999).

Thirdly, there is the matter of understanding what is at stake when one speaks of conversational rules and tries to uncover them. CA has, at times, been viewed as a resource for solving some problems associated with computer-mediated communication. Examples of work in this area include work such as Frohlich and Luff's 'advice system' (1990), which was designed to preclude or prevent certain kinds of response. Thus, if the system asked a question, users were forced into conditional relevance by giving answers to questions. In such projects, lessons from CA are learned in order to furnish rules for automated systems which might provide for instance, conversation-based ticketing information. Such work has proven controversial and the roots of that controversy should interest all of us who choose to work in this way.

The lines of the controversy have to do with different views of the notion of rule following and what is meant by the proposition that conversation can be said to embody a set of rules. At root, much as Graham Button argued (1990), following Wittgenstein, this has to do with a particular conception of rule-following contained in some conversation analysis, and one which many would reject. In that version, rules are thought of as basically causal and thus the rules of conversation in some way cause people to speak the way they do. Rather, Button argues, such rules should be thought of as rules in the sense (and this sense only) that they are descriptive of what people typically do; it implies something of the character of the behaviour in question, for example, whether it is done well or badly. Is a rule something that provides a causal relationship?

Well, it might be, but it doesn't have to be. One way of looking at the rules of conversation would be to view them causally, and if you can, then the sophisticated simulation of conversation is only a matter of uncovering every rule and its relevance. In principle, this may be no easy task, given that there may turn out to be a huge number of rules, but few would argue that the number of conversation-generating rules is that large. The 'Sundial' project, designed for airline bookings and enquiries had a similar structure (see Gilbert et al. (1990)), by including identifiable adjacency pairs, turn-taking mechanisms, opening sequences, closing sequences, and question/answer structures. Of course, if you take the view that breaking these rules is something that human beings frequently do then the possible value of such an analysis starts to look less substantial.

The issue does not disappear, we feel, when attention turns to the broader themes associated with interaction analysis. We should briefly characterise IA. IA is no single approach, but a broad commitment. It is associated with the work that came out of Xerox Parc, and with a number of well-known figures in the HCI and CSCW communities including Lucy Suchman, Brigitte Jordan, Jeanette Blomberg, and Charles Goodwin, as well as Christian Heath, Paul Luff, and others in Europe. It emphasised the value of the close video analysis of work sequences for design-related problems. Examples of this

kind of work include Goodwin's study of an airport (formulating planes) and Heath and Luff's study of the London Underground.

Briefly, the insights afforded by this perspective include

1. The idea that we can uncover a range of, and perhaps a grammar of communicative acts, which would include gesture, gaze, and the like (thereby, in principle, providing a logic of enquiry for all similar work)
2. That a focus on the detail of communication work has specific resonance for design, through its recognition of the semi-tacit nature of some communication

Ten Have asks the question, 'Would it make sense, then, to "apply" CA's methods and findings to this field of human–computer interaction or HCI?' (1999, p. 192). If we substitute IA for CA here and ask the same question, our answer depends on what it is that IA takes from CA and what it leaves behind. On the face of it, there is little in the claims made by, for instance, Jordan and Henderson (1995) to which we could object:

> Interaction analysis as we describe it is an interdisciplinary method for the empirical investigation of the interaction of human beings with each other and with objects in their environment. It investigates human activities such as talk, nonverbal interaction, and the use of artifacts and technologies, identifying routine practices and problems and the resources for their solution.

Furthermore, 'One basic underlying assumption in IA is that knowledge and action are fundamentally social in origin, organization, and use, and are situated in particular social and material ecologies.'

This sounds good. The position is clearly quite consistent with the ethnomethodological line that we advocate. Moreover, they are insistent on a relationship between IA as they practice it and some kind of ethnography:

> Another widely shared assumption among practitioners of IA is that verifiable observation provides the best foundation for analytic knowledge of the world. This view implies a commitment to grounding theories of knowledge and action in empirical evidence, that is, to building generalizations from records of particular, naturally occurring activities, and steadfastly holding our theories accountable to that evidence … analytic work, then, draws at least in part, on our experience and expertise as competent members of ongoing social systems and functioning communities of practice.

They further comment, 'Our own practice has been to do videotaping in conjunction with ethnographic fieldwork.' Nevertheless, we need perhaps to understand what might be entailed if we are to agree that this seems a sensible way to proceed. Hester and Francis (1999) have drawn attention to what they see as two developments. Firstly they argue that CA in some studies was being compromised by its incorporation into theorist-imposed sociological agendas and secondly that its focus on the sequential organisation of talk was being required to carry a far greater analytic burden than it was capable of bearing. It is on this latter point that we wish to focus. As Hester and Francis (1999) put it:

> Our second point is a concentration on matters of sequentiality and turn-taking alone whilst perfectly legitimate in themselves, cannot provide an adequate answer to the question of the recognisability of "institutional activities and identities".

They go on to suggest that such adequacy 'can only be achieved when a concern with sequentiality is combined with other organisational (e.g. categorical) features of such phenomenon.' Hester and Francis' critique of the Institutional Talk Programme (Drew and Heritage, 1992) in effect asks how we arrive at the categories we use in order to make organisation or institutional activities 'recognisable'. What Hester and Francis argue is that examples of analyses in this tradition actually draw on sociological categories rather than participants' contextual orientations. We make a similar point here: that studies predicated on some presumed relationship between IA and ethnography are in danger of conceptually driven readings which appear to emanate from the methodological concerns of the discipline rather than a concern for informing design.

The focus on interactional analysis has come under some attack, notably from Nardi (1996b). Her work provides us with an opportunity to discuss the relationship between ethnography and interaction analysis. This relationship has not, to our knowledge, been subject to careful scrutiny. Jordan and Henderson (1995), two of those most closely associated with the IA perspective, suggest that IA should be used in conjunction with ethnography. Thus:

> We rely on participative observation, in-situ interviewing, historical reconstruction, and the analysis of artifacts, documents and networks for *providing the framing context*. In the course of this ethnographic work, we attempt to identify interactional "hotspots" – sites of activity for which videotaping promises to be productive. Ethnographic information then furnishes the background against which video analysis is carried out while the detailed understanding provided by the micro-analysis of interaction, in turn, informs our general ethnographic understanding [our emphasis].

They advocate, then, some relationship between ethnography and IA. Even so, it is not exactly clear from the above extract what role ethnography is expected to play. There appear to be two possibilities. Firstly, it may be that ethnography and IA provide us with different and complementary analytic viewpoints, and thus feed from each other in providing design-related assessments or it may be that the ethnography merely provides a background

context for the serious analytic work of interaction analysis. Thus and for instance, Jordan and Henderson (1995) assert:

> ... much has been written about the complex organization of turn-taking in conversation. For IA the situation is ever more complicated because an IA turn-taking system has to take into account more than talk; it encompasses the whole range of behaviours through which people can take a "turn", that is, participate in an interactional exchange system. Not only "turns with talk" must be considered, but also "turns with bodies" and "turns with artifacts".

This presumption – that the situation or context for investigation will involve the turn-taking mechanism – explains in some part much of the analytic focus of Ruhleder and Jordan's study (1999) of 'time delayed' distributed interaction. This paper is indicative of the kind of study that results from presumptions about the relationship between IA and ethnography. We should note here that we are not in the business of criticising exemplary work. We chose it because it typifies the work done under the auspices of interaction analysis; it is a thorough and polished analysis of a highly specific set of interactional sequences, and explicitly recommends that studies of this kind be accompanied by something that looks like an ethnographic approach. This, specifically to engage with the problem of understanding 'what is going on', is something that video analysis on its own cannot do.

Furthermore, the paper addresses the application of technology in a distributed fashion and is therefore appropriate for exploring the methodological implications of moving out of the control room. The paper is concerned with the effect of time-delays on video-based communication systems and specifically addresses a video segment of premeeting and meeting activities between three software developers on the East Coast and three accountants on the West Coast, using videoconferencing technology.

The following extract serves to illustrate the type of problem they identify for analysis.

> Because of the delay of approximately one second, we noticed that what one side heard was different from what the other side heard. Silences were of different duration, cues came at wrong times. We identified 32 episodes within the 19 minute interaction which exhibited these characteristics and in which these characteristics were identified by multiple analysts without the aid of any special technological manipulation or assistance (slowing the sounds down, using a metronome etc.).

The following extracts from their discussion, which in keeping with the CA line focus on turn-taking and sequentiality, are indicative of the limits we are identifying with IA.

Talk is not just about the exchange of information, but about shared meaning making on multiple levels. The examples above illustrate how delay impacts the ability of conversational participants to create shared meaning through talk via remote communication technologies. In each case:

> Some kind of trouble arises.
> This trouble disrupts the turn-taking system.
> The trouble source *cannot be identified* by participants [our emphasis].
> Participants may sense that something might be wrong....
> ... The nature of distributed technology, however, may preclude people from identifying the trouble and making repairs.
> The potential consequence is a pervasive sense of unease.

We reiterate that this study is exemplary insofar as it achieves what it sets out to achieve. The points we want to make below have to do with the absence of what we would term an ethnographic sensibility from the analysis. Our point is that a number of possible questions are absent. In other words, there are things which we simply do not know and with which the ethnography could and should have helped. The questions might include:

1. Does the task-in-hand make any difference?
2. Does the status of the participants, construed by these participants, make any difference?
3. Is this work they could equally well do by using another technology (e.g. telephone), and if so why did these participants not opt for that?

If serious organisational tasks need to be completed, then members will use whatever technology is to hand to get the job done. If these people do not do so, then it suggests that the interactional problems they are experiencing are not terribly serious in the first place. If it is wrong to read the situation that way, then we should know why. That is, and in some sense, what seems to be missing here is some conception of an 'organisational context'. We are arguing precisely that the skills, knowledge, and competencies that members possess, and which enable them to orient to various here and now problems of work-in-organisation may not be directly visible in this here and now, given that some set of (unspecified) procedures has produced this particular context as the relevant context for analysis, but will be visible in other contexts within the organisational setting, contexts which the proficient ethnographer will have investigated and analysed. To put this another way, construing the relevant analysis as a matter of understanding interaction is one thing; construing it as a matter of understanding these interactional data is quite another. That is, we are never clear what kind of relevance criteria are applied such that we can justify applying these data to this technological problem. Construing the analysis as being a matter of understanding a job of work which takes place in the context of various organisational relevancies, and seen by members in those terms, entails seeing a range of other possibilities, including for instance how members define and orient to an organisational context.

Perhaps this lacuna is why Nardi can make the quite extraordinary assertion that, 'In situated action what constitutes a situation is defined by the researcher' (1996b, p. 82). We can only say, 'No it is not.' Indeed the purpose of ethnographic enquiry is to understand exactly what those involved define as the situation, inasmuch as this is the basis for action rather than any researcher-derived definition. Even so, we might ask why it is that we need understand gesture, gaze, glance, and the like as forms of turn-taking at all, but more importantly in a design context why we should presume that these mechanisms constitute the problem terms of computer use. The relevance of any context here is not that of context as a members' category, for that context would have to derive from how members construe and manage their work and we have been at pains to argue that the work is not necessarily in view in IA.

Our point here is akin to that made by Hughes et al. (1994), wherein they suggested several different ways in which ethnography might be used in relation to design. We suggest in addition that, whatever informing design might mean, its force has been the presumption that ethnography and design must be more or less tightly coupled. This may in part be because the analysis of interaction serendipitously coincides with a focus on certain kinds of technological problem. We want to suggest that in a period of time when the technologies in question may be only at the very earliest stages of development, or may not exist at all, we might opt for a much looser understanding of that relationship, facilitated by a better understanding of the relationship between ethnography and interaction analysis. For instance, a particular analytic problem might be posed for ethnographic studies pertaining to technologies such as 3G mobile technology[24] or multimedia resources envisaged in large-scale organisational contexts. Such developments in technology are moving us away from the co-located task-focused activities of the control room into the domain of geographically dispersed, distributed systems facilitated by computer-mediated communications technologies. These emerging technologies, and the changing contexts of use, are such that informing requirements may not be an appropriate way to think about the functions of ethnography. If that is the case then it may follow that some analytic choices within ethnomethodology may also be increasingly problematic.

This argument, as we stated at the outset, should be seen in the context of the ever-increasing complexity of design. The move to less bounded domains, we are suggesting, raises the prospect that what has been seen as an in-principle coupling of interaction analysis and design problems may turn out to be a serendipitous relationship between one set of analytic

---

[24]One international high-tech company with which the authors are familiar has recently set up an advanced products division. Their brief is to design new products based on breaking technologies. As one researcher there put it: 'How can we look at how people might use it when we don't know what it's going to be?'

interests and a specific set of problems to do with control room technologies. As we see a shift away from the highly limited domains of CSCW research towards more complex, and arguably more interesting, problems so we may see a progressive decoupling of this relationship.

In part, our concerns lie with when our analytic interests should become design-relevant, and what we see in IA is a rush to focus on presumed design-relevant matters which may, in highly complex organisational situations, miss the point. The point of the ethnographic stance we advocate is that it paints a picture of organisational complexity, richness, or contextuality which allows us to identify what matters might turn out to be relevant to design in the first place. We do this not merely by framing the work of IA, but by taking a quite specific analytic turn towards what work might be. Nevertheless, conversation/interaction analysis has undoubted relevance:

- It draws our attention to the merits of fine-grained sequential analysis.
- It sees at least a 'scenic' role for a wider ethnographic stance.
- It is of undoubted value in the analysis of a subset of design issues, those which relate to computer-mediated communication and to command and control problems.

4

Activity Theory, Distributed Cognition, and Actor-Network Theory

---

4.1 Activity Theory

Activity theory is yet another theoretical stance, or theory of practice, which has become directed at many of the seemingly obdurate problems of human-centred design. It is associated in origin with the work of Russian psychologists during the 1920s, notably Vygotsky (1978,1982) and Leon'tev (1974,1981). One thing to point out here is that its origins are completely separate from those of ethnomethodology and other situated analyses. Indeed, the origins of activity theory, it might be pointed out, were political. For Vygotsky it was an explicit reaction against the scientism of alternatives and was specifically a new form of psychology with a liberating potential. We do not claim to be experts in said humanistic psychology and describe the main tenets of the perspective because it has become widespread as a theoretical resource for interdisciplinary work. Moreover, its proponents typically appropriate fieldwork methods for their enquiries. As such, it should be understood both as a critique of the simplistic behavioural tendency in psychology, and as an explicitly humanistic programme.

For Vygotsky (1982), psychology should emphasise at least three primary elements:

1. It should be developmental.
2. It should relate 'elementary' psychological functions with 'higher-level' mental work.
3. It should take account of 'socially meaningful activity'.

Vygotsky was particularly interested in methodological issues, noting even at that early time that facts were 'theoretically laden'. Hence (Vygotsky, 1982), 'Any fact, being expressed in terms of these systems [introspectionism, behaviourism, and psychoanalysis] would acquire three entirely different meanings, which indicate three different aspects of this fact, or more precisely, three different facts.'

In part because of this, psychological investigation must be layered. It cannot restrict itself to basic functions such as attention, memory, and the like, but must also be aware of the inner evolution of psychological formations. In a nutshell, this refers to the development of concepts, which are most definitely part of the higher-level of cognitive, or mental, function. An initial finding was that thought and speech were not synonymous, and have different origins.[25] Rather, they merge at particular moments. In particular, they merge at the level of 'higher' mental functions, functions which form an existence culturally.

In certain contexts, then, thinking about matters (and we may impute from subsequent and more modern work, thinking about technology) can be preconceptual (sometimes referred to as spontaneous concepts, located entirely in reflection on immediate experience, and distinguished from scientific concepts). This has an immediate corollary in learning, in that this also can be systematically organised or spontaneous.

The best-known concept to emerge from this approach is that of 'zo-ped', or the zone of proximal development. In effect, it refers to the prescientific world of spontaneous concepts inhabited by children meeting the systematic organised world of the rational adult. Of course, it can equally well refer to the way in which the tyro user meets the expert. The point is that this meeting place is a rich learning experience: the learner learns by transforming the one into the other in and through the dialogue between learner and expert. In essence, then, activity theory orients to three elements: actor, object, and community. Its richness for CSCW lies in principle in its approach to technology as mediator of human activity, which in a dialectic relationship with the cultural world produces activity.

It is not entirely surprising, given this interest in concept formation, that activity theory has been of powerful interest in fields such as Computer Supported Cooperative Learning (CSCL) and to some degree in CSCW itself. (See Bannon (1991), Bannon and Kuutti (1991), Kuutti (1991,1996), Bardram (1997), Nardi (1996b), and Nardi and Redmiles (2002)). The continued development of activity theory has in part been a response to the perceived inadequacies of HCI. Part of the critique of HCI which they advance is a critique of 'ad hocery' insofar as research into HCI has been piecemeal, empirically derived, and predicated on no coherent set of assumptions about human behaviour. Put simply, one justification for activity theory is precisely that it provides a unifying theory for research into HCI (on the face of it, this seems like an odd criticism, given that HCI has been critiqued elsewhere, for instance by Bannon and by Winograd and Flores, on the grounds that cognitivist theory underpins its assumptions). Still, Kuutti (1996, p. 17) argues that

---

[25]This, we should point out, is a critique of the Sapir–Whorf hypothesis *avant la lettre*.

> ... one would assume that there exists a well-established body of harmonious scientific knowledge covering the basic foundations of the discipline. ... This harmony is, however, fallacious. Research is not ahead of practice-on the contrary. In fact, a considerable number of researchers have been studying successful solutions in order to understand why they are working.

Kuutti's point is that this body of 'harmonious scientific research' is not producing coherent and theoretically predictable results for use in practice. Critics of HCI, he says, 'would like to add to the research object the users and their actual work tasks' (1996, p. 19). He argues that this progression is one in which there is a gradual recognition of the 'perspectives' brought by users to the interface, but that attempts to produce results from this are problematised by the absence of 'any unifying background' (1996, p. 23), resulting in varying degrees of ad hocery.

We should note here that Kuutti is arguing that activity theory can add a dimension to cognitive approaches to HCI. It is not there to replace it. He further suggests that we can learn from IS research (see Bannon and Kuutti (1991)) in recognising the shift among levels that takes place, the levels in question being a technical level, a conceptual level, and a work process level. Activity theory then becomes a conceptual tool for unifying these levels. Activities, then, have levels and thus can be treated recursively (which, as we show, is where the notorious triangles come in). Participating in an activity is 'performing conscious actions that have an immediate defined goal' (Kuutti ibid., p. 30). However, and crucially, understanding these activities requires a frame of reference created by corresponding activities.

These views are supported by Kaptilinen (1994,1996a,b), who emphasises the way in which activity theory can be counterposed to some orthodox assumptions in HCI, most notably the shift from the individual human being and his or her relation to the computer interface towards '. . . a radically different assumption. It assumes that what is needed to make HCI a conceptually integrated field is a theory that describes and explains the larger context of human interaction with computers' (1996a, p. 45). That is, activity theory moves us towards real-world contexts of use, a context that is social through and through (or cultural historical). The relation between humans and computers is explicitly not symmetrical. Moreover, activity theory comes into its own because there has been a shift in the kinds of question asked about the design of computers, and these questions are not appropriately resolved at the cognitive level. (Kaptilinen also sees no necessary contradiction between activity theory and cognitive science.) The point is that these wider questions, which are largely to do with the developing influence of CSCW and/or organisational computing mean that, rather than the information-processing models of humans and computers, an approach to the behaviour of both in a wider environment is required.

Kuutti (op. cit.) further suggests that activity theory contributes three specific elements: multilevelledness. interaction in social context. and a dynamic.

It thus moves HCI's concerns onwards, from the 'human factor' to the 'human actor' as Bannon (1991) puts it. Kuutti asks why it is that, if operations are a natural and inevitable feature of actions, most computer systems are not designed with the action in view. He further suggests that we can understand what the role of IT is in various ways, including automating routines. providing data about objects, triggering predetermined responses, embedding rules, linking work tasks, and providing for a division of labour at the operation level, and so on and so on (see Kuutti op. cit. p. 36) and clearly sees activity theory as providing a conceptual framework for doing these things.

Here, activities and actions are distinguished. Activities, although realised in actions, specifically refer to conscious actions with defined goals (and manifestly, not all actions fit this criterion). Activity then is an analytical construct which relies on the recognition of shared goals in some way. Furthermore, activities (and not actions) are 'typically planned in the consciousness using a model (ibid., p. 31). This phase – the move from action to activity – is referred to as 'orientation'. Orientation is akin to the notion of 'resources' as suggested by Suchman (1987). Models and plans adopted in this 'orientation' are not to be regarded in any rigid way, and collapse into 'operations' as they prove to be adequate to the task in hand. Moreover, they can entail a return to the conscious level as the scope of operations is broadened. This is a critical feature of human development: as skills develop they entail an 'orientation-operation-unfolding' process.

Activity theory, then, implies a modest critique of cognitive science, suggesting that cognition as 'mental processing' is present only some of the time, and that internalist conceptions of cognition (whereby cognition consists of discrete and functionally interrelated, or modular, brain activities) are inadequate to our understanding of social behaviour. The claim is that activity theory rejects the dualistic conception of mind because internal states can only exist alongside external ones. Thus, according to Leont'ev (1974, p. 19) and quoted in Kuutti (1996, p. 33), '... a person's mental processes acquire a structure necessarily linked to sociohistorically formed means and modes, which are transmitted to him by other people through teamwork and social intercourse.'

Consciousness must be treated holistically, and located in ordinary and everyday practice. Activity theory, indeed, focuses on practice: 'understanding everyday practice in the real world is the very objective of scientific practice' (Nardi, 1996a, p. 7). Of course what any person does, if not a function of purely cognitive states, must be a function of other systems, and these are to be found in the material and social world according to activity theorists.

Activity here is a basic unit of analysis; a minimal meaningful context for individual actions must be included. Of course the big problem here is how one specifies what the context is to be: how it is constituted. To understand this, we need to get a picture of how individuals do anything at all in the world. Engestrom (1987,1990) and others (see e.g. Wertsch (1981), Cole (1984), and Bødker (1991)) have largely been responsible for developing a nuanced view of how activities might be structured. Broadly, for activity to take place there needs to be an individual, there needs to be a purpose, and there needs to be a context. The individual is the subject; the purpose is the object (necessarily mediated, but not necessarily material in and of itself. One source of confusion for those reading activity-theoretical pieces is that the term, 'object', does not in and of itself imply anything material at all. Although activities must necessarily be mediated by artefacts or tools, they are defined in, and constitutive of, the relationship between subject and object), and the context is the community. Of course, these three elements must exist in a relationship, and that relationship is triangular.

One has to bear in mind here that the interaction among these three elements can take place on various levels. Nevertheless, there is a set of relationships between each element, much as follows.

1. The relation between subject and object is mediated by the tool.
2. The relationship between subject and community is mediated by rules. (Rules cover a broad spectrum of norms, conventions, and procedures.)
3. The relation between community and object is mediated by the division of labour. Activities have outcomes, and these outcomes are transformations, delivered out of the division of labour of a community as it engages in this transformation process.

Activity theory begins the construction of context by pointing to the fact that activities are always, and inevitably, mediated by various artefacts or tools. An 'essential feature of these artefacts is that they always have a mediating role' (ibid. 1996, p. 26), paralleling the argument from actor-network theory. Activities are forms of doing directed towards an object (a purpose). Here there is a significant divergence from, say, ethonomethodological conceptions of doing, which do not necessarily involve any orientation to artefacts. Tools are both enabling and limiting (in line with the notion of constraints and affordances, as discussed by Gibson (1979)).

Along with this triangular structure, other features of activity theory should be borne in mind. First, it has a strong emphasis on development. Indeed, this strongly developmental aspect is arguably its strongest feature. This is visible, for instance, in the relationship between user and tool which must carry a history. Subject and tool are constituted in a history of use (as skills which are crystallised into the tool). In particular, users have very changeable statuses in their relations with artefacts; they begin as novices and become more expert.

These statuses are, of course, also strongly affected by the third point of the triangle, the community. This is why so much has been made of the aforementioned zo-ped, or the zone of proximal development, for it strongly suggests that our ways of doing, our skills and practices come, in part, from the way we learn from experts. A second major aspect of activity theory, then, is it places emphasis on learning. Third, artefacts, and in particular computer artefacts, radically alter our way of thinking about practice. This follows from the logically prior status of exteriority in activity theory, whereby doing precedes thinking. Because all doing is mediated by artefacts, then our way of doing, and our way of thinking about it (internalisation), must also be mediated. Fourth is the fact that the user is not merely an individual: users must be considered at the level of the group or the community or the organisation as well.

Activity theory, it is probably fair to say, has been adopted in a widespread way by practitioners in CSCW, although its purchase has been more limited elsewhere. Regardless, it is not difficult to find examples of its use, and useful sources include the CSCW special edition on activity theory (2002) and Bonnie Nardi's edited collection some years before (Nardi, 1996a). Specific case studies include, for illustrative purposes, Engestrom and Escalante's (1996) study of the 'postal buddy', Bellamy's application of activity theory to educational technologies (1996), Raeithel on design (1992), and Bardram (1997) on patient scheduling. Not least, what is evident from a review of this literature is that activity theory itself undergoes constant transformation as attempts are made to integrate it with realist epistemology (Spasser, 2002) and with actor-network theory (Engestrom and Escalante, 1996), as well as to introduce new concepts such as 'intensional networks' (Nardi et al., 2002) which are 'the personal social networks workers draw from and collaborate with to get work done' (ibid., p. 207).

To take but one example of activity theory's application, we might look at Bellamy's (op. cit.) use of an activity theoretical perspective to analyse educational technology. The role of technology in schools has often been seen as a progressive one (e.g. Papert and the constructivist approach). Because activity theory is based on the view that tools mediate thought, it should line up with this view, and to an extent does. Following Leont'ev (1981), mind can only be understood as a process of internalizing external activity, and activity always takes place in the context of an artefactual world. Bellamy points to the way activity has developed the concept of use by suggesting that it is not only the use itself, but the cultural context of the use that must be understood. He points to the way that one must analyse educational activity through this lens of the community, and identify, for instance teachers, administrators, parents, and students; but also a set of rules, explicit and implicit, and a division of labour. Change is produced interactively from the relationship among subject; object, and community. This occurs both at individual and community level.

Vygotsky's theory of zo-ped, which has to do with what novices can do on their own and what they can do along with an expert, reflects a developmental element to this and has been influential in the concept of authentic learning (Lave and Wenger, 1991). Lave and Wenger, as is well known, describe this community of varying tyros and experts as a 'community of practice'. Within this framework, and given the dynamic nature of activity, contradictions arise when there are ruptures between different activities, or at different stages of a given activity. Here, there is a focus on perceived problems, akin in some ways to the ethnomethodological focus on 'normal natural troubles'. Attention to these matters, according to Bellamy (1996, p. 131), gives us three principles of learning technology that can be derived from activity theory:

1. Authentic activity (similar cultural activities to those of adults; age appropriate)
2. Construction (tool-mediated)
3. Collaboration (between experts and learners)

We can see here how analytic attention is expanded, such that in the matter of education, the roles and work of other people, such as relevant adults, are treated as relevant, as is specific attention to the role of the tool and how it is used, along with the relationship between experts and learners. The power of activity theory, as suggested above, certainly lies in its corrective capacity vis-à-vis HCI and similar interdisciplinary arenas where cognitive presumptions have come to dominate. Where HCI has focused largely on the removal of error from operations, activity theory addresses issues that have to do with supported work and sensemaking, if you will, a broader focus.

Without a doubt, the long history of activity theory has provided us with an alternative view of human cognition, and one to which, at very least, other social approaches can be sympathetic. Even so, there are some general points to be made here about the role of theory that apply as much to activity theory as to any other approach. First, activity theory's approach to cognition – and this, we argue, is as true of distributed cognition – is deeply ambivalent. Much emphasis is placed on the intensional or goal-directed nature of human activity in this framework, and there does seem to be an intractable issue here in respect of ethnomethodology's position on motive (see Randall et al. (2001)). Furthermore, any doubts we might have do not lie in the broad sense of describing work in terms of relationships among subject, object, and community, for that seems unobjectionable. Rather, we are concerned with the relationship between the theory and its methods. That is, it seems to us that it is often the investigative stance, which we can broadly term ethnographic, which produces results for activity theorists rather than the theory.

This is more or less in keeping with what activity theorists themselves often say. Thus and for example, 'Activity theory is a descriptive tool that is useful for analysing and understanding collaborative work in general, independently of any specific field of application' (Barthelmess and Anderson 2002, p. 14), and, 'The value of any theory is . . . how well a theory can shape an object of study, highlighting relevant issues' (ibid.).

This bears some examination, for read in a particular way, the first of these two claims seems manifestly absurd. The idea that any description can usefully take place independently of specific settings is philosophical nonsense (at least from a Wittgensteinian point of view). Of course, the claim is not so strong. It is pointing to the prospect that concepts can be deployed independently of context, or if you like, to the value of generalisation. In turn, however, one might ask whether we are so saturated with a will to theory that we have lost sight of the important questions about theory, of which the most important is, 'What is it for?'

Halverson is one of the few in CSCW to ask questions of theory's purpose. She is insistent that we must ask what a theory is *for*, or what we are going to do with it. She identifies four basic needs in interdisciplinary work, which are descriptive power; rhetorical power; inferential power; and application. She suggests (ibid., p. 245) that,

> Theory in CSCW should provide a conceptual framework that helps us make sense of and describe the world. This includes describing a work setting as well as critiqueing an implementation of technology in that setting. Second, we need rhetorical power. Theory should help us talk about the world by naming important aspects of the conceptual structure and how it maps to the real world. . . . The third attribute is inferential power. . . . In some cases those inferences may be about phenomena that we have not yet understood sufficiently to know where or how to look. We may hope that inferences will lead to insights for design. Or we want to predict the consequences of introducing change into a particular setting. An important fourth attribute has to do with application: how we can apply the theory to the real world for essentially pragmatic reasons. We need to describe and understand the world at the right level of analysis in order to bridge the gap from description to design.

Such a position is unusually sophisticated and requires some careful thought. We note, for instance, that this characterisation of theory in CSCW makes no reference to predictive power. That is, whatever kind of theory we are discussing in CSCW and elsewhere, it is a weak conception of theory, one which might be consistent with Blumer's notion of 'illuminating' or 'sensitising' concepts (1969). Kuutti (1996), for instance, acknowledges that activity theory has no strongly predictive status, but acts as a clarificatory and descriptive tool. Indeed, he goes so far as to accept that it is not a theory at all, in the sense of theory as a body of accurately defined statements (ibid., p. 25).

We can have no in-principle objection to such a view of theory for, as already stated, it can be a useful signpost for those who need directions, or for that matter for those who are busily writing PhD theses and feel they need a crutch. At the same time, however, we do need to take the kinds of argument that Halverson adduces seriously. What exactly do we mean when we speak about descriptive power, rhetorical power, inferential power, and application? Description, after all, looks to be a simple business on the face of it. Our problem is the problem of relevant description, inference, rhetoric, and application, and how we go about deciding them. In each instance, we must ask whether any theoretical device can provide us with the answers.

These problems of relevance are manifold. They might include: what is our choice of setting to be and how (and by whom) is it to be determined? This might be a problem of inference. The apparently simple question disguises some difficult choices. Are we to choose a setting as an exemplar of something, and if so, of what? Is the example to be driven by an interest in a particular kind of work or by a particular kind of technology, or by some combination of the two? Different choices have profound implications, as is evident when we compare a literature which emphasises the problems of computer-mediated communication with a literature on, say, command and control centres. Our comments here are not intended to be critical but instead point to the ramifications of this choice. These decisions, as any practitioner will recognise, are important (although sometimes outweighed by practical considerations).

The first test of any theory, then, has to be whether it can help us choose between alternative prospects, or can give us any purchase on which approach might yield results.

Secondly, we need to ask which behaviours and technology uses in the setting turn out to be interesting. This is more directly a problem of description. The particular relevance of this kind of question is the infinite extensibility of the notion of artefact, for floors and walls are artefacts, and enable us to do our work, but few would assert that ethnography should involve staring at walls. At the same time, ignoring the fact that technologies consist of a great deal more than computers has arguably led to the belief that the paperless office would be easily achieved, inasmuch as it was presumed that the functionalities of paper were both obvious and easily replicated. Our question of any theory, then, has to be couched in terms of whether it provides us with a conceptual framework for deciding which artefacts are the relevant artefacts, and to which patterns of use we should be attentive.

Thirdly, we might reflect on what level of detail might be required of us, and for what purpose. Again, this is not intended to be a glib question, for at root it addresses the problem of concepts such as tools, division of labour, or rules. That is, it may have to do with naming. It would be foolish to believe that attentiveness to the division of labour, either between one person and another, or between persons and machines, is not relevant to the design problem, but our questions must address the problem of how the 'division of labour' is to be thought about. After all, economics furnished us with a set of formal descriptions of the division of labour from the time of Adam Smith onwards. What is important, empirically, is how that division of labour is in practice worked out, because many studies have shown that there can be a very significant difference between role structures as organisationally mandated, and how things are done in practice.

Exactly the same principle holds with the notion of rules. It is a common misconception, and one shared by Nardi, for instance, that ethnomethodology has no interest in rules, whereas activity theory brings our attention to them. For ethnomethodology, again, the interest lies in how people orient to rules. There may be a significant gap between the division of labour as a theoretical construct and a working division of labour as managed by people doing jobs, and a significant gap between the existences of rules and procedures as laid down and rules and procedures as implemented in practice.

Empirical work, of course, might well be aimed at understanding the importance of that gap in various contexts, for as Schmidt (1997) has pointed out, it will vary. These questions relate to 'application', in Halverson's terms, and application is, of course, the Holy Grail. Unfortunately, what the application applies to is the critical and 'wicked' problem, and has an infinite number of potential solutions, some of which will turn out to be better than others. The question for theory in this context is whether it can result in positive and relatively definitive statements about applicability, rather than the kind of cautions typical of ethnographic results.

Fourth, to what pattern of regular and unusual events should we be attentive? The theoretical insistence on attention to how activities are constructed through subjects, objects, and communities, and recursively to the division of labour, to rules, and to tools is valuable and illuminating, and we do not mean to suggest otherwise. Nevertheless, the theory does not, and cannot, tell us what to look for when we have to answer questions such as, 'Which activities?' This is because we simply cannot know in advance which activities are important, as distinct from which activities are common.

Neither are we likely, without a sophisticated knowledge of the domain, to be able to answer the kinds of 'what if' questions that designers are prone to ask, and which are an aspect of what Halverson calls 'Rhetorical' power, and which have to do with the imaginative reconstruction of scenarios. A part of this has to do with the degree to which descriptive work can be used comparatively, in other words, the degree to which it emphasises similarity and difference. Any cursory look at the idea of the 'rare but catastrophic' event and how it might be dealt with in the safety-critical arena shows us that activity theory, in and of itself, cannot provide us with a capacity to decide which events will turn out to be relevant to our problems. To be clear, this is not a specific criticism of activity theory, for we would contend that the same will be true of any approach, including ethnomethodology. What is at stake is the status of the claims made about concepts.

What Halverson (ibid.) calls 'Rhetorical' power, it seems to us, is largely a matter of the generalisability of concepts. Again, to make sense of an apparently simple matter, we have to step through a minefield. When we deploy concepts (as opposed to merely using words), presumably we are suggesting that some degree of precision should be attached to them, and that they should apply across some range of cases. Of course, all the problems come from deciding how big a range of cases might turn out to be appropriate and how precise we can, in practice, make our concepts.

One item of major importance is to understand and recognise the difference between the power of a theory to give a name to a recognisable phenomenon which might otherwise not be understood or recognised and the simple business of inventing neologisms. Recasting names does not constitute any kind of rhetorical power, and arguably the most worrying tendency in theoretical work is post hoc naming. That is, if the importance of a given phenomenon or range of phenomena is already recognised, nothing is served by recasting its name into activity theoretical terms, or indeed any other. If activity theory, however, is giving names to phenomena which are otherwise unrecognised or not understood, then it is providing a powerful service.

Regardless, activity theory has some undeniable value:

- It draws our attention to the developmental aspects of human behaviour.
- It locates cognition at least partly in culture and thus implies an ethnographic stance of some kind.
- It acts as a powerful reminder of the importance of tools in mediating action.

4.2 Distributed Cognition

Cognition is a fundamentally cultural process.

(*Hutchins (1995)*)

[Culture is] . . . that complex whole which includes knowledge, belief, art, morals, law, custom and any other capabilities and habits acquired by man [sic] as a member of society.

(*E. B. Tylor, quoted in Asad (1986)*)

Activity theory, it has been suggested, provides some pointers to what to study but is ambiguous about how to study it and even more ambiguous about the relationship between data and concept formation. At the outset, distributed cognition (DCog) would appear to have a similar problem. It, in the view propounded by Hutchins (1995), is very much predicated on the 'what has been left out' or residual model of culture but also appeals to what we might (roughly) call the semiotic model of culture as well. Certainly, we proceed on the assumption that signs and representations have a broad equivalence. They are also similar in respect of the importance of culture although they do not necessarily agree about what culture is.

All ethnography is based on the principle that culture in some sense is a significant aspect of our understanding of human behaviour. Indeed, for the discipline of anthropology, culture is a foundational concept and is only marginally less important in sociology. Nevertheless, the concept has been used and misused over time in such a variety of ways that it has arguably become little more than a gloss for different ways of dealing with residual information. One of the major features of DCog is that it tries to produce a positive view of what is entailed in cultural investigation, as we show.

Basically, social science conceptions of culture are typically counterposed with notions of structure or rationality. In other words, culture stands against the view that human behaviour, motivation, and attitude will be the same wherever we look. This gloss, however, disguises a series of problems involved in understanding how best to conceptualise culture and understand its impacts when design is the purpose at hand. Moreover, the methodological consequences of different theoretical choices are seldom examined in interdisciplinary communities. Thus and for instance, there has been a recent move towards ethnographic approaches in the information systems community (see Klein and Myers (1999)) in which 'interpretive' methods for the examination of culture are recommended.

Nevertheless, one finds relatively little examination of the different ways in which the concepts for so-called qualitative methods might be used and little understanding of the consequences of these different choices. Put simply, the term 'culture' can mean many different things and we need to determine which of the available meanings is likely to prove most useful. For instance, in the broad kinds of cultural typology we find in work such as Hofstede's (1980,1986,1991), currently fashionable in some IS research, the picture of culture is very much a broadbrush one, and in keeping with a residual view of culture as something left out when more rationalistic assumptions are made.

The questions that interest us have to do with what conception of culture is entailed in DCog, how it helps us make sense of variation and its effects, and how generally or locally these effects are manifested. In determining an appropriate sense of what 'culture' might mean, then, we should ask questions concerning how broadly or narrowly we set our sights. Our argument is that there is a certain ambiguity in DCog in virtue of the fact that it emphasises a material/semiotic view of culture but relies on fieldwork methods which imply a definition of culture as practice.

This may seem somewhat arcane, but there are issues of granularity here that are often overlooked. Anthropology, after all, has traditionally been interested in the differences between one culture and another, but fieldwork in design communities has seldom had that kind of ambition. Rather, it has been concerned – to the extent that generalisation has ever been an issue – with differences within the culture. This may seem to be a different kind of problem, but in fact is not. The greater the lines of variation in attitude, belief, behaviour, and practice we find within a culture then the less value that broadbrush characterisations of differences between cultures will hold, for the very assumption that there is a culture there in the first place begins to be challenged, or we need a very different conception of what a culture is.

The degree to which our interest lies in differences between or within cultures, then, leads to a problem with the term 'culture', which can serve a number of purposes, and all of them have to do with just how local or just how generic our picture of behaviour needs to be for us to reach sensible design conclusions. DCog in one respect starts from a similar picture of culture as ethnomethodology, that of 'culture as practice'. In its insistence on 'representation', however, DCog takes a rather different turn.

DCog is a relatively recent and as yet underused theoretical resource for CSCW investigation. The perspective evidently emanates from a dialogue with some versions of psychology, and not from a dialogue with versions of sociology. This is probably why, from a sociological point of view, many of its insights appear obvious, not to say derivative. We argue that it has a number of characteristics which are shared with certain common kinds of sociological or sociolinguistic positions, but it also has some distinctive features.

Firstly, it emphasises the systemic properties of cognition. Secondly, it is founded upon a view of representation which we term 'semiotic' and has some relationship with what is usually termed the 'representational' theory of mind. Thirdly, culture is material. Fourthly, it has an explicit methodological recommendation, to whit what is called, 'cognitive ethnography'.

DCog starts from the perspective that cognition and culture are two parts of a larger system. Its great insight is that cognitive processes take place both inside and outside the head. To put it another way, cognition and culture are intimately connected. For Hutchins, the marginalisation of culture by cognitive science has had reductionist effects, and has led to ignorance of context, or 'situatedness'. Hence (Hutchins, 1995, p. 354),

> The early researchers in cognitive science placed a bet that the modularity of human cognition would be such that culture, context, and history could be safely ignored at the outset, and then integrated later. The bet did not pay off. These things are fundamental aspects of human cognition and cannot be comfortably integrated into a perspective that privileges abstract properties of individual minds.

For Hutchins, the cognitive scientific insistence on mentalism leads to the consequence that too much emphasis is placed on the boundaries between the mental and other, wider, systems and hence cognitive science typically mistakes the properties of the wider system for those of the individual. Thus, Hutchins argues that this mistake can be seen in the assumption of 'primitive minds' in technologically primitive cultures. In this view, impoverished technology would be evidence of impoverished thinking. (One should point out here that this is something of a straw man argument in that various anthropologists have critiqued the notion of the 'primitive mind' over a long period of time.) Wider cultural properties, then, consist of, 'A complex functional system consisting of many media in simultaneous coordination' (ibid., p. 288).

Furthermore, systems have both computational and social properties. Here, the influence of at least some versions of cognitive science is evident for the mind, in these views, is a complex, modular, and functionally interrelated system. (See for instance Fodor (1989) and Sterelny (1990); for a more popular version, see Pinker (1997)). To be determined, therefore, is the degree to which, in DCog, any picture of the mind itself as a modular system is retained or whether the systematic approach to representation is passed entirely to the cultural system. It would seem that the answer is that both systems could be under investigation, as with (ibid., p. xvi) '. . . a conception of computation as the propagation of representational state across a variety of media. This view of computation permits the use of a single language of description to cover cognitive and computational processes that lie inside and outside the heads of the practitioners of navigation.'

At other points, what lies inside the head is de-emphasised (ibid., p. 49),

> I will attempt to apply the principal metaphor of cognitive science- cognition as computation- to the operation of this system. In doing so I do not make any special commitment to the nature of the computations that are going on inside individuals except to say that whatever happens there is part of the larger computational system. But I do believe that the computation observed in the activity of the larger system can be described in the way cognition has been traditionally described – that is, as computation realized through the creation, transformation, and propagation of representational states.

DCog strongly emphasises the notion of representation in its analysis, and as already stated this has something in common with semiotic views of culture as systems of 'sign'. It further has some relationship with what is usually termed the representational theory of mind, although a critical one. In our view, the issue of representation is DCog's strength and its weakness.

Equally importantly, culture is a great deal more than typical anthropological accounts would have it in that culture is material. Distributed cognition makes much of the idea that 'we cannot know what the task is until we know what the tools are' (ibid., p. 114) in much the same way that activity theory argues for mediation. In other words, understanding a task is a matter of understanding human activity in an environment, an environment that contains physical artefacts which themselves are culturally evolved.

Hence, distributed cognition

1. Relies on the notion of functionally integrated systems
2. Sees systems as having both computational and social properties
3. Sees learning as 'adaptive reorganization in a complex system' (ibid., p. 289)

Taken together, we begin to see what the task of the analyst might be. The system is a material environment which can take a symbolic form, according to the kinds of media used to make representations of it. There is a need, therefore, to understand the nature of the system in its widest sense, and the various conditions and artefacts that constitute it. These media have to be coordinated, and human beings, using their social experiences – knowledge, skill, expertise, and so on – work out ways of doing exactly that. (These ways get internalised and then become cognitive matters.)

DCog recommends a specific method, that of 'cognitive ethnography'. The benefits, for Hutchins, are clear (ibid., p. 371):

> Among the benefits of cognitive ethnography for cognitive science is the refinement of a functional specification for the human cognitive system. What is a mind for? How confident are we that our intuitions about the cognitive nature of tasks we do on a daily basis are correct? It is a common piece of common sense that we know what those tasks are because we are human and because we engage in them daily. But I believe this is not true. In spite of the fact that we engage in cognitive activities every day, our folk and professional models of cognitive performance do not match when cognition in the world is examined carefully.

Thus, for those who see cognition as a fundamental part of understanding human experience, and who recognise that attention to group behaviour is a matter of understanding context, distributed cognition provides a way of integrating two historically contrasting perspectives in cognitive science and social anthropology.

Distributed cognition has been criticised for colonising other approaches, notably ethnomethodological studies of work. It is certainly true that the notion that cognition is social is hardly original. It is central to both ethnomethodological views of cognition and to activity theoretical views. Nevertheless, where ethnomethodology rejects any relevance for the idea that cognition takes place in the head, distributed cognition, like activity theory, does not. Unlike activity theory, however, which is explicit about the move from 'lower' to 'higher' mental functions as being precisely a move from 'in the head' cognition to culturally determined cognition, the position in distributed cognition is less clear. What its defenders would argue is that by retaining a conception of 'cognition in the head' it provides a means for relating 'mental' processes to cultural processes.

There is some ambiguity in our view in the literature about the nature of this relationship, but if our position on it is accurate, it constitutes the main point of departure from ethnomethodological studies, in that ethnos for the most part would have little interest in what goes on 'in the head', following Garfinkel's (1963) formulation that 'there is nothing in the head except brains' (1963: 190).

Having said all that, we should take DCog seriously, for it offers some very straightforward advice about how to proceed with fieldwork, and it may not be bad advice. It suggests that the topic under investigation ought to be that of representation, with the appropriate cautionary note that representations are not necessarily to be found 'in the head' but in objects. The distinctiveness of DCog lies in our view in the following.

- It focuses ethnographic attention on representation and the variety of representational structures to be found in the ecology.
- It also locates cognition at least partly in culture and thus implies an ethnographic stance of some kind.
- It demands a systematic view of cultural properties identified.

4.3 Actor-Network Theory (ANT)

> *There are four things that do not work with actor-network theory; the word actor, the word network, the word theory and the hyphen! Four nails in the coffin . . . there is life after ANT. Once we will have strongly pushed a stake into the heart of the creature safely buried in its coffin – thus abandoning what is so wrong with ANT, that is "actor", "network", "theory" without forgetting the hyphen! – some other creature will emerge, light and beautiful, our future collective achievement*
> *(Latour, 1999 in Law and Hassard (1999))*

It was Bruno Latour, somewhat bizarrely, who first pointed to the 'missing masses' in sociological work and thus brought a distinct way of thinking into the general 'there's something wrong with sociology' school of thinking. Remarkably enough, this school has been hugely influential within sociology, perhaps indicating that it is appreciably less radical a divergence from sociological orthodoxy than it thinks it is. For Latour, typical sociological explanation was as guilty of determinism as the so-called technologically deterministic work identifiable elsewhere. As such, his work was part of a general programme to reinstate some consideration of the relationship between social and material processes, and in particular to give attention to the ways in which technology is shaped by 'social processes' surrounding the development and introduction of new technological forms. Key to this is the notion of heterogeneity, in that 'social processes' can refer to a wide range of economic, cultural, organizational, and political factors.

Actor-Network Theory (ANT) developed out of two recent tendencies. These are the history of science and the 'social construction of technology' (MacKenzie and Wajcman, 1985; Bijker et al., 1987). These positions challenge the view that, firstly, science and, secondly, technology can be viewed as independent of social arrangements. In contrast, science and technology, in these views, must be produced within a framework of these social arrangements. In order to avoid either the charge of technological or social determinism, these perspectives propose some kind of mutually constitutive influence. The claim within such arguments is an insistence that the content of technology is the matter of sociological interest, and that it is in this regard that previous theories have been lacking, caught in the jaws of 'the wholism/individualism dichotomy'. Thus, 'To study technological projects you have to move from a classical sociology – which has fixed frames of reference – to a relativistic sociology – which has fluctuating referents' (Latour, 1996).

By way of contrast, these arguments set out to provide a corrective to the general orientation to a technologically deterministic frame (whether stronger or weaker in this regard) in the work of their predecessors through the deployment of a new set of analytic concepts that link together technical and nontechnical elements in a network of heterogeneous elements.

Delineating the important features of actor-network theory is difficult. Having been created, it has shifted focus a number of times, been critiqued (to death apparently) by its original creators, but it has not been abandoned but seemingly morphed into 'after ANT' (Law and Hassard, 1999) where, although the focus and objective may be different, many of the same analytic techniques can be discerned. It clearly remains a powerful, popular, and influential approach to understanding technology and sociotechnical change.

Actor-network theory (Callon, 1986a,1986b; Latour, 1987,1996; Law, 1992a,1992b,1999; Law and Hassard, 1999) largely grew out of various debates in the social studies of science and technology, although its impact as a mode of analysis has spread to a number of other fields (Williams and Edge, 1996 [information systems]; Bloomfield and Vurdubakis, 1997 [IT, organisations, and management]; Michael, 1998 [social psychology]). It attempts to explain and interpret social and technological development by integrating human and nonhuman elements into the same conceptual framework. Actor-network theory is an approach to structuring and explaining the links between society and technology, documenting how technology becomes accepted and used. It focuses attention on the sociotechnical networks that engineers and scientists create to get their projects done and is concerned with the processes by which scientific disputes become closed, ideas accepted, and tools and methods adopted, that is, with how decisions are made about what is known.

105

Actor-network theory collapses any distinction between the social and the technical, replacing these categories with the notion of physical and social actors (or actants) involved in the development of technological systems through their assembly into a network. Actor-network theory can therefore be regarded as a systematic way to emphasise and document mundane structural and interactional features of scientific and technological achievements. It is based on a number of essential related concepts. 'Actor', or 'actant', for, example, refers to 'any element which bends space around itself, makes other elements dependent upon itself and translates their will into the language of its own.'[26] Actors are both human and nonhuman stakeholders who pursue interests that may encourage or constrain technology (Monteiro and Hanseth, 1996; Walsham, 1997). One of the key elements of the ANT agenda is this rejection of the primacy of human elements in the sociotechnical scenario, adopting the notion of the actant to underwrite their identification of seamless webs of human and nonhuman elements, claiming that it has thereby, '. . . opened the social sciences to non-humans . . . [and] freed them from the sterile individualism/wholism dichotomy . . .' (Callon, 1997).

This approach of not distinguishing a priori between social and technical elements of a sociotechnical web potentially increases the level of detail of the network mechanisms at work. Examples of actants would include humans, collectivities, texts, and technical artefacts. Such actants have interests and through attempting to create an alignment of interests, in a process of translation, they produce an actor network: a network of interests that becomes stable as it is aligned to the technology, achieved through the translation of interests and the enrolment of actors into the network. The process of translation itself consists of problematization, interessement, and enrolment (Callon, 1986a; Latour, 1987). Problematization is when a 'focal actor' defines identities and interests consistent with its own, interessement involves convincing others to accept this view, and enrolment is when this process is achieved. Irreversibility reflects the degree to which it becomes impossible to return to a point where alternative possibilities exist.

Inscription refers to the process of creating technical artefacts that would ensure the protection of an actor's interests (Latour, 1996) and the ways in which technical artefacts thereby embody patterns of use: 'Technologies . . . simultaneously embody and measure a set of relations between heterogeneous elements' (Akrich, 1992, p. 205). Inscriptions give a particular viewpoint precedence. In this sense design involves the inscription of a particular vision of the world into a newly designed artefact and is part of an attempt to anticipate and promote if not restrict future patterns of use. Inscriptions – including texts, but also images of many sorts, databases, and the like – are central to knowledge work. Inscriptions are central to the process of gaining credibility: they present work in such a way that

---

[26]Callon (1986a) and Akrich and Latour (1992) provide detailed definitions of ANT concepts and terms.

its meaning and significance are irrefutable. They carry work to others, thereby making action at a distance possible and stabilising work.

Through constant negotiation between diverse actors around 'inscription' and 'translation', actor networks are established; Latour (1996, pp. 106–107) asserts that these efforts need to be constant in order to form 'alliances' that keep all parties 'integrated' within the network, despite the changes in their orientation to the network:

> [The actor network] can never be fixed once and for all, for it varies according to the state of the alliances [within it] ... each element ... can become either an autonomous element, or everything, or nothing, either the component or the recognisable part of a whole.

Order is, then, never fixed, but constantly open to negotiation and renegotiation, reinscription, and retranslation by actors within the network. In this vein, Law (1991) discusses Hughes' history of the electrification of several countries, highlighting the sociotechnical order emerging from this process as an important achievement, that sociologists would do well to learn from. As Law (1991, p. 10) puts it:

> Here the distinction between humans and machines, though present is subordinated to another concern – that of exploring the development of a complex socio-technical system. Hughes is careful to avoid suggesting that either the technical, or the social, is determinate in the last instance. ... Hughes' version of the "social order" – his answer to the problem of what it is that holds overlapping bits of the social together – is to imply that the social order is not a social order at all. Rather it is a sociotechnical order. What appears to be social is partly technical. What we usually call technical is partly social. In practice nothing is purely technical. Neither is anything purely social. ... [Hughes'] discovery of the sociotechnical, strikes me as a finding of absolutely major importance. And it is one that has not been assimilated to the sociological imagination: for reasons that I do not understand, the idea that wherever we scrape the social surface we will find that it is composed of networks of heterogeneous materials remains foreign to most forms of sociological practice."

As an exercise in forgetting (ignoring a longstanding and honourable tradition that is, if not always to the fore in sociology certainly there in social psychology, as evidenced in the work we cite above in respect of what preceded participatory design) this is quite staggering. The suggestion that the sociotechnical is a recent discovery is, we think, insulting to a very large number of researchers (not least Karl Marx). This is not to say that ANT simply duplicates other sociotechnical insights for it may not. That is, it may deal in the relationship between the social and the technical in a different way to that which we have hitherto seen.

Methodologically, ANT has two major approaches. One is, as Latour suggests, to 'follow the actor,' via interviews and ethnographic research and

ANT has motivated a number of interesting and insightful ethnographic studies (Mort 2003; Law 1994; etc.). The other is to examine inscriptions. Ethnographic approaches are deployed because of the belief that any analysis requires an understanding of particular specific contexts and therefore must start at the local level in which networks are embedded.

In terms of investigation and analysis a number of stages can be identified. These include: identifying and investigating stakeholders and their rational, organizational, and individual interests: this incorporates analysis of documentation, attitudes, relationships, roles, power, and influence, considering communication lines and stakeholder interactions. The identification of links between stakeholders helps identify the development of an actor network and the various alignment strategies. This process, of identifying the stakeholders, decisions, and technologies historically and currently implicated in the actor network, helps provide some indications of irreversibility, and identifies promoters and inhibiters and actions designed to promote the alignment of the network so that any technical adoption or deployment is aligned with appropriate organisational structures to facilitate social acceptance.

During its relatively short-lived career, ANT has stimulated widespread debates (Walsham 1997; Law 1997,1999; Star 1991). Amongst the principal criticisms are ANT's lack of political (or design) relevance, whereas Monteiro (n.d.) questions its all-encompassing claims: 'the seemingly (implicit) assumption that ANT can be used for everything – urban transportation, microbes, and hotel keys alike.' Furthermore, in discovering and documenting key actors and interests and elucidating how the aims and goals of projects are realized there is a danger that ANT studies, in practice, overemphasize goal-directed actions, the 'managerial, engineering, Machiavellian, demiurgic character of ANT' (Latour 1999), and thereby gloss cultural, nonutilitarian, employment of technology.

In ANT terms, design is all about translation and inscription, as Akrich, (1992, p. 206) claims:

> "users'" and others' interests may ... be translated into specific "needs", the specific needs are further translated into more general and unified needs so that these needs might be translated into one and the same solution. When the solution (system) is running, it will be adopted by the users by translating the system into the context of their specific work tasks and situations ....In such a translation, or design, process, the designer works out a scenario for how the system will be used. This scenario is inscribed into the system.

However, whilst ANT may well tell us, retrospectively (and perhaps a little conspiratorially), about how particular designs and technology configurations come to be accepted and promoted, it appears to have little else to contribute to the actual, realtime, real-world process of designing the technologies themselves. This, because as Button and Sharrock (1997) summarise (quoted in O'Brien (1999)), ANT is very much sociological 'business as usual':

The attempt to employ vernacular terms to identify "agents" occupying positions in an extended network are not unlike earlier efforts by sociologists to define variables and link them together in causal models. In both cases, difficulties arise when natural language categories are literally "pinned down" to compose a stable distribution of the nominal "entities" (actants, factors or variables according to the case), which act as constituents of a map or model.

Claims that the ANT approach develops qualitatively better explanations of the ways in which webs of technical and nontechnical actants form structures of social action, comes from the perspective of issues produced by the social sciences, sociology's big prize, rather than any problems encountered in technology design and use. Crucially for issues of technology design, usability, and use, the ANT approach cannot be a means of understanding the social organisation, the lived detail, or the content of the technology as it is encountered by those on the ground. Nevertheless, its possible merits may include:

- That it provides an explanatory account of the development of new technology.
- It recommends a wider treatment of ethnographic issues than those normally encountered in design-related work.

4.4 Ethnomethodology

In advancing some version of ethnomethodologically informed ethnography and relating it to other and different approaches, our emphasis is on relevance. Our concern is with why an ethnomethodological approach is particularly relevant to informing ethnographic studies of work, technology, and organisations for design purposes. In trying to do so, we tread a path that many others have trod, including for instance Dourish (2001). We reiterate that ethnography or fieldwork is a broad and not especially helpful gloss on a range of observational practices and many of the studies which result from at least some analytic choices have the character of 'scenic' work, whereby what is discovered is some general pattern or tendency in cultural life. That is, the ordinary practicalities of activities are seldom visible in such accounts.

Again, in suggesting the value of ethnomethodological approaches here, we are explicitly not contrasting ethnomethodology with other theoretical tendencies, because ethnomethodology, at least in most of its forms carries little or no theoretical baggage. That is, it provides no alternative to the conceptual work that is done by theories such as activity theory or distributed cognition. It stands in no clear relation to problems of, for instance, grounded theory. Rather it consists, purely and simply, in a set of analytic choices. This point, deceptively simple, proves extraordinarily hard to grasp for researchers within the social sciences, let alone elsewhere. These choices in turn are not founded on philosophical beliefs about how the world must 'really' be but a concern for the ordinary, practical commonsense reasoning procedures which make up people's understandings of social life, the resources they use to make sense of aspects of the social world.

Thus and for instance, where many sociological and anthropological debates have turned on the impossibility or otherwise of experiencing another's experience, and thus of interpreting another culture (or even gender/race), for the ethnomethodologist such issues are nonsensical. Instead, he might concern himself with the ordinary difficulties rather than impossibilities of such an enterprise on the assumption that experience is a difficult/meaningless concept when applied philosophically whereas understanding is not. Therefore we can legitimately, in principle, concern ourselves with the difficult but not impossible business of trying to understand any form of human behaviour. The idea that we may not understand what is 'really' going on is irrelevant, because the business at hand is to produce a plausible account which is, to use ethnomethodological jargon, 'uniquely adequate' and which can be understood to mean, 'can be judged for accuracy and completeness by those people who are the subjects of, or interested parties in, the enquiry.'

This in turn raises another prospect, which has to do with the degree to which sociological concepts, or those from any other human science are privileged concepts in the context of something like HCI or CSCW. After all, it is an aspect of occupational psychosis that concepts successfully deployed for entirely disciplinary purposes will continue to be deployed no matter what the context for new enquiry might be. We see this in sociology, where the study of any new social setting is an opportunity to identify the sites of generic, abstract social processes, for example social control or domination or surveillance. Sociology's purpose in surveying actual social settings is consequently to minimise the differences between them, to abstract from the data ways that exhibit the commonality of such processes, and to make the case that these are generic.

The ethnomethodologically informed ethnographic approach, in contrast, has been particularly focused upon the distinctiveness, the specificity, of the setting. This is because in the organisation of practical conduct, although there may be abstract general similarities between one setting and another, it is nonetheless unavoidable that one must come to terms with the particularities of the setting if the day-to-day affairs of the setting are to be carried out. In terms of many sociological strategies for generalisation, the fact that people are engaged in a particular kind of work is only an analytically incidental feature of what they are doing.

The ethnomethodologically motivated approach has every reason to attend to the distinct character of the work in the setting, to give priority to the fact that these persons are, for example, authorising a bank loan or completing a standing order, and for directing its attentions to the activities which specifically distinctively comprise those particular types of activity and, thus, to give detailed characterisations of, and to seek to understand the particular circumstantial conditions for, carrying out those activities in actual cases. The relevance of this to an understanding of work, technology, and organisations has been, then, in the engendering of studies directed toward understanding how the work gets done, and thus to describing the detail and intricacies of working practice for their own sake.

Again, and for the sake of clarity, there is a frequently expressed view that ethnomethodology is implacably opposed to any form of generalisation, and that this must limit its uses in an interdisciplinary medium. It is not. Ethnomethodology has problems with the status of enquiry in the human sciences insofar as it doubts the sense or usefulness of the supposedly analytic categories generated by, for instance, sociology and for that matter psychology. In a book of this nature, there is no purpose in rehearsing difficult arguments here because they do not pertain overly to the business of getting field studies done. Suffice it to say that the ethnomethodologist will see much of sociological theorizing as trivial, irrelevant, and trading on the illusion of the technical term as opposed to commonsense terms. It thus raises a number of issues in respect of the status of generalisation, and does not see generalisation as the immediate or indeed as a necessary part of its enquiries, but provides no principled argument, especially in the context of interdisciplinary enquiry, as to why some ordinary, commonsense, and general categories might not be brought to our understanding of a domain (and domain itself is an example of just such a generalisation). What such categories do not do is drive or determine our understanding of what is going on within the setting.

We have alluded to the postmodern turn above and suggested that it can be placed squarely within sociology's longstanding and notorious tradition of debunking, from which ethnomethodology fundamentally dissents. Constructionists seek to dispute the commonsense understandings that members of society have, often amounting to the suggestion that members of society do not know what they are doing. The task constructionism sets itself is, of course, to challenge members' understandings, to show how they are wrong and to present alternative, and authoritative, conceptions of both the way things are and how they got to be that way. These studies claim to show that what appear to people as commonsense or obvious – for example that death or disability is a physical and biological event – are nothing of the kind but instead interpretative constructions, that can, therefore, be constructed differently, so that death or disability becomes a social construction (Woolgar 1987,1988; Shakespeare 1993).

Sharrock (1995), following Bittner (1973), views this development as part of the reaction against the concept of 'objectivity'.

> The reaction against "objectivity" . . . was to move in a "subjectivist" direction, to denounce all notions of objectivity, and to purport to root social phenomena in and to explore the dimensions of subjectivity. These tendencies were, in effect, to deny the existence of social reality, to make social reality a matter of individual determination – it was up to individual's to define social reality as they will.

The result of this move, however, has been a shift away from a careful concern with the research setting and its members to a focus on the researcher and the research act itself, and the subsequent endless navel gazing, confessional tales, and dreadful attempts at poetry and other forms of narrative reconstruction. The constructivist view contrasts with ethnomethodology's commitment to indifference, that attempts neither to undermine nor to support the everyday realities to which the members subscribe but to investigate, describe, and understand them. Sharrock (1995) continues,

> Bittner, arguing on behalf of ethnomethodology, sought to distance it from just those tendencies, and to do so by arguing that the retreat from "objectivity" as defined by those in the positivist traditions should not be toward "subjectivity" but toward "realism" – not realism, in the metaphysical sense, of asserting the existence of an external reality, but "realism" in the phenomenological sense of faithfulness to the portrayal of its subject matter, a devotion to capturing society as it is actually experienced "from within."

Bittner suggests that fieldwork strategies that have focused on detailing the experiences of the researcher are inclined to perpetuate that impoverishment in the portrayal of members' experience and represent a move away from a faithful description and rendering of the experience of members. In this way phenomena, the everyday occurrences in the setting, are divested of their massive sense of reality to those who routinely and necessarily inhabit that setting.

Bittner's argument, that the ethnographic turn to subjectivity involves increasing, almost exclusive, emphasis on the fieldworker's experience and point of view has been readily confirmed by the growing chorus for 'reflexivity' in sociology in general and ethnography in particular. (May, 2000; Woolgar and Ashmore, 1988). However, the focus on the fieldworker's standpoint as the focus for consideration of how social reality is engendered tends to overlook the extent to which the fieldworker's point of view is a peculiar one. Although ethnographers may attempt to sensitise themselves to members' points of view, as Sharrock (1995) reminds us,

> . . . The fieldworker's occupation of that point of view is a temporary matter. . . . The fieldworker does not, however, characteristically occupy the point of view. . . . The fieldworker simulates certain aspects of that view, but adopts it only for the purposes of the research, and as one which is freely taken up and from which it is equally possible readily to withdraw.

In contrast, for members their 'native' point of view is not something to which they have a contingent relationship, one that they may freely take up, abandon, or exchange. In the setting of the bank we studied, for example, the native point of view is their life, something they have to take very seriously and not something they can play with or relate to on a 'take it or leave it basis.' In the bank, the ways in which matters appear, for instance, to a bank manager (e.g. in terms of loans, overdrafts, repayments, etc.) are mandatory for the manager and for others organisationally involved in the situation; these are the objective and (legally) binding ways of doing bank work. As a highly distributed organisation the bank is reliant on the manager (and all its officials) acting in particular ways; indeed it can be a disciplinary matter if he fails to act accordingly. Bank personnel as a general rule cannot, except in their dreams (and often not then), playfully adopt a different point of view just to see what would happen and the idea that things 'could be otherwise' is a possibility too childish to entertain.

As Gould et al. (1974) note, there are particular problems in ethnography's claim to describe events as they are seen or experienced by social actors. Asking people to explain what they are doing turns members into informants (Sacks, 1992) and produces a 'perspective of action' whereby settings are made meaningful to outsiders rather than a 'perspective in action' where meaning unfolds in naturally occurring interaction. Furthermore, there are some difficulties involved in seeking to understand the actor's perspective (Emerson, 1981, p. 357):

> They treat as a "perspective" what actors on most occasions view as the way the world is. The field worker, then, does not produce a description from the actor's point of view, but a description of the actor's point of view from the point of view of a sociological observer. This is true even if the observer seeks to empathise closely with actors' concerns and meanings. As a consequence, field-work descriptions tend to depict social life as perceived events and meanings, ignoring or distorting the lived reality of actor's worlds.

The emphasis in recent ethnographic writing on the reflexive experience of the fieldworker, in that the fieldworker's history, attitudes, sexuality, and so on have an impact on her perception of the setting, leads to an underestimate of the extent to which the experience of those under study possess traits of depth and stability. In these circumstances, notions that 'it could have been – it could be – otherwise' are sociological fantasies. However, to critique constructionism is not a recommendation for accepting accounts at face value. Ethnomethodologically informed ethnographers choose instead to adopt a stance of indifference to such questions so that issues of questioning or supporting an account do not arise. Thereby issues of truth and falsity and the endless debates of objectivity/subjectivity, the possibility of value neutrality, the researcher–researched relationship, and more are

113

avoided. When considered from the viewpoint of sociological research, 'social reality' is clearly not the same thing as social reality for the purposes of everyday life. As previously suggested, the actor cannot, under the auspices of the natural attitude, systematically adopt the sceptical stance found under the auspices of the theoretical attitude; we accept, rather than systematically doubt, everyday appearances.[27]

Fortunately, ethnomethodologically informed ethnography avoids these debates by refusing to buy into many of the dichotomies of traditional social science – objective/subjective, structure/agency, and so on – that create many of these problems in the first place. In its view, the production of valid and useful ethnographic accounts relies initially on the ambition of the unique adequacy requirement. This insists that the researcher should try to develop a vulgar competence in the setting itself, in order to understand life as practitioners themselves comprehend and practice it and to be able to describe in the language of the setting. As Garfinkel and Weider (1992, p. 182) put it,

> ... for analysts to recognize, or identify, or follow the development of, or describe phenomena of order in local production of coherent detail the analyst must be vulgarly competent in the local production and reflexively natural accountability of the phenomena of order he [or she] is "studying."

As Crabtree (2003) argues, the issue is one of the 'probativeness' (Garfinkel and Wieder, 1992) or of descriptive adequacy. Understanding culture requires little more than a mundane competence in the practices of the domain such that the researcher can deliver an account that is intelligible to competent members. This is far from arguing that anyone who is not a bank worker (scientist, disabled, woman) is unable to write about, analyse, discuss, theorise, and so on these matters.

To conclude this argument, the ethnomethodological endeavour lies in describing how members (not researchers or sociologists) manage to produce and recognise contextually relevant structures of social action. The warrant for ethnomethodologically informed ethnography is that of 'probativeness' or 'faithfulness to the phenomena,' that the description of the situated organisation of that activity in its detail makes that real-world activity mutually intelligible. The description should consist in the witnessable methods of practical reasoning employed to accomplish activities.

---

[27]However, this concern with the natives' point of view, with the difficulties of uncovering, displaying, and understanding a setting and way of life that is different, if not alien to the researcher, can also produce some unfortunate arguments about both how ethnographic research can be done and who is entitled to do it (Dartington et al., 1981; Miller and Gwynne, 1972; Oliver, 1992). This entails disputes about not just what is investigated but how research is conducted; arguments about objectivity and subjectivity, involvement of the subject in research, and so on. Such positions are redolent of Becker's view of 'understanding' and we need to bear very much in mind that there is an alternative, cast roughly in the manner of Geertz.

Ethnomethodology can thereby avoid the sorts of dilemmas that perplex other sociologists, the dualisms that both fascinate and perplex mainstream social science. As Sharrock (1995) writes,

> The conduct of ethnographies as we do them does not leave us exposed to the charge that we are perpetuating a now outmoded practice of ethnography, one which, in the light of relatively recent developments in sociology, stands revealed as perpetuating the illusion that there is a reality "outside the text," that there is a "real world" out there to be studied. We have sought to do no more than illustrate that our own lines of argument are not elaborated in ignorance of those recent developments, but, to no small extent, in defiance of them....

Having said that, understanding ethnomethodology is no straightforward matter. As interdisciplinary practitioners will have noted, it has a jargon all of its own, one which is sometimes every bit as obscure as that of the rest of sociology. Equally, it comes in a number of versions, including ethnomethodological studies of work, conversation analysis, institutional talk, and, latterly, interaction analysis. We discuss all of these alternatives, at least briefly, but should equally make it clear that our own version is very much in the ethnomethodological studies of work tradition first formulated by Garfinkel (1986). Even so, and as should be obvious from our comments thus far, we are asking our ethnographies to do more than Garfinkel for one would demand or want, to the extent that it is open to question whether some parts of what we might want of a design ethnography might be termed ethnomethodology at all. This is, of course, why the neologism – ethnomethodologically informed ethnography – was coined.

We cannot cover the whole of the literature on ethnomethodology, and we do not attempt to do so. Rather, we try to bring out some of its fundamental features and key terms, in particular, its interest in language, in context, the notion of accomplishment, and of lived experience. Associated with this is a set of analytic commitments, such as to unique adequacy, the processual or sequential organisation of interaction, warrantability, data-driven sociology, and so on.

Ethnomethodology is generally held to have originated with the work of two American sociologists, Harold Garfinkel and Harvey Sacks, in the 1960s. In fact, its origins can be traced back to what is usually called phenomenological philosophy, and to Alfred Schutz (1970,1972). One aspect of the ethnomethodological programme that tends to be lost in CSCW (and it is probably just as well) is the radical nature of its relationship to other disciplines such as sociology and psychology. Its stance on problems such as meaning, cognition, and behaviour is at variance methodologically and perspectivally with the standard disciplinary assumptions of psychology and sociology. In a nutshell, ethnomethodologists (to a greater or lesser extent) would argue that most human science disciplines confuse theoretical/

conceptual matters with practical/empirical matters (in much the way described by Peter Winch (1958)), and are imbued with dubious philosophical commitments of one kind or another. Ethnomethodology, in contrast, refuses any epistemological or ontological commitments except those used by people in their practical affairs. They assume the world is objective; thus the ethnomethodologist does too and limits enquiry rigorously to what is directly observable and (in our version) what can be plausibly inferred from observation on a known-in-common basis.

Another way of phrasing these different commitments is in terms of theoretical concerns with what can be objectively known: a scientific world-view, if you will. This evolved from the rationalism of Kant and Descartes in the eighteenth century, who had as their topic of enquiry what can be known and how it can be known. That is, they were concerned with the construction of an epistemology. In contrast, the phenomenologists rejected the notion that it is possible to know an objective reality derived from logic or from the senses. Rather, they were concerned with the prospect that what we know is inevitably constructed from our experience. This experience may be made up of many things, but for instance always includes the things we do, concepts we use, and the words we deploy.

The phenomenologists started from the view that human beings typically orient to the world with what is called the 'natural attitude' (Schutz, 1972), which refers to the way we mundanely, ordinarily, without any problems, see the world as made up in a particular way. The point is that the natural attitude contains no doubt about the way the world is, whereas philosophy and psychology are based on doubt concerning it. Rather than doubting whether the world is 'real', the phenomenologists were interested in analysing the natural attitude, if you like, in understanding what it is like to experience the world the way people experience it, and suspending any beliefs concerning whether it is 'really' like that.[28]

This means that, if we are to understand social behaviours, it is not enough to observe them directly, for what they mean must depend on our knowledge of the culture we inhabit or are trying to 'learn'. As Schutz (ibid.) puts it, '. . . we have no means of knowing that the meaning-context which we think appropriate is at all the same as what the actor had in mind. . . . It suffices at the moment that we have proved the impossibility of motivational understanding on the basis of observation alone.'

That is, we have to impute some motive, desire, rationale, or whatever, to the actions observed in order to make sense of them but one can only do so contingently. This in effect is what Garfinkel meant by the 'documentary

---

[28]Indeed, and subsequently, not only Schutz but others as well, pointed out that even science depends on preinterpretation. In other words, all thinking activities, whether scientific (and thus supposedly objective) or commonsensical, rely on our known in common views of the world. The implication of this is that our understandings are founded on intersubjectivity rather than subjectivity.

method'. This point cannot be overstressed because it means that our 'sensemaking' work is always commonsense work. Again, it is important to understand that this appeal to common sense is not part of a contrast pair. It is not, that is, of the variety, 'it's just common sense' as opposed to other, perhaps scientific, practices. It is to say only that all human behaviours, science included, can be understood as a set of practices founded on what are shared, known-in-common, assumptions about how this particular bit of the world (in this case, the science lab) works. Common sense is how we make the world and, just as important, it is largely unproblematic. We do not for the most part have any trouble understanding the world, and thus have no need for any further investigation of how understanding is possible. This is not to say that interpretation is never done, for our understandings of the world are contingently valid and open to correction.

An initial relevance to CSCW concerns can be identified in phenomenological perspectives insofar as they point to the ways in which people are able to draw on their common sense to make sense of what is going on. They do so through typifications which have to do with their stocks of knowledge about the world; this includes knowledge about, for instance, objects (know what) and recipes (know how). These stocks of knowledge are contingently valid; that is, they are treated as right until something crops up which makes them problematic. Moreover, stocks of knowledge are not normally consulted, because we simply take them for granted in most circumstances.

One obvious task for the ethnographer, then, is to take knowledge seriously. We should emphasise that this is nontrivial and it was the point of our discussion in Chapter 1. The very fact that actors take their knowledge for granted means that eliciting knowledge is not always straightforward. Belatedly, it seems that even the knowledge management literature is catching on to this in and through its use (and misuse) of Polanyi's (1966) concept of 'tacit' knowledge.

Schutz (ibid.) emphasises that no two people can have identical viewpoints, for their biographies diverge, but the interesting feature of the social world is how we can behave, more or less, most of the time, as if our perspectives are the same. Intersubjectivity relies on two fundamental assumptions on the part of actors that are part of a general reciprocity of perspectives. We assume, until it is proven otherwise,

1. That if we stand in the place of the other person we will see and think about things in much the same way as we see and think about them now. We will share, that is, typifications.
2. That, although our personal biographies make us different, we are sharing a common perspective on the world when we interact. That is, we are selecting shared and common objects and features about which to speak.

117

Just as important, there is no guarantee of this shared world; it is actively sustained by participants to it. This is ethnomethodology's starting point, for it asks the question, 'How do people achieve and sustain this known in common, typical, world as a matter of ordinary, practical, purpose?' For Garfinkel and Sacks, then, the fundamental problem is how people maintain orderly conduct: how they produce order in and through their intersubjective action. Ethnomethodology, then:

- Focuses on the mundane and practical ways in which people make sense of what they do
- Emphasises the moment-by-moment, sequential organization of their activity

4.4.1 Ethnomethodological Studies of Work

The approach to ethnography best known in design-related communities is probably the one that derives from the 'ethnomethodological studies of work' programme. This approach is associated in CSCW with work done at the Lancaster school in the United Kingdom and at Xerox Parc in the United States. This programme of study was formulated by Garfinkel, along with Michael Lynch and Eric Livingstone. It is predicated on what Garfinkel termed the 'missing what' of most sociological enquiry into work. That is, the sociology of work, much though it might have contributed, tells us little about the nature of work itself, the nature of work as moment-by-moment 'lived experience'.

In contrast, the ethnomethodological studies of work programme takes as its *only* topic, how members accomplish their world of work.[29] The stress is important, for it implies no commitments of any kind as to the merits or otherwise of members' world views, attitudes, assumptions, and so on although, and here is a point of divergence from a strict interest in the sequential organisation of work, we feel that for interdisciplinary purposes we might want to report what members say about these things. That is, one of the problems surrounding the need to pay account of culture (as Beyer and Holzblatt suggest) is that the term itself has a multitude of different meanings.

One orientation to it is very much in line with the idea of culture as characteristic or typical attitudes, beliefs, values, and so on. We want here to explicitly resist the idea that ethnography is a method for uncovering attitudes, values, and beliefs for such matters are not observable at all.

---

[29]Although 'work task' here must be understood in the most general of ways. As we try to show, 'work' for the ethnomethodologist can be any piece of social interaction.

Moreover, the idea that these attitudes, values, and beliefs can be reported at all in a systematic way is a dubious one, as postmodern accounts have shown. We can, however, and should insist on reporting on what is said and done because it confers a clear standard of evidence on our work.

Ethnomethodology sets a standard for how this should be done through its insistence on unique adequacy. Much has been written about this concept, although very considerable confusion surrounds it. We suggest that it is best treated as an ambition. For Garfinkel, if we treat members' commonsense methods as being equivalent to our professional sociological methods (it being the case that there is no time out from commonsense judgements, as studies of professional coding practices have shown), then members' judgements about the adequacy of any account of their work must be as good as anyone else's. Actually, more or less by definition, they will be better. It follows, then, that a good measure of the adequacy of any ethnographic work lies in members' reaction to it. Nevertheless, unique adequacy must itself be a commonsense category: there is no ultimate objective test of it. After all, anything that members might say to us about the quality of our work will itself be, as ethnomethodologists like to say, recipient designed.

Related to this is the equally confusing notion of the hybrid discipline of which Garfinkel also speaks. The hybrid in question is between 'outsider' and 'insider' accounts. It would seem that the best description of the processual or sequential character of work should be provided by someone who can do the work. Of course, they would have to be professionally motivated so to do, as sociologists typically are. Therefore, some combination of the domain expert and the professional description ought to provide us with a pretty good description of work.

Again, however, we must distinguish here between ethnomethodology's debate with sociology over method and theory, and ethnomethodology's role in the design process, for they may be quite different. There is no reason to presume here, for the purposes of understanding design-relevant matters, that a hybrid ethnography will be required, nor that whatever account is provided should meet unique adequacy requirements as they apply to members. This is because, in anything other than limited domains, the existence of a division of labour in complex organisational settings is bound to restrict our competence.

There may of course be some kind of unique adequacy test as applied to designers' views of ethnographic enquiry. Our caution here has nothing to do with reservations about ethnomethodological accounts, but with the prospect that terms that ethnomethodologists habitually use might get reified into a programme. One could, if so minded, interpret the 'unique adequacy' clause to mean that the best ethnographies for design will be done by those familiar with the job in hand, and therefore that we should always appoint domain experts to the task. Not so. Firstly, we might consider whether unique adequacy is an injunction or an ambition. In our view, and as already stated, it is the latter. That is, it is an internal test applied by ethnomethodologists to ascertain the merits of any particular ethnomethodological enquiry. In and of itself this has no necessary relation to any design concerns. As something to aspire to, it makes a degree of sense in design-related endeavour because it acts as something of a guarantor of detail and of taking real-world activity seriously.

In sum, and put simply, ethnomethodology means people's methods. It involves seeing things from the point of view of participants and trying to understand how their form of life can be construed as the outcome and accomplishment of their interactions. Taken together, these points indicate what an ethnomethodologically informed ethnography would look like. They suggest it would be an analysis which is interested in how people conduct working life in real settings, doing what they do in the mutual accomplishment of sometimes divergent intentions, treating work as socially organized, and interested above all in how it is socially organised in that setting. This means looking at the actual working division of labour as routinely manifested in peoples' meaningful orientation to their work. One important feature of this is that it would not treat work and technology as analytically separable. It would treat technology as technology-in-use.

The ethnomethodological task, therefore, is merely to report in adequate detail how members go about doing what they construe as the thing to be done. The relationship between ethnomethodology and design, then, on the face of it looks slightly puzzling, inasmuch as design must be about commitments. We have already alluded to this and we have more to say about this at a later stage, but we can imagine a number of possible reactions to design on the part of the ethnographer, ranging from: 'We just provide the data; leave the rest to designers,' through 'Start innocent, become informed,' to, 'We all do design now.'

To put it another way, ethnomethodologists in design can either restrict what they do to ethnomethodological enquiry, or put on another hat when they get engaged in the design process. We might ask how many possible hats we can be asked to wear (because, of course, there are lots of hats).

Everyday Work as Accountable and Cooperative Activity

Our stance is that certain ethnomethodological commitments should be foundational to ethnographic practice in design, that these commitments have no necessary relation with other commitments to be found in varieties of ethnomethodology such as conversation analysis and interaction analysis, and sit comfortably with some, but not all, forms of generalisation.

Ethnography in this version is interested to understand how people make sense of mundane activities and how they make those activities accountable to others. For ethnomethodologists how people go about making sense of the social world represents mechanisms through which social structure is created, ordered, and sustained. As the social order is continually constructed and reconstructed, so people, as practical sociologists, are involved in a constant, if taken for granted, process of inference and understanding, so that they are able to act successfully in relation to others for everyday practical purposes. Members must be able to make the social organisation of their mundane activities visible, accountable, and observable-reportable to each other. The methods that members use to make sense of what is going on are publicly available resources for the observer.

Consequently, ethnomethodologically informed ethnography is particularly attuned to revealing cooperative aspects of working life: how people reconfigure their arrangements in the face of contingencies and circumstances as they arise. Social activities are concerted activities. The concern to understand just how such working together takes place (as opposed to why it takes place), and how people manage to make their activities fit together whilst doing those same activities, appears the province of ethnomethodology.

Its concern with the question of how concerted actions are conducted, and the associated emphasis upon the accountable character of work, has combined to give studies a focus upon the ways in which the pattern of complex activities are made visible to those carrying out those activities, to the ways in which people placed within some complex of action can figure out what is happening around them, and how they can fit their own activities into that complex, both when, for example, the pattern of activity is a localised one, within their visual field, where the participant can directly monitor those activities which are relevant to their decision as to what to do next and when, on the other hand, they are engaged in patterns of distributed activities, and where they cannot immediately monitor the activities of other, collaborating, parties but need, nonetheless, to know in some more-or-less specific sense what those others are doing, so as to shape their own activity into the relevant pattern.

The explication of sense-making machinery has often invoked work activity as a manifest 'working division of labour' (Anderson et al., 1989). Ethnomethodologically informed ethnography seeks to understand the organisation of work, its flow, and the division of labour from the point of view of those involved in the work. Because work settings are organised around, through, and within a division of labour, work activities are necessarily seen as interdependent. Understanding how people coordinate their work in realtime, moment-by-moment, how they orient to the 'working division of labour' to make sense of what they are doing, is a feature of ethnographic explication.

Ethnomethodologically informed ethnography approaches the flow of work (rather than the disembodied idealisations of workflow) as an accomplishment, a collective achievement. Individuals perform their tasks within

121

the context of others similarly doing their own tasks, within sequences of activities, but the actual work requires individuals to determine and display how their work fits into their responsibilities, their relevances, and how this will fit with that of others. Anderson et al. (ibid.) call this an 'egological' viewpoint: a view of the world of work and its organisation from the perspective of individuals cooperating and coordinating their activities with others (we make use of these concepts extensively in a subsequent chapter).

Although individual workers have individual tasks to perform, they are also, and necessarily, individuals as part of a collectivity, and much of their work consists in the ability to organise the distribution of individual tasks into an ongoing assemblage of activities within a working division of labour. Individuals, that is, orient to their work according to 'egological' principles and their own horizons of relevance, but have to be attentive to the work of others in order to organise the flow of work in a coherent way. This focus has arguably provided an important analytic tool for the examination of work as lived experience, providing important clues as to both how work was accomplished and, perhaps, why work was done the way it was.

4.4.2 Ethnomethodologically Informed Ethnography: Clearing up Confusions

> *I want to encourage the sense that interesting aspects of the world, that are as yet unknown, are accessible to observation.*
> (Sacks, 1992, p. 420)

This section is primarily concerned with documenting in outline the analytic purchase of ethnomethodologically informed ethnography (something we follow up in Section 3) and, in consequence, its utility for describing and understanding everyday organisational, and other, activity. We have seen above that an ethnographic stance entails some minimum orientation to viewing the social world from the standpoint of its participants, but that equally there are many different routes towards this simple commitment. One approach to this is the ethnomethodological one, in which members' methods for accomplishing situations in and through the use of local rationalities become the topic of enquiry. For ethnomethodologically informed ethnographic enquiry, members and their subjective orientations and experiences are central. Observation focuses on the places and circumstances where meanings and courses of action are constructed, maintained, used, and negotiated.

> We are concerned with how society gets put together; how it is getting done; how to do it; the social structures of everyday activities. I would say that we are doing studies of how persons, as parties to ordinary arrangements, use the features of the arrangement to make for members the visible organised activities happen (Garfinkel, 1967).

The mere fact that people are doing it justifies the attention being given to it by an ethnomethodologically motivated ethnographer. In this way the false starts, glitches, diversions, distractions, interruptions, and digressions which are aspects of all activities are notable features of the phenomena; not, so to speak, noise to be eliminated from the data in order to reveal essential or sociologically relevant aspects of the data.

4.4.3 Why? Questions

We have suggested that ethnomethodology is typically concerned with trying to understand how people do what they do in a detailed and orderly way. It may be thought as a result that ethnomethodology has no interest in 'why' questions. This is not true, although much hinges on what kind of 'why' questions we are considering. Thus and for instance, questions about causes, motives, and generalisation very much hinge on what kind of cause, motive, and the like is our concern. As all philosophers know, cause can have a range of technical meanings and, as all cognitive scientists know, so can motive. Ethnomethodologists are not interested in any of them. Notions of cause and motive are ordinary commonsense terms used by members to infer various things about what is going on. Ethnomethodologically informed ethnographers are entitled to draw these ordinary commonsense inferences because they too have the (vulgar) competences of members after having investigated the setting in question in the way recommended by ethnomethodology.

4.4.4 Perspective and Practicality

The above review of assorted theories, perspectives, orientations, or what have you should indicate a number of commonalities and lines of dissent. We are not here trying to persuade readers of the superiority of one perspective over another, but to show some of the consequences of adopting one stance in preference to another. We have tried to avoid an unnecessarily critical tone, and see much of value in all of these more or less theoretical perspectives. We have also been at pains to show that all the perspectives in question can exist comfortably with some conception of ethnography, although none fully explains what it is that ethnography might contribute to analysis within a theoretical framework.

Indeed, the contrast between fieldwork and ethnography we discussed earlier raises its head again here, for one of the decisions that any theoretically informed observer must make is whether her concepts – the way in which she organises the data she has collected – are given by the data or by the theory. If the latter, then observational methods are simply superior techniques (in much the way that Beyer and Holzblatt (1998) suggest) and as such ethnography or any other form of fieldwork must be considered purely and simply as method. In the former case, however, ethnographic results implicate their own analytic procedures (i.e. whatever concepts are produced are data-driven). In this sense, the ethnography itself generates the analytic insights and hence the relevant concepts.

The problems with each are obvious. If ethnography is merely a method, then the spectacle of researchers shoehorning their data into pre-existing categories, determined to make the data fit, is raised. The danger is evident: that fieldworkers fail to see what is in front of their eyes because they have already decided where to look and for what to look. On the other hand, data-led approaches produce a vast range of concepts, with little or no consistency from one piece of work to another. Comparison between one case and another is difficult. Put simply, one approach leads to similarity being overstressed, the other to difference being overstressed. Across the range of theoretical devices we have discussed, the relationship between data and theory is complex and the ramifications of our choices significant. Ethnomethodologists ask, legitimately in our view, what are theories for, whilst those with a more theoretical orientation ask, equally legitimately, how do you generalise from your results.

Asking what a theory is for might seem a trivial and unnecessary question. However, it may be necessary in situations where the theories and perspectives in question have arrived out of broadly disciplinary concerns and yet are being applied to interdisciplinary purpose. (Ethnomethodology, activity theory, and distributed cognition all came about initially as critical responses to orthodoxies in sociology and psychology. Actor-network theory developed as a response to what was seen by its proponents as either naive technological, or naive social, determinism in sociology.) Theories imply some kind of generalisation by definition and this is normally held, in outline, to be their purpose. Of course, whether this kind of generalisation is appropriate for that kind of purpose is not straightforward. It is not at all evident that concepts developed to deal with infelicities or lacunae in existing sociological or psychological theory are necessarily relevant to design and construction problems or the kind of generalisation appropriate here.

For this reason, one of the decisions all of us must make in respect of theory (should we want to argue theoretically), concerns the status of our theoretical choices. Our own conviction, as mentioned above, is that any theoretical choice in interdisciplinary work should be on the basis that the theory illuminates or sensitises (Blumer, 1969). That is, general but often loosely formed concepts can help orient the researcher to the kinds of problem he might face, and in particular might help him determine what the relevance of his enquiries might be. Seen in this way, all of the above theories and perspectives might have a more or less useful status. On the downside, of course, is the obvious consequence that theory seen in this manner meets no scientific criteria, produces no predictions, and admits of no precision in measurement.

Our point is that the majority of approaches we have discussed in the last two chapters are of exactly this kind, admitting concepts with imprecise definitions, where only loosely organised conceptual relationships are possible. They serve, above all, to orient the researcher. Even if these theories or perspectives are similar in this respect, however, they may be different in others. The kind of orientation involved in any given theoretical commitment might be very different:

- Activity theory seems to remind us of the need, above all, to adopt a developmental approach, to retain a sense of history.
- Distributed cognition stresses 'systems' and system relationships and above all reminds us that structures of representation are important in understanding and interpreting information.
- Participatory design reminds us of the various stakeholders in the design process, and in particular that some voices are regularly silenced.
- Actor-network theory orients us to the closely intertwined nature of outcomes, whereby neither changes in the technology nor changes in the social/organisational world can successfully predict the future, and above all reminds us of the massive contingency of outcomes.
- Grounded theory speaks powerfully to the limits of scientific enquiry as conventionally conceived, and forces attention to the emergent relationship between data and theory.

All of these foci are useful, but we should not forget that these evident differences have some impact on the relationship of theory to design, in at least the following ways.

Orientation to Change

It should be apparent that the perspectives described above differ radically in their orientation to change, although they all have in common their treatment of design as being a social, cultural, or organisational issue. In this respect, as we have pointed out elsewhere (Harper et al., 2000) participatory design is unlike the other approaches in that it is unapologetically and explicitly about change. This up-front approach to intervention makes it similar to business process re-engineering (although only in this respect), whereas other perspectives seem to accept a more modest remit.

Grounded theory, for instance, is clearly evolutionary in the sense that it anticipates that theories will build in relation to the way in which data come to be organised. Although grounded theory hardly dominates the world of HCI and CSCW it would carry an obvious implication for interdisciplinary endeavour. That is, if the purposes of enquiry are to be evolved by all parties to the enquiry then all must share an equal responsibility for deriving the sense of relevance that should eventually evolve from ethnographic enquiry. Certainly, it would seem to be foundational to such a view that too precipitate a view of strategy would be extremely risky.

Ethnomethodology has the most controversial approach in that, in some versions at least, ethnographies should in the first instance be innocent of design concerns. This view holds that taking on the concerns of designers at an early stage is an analytic error, because it means moving towards some kind of theoretical perspective before discovering what the data are telling us. It is perhaps this stance more than any other that has led to ethnomethod-ologically informed ethnography being labelled conservative in the design sense. It further refuses to theorise about how one eventually does go about orienting to change, contenting itself with treating the relationship with designers as an entirely practical matter. Of course, and unsurprisingly, we view this as a strength rather than a weakness, for our claim all along is that these issues can be reduced to the problem of timeliness.

The point is that these different takes have consequences for the emergence of lines of enquiry. Fieldwork under the auspices of, for instance, business process re-engineering, is going to be very much a matter of fitting evidence to conceptual categories that are systematically applied. Furthermore, fieldwork of this kind is going to constitute management information, and explicitly so. The existence of other versions is unlikely to be seen as relevant here. PD in some respects takes an entirely similar, if structurally opposed, view. The others position themselves at various points in between strongly motivated approaches of this kind and ethnomethodology's sometime claim to unmotivated looking.

Nevertheless, all these perspectives have one thing in common: the argument that the classic structured approach to design exemplifies hard systems thinking, and seriously underestimates the requirements problem. Of course, this is not to trivialise the work of software engineers. It has long been understood that poorly understood domains require a complex and iterative approach to requirements. (Checkland's 1981; Checkland and Scholes, 1989) point, however, and it is one that several sociologists in CSCW have also made, is that the problem is precisely an analytic one. Put simply, how to go about understanding the problem must precede decisions concerning what to do about it. The reason we emphasise this point so strongly is that examination of various candidate solutions to the design problem, as we hope we have shown, indicates that each is founded on a rather different set of analytic assumptions.

Formal Versus Informal

Following Suchman's deployment of ethnomethodology for system design purposes in 'Plans and Situated Actions,' there has been much debate in

CSCW concerning the relationship between the 'plan' and 'action'. (Discussion of this theme goes on: see Schmidt (1997) and Bardram (1997).) Suchman herself has pointed out several times that her conception of this relationship has been misunderstood by commentators. Methodologically, whatever the status of the two, this can be glossed as posing the field of study as being precisely about the connection between formal and informal processes (although ethnomethodologists including Suchman would strongly resist this separation). In many respects, all the perspectives discussed above can be seen in these terms. Even BPR emphasises the need to study 'work arounds', albeit with a view to formalising informal activities. The main difference with the other approaches is the degree to which this analytic problem can be seen as the relationship between individual and system, or individual and culture (or rules) in the way that distributed cognition and activity theory variously stress, or as collapsing the distinction entirely, rejecting notions of individual cognition and of system, and substituting accomplishment (ethnomethodology).

Problem Specification

The effect of interdisciplinary claims on design is to make it an ever more complex problem. The problems which software developers are asked to solve today are in any case often immensely complex without this complication. Systems of a radically different kind, of a new order of complexity, which are distributed, and so on, all share the common feature that there is often no stable or pre-existing 'successful' system to serve as a basis for the software, a condition which applies particularly to CSCW systems. That is, establishing the services the system should provide and the constraints under which it must operate (requirements capture and analysis) is a matter of discovering the nature of the problem before one begins to define a solution.

As has been noted elsewhere (see Rittel and Webber (1973) and Checkland (1981)), the root of the problem lies in the nature of systems and how we think about them, and here 'systems' refers to the organisational complex rather than to the technology. For Rittel and Webber, the main difficulty is that the problems being tackled are usually 'wicked' problems, a 'wicked' problem being one for which there is no definitive formulation. The theoretical stances rehearsed above all show different orientations to problem specification.

On a wholly artificial continuum, we can see that some managerialist approaches take a hard analytic position, in that, for instance, process problems are regarded as self-evidently the most serious, regardless of context. That is, they derive from the viewpoint that the task starts with the construction of a solution rather than the identification of the problem. As Rivett has argued, formal models of decision making tend to ignore the fact that change is, 'A complex process which is a mixture, in practice, of fumbling, mind-changing, chaos and political intervention' (Rivett, 1983). In sum, hard systems thinking arguably has trouble coping with contingency. Perhaps one of the reasons for the (small) popularity of Glaser and Strauss' perspective is their commitment to the evolving nature of theoretical work, and its contingent refining. Certainly the most radical version of problem specification is that of ethnomethodology, in that it refuses to treat any phenomenon as a problem in any sense other than the way in which it is treated as such by participants to the work.

The issue of problem formulation, then, seems to get more rather than less complicated. In the specific context of system design, the complexity of the problem space may be a function of any number of different technical, human, and organisational issues. However, if we see all the perspectives we have discussed as emphasising (in their different ways) the importance of relating what people actually do to the issue of organisational goals, rules, purposes, and what have you, then we can derive the following basic points from any and all of them.

a) Large software systems are usually required to improve upon the *status quo* where either no system or an inadequate system is in place. Although difficulties with the current system may be known, it is hard to anticipate what effects the 'improved' system is likely to have on an organisation. It is a critique of ethnomethodological stances, for instance, that they do not deal systematically with problems of this kind. Nevertheless, the problem of when one is adequately prepared to make guesses, informed or otherwise, about the consequences of new technology, work practice, and organisational form is a vibrant one, not least when it comes to evaluation.

b) Large systems usually have a diverse user community who have different and sometimes conflicting requirements and priorities. The final system requirements are inevitably a compromise. Many of the perspectives we cite are, at root, methods for understanding the different viewpoints organisational members might have. It is arguably a weakness of BPR that it underspecifies alternatives to the management view.

c) The procurers of a system (those who pay for it) and the users of a system are rarely the same people. System procurers impose requirements because of organisational and budgetary constraints. These are likely to conflict with actual user requirements.

d) The iterative nature of the requirements process, from capture to specification, and the attendant problems of communication, understanding, contractual obligation, and so on, require us to orient to complexity.

Task, Organisation, and Culture

Our aim in this book is not necessarily to privilege one perspective above others (although it would be foolish to deny we have our preferences), or to suggest that the long sought magic bullet might be found among these candidates, but to emphasise that it does a different kind of analysis, analysis which is likely to prove relevant to systems design as the design process itself orients more and more to business and organisational issues. One way of thinking about the relative merits of these different perspectives is to think about their analytic consequences for separating (or not, as the case may be): task, organization, and culture.

Doing real-world studies, under whatever auspices, could be seen as providing tools for getting to grips with each of these concepts. Whether they all do so equally well, or in the same way, is debatable.

a) Task issues. These are, to put it simply, to do with understanding what gets done, and how. It is quite clear that perspectives such as ethnomethodology and distributed cognition make much of their analytic power for this purpose (as of course do other more orthodox cognitive perspectives). It is an entirely fair question to ask whether all perspectives are equally valuable for uncovering the level of the task. It would seem to us that granularity is more endemic in some approaches than others.

b) Organisational issues, at the very core of CSCW and information systems work, are increasingly being defined according to a variety of change management philosophies, theories, and practices which have their roots in some classic sociologies of the organisation. They provide strong versions of what it means to understand the organisation, at least as constituted in rules, processes, and procedures. One question, then, that we might ask of our candidate perspectives is whether they provide useful alternatives.

c) Organisational culture is one of the great mysteries of organisational theory (which probably reflects the immense confusion concerning culture to be found in the sociological and anthropological literature), and it is not the place here to recount the debates between rationalists and others in this context. Suffice it to say that the Human Relations School and the various versions of sociotechnical systems theory that have followed upon it have had a profound impact on recent organisational concerns with the notion of culture, concerns which are shared by assorted writers in CSCW. Organisational culture is not easily defined but a useful definition is: '. . . the solutions to external and internal problems that have worked consistently for a group and are, therefore, taught to new members as the correct way to perceive, think about, and feel in relation to those problems' (Schein, 1985). Understanding the relevance of such

129

a vague concept is difficult in the extreme, but some of our competing viewpoints make much of it (activity theory being one). Much of this interest in organisational culture comes from the prospect that changes in cultural expectations can be managed and controlled. If so, it is generally accepted that changing a culture is especially difficult, because of the very pervasiveness and subtlety culture possesses. Nevertheless, this interest has burgeoned, not least in and through the advent of recent interest in the role of 'networks' both in and outside organisational contexts.

In many ways, of course, the issues we recount above have to a greater or lesser extent been the concern of CSCW for some time, and much of the research that has been undertaken in CSCW has attempted to orient to some notion of organisational context in and through analysing task, organization, and culture. Many examples of what we can conveniently term evaluative ethnography now exist to illustrate the point (see e.g. Orlikowski (1992)). It would not be terribly controversial by now to argue that such studies have provided an excellent method for the critique of existing systems, and serious attempts have been made to integrate them into the design process itself, not without some difficulties. (see Hughes et al. (1992) and Bentley et al. (1992)). This would appear to be the kind of logic, for instance, behind much of the interest in pattern languages today (see e.g. Crabtree (2003)).

Fieldwork, potentially, has a significant role to play here in providing a contrast between the definition of problems given from the outside, whether by systems designers or change management specialists, and the problem seen from the point of view of the person(s) doing the work. Problems seen this way, from the participants' point of view, help us gain purchase on some features of work that are commonly overlooked, notably as we show, how the flow of work is distributed according to the principle of 'What should I do next?' and consequently on the problem of, for instance, interruption. Equally, where many techniques exist for assessing the frequency with which problems arise, little emphasis is placed on their significance for participants to the work outside the CSCW arena.

What is less clear is how to relate problem-solving strategies to context. At this point, we simply wish to suggest that the detailed and focused analysis of ethnographic data can help us understand how knowledge, skills, and expertise can be deployed by members to solve problems of task, organization, and culture. In this respect, ethnography acts in contrast to orthodox conceptions by placing skill, expertise, and experience in contexts which participants to the work would recognise. That is, it can describe participants' orientation to problems such as 'Who or what do I need to help me and how?' The existence of patterns of skill and expertise is, of course, of fundamental importance to the allocation of function problem in systems design.

Ultimately, all the theories we have discussed can be seen as correctives. They challenge and interrogate other perspectives which have proven inadequate to the kinds of task endemic in design. Of course, like all correctives, they will prove most useful to those who need correcting. Where activity theory, for instance, was originally a corrective for behaviourist psychologies, it has very much become one for HCI protagonists who have become fixated on the logic of the task. Distributed cognition, equally, seems to be fixed on correcting that vision of human behaviour which sees it as springing from mental processes alone. Participatory design corrects the view that design is a technical matter, pointing to its political ramifications and to the very partial view of the world held by organisational managements.

Generalisations

The assumption that human activities are socially organised and so, from the outset, are committed to inquiring into patterns of social life is foundational to the practice of ethnography. Unlike other methods which tend to use more formal instruments of data capture and analysis, the ethnographic method relies on an observer going into the field and learning the ropes through questioning, listening, watching, talking, and so on, with practitioners. That said, these enquiries can, in principle, be into an enormous range of matters which might be of interest in principle. They might, for instance, be enquiries into beliefs and attitudes, the symbolic universe of a culture, customs, law, gender relations, and so on. They do not have to provide detailed pictures of patterns of interaction and collaboration.

Our argument, however, is that these latter interests, and unlike those of sociology, are absolutely foundational to fieldwork-for-design. The task of the fieldworker is to immerse himself or herself into the work and its activities with a view to describing these as the skilful and socially organised accomplishment of parties to the work.

One obvious consequence of this is that, in the first instance, data collected will be of the messy and unstructured variety. It may include interviews, observations of work sequences, anecdotes, speculations, and so on. The data gathered, in other words, usually take the form of fieldnotes but are increasingly also supplemented by audio and video data. Again, however, the messy and unstructured nature of much ethnographic data is not a necessary outcome of ethnographic work: it is more often an outcome of a historically evolved way of doing things.

Part 2
Methods for Social Investigation: Practical Issues

5

Ethnography and Its Role in the Design Process - 'If You *Must* Work Together'

Whatever humans do can be examined to discover some way they do it.
(Sacks, 1984b, p. 22)

When in doubt collect facts.
(Barley, 1983, p. 3)

It is probably safe to assert that most sociologists live their intellectual lives in a world populated principally by other social scientists and their work.
(Glaser and Strauss 1967, p. 161)

The various candidate theoretical perspectives just discussed, their analytic recommendations, and the confusion surrounding the status of fieldwork in the social sciences all tend to suggest that the hype surrounding ethnography in HCI and CSCW is misconceived. Nevertheless, recommendations to do ethnographies as a means to overcome the perceived shortcomings of other methods are now to be found in a wide range of disciplines, not only these. It is almost as if a commitment to some kind of naturalistic enquiry is now a sine qua non of CSCW research, despite the fact that at supposedly interdisciplinary conferences, audiences divide according to whether it's a 'techie paper . . .' or 'another ethnography paper . . .', implying that a certain cynicism has crept into what initially looked, for all the world, like a marriage made in heaven.

There may be a number of reasons for this dismay, including the prospect that expectations were too high at the outset, that the practical problems of integrating fieldwork into highly structured design environments proved too difficult, or that there was a misconception in the first place about what might be achieved. Regardless, our focus from here on is on the practical and analytic work done by ethnographers, because we believe that much of the gap between expectation and reality is an analytic gap. That is, either ethnographers are not very good at explaining the analytic devices they use, and the reasons for using them, or computer scientists find it difficult to map these concepts onto their own understanding of the world. We believe too little attention has been given to the analytic auspices under which fieldwork takes place, and to the practical problem of 'what is it for?' in the system design process. That is, and some years after Suchman (1987) published *Plans and Situated Actions*, the role of fieldwork has yet to come to maturity in the systems design process.

Without wishing to critique specific pieces of research, we believe that too often ethnography is regarded as either:

1. Merely being the same thing as hanging around picking up pointers about what's really going on, or
2. Regarded as a useful method for collecting data which is sociologically interesting, and to which a systems 'spin' is only subsequently given.

In any event, the problem of how to relate ethnographic fieldwork to system issues is an obdurate one. To deal with the issue of hanging around first, our stance in the following chapters is that it is analysis that underpins the success or failure of fieldwork results for system design. 'Hanging around' is all too easy to do, and it is not stretching the point too far to say that data collection in and of itself is easy, especially in the days of video.[30] Of course, the critical decisions that are to be made concern what kinds of data are to be collected, how they are to be organised, what the role of conceptualisation might be, and how it might be represented to other interests in such a way that its relevance will become apparent. We endeavour to defend an ideal position which involves only the gradual acceptance of design issues in data collection and analysis, in line with the theoretical position adopted by Glaser and Strauss but also central to the ethnomethodological approach to the social world encapsulated in the idea of indifference. We also recognise and discuss the degree to which we can meet this ideal in a range of contexts.

Analysis is also the key to the second issue. We are not the first, no doubt, to scratch our heads in confusion when trying to understand what the design relevance of a given piece of data might be, or to be nonplussed at what appears to be some trivial recommendation at the end of a lengthy enquiry. There may be a dangerous tendency in ethnographic enquiry, and it is that it simply gives sociologists and others a chance to do sociological or similar work under the pretence that it has some design-relevant

---

[30]It was never very difficult, even in the days of pen and paper. Indeed, we recommend that pen and paper continue to be used where possible in the setting, or as much as possible shortly after visiting the setting.

consequences. Again, we do not wish to enter into a debate about who might be guilty of such egregious behaviour, and when.

Our intent is not to point fingers at the work of others, but rather at the dangers inherent in precipitate conceptualisation. We argue below that ethnographic 'failure' may come in part because there can be a tendency to believe that it functions as a naturalistic alternative to laboratory work, in which the hypothesis to be tested is somehow more contextual than it is in a laboratory. Our point is that there is no hypothesis to be tested, no concepts are given such that we know in advance where to point our cameras and/or pens to find behaviour exemplifying the concept in view, and it is not always apparent what the setting in question exactly is. All of the theories and approaches we have considered share one common ground, which is that they all orient critically to the 'rational person' argument. They take seriously the sociological position which originates with Durkheim and Weber, and is highly visible in, for instance, Parsons (1937). Put simply, this position holds that rational self-interest cannot, on its own, explain behaviour because values, beliefs, and attitudes must underpin any behaviour – however motivated – and these are culturally given.[31]

More radically, of course, the focus shifts away from any concern for determining factors in behaviour and towards a concern for culture as practice. The turn to situatedness is inescapably a critique of the rationalist strand of enquiry in, for instance, organisational theory, cognitive psychology, and system design. We say this not to criticise or debunk these latter perspectives, but to point out that the issue of complementarity remains a vibrant one. 'Situatedness' in CSCW runs the risk of being a catchword, rather than a serious alternative to the top-down or decompositional models, commonplace in most disciplines. In particular, the matter of how business strategies which are inherently 'planful' relate to the situatedness at the heart of ethnographic studies is likely to prove critical (see Randall et al. (1995b) and Harper et al. (2000)).

5.1 The Purposes of Method

A variety of so-called methods has emerged to support the capture of users' needs and the development of systems requirements. Each of these methods has it own strengths and weaknesses which are not always clearly perceived. It is vital to understand from the outset of any discussion of methods which

---

[31]Such a view is often accused of being a standard social science model, and for refusing to accept the role of nature in defining motive and purpose (what Pinker (2002) has recently termed the 'blank slate' position, with cavalier disregard for the actual positions that social scientists take). To be clear, we are advancing no such view here. Like Durkheim before us, we are merely bracketing questions of drive, motive, and need as 'mental states' or 'biological drives'.

tackle the problems of capturing users' needs that there is no silver bullet to solve all the problems of systems design (Brooks, 1987). This is particularly true in the case of the highly interactive systems which predominate in CSCW and are formulated upon understanding the needs of their user community. The question to ask about any method is, 'What purposes is it designed to serve?' In the context of CSCW this is essentially a matter of establishing effective interdisciplinary communication.

One can begin to answer this in a way that we have already deployed by noting that all methods have analytic purposes. They are informed by foundational principles, sets of assumptions, and conceptual frameworks which serve, sometimes implicitly, to shape the kind of questions the method is seen as capable of answering.

We are adamant that, in the context of CSCW, or wider HCI, the method must serve the practical purposes of system design. It is this which makes CSCW an interdisciplinary endeavour.[32] This means that the primary purpose of ethnographic work in CSCW method must be to identify, describe, and analyse relevant aspects of work and its activities so that design is adequately informed. However, adequately informing design, especially using soft science methods, is not straightforward. System designers tend to require formal or at least systematic procedures, a requirement that the kinds of data collection method associated with ethnography seem to have had some difficulty meeting.[33]

In any event, the generally held view is approximately that we can and should inform system design by refining our methods of data collection and analysis, and perhaps that some kind of theoretical perspective might allow for kinds of generalisation that will further illuminate the process. We are less sanguine, and believe that good practices have to do with experience, goodwill, and the resolute insistence that the dialogue will continue. It should be obvious that where illumination, sensitivity, sensibility, and understanding are key concepts in one version of ethnography or another, there can be no programmatic solutions to the business of integrating its results into the design process. In what follows, therefore, we do not want to institute the very programme we are critiquing here. Our remarks concerning practical issues and analytic/theoretic problems should never be read as putative solutions. They are at best recommendations or advice. The relationship between specific ethnographic results and a particular design problem will always be uncertain. Even so, an effective dialogue between the human and the computer sciences is likely to produce the best understanding of just what a method can and cannot deliver.

---

[32]That does not preclude a secondary, more critical, role of course (see Suchman (1994) for an example of such a critical view, and Agre (1995), Malone (1995), Button (1995), Harper (1995), and Randall (1995) for responses).

[33]There is no logical reason why this should be so. Nevertheless, attempts to formalise carry heavy risks, including that of presenting a highly selective and erroneous characterisation of work.

5.2 Practical Matters

For the reasons we outline above, those searching for the section on 'how to do it' may risk disappointment. This is for the simple and evident reason no single way to do it exists. We have been at great pains, thus far, to stress that analytic choices are by far the most important matter to contend with, much more so than difficulties concerning access, technology, duration, and so on. This is not the same as saying there are no practical considerations to be dealt with and we do, where appropriate, deal with them. Nevertheless, it is well worth stressing this point. What distinguishes ethnography from other forms of enquiry is that there are not, and cannot be, any stepwise procedures that determine 'what to do next'. In that sense ethnography is not a method at all.

This chapter and the next nevertheless provide some ordinary practical recommendations associated with going out and doing it. It is predicated on the view that the first professional crisis ever experienced by the tyro ethnographer is one of confidence. So is the second. And the third. Most of the problems that ethnographers experience are eventually resolved through good-natured persistence. To put it another way, fieldwork is easy to do but also easy to mess up. What we have to say about the practical issues, then, should not be taken as programmatic recommendations, for no such recommendations ever suffice, but as suggestions concerning how to avoid messing up. Indeed, our only claim to experience is a claim to having made a number of mistakes, which in turn gives us the right to suggest to others how to avoid making them.

As indicated, the ethnomethodological emphasis on 'real-world, real-time' work stands in rather stark contrast to many sociological accounts of social life in general and (perhaps) the everyday world of work in particular. Conventional sociological accounts portray a world in which not only does '"homo sociologicus" neither laugh nor cry' (Williamson, 1989) but he does not seem to do much that looks like work either. This is a world not only stripped of the relentless and familiar tedium and repetition of routine work, but a world in which the practical accomplishment of work, the skills and competencies that workers routinely and visibly bring to their jobs, is largely absent. Consequently, although there are many sociological studies of work, they often seem to have very little to say about the actual work which goes on within the setting under study, about what makes this work 'bankwork' or 'insurancework' or for that matter the work of ongoing organisation done using a mobile phone in meeting up with friends.

In the process both the worker and the fashion in which work is accomplished effectively disappears into theoretical abstraction. The desire to be attentive to the work is, therefore, one of the motivations for the use of ethnomethodologically informed ethnography. In contrast to a common sociological attitude which views specific social settings as sites of generic, abstract social processes this approach is particularly focused upon the distinctiveness, or the specificity, of the settings under study.

5.2.1 Ethnography, Data, and Design

Whatever the ostensive analytic claims, ethnographic analyses of a nontrivial nature generate a large amount of information. For example, the fieldnotes generated during the Lancaster ATC study came to some 600 pages plus several tape recordings. These data were collected mainly through the use of handwritten fieldnotes and interview transcripts. The problem escalates when audio/video recording devices are used to collect data. During their study of London Underground control rooms, for example, Heath and Luff (1991) collected several hundred hours of data on videotape. In addition, most ethnographers would agree with the assertion that, no matter how much is recorded, they always know more than is present in the recordings.

The data collected during the study of ATC ranged from specific observations of particular activities to anecdotes and 'war stories' told by workers to the ethnographer. Data varied from being very detailed in parts to sketchy in others, and inevitably there was a significant amount of duplication. Misunderstandings in earlier observations were often clarified later in the transcript as the ethnographer became more familiar with the work taking place. In addition, there was no indication of the relative importance of the different observations; all data were treated as being uniformly relevant and recorded as such. This is summarised by Procter and Williams (1992) when they say:

> Ethnographic data is typically rich, but informal, poorly-bounded and perennially pointing to the provisional, partial and incomplete nature of any account of a social situation....

Ethnographic data might therefore be, in the first instance, ill-matched to designers' agendas, which are focused around finding solutions to well-defined problems. This mismatch is usually traced to three fundamental differences, even tensions, in the two approaches:

- Ethnographers are concerned with analysis; software engineers are concerned with synthesis.
- Ethnographers avoid making judgements about the work; software engineers often have to.
- Ethnography is a prolonged activity; software engineers require information quickly.

5.2.2 Analysis Versus Synthesis

The differing perspectives of the disciplines of ethnography and software engineering are summarised by Hartson and Smith (1991, p. 53):

> In the cooperative development activity of behavioural scientists and computer scientists, a gap exists between the skills and goals brought to the task by each of these roles.... The behavioural scientist, trained in analysis and evaluation, is now part of an environment primarily intended for synthesis and design.

In the context of the analysis of work, ethnographers are not concerned with finding improved ways of carrying out the work or posing 'solutions' to observed social problems. This is a key issue, for much of the attraction of the more change management-oriented approaches is precisely that they do offer the appearance of solutions. This is not out of innate conservatism but out of a recognition of complexity, a will to avoid snake-oil solutions, and above all the awareness that promises made are not promises kept.

In contrast, the development of computer systems has historically been based on an engineering-oriented approach, although creativity seems to be a growing theme in some software development arenas. A key part of the engineering approach is the notion of abstraction, that is, the hiding of detail of appearance, representation, and implementation using higher-level constructs. The discipline is very much one of synthesis, involving the construction of complex systems from smaller simpler components.

5.2.3 Nonjudgmental Versus Judgmental Investigation

It has been shown in the previous section that ethnographic methods of analysis are concerned with providing a rich detailed description of the social organisation of a particular domain. This leads to various problems. One is that some versions of fieldwork are manifestly nonjudgemental. Ethnomethodologically informed ethnographers regard all events, conversation, and the like as being equally relevant and take great pains to avoid making judgements with respect to the relative importance of each fragment of information. In contrast, fieldwork under the auspices of, say, BPR or participative design may not. Our commitments are obvious, but we should stress again that the issue of 'judgement' or strategic intervention is, in our view, less an 'in principle' concern than it is a concern for when judgement can most sensibly be made.

On the other hand, designers are forced to make judgements regarding what is and is not important when designing computer systems, often with incomplete information. System development is often constrained by cost, hardware availability, memory limitations, and so on, and it is not possible to address all the requirements identified during the requirements investigation process. In addition, it is common to discover conflicting requirements for computer systems, particularly where different groups of end-users are involved.

The contrast between the two approaches of software engineering and ethnography can again be highlighted using an example from the ATC project. We wished to provide an electronic display system to support work currently carried out with the use of paper-based information. Quite early on in the project, it became clear to the software engineers that the mass of information emerging from the ethnographic study had to be structured in some way. It was going to be impossible, given our hardware, manpower, and time constraints, to address all of the issues revealed. The software engineers asked the ethnographer to try to categorise the activities they were recording in one of four categories:

- An unimportant activity which need not be supported in an electronic system
- An important activity which need not be supported in an electronic system as the activity is a consequence of the existing nonelectronic system
- An important activity which must be supported in an electronic system but can be supported in a different way to that used in the current paper system
- An important activity which must be supported in exactly the same way as the current paper system

The ethnographer's own methodological point of view which treated the system as a fusion of working practices and technology made it difficult for him to draw the distinctions necessary to answer such questions. For example, deciding what were the 'important' activities, irrespective of automated support, was not straightforward. Was 'idle chat' amongst the controllers 'unimportant' and, if so, in what sense? Even though such talk might not be related to the specific tasks of controlling, a case could be made that it was important for morale, the sharing of experiences, providing support, and so on. The difficulty of fitting ethnographic data to such questions, however, is pointed to by these extracts from the ethnographer's notes at the time:

> Coordination is clearly a very important function in controlling work- so much so that the rules laid down in the manual specify the codes for indicating that coordination has been done, and by whom. At the same time, it takes up a lot of controllers' time and generates some irritation. Controllers, however, talk about the problem of altering coordination strategies. They argue that one such strategy is to alter the dimensions of sectors (something that happens anyway on an expedient basis when sectors are "split" or "bandboxed"). Bigger sectors mean less coordination; smaller sectors,

more. At the same time, however, the bigger the sector, the greater the number of planes in it and the more work required of the controller. I also spoke to a guy at Bournemouth (the Training College) and he said that no-one had ever plausibly shown why the measured amount of coordination doesn't reduce in a linear fashion as traffic reduces. I argued to him that it was because of all the justification/ explanation work that goes on at the same time – I think this may be important. It seems to raise a wider issue that has to do with controlling culture.

Here, the ethnographer has begun to recognise that coordination is in some way both a problem and a solution to the business of keeping traffic moving. At a later stage, analysis of these issues led us to think in terms of a culture of support and the degree to which particular technologies might add to or attenuate this culture.

5.2.4 The Prolonged Nature of Ethnographic Analysis

It is not uncommon for ethnographers to spend a number of years engaged in fieldwork and subsequent analysis, although the rise of the 'quick and dirty' (Hughes et al., 1994) as we show below has rather changed the landscape. In general, software engineers require information in a much shorter length of time than is needed to perform a thorough ethnographic analysis, resulting in demands being placed on the ethnographer to provide rapid assessments of her work. Traditional approaches to system development require a thorough analysis of requirements before any preliminary design is carried out. Although a prototyping approach to system development can alleviate this problem somewhat (as described later), the use of requirements documents as the basis of client–contractor agreements means that requirements capture and formulation still needs to be carried out as a distinct initial exercise. We believe that ethnography can perform many different possible functions; key to this is the belief that it can have many different relations to design. If so, it would indicate that we need a more nuanced view of the circumstances in which the leisurely ethnography is possible and those in which it is not.

5.2.5 Problems of Working Together

In addition to the problems discussed above, practical problems result from the collaboration of different disciplines such as sociology and software engineering. In our view, the practical problems are by far the most important to resolve. One such problem is that of communication. It is often difficult for experts to articulate their expertise to someone not expert in their fields. This will be as true for ethnographers and designers as anyone else.

Both use normal English words as jargon terms. The problem is compounded when the disciplines attach different meanings to the same words or terms. Examples of terms which hold different, discipline-specific meanings for sociologists and designers are 'semantics', 'abstraction', 'model', and, latterly, 'ontology'. These linguistic difficulties are indicative of the differing sensibilities to be found in different disciplines. Indeed, Stanley Fish (1994), a literary theorist, would go further and describe them as different 'logics'. For Fish, doing interdisciplinary work is very hard indeed, precisely because the assumptions, way of talking, 'logics', and purposes were brought from our own disciplines. Nevertheless, if we are to do interdisciplinary work, these problems have to be resolved.

5.2.6 Time and Cost

The issue of time and cost relates closely to our early question about 'where to start' as against what we called the 'view from nowhere'. It is sometimes argued that ethnography is time consuming and expensive. We are not convinced by the expense argument, because in our experience ethnographers come very cheap, but the former presents a more intractable problem. Our view is that time can be an issue in certain circumstances. At one extreme, for instance, if we examine the concurrent ethnography conducted in a technical domain by an ethnographer with no previous domain knowledge, the ethnography in question will certainly take a long time.

A ready understanding of some domains, especially where they are tightly bounded, involve relatively small numbers of participants and have limited technical elements, may be possible in fairly short periods. (Our Building Society study, which focused on the work of cashiers, was completed in about four weeks and the analysis was completed in another three.) What we later call 'scoping' ethnographies, for instance in public or private domains with which we are all familiar, might take relatively little time. Time available will evidently vary with the project model being used.

5.2.7 The 'In the Head' Nature of Some Data

This very much relates to our early question about orienting to ethnographic data. Recording data in themselves, as we remark in subsequent chapters, can be done in any number of ways. However, and it is important to note it, the presentation of data and assessment of their significance relies very much on interaction between the ethnographer and designers. One of the commonplace sentiments expressed by experienced ethnographers is that they, 'always know more than we know'. In other words, ethnographers are carrying a wealth of domain knowledge, the relevance of which has yet to be identified and established. In turn, this leads to the problem of the 'ethnographer's fatal accident' in which the sudden unavailability of the individual in question could be fatal to more than that person.

The solution generally proposed for this problem involves the maintenance of the ethnographic record in some kind of structured form through technological support. Again, in academic research environments, the consequences of the loss of an ethnographer may not be that serious (others can be appointed and more often than not there will be enough time to produce results) but in commercial work, involving large teams of designers, the logistics may be complex. Much of the recent work on pattern languages is motivated by this kind of problem. Nevertheless, whether it is actually a solution remains to be seen, for it will depend on the use to which designers put the patterns. There are reasons for believing that negotiations of belief across cultural or practice communities may also be difficult to achieve without active involvement by the ethnographer, for there are various ways in which the ethnographer might be unique. He might, for instance, be the only person with an understanding of a range of organisational roles; the only person with in-depth organisational knowledge, and the only person able to bridge design views and domain views. Here, we are referring again to the nebulous concept of sensibility.

5.2.8 The Distributed Nature of Many Activities

Hitherto, ethnographic research has largely been a single-person activity, whereby the researcher spends a considerable amount of time getting to know a particular domain. In organisations where, for instance, much daily contact is by e-mail, telephone, or what have you, observation by one person becomes increasingly problematised. Or at least, so it is sometimes argued. Indeed, the obsession with the idea that something has fundamentally changed with the advent of technological affordances such as online communication, information-sharing, or community activity has led to fashionable treatments of notions such as the virtual ethnography.

The idea that some special kind of difficulty is entailed here is laughable. Ethnographers of community in the past had to struggle with issues of privacy and the invisibility of much social life because it took place behind closed doors. Ethnographers of the organisation have long recognised the problem of the telephone conversation. What is new is not the uniqueness of the technology but the unfortunate way in which sociological concepts such as community and identity have infused debate over new technology without serious attention being paid to the intellectual auspices of these terms.

This is not to say there are no practical difficulties involved in ethnography of complex distributed settings, for there are. Our point, though, is that these difficulties do not require special methodological solutions. Instead, they require the same attention to documentation and other traces as was recommended by Chicago School sociology, the employment of ethnographers at both ends of distributed communication, the reconstruction of conversations through subsequent enquiry, and so on. Perhaps the most difficult practical task is tracing sequences of activity as they are prompted by enquiries or requests on the part of outsiders from widely disparate locations. This can be difficult to say the least (especially in situations where privacy requirements mean that calls cannot be recorded). Even in this situation, we have found that the simple expedient of asking the call receiver what the conversation was all about often produces valuable information, in other words, commonsense strategies.

5.2.9 The Problem of Formalisation

Procedures for rendering data into formal notations which are complete and consistent must be developed if ethnography is to fit. This has turned out to be an intransigent problem which continues to exercise the minds of researchers. We doubt that in any case this is the primary value of ethnography. We believe that the main value remains in high-level descriptions of what it is that systems will have to do, what problems have to be dealt with, and how to make sense of the problem of reducing complexity/contingency/unpredictability. It is still very much a matter for debate exactly what it is that ethnography contributes to the design process.

Having said that, there is no in principle reason why ethnographic data should be unstructured. It can be formalised, just as any other data can be formalised. Most computer support for ethnographic work is predicated on exactly that principle. Of course, all the relevant issues have to do with the kind of formalisation required, and whether it is adequate to the designers' task. Any number of attempts have been made to deal with this issue; see, for example, Calvey et al. (1997), Hughes et al. (2000), and more recently technomethodological attempts to rethink the foundations of the problem (see Button and Dourish (1996,1998)).

In sum, then, many matters need to be resolved, at least on the practical level. We suggest below that they can be, in two different general ways. The first is to understand what is expected from the fieldwork, to answer, that is, the question, 'What are workplace studies for?' posed by Plowman et al. (1995). The second is to try to take the issue of how to use ethnographic insights and data in the design process. Of course, the results of ethnographic enquiry can be, in principle, used in any number of different ways. We now turn, therefore, to discussing the different possibilities as to purpose, or function.

5.3 The Purposes of Fieldwork

We are doubtful as to whether it is sensible to simply regard ethnography as a method that can be unproblematically incorporated into the requirements capture process. It is more a matter that is best described as a method which can inform design by identifying the problems and concerns which a system has to accommodate if it is to effectively support work activities. As Procter and Williams (1992) put it:

> Human behaviour in organisations is complex and subject to a broad range of influences, is often poorly defined, hard to predict and highly contingent. As such it is impossible to capture and represent human social behaviour formally by the kinds of quantitative methods of mainstream HCI. It arises in interaction with others – and cannot be derived simply by scaling up from individual responses.

In which case, this is the problem CSCW must face up to and, as such, is not so much a failure of its methods or its ambitions but of the conditions of their realisation. Over many years, we have argued that these purposes should not be unnecessarily limited, and especially not by the 'implications for design' clause (see also Dourish (2006)). That is, we need to identify the general purposes (and they are several in our view) that ethnography might have.

5.3.1 Establishing and Maintaining a Corpus

Ethnographic studies taken as a whole can begin to give us some purchase on similarity and difference – and thus take steps towards some kind of generalisation – in environments where similar types of system might be deployed. An example would be the way in which command and control systems are used in particular contexts. After all, in CSCW and elsewhere we now have ethnographic studies of air traffic control done in a variety of locations and by several different research groups (see for instance Hughes et al. (1992), Halverson (1995), Sanne (1999), and Berndsson and Normark, (1999)), of emergency service work (Artman and Waern, 1999; Martin et al., 1997; Bowers and Martin, 1999; Petersson et al., 2002), and of other command and control locations (see for instance, Goodwin and Goodwin, 1993; Heath and Luff, 1992; Watts, et al., 1996).

The gradual development of a corpus in theory allows for two important things to take place. The first is that we can compare insights into very similar kinds of work in different locations and thus assess, for instance, the degree to which plans and procedures underdetermine work in different locations (and thus perhaps figure out why). The second is that we can begin to compare areas of work which may have both a degree of similarity and a degree of difference.

The point here is that the fieldworker entering a 'similar' domain can be prepared for the subtle variations to be found in their domain by reference to an existing literature of a type. In many ways, however, this neat and simple idea opens up a can of worms about the question of generalisation, for no corpus has more than a very limited value unless there is some means to index it. Of course, such an index implies a commonality of concepts which in effect constitute generalisations. Several issues are raised by this and none have been successfully answered.

5.3.2 Sensitizing Design

Whether the conduct of ethnographic investigation can ultimately do much for requirements gathering, there is little doubt it has the merit of sensitizing designers. That is, we cannot know in advance whether problems of context will turn out to be important, and if so for whom, but the simple recognition that they might has to be a substantial analytic gain. This falls short of the recommendations of technomethodology, which turn on ways in which ethnomethodological thinking might be embedded in design (Button and Dourish, op. cit.), but nevertheless also appeals to the idea that alternate ways of thinking might themselves be important to design. In turn, this raises the prospect that a function for ethnography that has seldom been recognised is that of the 'scoping' function. Of this, more below.

5.3.3 Informing Requirements

The form of data which results from an ethnographic observation of a particular domain tends to be, as everyone knows, messy and unstructured. Such data, compounded by the fact that they are often anecdotal in nature, sharply contrast with the clear and concise structured information which results from a successful application of a traditional domain analysis/ requirements capture method. Although ethnographic data may contain information pertinent to many different kinds of requirements, such as ergonomic considerations, functional/nonfunctional software requirements, requirements for staff training, and so on, finding this information amongst the mass of material is not an easy task. At least, that would be a fairly conventional view of the problem. Some thought, however, suggests otherwise. To make it explicit, there is absolutely no logical reason why ethnographic data should be messy and unstructured. The 'structuring' of data is, in fact, analytic work being undertaken. Because ethnographies, too, entail analysis then their data too, in principle, can be structured.

Of course, it sometimes turns out that the data presented in the real world are messy and unstructured. The reasons for this are not what they seem, however. In our own experience, ordering or structuring data is (although difficult to do) a key part of enquiry. It is important, far too important, that is, to do casually. If we remind ourselves that the structure of data reflects the analytic work we do, then it should be apparent that it matters hugely when we do this analysis and it matters hugely who does it. Designers who have recourse to the 'what's this got to do with me?' get-out clause would be designers who refuse to engage in design. They would be limiting their remit to the building of solutions without being willing to engage in a formulation of the problem. They would be bricklayers, not architects.

5.3.4 Orienting to Purpose

Goodwill

The sensitivities or sensibilities referred to in various places in this tome gloss the simple fact that learning to work together is a matter of goodwill and mutual respect. Social scientists need to recognise how difficult a task design is, and orient to that fact. It does not help interdisciplinary collaboration when design is described as being contingent on the moral or intellectual failures of designers. (If we appear to do so in our caricature of the designer as bricklayer, we should stress that in our own collaborations we have never met anyone who fits this description.)

Our experience is that designers normally have sophisticated understandings of the moral consequences of their work, and frequently agonise over their position in the design space. Their willingness to engage with often tiresome 'sociologese' in order to come to better conceptual understandings is laudable and puts the sociologist to shame. Equally, however, designers need to recognise that social scientists, for the most part, are not being critical out of cleverness, but are trying in a principled way to provide a different purchase on problems. Talking to each other regularly is the most effective way in which mutual respect is garnered. The debriefing session, along with the other benefits it confers, is one of the most important ways in which we learn to understand each other (Hughes et al., 1993), and has become central to the task as defined by others (Beyer and Holzblatt, 1998; Crabtree, 2003).

Addressing the Problems Using an Iterative Approach

The problems outlined above have detailed the difficulties for systems developers to use ethnographic data to derive system requirements in a structured way. There does not yet exist a theoretical framework for understanding

149

the interactions among task requirements, the work organization, and the computer system which produces perfect answers.

It is now accepted that because of the problems of modelling users, and the poor understanding we have of human–computer interaction, it is impossible to get requirements correct the first time when developing interactive systems. Attempting to formulate definitive requirements for these systems a priori of any design and implementation will result in poor specifications and costly changes as errors are discovered later in the process (Boehm, 1981). This is not to say that specification is not important in interactive systems design; rather that detailed specification and design decisions should be deferred as long as possible.

The problem in specifying user interfaces for interactive systems has led to the advocation of an iterative approach to requirement capture. This approach is based around two component stages of evaluation and refinement, where the interface is successively evaluated and refinements made in the light of these evaluations. Development follows this cycle until the interface is considered acceptable, at which point the prototype system forms the basis of the interface specification. This 'HCI prototyping cycle' is presented in more detail in Figure 5.1 (Bentley and Randall, 1994).

The nature of ethnographic analysis is one of evolving understanding as the study progresses, with previously held assumptions being confirmed, clarified, or invalidated. The timescale involved in developing a good understanding of the social processes taking place is such that an approach to systems development based on rapid prototyping, informed by a progressing

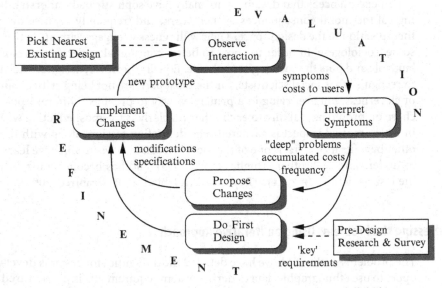

Figure 5.1 The HCI prototyping cycle. (Bentley and Randall ibid.)

ethnographic study, is suitable for the design of systems to support collaborative work. The advantages of such an approach are described by Hartson and Smith (1991, p. 54) when they say:

> Through rapid prototyping, an early opportunity is afforded the behavioural scientist to build good human factors into an interface design. By building ease of testing and modification into a prototype, the computer scientist is providing human factorability. Rapid prototyping is an important factor in harnessing the sometimes opposing forces of these roles in helping them work together.

One approach to integrating ethnographic analysis with rapid prototyping is presented in Figure 5.2, which shows the development model for the ATC project and which we (and others) have used many times since. Initially, a generic system prototype was built which reflected early understandings of the application domain. This prototype was refined and new prototypes produced in line with the results of evaluations. During the early iterations of the cycle, the ethnographer was responsible for evaluating system prototypes, allowing gross errors in the design to be revealed. As our understanding of the application domain grew, it was possible to expose the prototypes to end-users.

An important part of this development process was the regular debriefing meetings which took place between the sociologists and system developers. During these sessions, the ethnographer discussed his findings and was questioned by other team members. The system developers' questions focused on the system requirements and, whilst it was rare to identify an explicit software requirement during the debriefing meetings, the developers gained an intuitive impression of facilities required by controllers. At the same time, the developers identified particular areas of interest and problems which should be investigated in the next phase of ethnography. Thus, the ethnographer was informed of the system requirements and focused his observations to answer the questions posed by the designers.

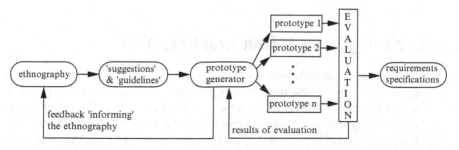

Figure 5.2 Ethnography and prototyping. (Bentley and Randall ibid.)

Our development model utilises prototyping tools to aid the rapid production and refinement of system prototypes. This model of system development, called 'cooperative prototyping' by Bødker and Grønbæk (1991), combines the use of computer-based tools for exploratory programming with user participation in the development process. It allows refinements to be made quickly and for rapid switching between alternative prototype systems.

Analytic Complementarity

It is already implied in much of what we have already stated, but the point of ethnographic fieldwork lies, whatever the analytic auspices, in what it provides that cannot be derived from conventional requirements gathering techniques. Ethnography provides no special insight into process, business process, data flow, or data structure, or indeed any other category associated with structured system design and business change methodologies. To state the obvious, therefore, it can (and perhaps should) be used in conjunction with methods for uncovering precisely those things.

Ethnography provides a picture of the social reality of work and interaction, one which may reveal a great deal not covered by more formal analytic procedures. It is worth stating here that it follows that, although ethnography has for historical reasons been associated with interactive or CSCW systems, there is no particular reason to suppose that it should be. Analysis of work, it seems to us, has a payoff for almost all computer systems. This forms part of a puzzle in respect of the sometimes narrow definition of CSCW systems insofar as we see too little of the ethnographic imagination deployed on, for instance, the use of database systems, and for no good reason that we can see.

In sum, much of what has been said in the literature about ethnographic practice tends to exaggerate or overpronounce on its character as a sociological method. After all, what we are talking about here is its character as a method for informing design problems. The character of ethnographic work will, to some extent at least, be altered according to what kind of purposes are envisaged for it. These purposes, it turns out, may be many and varied.

5.4 Developing Forms of Ethnography for CSCW

Ethnographic methods have always been utilised, deployed, and adapted in a variety of ways. These multifarious ways often depended on very practical or serendipitous aspects of the research process such as the complexities of obtaining fieldwork access, prior relationships with organisations, professionals, and other interested parties, and so on. The variety of uses to which they have been put does not constitute an obvious research typology, such as those that are frequently produced for participant observation stud-ies,[34] nor is it mutually exclusive. Instead it suggests an orientation to a range of practical factors such as available time in the field, and the availability and suitability of existing data. Nevertheless, and probably because much of early ethnographic work in CSCW concerned itself with the co-located, 'shared goal' work associated with control rooms, suggestions as to the way in which ethnographic studies might be used have, in fact, taken on the rough status of typologies. The broadly different uses of ethnography iden-tified by Hughes et al. (1994), for instance, prompted a vast number of self-identified quick and dirty studies. Hughes et al. actually include:[35]

- *Re-examination of previous studies:* Here previous studies are re-examined to inform initial thinking. So, for example, the bank studies we have reported on (Harper et al., 2000) depended initially on a general perusal of paperwork studies in order to inform the observation of the paper record-keeping in the specialised 'Mandates' section in the bank. Put simply, much as software can be reused, so can ethnographic studies. There is one caveat here, which is that the flavour of reuse may vary according to who is reusing. Different factors may matter when reusing the studies of others to those which are important when reusing one's own material. We feel one is on safer ground with the latter.

- *'Quick and dirty' or 'lightweight' ethnography:* Here brief ethnographic studies can be undertaken to provide a general but informed sense of the setting. Quick and dirty studies can be a precursor to concurrent ethno-graphies, providing early but useful information, or they might follow from concurrent ethnographies, drawing on background knowledge obtained from them.

- *Concurrent ethnography:* This is the idea of an ongoing ethnography that adapts its focus over time. Here design is influenced by an ongoing ethno-graphic study taking place at the same time as systems development. In the SYCOMT research project, for example, after a period of general observa-tion of everyday work the research focused on the Lending process and the design of systems to support lending across the organisation. As these were developed and deployed further studies informed the iteration of design.

- *Evaluative ethnography:* Here an ethnographic study is undertaken to verify, validate, or evaluate a set of already formulated design decisions. Work we have undertaken in recent years on smart homes and the use of mobile phones might both be loosely characterised this way.

---

[34]For example the common distinction between overt and covert observation or Gold's (1958) typology based on various identified relationships between 'observation' and 'participation'.

[35]These types of usage are primarily a product of and relate to the use of ethnography within 'design' projects.

Throughout this rather loose separation of types there is an emphasis on a range of design-related issues. We have a number of observations to make about a very rough, not to say crude, set of distinctions. First, these categories should not be read as if they were mutually exclusive ways of using ethnography; some of the uses could be, and were, harnessed together and the differences between them seen as differences of emphasis rather than sharp demarcations. Design, as in so much else, is a matter of responding to contingencies of various kinds. What is also important to note is that the scheme recognises that design objectives are themselves various and that this will have a bearing on the role of ethnography. In other words, although not necessarily buying into the picture of the design process as a series of discrete, clearly delineated, and phased steps, it undoubtedly has different objectives at different stages and, accordingly, implications for how design needs to be informed by relevant information about the domain. In this way we are attempting to move away from the misconception of ethnography as simply and exclusively involved in the requirements phase of systems design.

5.4.1 Re-Examination of Previous Studies

The approach to ethnography characterised as the re-examination of previous studies is intended to address one of the major problems that arises when new approaches, new methods, and new systems are proposed. That is, lack of experience can be compensated for by examining what is already known. The corpus of case studies, examples, exemplars, and so on, can be used as sensitising material. We should not forget that ethnography is a method which has been used for many decades in sociology and anthropology, producing studies related to work and occupations which can, in principle, be informative for design. For instance, many of Erving Goffman's (1968,1969) insights have proven useful in studies of CMC, and may yet turn out to be useful in studies of life in public places and the role of mobile technologies. Consequently the re-examination of previous studies takes on some of the characteristics of a preliminary, focused literature review intended to sensitise the research to a range of relevant design issues.

In the case of Hughes et al. (1994), previous ethnographic studies were used to inform the preliminary design of a Shared Object Service (SOS) platform which, among other things, was intended to handle documents in a wide variety of domains. It was felt that much could be learned by using available studies, even though they had not been carried out with system design in mind, looking for exemplars exhibiting some of the varieties of document production, management, and use as socially organised features of the work. Such an approach also offered the possibility of uncovering some properties that generally hold true and consequently this use of ethnographic materials may be especially useful where obtaining sight of general infrastructural CSCW principles is the prime goal.

In drawing on various studies of paperwork Hughes et al. identify a number of sensitivities for design, the importance of history and record of use within the information store, the prominence of nonrealtime interaction and the need for effective and dynamic management of access to shared information, the need to manage considerable heterogeneity as part of the shared object service, and to provide facilities that maintain links between electronic and paper records. Consequently reanalysing ethnographic studies could prove a useful way of sensitising designers to the socially organised character of a considerable variety of settings. Although clearly not a substitute for the more directed uses of ethnography (when there are specific design issues to address) such an approach may perform a useful role in making designers aware – sensitive – to what to avoid and what the more specific issues might be.

As already indicated, of course, this re-examination is not the same as developing a corpus, because any fully fledged corpus of case studies must ultimately come with an index of some kind if it is to prove useful. Researchers will need to know not only what previous studies they might be looking at, but also what orientations are embedded in them. Without question, this is one of the roles that theory can play: as a means to organise data under headings to aid others in knowing where to look when examining prior material. Of course, it requires a consistency that is not provided in a market with so many competing approaches. We would tentatively suggest that this kind of re-examination can be done for three broad purposes: empirical, conceptual, and comparative.

5.4.2 'Quick and Dirty' or 'Lightweight' Ethnography

The phrase 'quick and dirty' implies that many of the implications of a traditional social science approach to ethnography need no longer be a problem, for somehow it will be possible to do ethnographic work in a short space of time, and although the results will be a little rough and ready, they will satisfice for at least some purposes. That would certainly appear to be the case, inasmuch as quick and dirty ethnographies have sprung up like genetically modified Japanese knotweed. It is worth, then, laying out exactly what can be achieved with this highly limited approach to fieldwork, and what cannot. It not only seeks relevant information as quickly as possible but accepts at the outset the impossibility of gathering a complete and detailed understanding of the setting at hand. The focus, then, is on informing strategic decision making to select those aspects of the work setting of particular importance in informing design.

There are two points of comparison with what might be seen as traditional ethnographic approaches. First, quick and dirty ethnography is capable of providing much valuable knowledge of the social organisation of work of a relatively large scale and distributed work setting in a relatively short space of time. Indeed, it can be argued that the payoff of the quick and dirty ethnography is proportionately greater in that, for the time expended on fieldwork, a great deal is learned.

Second, such knowledge can be built upon for a more focused examination of the detailed aspects of the work which is more typical of what we call 'concurrent ethnography'. What the quick and dirty fieldwork provides, according to Hughes et al., is the important broad understanding which is capable of sensitising designers particularly to issues which have a bearing on the acceptability and usability of an envisaged system rather than on the specifics of design. Both aspects, of course, are important. Quick and dirty ethnography is then capable of providing an informed sense of what the work is like in a way that can be useful for designers in scoping their design and in providing designers with a better sense of the setting and its work activities.

One example of just such a quick and dirty approach, aimed at developing a sensitivity to the work context within which IT changes were to be implemented, is the ethnographic study of a small office reported in Rouncefield et al. (1994). Because the setting was so small – a single room with three workers – a week-long ethnographic study with follow up informal interviews was deemed sufficient. Despite the quick and dirty nature of the study, the process of work in a small office and its recurrent features, notably the massive volume of paperwork, the importance of local knowledge in the accomplishment of work, and the phenomenon of 'constant interruption', are depicted and despite the obvious contrasts with large-scale work settings analysed in other ethnographic studies, similar features of cooperative work can be observed.

Whilst acknowledging the limitations of this study and the obviously mundane or routine character of small office work, we should not ignore the apparent typicality of this setting for many workers and the consequent importance of any lessons learned. Without being too grandiose, although both this study, and the office concerned can be characterised as small, the problems identified may not be; rather they seem generic to the whole issue of the implementation of IT. The particular issue that this study drew attention to was that moving to greater levels of IT will also involve a reconfiguration of the local knowledge which is essential to the working of the current system. It is therefore important to recognise that embedding a system into work activities, achieving a level of routine-ness, generating relevant local knowledge, gearing the user into the work, and so on, are all likely to take time. Consequently the adoption of some element of IT is never simply a matter of switching on a PC the first thing in the morning as opposed to reaching for a pencil. It will also involve subtle changes and adjustments in the sociality of work.

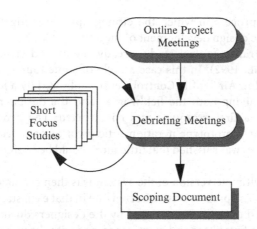

Figure 5.3 Quick and dirty ethnography. (Bentley and Randall ibid.)

The quick and dirty ethnography (Figure 5.3) has proven to be popular, if sometimes misunderstood. Perhaps here we should point to two quite different versions of quick and dirty. The first is based on the simple fact that to some degree it is possible to undertake this kind of ethnography because the ethnographer is already familiar with large parts of the domain. She is simply applying existing knowledge to some previously unexplored aspect. Evidently, when this is the case, there is no great need to relearn a range of organisational features (for instance, standard documentation or process) and thus the ethnography might be done quickly.

Quick and dirty, however, might have a quite different sense, which has to do with the state of the relevant technology or the degree of domain knowledge. Here, at least at one extreme, we might more properly speak of 'scoping' ethnography. We mean that, in some circumstances, the kind of requirement analytic work expected of concurrent ethnography would not be possible because no coherent view exists as yet of what kind of technology might be appropriate for this domain, or indeed what the characteristics of the domain might be.

Thus, so-called quick and dirty ethnography too might take various forms, depending on the purposes of its deployment. It might be scoping where existing knowledge is very sketchy; it might be additional, in that it builds on what is already known, or it might be comparative in that it extends enquiry by interrogating existing concepts in new areas. We expand on this below.

5.4.3 Concurrent Ethnography

Concurrent ethnography is perhaps the one most commonly associated with design and the one most commented on (Hughes et al., 1992). It is a sequenced process in which the ethnographic investigation of a domain precedes the design development of the system. This is the method followed in the air traffic control study already mentioned (Hughes et al., 1992; Bentley et al., 1992). In this case a cycle of some four weeks' ethnography in the London Air Traffic Control Centre, followed by a lengthy debriefing session involving both the fieldworker and the designers was the norm. Meanwhile, a first prototype was constructed. The process of fieldwork > debriefing > prototype iteration > fieldwork was repeated several times until the team was satisfied that little more could be usefully gained by more fieldwork.

The penultimate version of the system was then evaluated using working controllers. The process was a directed one in that each stage of the fieldwork was intended to target issues raised by the designers during the debriefings, although the first phase was more concerned with the very important task of the fieldworker familiarising himself with the setting and the work of the controllers.

What the ethnography especially provided was a thorough insight into the subtleties involved in controlling work and in the routine interactions among the members of the controlling team around the suite, subtleties which were rooted in the sociality of the work and its organisation. The vital moment-by-moment mutual checking of what was going on by the various members of the team had been missed by earlier cognitive and task-analytic approaches to describing controlling work. We also learned that there was a declining rate of utility for the fieldwork contribution to the design,[36] that, although there is always more to learn, the payoffs for design, at least

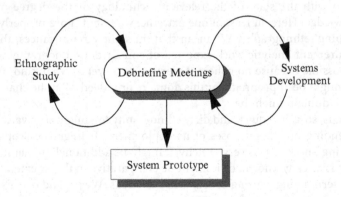

Figure 5.4   The use of concurrent ethnography. (Bentley and Randall ibid.)

---

[36]This is not to say that there was not more to learn or that we could not have learned more sociologically, only that in terms of the project the 'fine tuning' of the design needed to be informed by experts actually using it.

in this case, came relatively quickly in comparison with social research uses of ethnography.

Again, however, those who have followed have often ignored the fact that this study rehearsed (see Hughes et al. (1992) and Randall et al. (1993)) the problems involved in this kind of design relationship. The nature of these problems will also vary according to aspects of the research context. They include the difference between academic and commercial research settings, scale and distribution of research project, and type of design team.

5.4.4 Evaluative Ethnography

Although undoubtedly 'evaluation' has taken on some of the characteristics of an advertiser's weasel word, few practitioners in CSCW would wish to contest its importance, and we have used ethnographic techniques in evaluation in a number of ways. It should be acknowledged at the outset, however, that the evaluation of CSCW systems is especially difficult, not least because of uncertainties over both what exactly constitutes an evaluation, how it should be implemented and when and where it should take place.[37] In particular, in the context of CSCW, as a number of writers have suggested (Twidale et al., 1994, p. 441):

> There is a pressing need for the reappraisal of evaluation philosophies and techniques. In particular, the view that evaluation should be regarded principally as a summative process which takes place at a given stage in the software life cycle and which yields "objective" results is, we believe, deeply problematised by CSCW's interest in the "real world" context of use.

In a similar fashion Bannon argues that design, use, and evaluation should not be viewed as distinct activities, but as being necessarily interwoven and that 'evaluation' issues, informed by the context of use, should effectively saturate the design process.

Evaluative ethnography can also be considered as a more focused version of the quick and dirty approach in that although it does not necessarily involve a prolonged period of fieldwork, it can be directed/focused at a 'sanity check' of an already formulated design proposal; that is, it is used in evaluating a design.

The example we use is research that involved approximately three weeks of fieldwork in two branch offices of a building society. It was commissioned by a computer company to check out, using ethnography, some

---

[37]Grudin (1988) cites the difficulty of evaluation as just one contributory factor in why CSCW systems fail to deliver the benefits intended. Indeed, we may regard all his case studies as examples of a failure to adequately determine what is being evaluated, when it is appropriate to evaluate, and what methods are likely to prove suitable when the focus of evaluation moves from system functionality to system use.

aspects of a model the company was interested in using for IT developments in the financial sector. In particular, we were asked to investigate customer relations at the front desk and mortgage processing. In the relatively short period of fieldwork, it became clear that the model on offer had almost wholly ignored the character of front desk work in branch offices, representing it as a series of information flows and tasks which could be unproblematically instantiated in the real-world conditions of branch work.

Although only a very brief characterization of the results of the ethnography, the findings were sufficient to suggest that the model was, in significant respects, deficient. Such a conclusion was not necessarily of much comfort to designers who had, no doubt, spent many hundreds of 'person hours' developing the model. However, although in this case it reinforced the computer company's initial concerns, so much so that they withdrew from the negotiations to purchase the model, it is not difficult to see this use of ethnography in a more positive light. Independently of the commercial pressures that surrounded this project, the approach identified here could well be used to develop and improve system development.

The immediate point we want to make, which is reinforced by the findings of Twidale et al. (1994), is that 'ethnography as evaluation' could be developed as a systematic means of monitoring systems in their use. Although human beings have an extraordinary ability to make do with the technology with which they are provided, ethnographic studies could be useful in tweaking existing systems and/or to inform the design of the next generation of systems.

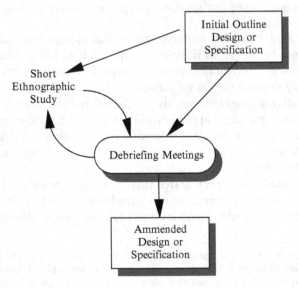

Figure 5.5 The role of evaluative ethnography. (Bentley and Randall ibid.)

This use of ethnography may be of major relevance to many of the organisational contexts of IT use, in which nothing is ever ideal. Investing considerable amounts of money in a new system is not an option for every organisation, and those who do often live to regret it. However, this proposal of continuous but modest redesign through periodic ethnographic field studies of system use may have considerable benefits if appropriately managed. And, again in support on one of the main tenets of CSCW, ethnography's focus places particular emphasis on the social context of innovation rather than simply allowing the technology to drive the innovation. It is in this context that the proposal for continuous but modest redesign, other things being equal, allows for persons using a system to make contributions to its evolution and contribute their skill and experience to the next generation of systems.[38]

5.5 Extending Ethnography's Remit

Valuable though the characterization of different kinds of ethnography undoubtably is, we have tried to show that it can be decomposed to some purpose. In addition, there are factors which do not directly relate to the purposes of enquiry that also might affect the form that the enquiry takes. These, for instance, include the following.

5.5.1 Academic Versus Commercial Arenas

Although ethnography as a method is commonplace in research arenas, and is increasingly being advocated for use in commercial work (see for instance Beyer and Holzblatt (1998)), several problems arise in this context. The kinds of question we have in mind are issues of the use of ethnographic material, and indeed of the ethnographer, in large design teams, with all of the associated problems of agenda management, cultural difference, and so on.

It remains the case that the majority of ethnographic enquiries have taken place in an academic, or at least research context rather than specifically oriented to commercial product design. This in turn implicates a whole set of deeply problematic issues around the relationship between ethnographers (or ethnographic data) and the ever more complex and large-scale business of doing design (especially when, as is now frequently the case, design is being done in a highly distributed way and where it

---

[38]There is a whole host of sensitivities in this which go beyond the confines of system design, namely, the willingness of people to participate given that one of the options of such investigations is to use systems to dispense with labour. This issue, of course, is not peculiar to ethnography.

involves an ever-increasing range of organisational interests from accountancy to aesthetics). Furthermore, the problem space has shifted, especially in the context of the design of technologies for distributed working and mobile technologies. This has led to a number of different, and highly ingenious, ways of collecting data, as we show.

5.5.2 Applying Research to Systems Design and Change Management Issues

The arguments for exploiting ethnography are also the arguments for bringing in a perspective that enables system designers to take account of the socially organised character of work. What we signal by the phrase, 'the socially organised character of work,' are those aspects of work which are features of the collaborative nature of work and its activities, aspects which include more than one might conventionally think. It is axiomatic for sociology that much of human life involves interaction with others and that our individual activities are oriented to this fact. Our actions are embedded in a network of relations with others, relations which can vary in scope, intensity, affectivity, formality, and more. Thus, in work a familiar network of relations is the formal organisation, be it a firm, a professional agency, a corporation, a political party, and so on. However, equally important are the plethora of informal relations which enable work to take place.

The importance of this for both HCI and CSCW can be illustrated by Procter and Williams' well-known (1992) remarks on the problem of defining the user:

> ... when HCI practise is placed within an organisational context. . . . Is the user the "end user", the person who directly interacts with the computer or the "client", the person who commissions the system? There is insufficient acknowledgement of the complexities of organisational life, and that the requirements of various interested parties might conflict.

'Insufficient acknowledgement of the complexities of organisational life' is as good a motto for ethnographers as any other.[39] What they are pointing to are the problems that emerge when HCI moves away from the comfortable picture of the user as the individual sitting in front of a VDU to take into account the wider context in which individuals work. In this respect, as a number of commentators have noted, we still do not have an adequate picture relating to who these users are and how they interrelate.

This very problem has plagued the requirements process from the earliest days of systems development and, as we saw in the previous section, is

---

[39]With the possible exception of, 'Ethnographers like to watch. . . .'

hardly dealt with in a nuanced way. Clients, for example, are not always users and, indeed, may not even know who their users are. Users may know who they are, individually and in small co-located groups, but have no idea what the relevance of other, more distant, patterns of use might be. Users may know what they have to do, but may not find it easy to articulate what they know. Matters are complicated by the fact that organisations often give rise to vested interests which influence not only the impetus for change but also the direction. Equally, the existence of organisational cultures, social networks, and so on, may imply a need to move ethnography on from a more or less objectivist approach to the detail of interaction. One could add more but, it is hoped, the point is clear.

It seems, and of course we would wholeheartedly agree in principle, there is a prima facie case for ethnographic investigation of the issues which bedevil the systems design process. However, recognising a need is by no means the same thing as providing a solution. If we are to address the problem of integration, then a whole gamut of related problems, some of which are examined below, need to be addressed.

5.6 Refining the Framework: Technology and Development History

Whatever the merits of the above framework, one thing is absolutely clear about it: that it distinguishes between one type of ethnography and another on the basis of purpose. The 'Moving Out of the Control Room' study has become a very popular resource for those wishing to characterise their own work, or locate it in a literature. We certainly believe that it raises a number of interesting and contentious issues. Here, however, we want to move beyond 'moving out' by detailing some of the other dimensions and features that may alter the relationship between ethnography and design. We start from the more or less uncontentious view that this relationship can never be determinate, and the rough framework we provide here is largely based on our own experience. We suggest that we might think about ethnography and design along four dimensions. These are as follows.

5.6.1 Purpose of Enquiry

The purposes of ethnographic enquiry, and again we should stress we are not trying to develop a fully fledged typology here, are many. We have suggested that each of the types of ethnography referred to above might have more than one purpose. The re-examination of existing studies, for instance, could be done for empirical (finding out what is known), conceptual (figuring out what to look for), and comparative (establishing similarities and differences between current work and previous studies) purposes. We stress again that re-examining one's own studies is very different from examining those of others, inasmuch as the former may utilise knowledge which is frequently in excess of what is published. Examining the studies of others might involve all three purposes. Re-examining one's own material, we think, is most likely to be done for conceptual and comparative purposes.

So-called quick and dirty ethnography too might take various forms, depending on the purposes of its deployment. It might be scoping where existing knowledge is very sketchy; it might be additional, in that it builds on what is already known, or it might be comparative in that it extends enquiry by interrogating existing concepts in new areas. The scoping ethnography is perhaps one that fits best with the 'innocent' to 'informed' strategy. By definition, a principled refusal to take on design issues in the first instance involves a more or less leisurely approach to ethnography. This may be possible where no immediate product is envisaged, but rather the scope of possible products is being investigated.

Concurrent ethnography is unlikely to take all these forms, and in particular is unlikely to have a scoping or comparative function. It is, however, very likely to take this additional form, building on what is already known, or a conceptual form if no previous work is available. It may also take on an extra aspect here, in that what is already known may be of the managerialist form associated with BPR or what have you, and hence it is likely to have a complementary form, characterised by the analytic alternatives we discuss later. In any event, the concurrent ethnography is also likely to be one where the 'innocent' to 'informed' strategy is possible, in limited circumstances. Here, the evolution of the necessary concepts and relevancies will be a product of the developing interaction between the ethnographer and others. Again, however, the likelihood that this will be possible in commercial arenas with serious deadline pressures is remote and, thus far, only academic environments have proven suitable for the 'innocent' to 'informed' approach.

Evaluative ethnographies by definition could not involve scoping, but do very much contribute to additional knowledge of known domains, at least where they build on ethnographic work in the same domain. They can also, however, take another more critical form. That is, their purpose might be closely tied to showing how previous assumptions turn out to be incorrect or naive.

5.6.2 Status of Technology

It seems to us that the relationship between ethnography and design rests to some degree on the status of the technology implicated in the design objectives. Closely allied to this is what we term development history.

By development history, we mean those issues that relate to how mature an application might be, or how well understood its role in the workplace is. These development stages may involve differences along more than one axis, but we can at least suggest some sources of variation. We feel there will be considerable differences involved in, for instance, the following scenarios.

1. The technology in question may not exist at all, in which case the kind of ethnography appropriate for investigation is the scoping ethnography. Thus and for instance, ethnographic work in domestic and public settings can currently be considered as being of this type, because it relates to technologies which at present are only envisaged. In many ways, this provides more flexibility and imaginative opportunity than any other kind of ethnographic work, because very often there may not even be a self-evident domain for investigation. The idea of public settings, for instance, hardly constrains enquiry in any way and thus imaginative approaches to the problem of what to study and how to study it might seem more applicable.

2. It may exist as a research technology, but never have been put to any real-world use. It is in this context that the ethnographer as bridge comes into his or her own, because it is likely that she or he will already have a familiarity with the technology in question, including all its quirks, and thus is well positioned to deal with a designers' lack of familiarity with domain problems and with users' problems with the technology. The evaluation of the MEAD system referred to above is an example of this kind of work, and the additional or comparative forms of quick and dirty or the critical evaluative ethnographies may be well suited to this kind of problem.

3. It may have existed for some time, but have well-known problems. Much of the work on computer-mediated communication, and especially work on videoconferencing (see Ruhleder and Jordan (1999)) can be considered as being of this kind. Here, and although there may be some dangers in this, it is likely that ethnographic studies will begin to concentrate on some quite specific interactional matters. It is, in our view, no accident that conversation-analytic versions of ethnography have proven most popular and useful in this context. Here, combinations of the conceptual and comparative re-examination of existing studies and the additional form of the quick and dirty might be particularly appropriate.

4. It may be considered ripe for radical redesign. This may have to do with new generations of technology with the same broad functionalities, or envisaged for use in the same domains (see Petersson et al. (2002)), or it may involve taking a well-known technology and considering whether its use can be extended into a new domain which has apparent similarities with some others. Undertaking an ethnography with a view to

165

understanding what version $N + 1$ of an existing technology might look like would be another example of this. Various studies into, for example, emergency service work would fit into this problematic (see Whalen (1995), Martin et al. (1997), Martin and Bowers (1999), Artman and Waern (1999), and Juhlin and Weilenmann (2001)). We feel that combinations of conceptual approaches to existing studies, comparative forms of quick and dirty ethnography and critical evaluative ethnographies would be useful in this context.

5.6.3 Type of Domain

A further issue relating to the form an ethnography might take is that of the domain to be studied. The domain itself might:

1. Be small and self-contained, and be defined by relatively clear coordinative tasks, as with the classic control room studies (see for instance, Heath and Luff (1991,1992) and Hughes et al. (1992,1993)). It is hardly surprising that ethnographic enquiry in the early days of CSCW focused on these domains (and on item 2 below) for they constitute manageable domains for initial research. Nevertheless, they are not necessarily ideal exemplar domains for ethnographic research. They focus on highly coordinated types of work with teams of people doing similar jobs. They tend to be small-scale, and involve observation of relatively small groups of people. Hence, many of the problems associated with more complex organisational sites are not present. Given the existence of a body of work of this kind, it would seem that the purpose of further research in this context is likely to be comparative, establishing the relative importance of various similarities and differences.

2. Be small and self-contained, but involving knowledge work where the notion of task may not adequately account for the work being done. Small office studies might be considered as being of this kind (see Suchman (1983) and Rouncefield et al. (1994)). These studies have provided the impetus, arguably, for at least one very promising strand of research. This is to do with critical reflection by CSCW practitioners on the various orthodoxies of office de-skilling/paperless office/organisational memory/knowledge management which, in their turn, have exercised management and organisational theorists. This has led to concepts of knowledge work which emphasise issues such as tacit or local knowledge, and thus they are slowly becoming more central to the CSCW research arena. Ethnographies in this context have tended to take a critical and conceptual form, above all, in that they tend to be done in response to prevailing orthodoxies concerning, for instance, office automation or knowledge management.

3. Involve a widespread and complex division of labour. Ethnographies of this kind remain rare, in our view. This probably has a great deal to do with the nature of grant funding as much as anything else, inasmuch as it is easier to get research grants for focused study than it is for long-range, general study. Nevertheless, it comes at a cost, because arguably CSCW lacks any coherent view of the organisation as a result. We are of the view that there is a pressing need for this expanded interest, not least because such studies exemplify situations where the ethnographer is in an unquestionably unique position. No one else in an organisation, after all, has the license to roam that the ethnographer has, and thus the full range of skills and knowledge deployed are unlikely to be visible to anyone else. Although we have few examples to draw on, our instinct is that organisational ethnographies of this kind are likely to emphasise conceptual matters, and in particular complementary analysis (Harper, 1998).

4. Involve distributed working, with separation of personnel or function. This might properly be considered a subset of item 3, in that for the most part it references organisational work of the most modern kind.

5. Involve work which is tightly or loosely coupled with the technology.

6. Involve undertaking an ethnography with a view to understanding the uses of technologies for mobile working.

7. May not involve any specific domain at all.

Related to this is the degree to which technologies are envisaged as having application in specific domains, or to have more generic purposes. We might think of this as having to do with the scope of the technology. It may be, for instance, appropriate for use in small, well-defined groups or be appropriate for use in large-scale, organisationally complex settings. It may be that our problem is understanding the uses and limitations of one specific iteration of a technology in one context, integrated technologies working in a complex organisational environment, or many largely unintegrated technologies (with concomitant legacy problems) being used in a complex organisational environment (see Harper et al. (2000)).

5.6.4 Type of Design Team

A final dimension across which ethnographies might vary is the nature of the design team for which the ethnography is designed: a range of experiences, including collaborations between academics for academic research purposes, between developers and social scientists in a commercial context, or on a consultancy basis whereby commercial and academic interests might be involved. Similarly, the scale of the design problem and the coordinative aspects of working on large-scale design problems will have an impact on the kind of ethnography in use. Various models for ethnographic enquiry may be implicated, depending on the arrangement in question. Thus, where academic research might facilitate the 'innocent' to 'informed' approach we have discussed, this is unlikely to be acceptable in any commercial investigation where time and money pressures, as well as problems of coordination will suggest a much more directed form of enquiry.

Even in those areas where academics and commercial interests work together a range of issues including the purpose of the enquiry, the language, the site, and so on may all be influenced by the fact of commercial involvement. Indeed, we may venture to suggest that this is the most difficult form of relationship. Rationalist organisational assumptions have it that in principle the organisation and its representatives will have a set of specific goals and envisage specific tasks for the completion of those goals. Academics, in this version, may have skills not easily obtained elsewhere and are therefore hired in order to deploy those skills.

We have reason to doubt this picture. Having severally and jointly worked on a number of different projects which include a commercial and academic relationship of a kind, our feeling is that organisations and their representatives sometimes have only fairly vague ideas about what the purpose of any given research relationship may be. More problematically, functional divisions within the organisation might mean that assumptions about purpose may vary from department to department, or role to role.

Clearly, if we need frameworks for types of ethnography at all, they will be complex. This preliminary attempt at a more nuanced view of the ethnographic range is intended only to point to some of the dimensions of this complexity. It is not intended to provide yet another spurious typology. Our point is that, buried in these different attitudes to ethnographic practice is the fact that important choices have to be made, often in circumstances where the ethnographer will have incomplete knowledge about the purposes and form of the envisaged enquiry. To make matters more difficult, our *naif* will also have to confront a range of irritatingly practical matters in order to get underway. We turn to these now.

Ethnography and How to Do It

6

*The concern to balance detailed documentation of events with insights
into the meaning of those events is the enduring hallmark of ethnography.*
(*Fielding 1994, p. 154*)

Who would you rather believe? Me, or the evidence of your own eyes?
(*Groucho Marx*)

The relevant question here concerns what is done when we do ethnography.
Nevertheless, there is more than a little irony in our chapter title, for the
character of ethnography is such that no one, no matter how practiced, can
tell anyone else, no matter how naive, how to do it. We can only characterise
the pitfalls and describe 'good practice' as we see it. This is because ethnography is only in the very weakest sense a method at all. As we have seen,
ethnography is a qualitative orientation to research that emphasises the
detailed observation of people in naturally occurring settings. We have
traced its development from the likes of Malinowski and other anthropologists, through what is usually glossed as the Chicago School and onto the
wilder shores of postmodern ethnography. In so doing we have tried to
make it clear that the significant kinds of variation we see in ethnographic
enquiry are analytic variations. Even so, all share a common conviction,
which broadly has to do with the idea that only through living with and
experiencing 'native' life in its own environment could a researcher really
understand that culture and way of life and move away from the notion of
anthropology as 'strange tales of far-away places'.

Within mainstream sociology, ethnography has often been presented as a
methodology of last resort, used primarily for obtaining information about
groups and culture – usually 'deviant cultures' – that are impossible to investigate in other ways and to some degree this has been one of its values in
CSCW. We have suggested that the main virtue of ethnography-for-design is
its ability to make visible the real-world sociality of a setting. That is, it
is capable of producing detailed descriptions of the workaday activities of

social actors within specific contexts (Hughes et al., 1992,1993). The fact that it is a naturalistic method provides the rationale behind an insistence on the development of an 'appreciative stance' through the direct involvement of the researcher in the setting under investigation. It is, as Fielding (1994, p. 156) suggests, 'a stance which emphasised seeing things from the perspective of those studied before stepping back to make a more detached assessment. ... mindful of the Native American adage that one should "never criticise a man until you have walked a mile in his moccasins."'[40]

Our 'methods', so to speak, are those of understanding, common sense, and goodwill. The primary difference between the ethnographer and the casual observer of any setting is the decision to take a long, detailed, and rigorous look at what's going on. Much of what we have to say below has to do with these simple principles.

Although ethnographic methods can take a variety of forms, all ethnographers would agree that the researcher's immersion in the setting is the chief characteristic of ethnographic research, and the detailed observation of circumstances, practices, conversations, and activity that comprise its real-world character. Over the years ethnographic researchers have gained a great deal of practical experience of the problems in using the method. Unfortunately, given the need to make academic careers from their findings, they have also tended to methodologise their procedures – turning commonsense decisions into methodological injunctions. We would like to think we are not guilty of this, although we probably are. It is, of course, important that these practical problems are considered when both planning and undertaking an ethnographic study. This section briefly reviews some of the common problems associated with doing an ethnographic study. These are not the sole problems associated with the organisation of a study but are illustrative of those that most commonly effect ethnographic studies.

6.1 The Practical Problems of Ethnographic Inquiries

6.1.1 Access

Access is one of the most puerile and written about issues in ethnographic research. Problems are all too often exaggerated. In practice, the problem of access turns out to be a cluster of, for the most part, manageable problems which include gaining entry to the work setting, gaining acceptability, being able to 'hang around', and more. They also include problems that might arise from sponsorship and association with particular vested interests. Even if entry is successful, some areas might be regarded as 'sacred' and off limits to the observer. In any organisation there are likely to be gatekeepers who can

---

[40]This has the added advantage – as the old joke goes – that when you do come to criticize him you're a mile away ... and you've got his shoes.

block off access. There is also the question of whether the ethnography needs to be open about the purposes of the study or clandestine. In the context of CSCW, even when invited into an organisation, this can present problems vis-à-vis different groups within the organisation. Oddly enough, a reverse gatekeeper function is often recognised by ethnographers, in which people being observed insist on determining your focus of interest on your behalf. It is good policy to go along with this, because failure to do so can result in a loss of goodwill, even though this sometimes means time will be wasted.

Nevertheless, mundane problems of access do occur. They include the following.

Complex Organisational Settings

Organisations are complex and this is often manifested in the sheer difficulty of finding someone who is able to take responsibility for a decision about access. Here, one often has to take on trust statements of the kind, 'It's not really me who deals with this kind of thing, but I'll pass it on to someone who might know who does.' There is absolutely no general solution to this kind of problem when it arises. Finding the right person may be a question of finding someone in authority or of finding someone who, for whatever reason, thinks that your proposal is interesting and is willing to sponsor it to others. Even so, obtaining formal permission can be a prolonged business. In the case of the air traffic control study this took many weeks talking to various groups and managers within the Civil Aviation Authority (CAA). Because the study was built on a previous investigation at least the research team had an initial contact in the organisation which was useful in directing them through the various people who needed to be informed and whose agreement would be necessary. Much of the activity involved in obtaining permission was speaking to the various interested parties to inform them of the objectives of the research, reassuring them about the low level of intrusion that the fieldwork would involve, and establishing the team's own credentials as serious academic researchers. This took various forms, sometimes one-to-one interviews with CAA representatives and sometimes presentations to groups of them.

One essential outcome of these meetings was an introduction to the line management at London Air Traffic Control Centre. Although we had the blessing of the relevant senior managers in the CAA, it was made clear that we would also need to obtain the agreement of the local line managers which necessitated a further round of presentations and interviews. Although there were clear benefits in having already obtained the support of the CAA, it could not be taken for granted that local management would simply accede to the research without further ado. The fact that we had undertaken a previous study without any undue mishaps helped, but ermission at the local level could not be taken for granted. As it turned out, once the team had talked to local management and to the local representatives of the controllers' trade unions, permission was given and arrangements made to facilitate the fieldwork. Even so, when one of the fieldworkers entered the operations room for the first time, and introduced himself to the Watch Leader, he was greeted with, 'Who did you say you were? No one's said anything to me. . . .'

Our experience is that good-natured persistence solves most of these difficulties. Specific difficulties arise, however, when a research interest is generated by some issue that is newsworthy. Just as researchers might begin to take an interest in something like ambulance work as a result of a disaster, so might organisational members show understandable reservations for the same reason. Times of organisational transformation and political unrest make access more difficult. Another problem which can arise lies in another kind of organisational complexity, which has to do with different kinds of occupational role. Medical research, for instance, demonstrates the problem in that hospital management, professionals, and workers all have different but nonetheless deeply felt interests in what is being studied. This means that medical work is in some senses unique, insofar as it is one of those domains where 'ethics' becomes an explicit issue (and even more so when these issues, as they do from time to time, become 'newsworthy'). So much so that research has to be validated through 'ethics committees' in most countries. Similar difficulties can arise, for obvious reasons, where certain kinds of client group are involved. One of us, quite recently had the experience of being told that although the observation of young children was acceptable (various bona fides having been given) in a school, the videotaping of their behaviour was not. At the time, the ethnographer (a middle-aged man) was more than a little puzzled by this absolute ban, until he remembered that paedophilia had been something of a moral panic in the British media in the preceding months.

Knowing Organisational Members

Clearly, the site of the research has everything to do with the nature of the research and the problems it intends to address. Where it involves (as most of the ethnography in the context of system design inevitably will) research into an organisation such as a hospital, a command and control centre, or a factory, then problems of access can sometimes, and for obvious reasons, be difficult. The site may be dangerous, it may be confidential, or there may be so many people in the workplace that it proves difficult to communicate why an ethnographer is there. In our own case, we have spent many weeks trying to gain access to sites even when we have been invited to come and do the research. There are two distinct aspects of access that are relevant:

- Getting permission for the research
- Getting accepted in the research site

Obtaining permission is usually a matter of going through 'official channels' and arguing one's case to the relevant authority. In our experience, this typically involves explaining the nature of the research and offering convincing assurances that the research will involve a minimum of disruption. Depending on the organisation, this process may involve meetings with a number of authorities in order to preserve departmental responsibilities and prerogatives. However, finding who the relevant authorities are is often not straightforward. In this respect, 'sponsors' can be invaluable inasmuch as they are likely to know not only whom to see but how to go about presenting the case. In a research project involving gaining access to the police at Lancaster, the researchers were fortunate in having the support of a Chief Superintendent (a senior police officer) who smoothed the way with the Chief Constable (chief of police) of the area and, once permission had been obtained, enabled contacts with relevant divisional and departmental heads.

Such a sponsor can be invaluable not least because within most organisations access can be frustrated or facilitated by gatekeepers, that is, persons, and they need not be formally powerful, but who can make life very difficult for any researcher. Often this is a matter of acknowledging the prerogatives of, for example, departmental heads and representatives of staff. It is important to remember that even top managers have to work day to day with the people under them and they are unlikely to jeopardise effective working relationships for the sake of an academic research project and can create difficulties even where there is a commercial imperative.

The general point is that relations between the hierarchies within an organisation are as much infused with proprieties, reciprocities, and the need to maintain good working relationships as they are with power and authority. One consequence of this obvious fact is that the experienced ethnographer quickly recognises the importance of good relations with routine administrative and clerical staff, especially in 'front desk' roles for those people can both make life extremely easy and extremely difficult. In any event, managing relations with such organisational members is for the most part very straightforward and easily subsumed into the general principle of politeness.

Even when the research is invited, it is recommended that permission be sought from all the likely parties to be affected. Gatekeepers, after all, can be found at all levels. In the ATC research satisfying the trade unions' representatives of the objectives of the research was vital, not least because, at that time, LATCC had been the subject of a management consultant study which had concluded that ATC was overstaffed. And, equally to the point, a fieldworker will be spending some time studying the activities of various groups of people and will depend upon their goodwill for the effective performance of the study, so time spent informing them and reassuring them is not only a matter of courtesy but also likely to result in more effective relationships with them. It is important to remember that the process of gaining access is not simply 'something that has to be done' and 'something that is a bloody nuisance'. It can also be highly informative about the nature of the organisation and tell one a great deal about the setting and its character.

The Sacred and the Profane

The French sociologist Durkheim's sharp distinction between those matters that are 'religious' and thus generating powerful emotional and moral commitments and those matters that are just 'ordinary' features of working life has a certain relationship to organisational ethnography. Some things appear to be 'off-limits' at the outset and fieldworkers must accept this. Just as important, the sacred quality of some aspects of work has some practical consequences in terms of the kinds of respect that are due. Practiced ethnographers are used to their informants making judgements about what will be interesting to the ethnographer. It frequently happens, for instance, on hearing that the ethnographer is interested in 'technology' that the invitation will be proffered to 'Have a look at ours' on the grounds that 'You'll find it really interesting.' This raises the spectre of what we call the 'reverse gatekeeper' and which has little practical importance other than it calls for some forbearance on the part of the ethnographer. Put simply, and despite the above, ethnographers for the most part experience their subjects as being only too willing to participate in their research. Rather than creating difficulties through suspicion and distrust, people for the most part are pleased that someone is taking an interest in what is, for them, a quite ordinary and mundane business. As a result, they want to help. Of course, this is a consummation devoutly to be wished, but it does mean that once in a while the ethnographer has to practice the art of maintaining the fixed smile and avoiding glassy eyes while someone explains to them in enormous detail the workings of some technology, or their relations with other individuals. That is, ethnographers sometimes have to put up with what may well turn out to be irrelevant material with good grace.

Ongoing Gatekeeping

In an organisational context these can include different managerial sections, secretarial staff, 'shop floor' workers, and more. In other words, gatekeepers are not always the high-status members of an organization, quite the contrary. One consequence of this, especially in large organisations, is that dealing with gatekeepers is an ongoing business. In the ATC study, the patterns of shiftwork were such that on any given day the ethnographer could meet a controller who was not a member of the 'watch' with which he was familiar (so-called 'spinning'). This meant that, even six months into the ethnography, the ethnographer would occasionally be met with the question,

'Who are you and what are you doing here?' and a well-rehearsed, 'Oh, my name's . . . I work at . . . We're just interested in . . . X knows about us/has given us permission . . . We won't get in your way . . . ,' was the regular response. The ethnographer in this case reports that he felt that he was finally a 'member' of the organisation when another controller responded to such a question with, 'Oh, that's just Dave . . . He's part of the furniture . . . Don't worry about him . . . ,' before he could provide his rehearsed answer.

This pattern of questioning is even more likely in large organisations where the ethnography is going to range over a wide area, for instance in several different departments. Any ethnographer of organisations quickly recognises an almost universal fact of organisational life, which is that members of any particular unit or department will have little or no idea what goes on in adjacent units or departments. (One of the major values of ethnography is precisely that a view of the whole organisation can be obtained, one which is not available to other organisational members.) Of course, this means that moving from one part of the organisation to another means beginning the whole business of explanation and pre-emptive excuse again.

This is not to say that gatekeepers do not sometimes put up insurmountable problems. From time to time, suspicion and hostility are ingrained in an organisational culture. This can happen, for instance, in cultures which are competitive, or involve difficult relations with outside agencies or with the public. One of us, for example, has the experience of only being allowed to investigate on condition that no recording of any kind, including note-taking, was to take place during the actual observations of work. On other occasions we have encountered individual paranoia, in one instance taking the form of an objection to the presence of the ethnographer because of the shoes he was wearing. These problems, when they arise, do not arise in a predictable way. Many ethnographers, for instance, have experienced difficulty in observing classroom or staffroom behaviour amongst teachers because they have failed to establish the necessary trust. Others, however, have not and report that access was straightforward. Luck may be a relevant matter here.

Insiders and Outsiders

This raises a gamut of issues around insider/outsider accounts and overt/covert research which again has been endlessly discussed and with which we have relatively little patience. Ethnographers have normally been 'strangers' to the domain in question but in CSCW and HCI research it has become more common to see insiders (current or past) do ethnographic research. Indeed, Garfinkel (1967) (see also Shapiro (1994)) has argued for a kind of hybrid ethnography which might marry reflection and experience with observation. Insiders, of course, can lay claim to much of the expertise associated with the domain and already know about important features

175

of the job in hand. As a result, the learning curve is less steep. In contrast, some have argued that there is an advantage to outsider accounts, notably that a more dispassionate account will be provided and there is less risk of 'going native'. The difference may seem trivial, and the risk of going native is nigh on nonexistent if one takes ethnomethodological injunctions seriously, but when time and cost considerations prevail, the issue of existing expertise against naivete starts to become important. One important feature to be stated is that even the insider will know only a limited amount about the organisation under investigation. Indeed, it is a great merit of ethnography, as we have already pointed out, that few organisational members acquire an overall picture of the kinds of coordination and cooperation necessary to get tasks fulfilled for the simple reason that they are too busy attending to their own work. The ethnographer is in the remarkably privileged position of being able to range across the whole organisation, investigating matters that are opaque from any single perspective.

Acceptance

Closely connected with the business of gaining access is that of gaining acceptance. This is sometimes called the problem of 'rapport'. Unfortunately the problems involved are all too frequently exaggerated and claims that the ethnographer has to adopt a studied and neutral stance, much like Rodin's 'The Thinker' personified or risk going native are best taken with a pinch of salt. This is not to deny the fact that there are decisions to be made about involvement. From the design point of view, we feel, the concern is not so much to ensure that the ethnographer is 'one of them' as it is to ensure that his or her views are treated with respect by those observed. By respect is meant that the ethnographic analysis is treated as cogent, accurate, worth taking heed of, and is, in short, sufficient on which to base work process of systems design decisions.[41]

Here the issue is whether the ethnographer is entitled to have a view, whether that view looks cogent to the subjects of the enquiry, or whether it will be rejected out of hand. The question is not just to do with how thorough an ethnographer has been in her program of work (how many individuals she has interviewed and the extent of the observation of the information life-cycle, and so on). The issue is what activities an ethnographer will need to undertake for her views to be treated as from the inside rather than as from the outside of work. This is not an empirical question. It is a moral one. For example, Harper's (1998) study of the International Monetary Fund reveals how many members of the organisation were insistent on the impor-

---

[41]Gaining the respect of those studied can be very difficult when an ethnographer has been 'tainted by technology'. See Harper (1996).

tance of missions to the work of the IMF. His point is that, regardless of the value of participating in a mission for research purposes, his own status in the organisation was transformed once he 'went on one'. He refers to the way in which interviewees were more forthcoming and materials became more accessible as what he was doing came to be regarded as 'serious business'.

Air Traffic Control affords another example of this kind of acceptance. Here, the simple fact of persistence, spending months observing highly technical and tedious work (from an outsider's point of view), was probably key to the success of the ATC study in respect of the fact that the ethnographers' willingness to participate in unsocial hours, such as the night shift on Saturday, (and stay the full length of the shift) was critical in getting a certain level of respect. In this domain, which had something of an 'us and them' culture, it turned out to be important that the ethnographers could demonstrate that they 'really wanted to know' and they did so by their faithfulness to shift patterns.[42]

In contrast, other domains do not seem to require the same faithfulness. Office life, for instance, is broadly uneventful and mundane. Office workers sometimes find it hard to believe anyone could possibly be interested in what they do, and, 'You don't really want to know,' is a common response early on. Arguably, this is a domain which is best come to as a stranger, for the very fact that it is, for members, boring and unremarkable means that 'taken for granted' or 'seen but unnoticed' has to be taken literally here. Office workers find it more difficult to talk in detail about the work they are doing than Air Traffic Controllers do. Again, though, there are simple remedies. Offering to do some of the work is one. Expressing surprise at the complexity and difficulty of the work is another. Trading on the role of the 'naive observer' whereby one's inability to understand anything that goes on is made manifest, is a third.

Sometimes the ethnographer simply has to wait. In police work (Harper, 1991), for example, the induction does not occur when the ethnographer turns up for night duty, nor when he or she helps break up a pub brawl. The transformation comes about when the ethnographer is taken to a domestic dispute. Such a dispute gets its name because it involves people co-habiting in some form or another (either as married couples or otherwise). The ethnographer will only be taken to such events once the police officers trust in the ethnographer's ability not to make premature judgements about who is or is not at fault. These matters are nearly always very difficult to determine in 'a domestic', and it is often very divisive to try. What the police officers need to do, and require the ethnographer to do, is to grieve with the victims over the damage they have had done to their bodies and the mess they have made of their lives.

---

[42]ATC is one of those domains where organisational members show a surprising knowledge of academic research. Many controllers could rehearse research 'insights' into stress, motivation, '3-D abilities' and so on. They were universally scathing about the nature of this research because, 'It usually means someone dishes out a questionnaire. You never even meet the person who wants to know. It goes straight in the bin.'

The point of these inductions, the ritual transformations of identity that they involve, is not that they are interesting unto themselves (though they often are), it is to ensure that what the ethnography delivers in terms of findings gets taken seriously. It is only once these inductions have been gone through that the ethnographic materials come to take a place at the table alongside the more traditional views of authority on system and work process design. This is not to say anything about whether these findings will be properly understood or that they will jostle other views (say produced by BPR consultants) off the table. Getting the implications of the ethnographic research to have an effect requires further skills of exposition, persuasion, and discussion that we discuss later.

6.2 Some Lessons

Ethnographic research involves making an incursion into other people's lives, into their organisational lives. Although those involved in the research may well have spent a great deal of time setting up the ideas, applying for funding, appointing staff, and so on (so much so that it can easily become a major focal point of life), these are not likely to be considerations of much relevance or concern for people in the organisation in question who will have their own preoccupations, troubles, and interests. This does not necessarily mean that senior managers of organisations are always going to be unsympathetic, or even antagonistic, but it does mean that researchers need to be mindful of the fact that they are in a dependent and subordinate position and to recognise that it is up to them to persuade and not to demand. This may seem an obvious point but it does have some very practical implications which we sum up as follows.

6.2.1 Gear Fieldwork Requirements to What the Organisation Can Reasonably Provide

What this means is that permission is more likely to be forthcoming if there is a strong reassurance that the research will not involve too much disruption to organisational routines and responsibilities. This is an issue which needs to be considered early in the planning of the research.

6.2.2 Do Not Dissemble About Requirements

Despite the natural inclination to understate fieldwork requirements in order to facilitate permission being granted, it is wise to be as clear as possible about what is needed even though this might occasion some reluctance on the part of the organisation. Although some negotiation is normally possible and, indeed, if the fieldwork is going well the possibility of extending it is often not much of a problem, it is important to be clear at the beginning to avoid possible repercussions later. Also, although in some cases there may be only one possible place to do the research (air traffic control, for example), it is important that the design team evaluates the consequences for the study of what the organisation can provide. If access to any particular site is less than is required for the research, then it may be worth thinking about another research site or, if this is not an option, reconsidering the research objectives.

6.2.3 What Is in It for the Organisation?

Although it is not the case that organisations always demand a strict quid pro quo for granting permission, it is helpful to think about how the organisation (and/or the managers), could benefit from the research. In the case of air traffic control, there was, to a large degree, a strong commonality of interest in controlling even though the research was not practically addressing the controller's problems. Nevertheless, the willingness to share information and results was an advantage. Not all research, of course, is so closely tied to organisational interests as it was in this case. Nor is it always a matter of an instrumental exchange. Very often a willingness to give a presentation on the research, or to cite the organisation in any published papers, and the like, can be sufficient.

6.2.4 Be Clear About Arrangements

Once permission has been granted it is important to establish clear contact points, dates, and other arrangements that will be necessary. Sometimes organisations may nominate a person who will take responsibility for making such arrangements, but in other cases it is important to obtain names and means of contact for relevant people and to follow these up as quickly as possible.

6.2.5 Organisations Have Their Politics

An inescapable fact of organisational life is the politics that surround much decision making and negotiation. There is little that the research team can do about this except as far as possible to resist being drawn into it. It is particularly important to fully appreciate the nature of the relationship between the separate units of the wider organisation.

6.2.6 Try to Get Direct Access to the Research Site

As far as possible, researchers should endeavour to get direct access to relevant personnel in the research site rather than through intermediaries. This minimises the risk of misrepresentation and any potential overselling of the benefits of the research to the organisation. However, such arrangements are not always possible.

6.3 The Role of the Fieldworker

> *When you marry, marry a lady anthropologist. She will have been trained for years never to interrupt you and to say only just enough to keep you talking.*
>
> (Quoted in Barley (1987))

> *The purpose of ethnographic analysis is to produce sensitising concepts and models that allow people to see events in new ways. The value of these models is to be judged by others in terms of how useful they find them.*
>
> (Hammersley 1992, p. 15)

In a sense, the ethnographer has no fixed role to play in the ethnography, because whatever role is worked out it will be through interaction with subjects. The fieldworker becomes involved in the setting and the activities being studied in order to gain the same perspective, as far as this is possible, of the actors concerned. This counteracts the temptation when studying others' lives to read things into them. This is the reason why ethnomethodologically informed ethnography insists on approaching the investigation of a setting without theoretical preconceptions as to what will be found, because the social world is not organised in ways that analysts and researchers want to find it. However, things that are familiar are extremely difficult to see clearly because of their very familiarity. The apothegm, 'It is not the fish that discovers the water,' aptly captures this feature of ethnographic enquiry; drawing attention to the difficulty of seeing things which are right in front of one's eyes.

In terms of the practicalities of ethnographic work, Evans-Pritchard, the famous anthropologist, wrote of how he sought some insight on how to do fieldwork from other noted anthropologists and received advice that amounted to little more than 'Don't drink the water and leave the women alone.' Although this remains very good advice it should also be understood that ethnography is neither an esoteric procedure requiring immense amounts of training, nor is it searching for things that are hard to find. Nor, however, is it simply 'hanging around', or as Button and King (1992) put it, '*Hanging around is not the point.*' Hanging around is a means to an end, uncovering the sociality of work.

Much of ethnographic practice is simply about presenting oneself as a reasonable, courteous, and unthreatening human being who is interested in what people do and then shutting up, watching, and listening. Ethnography requires simple abilities, including an ability to listen, show an interest in what people do and what they have to say, and tolerate long periods of boredom. Ethnography is an immensely ordinary activity requiring ordinary mundane skills.

> *The important thing about the ethnographer is not that he or she brings particularly arcane skills to the collection of data [many of those are the skills of office administration, cataloguing and classifying documents and records], but that they bring the willingness to pay attention to people's activities, to attend in detail to how people actually go about their affairs, however ordinary and otherwise unremarkable these affairs might be.*
> (*Hughes and Sharrock, 2002*)

What an ethnographer does is what any other person in the organisation being studied is likely to do: watching, talking, sitting in meetings, and learning his way around the organisation. And it is not difficult. The data are not hard to find; the fieldworker does not need to *look* for them, for the data are right there in front of him. As Sacks (1984a) puts it 'there is order at all points.' Consequently there is no need to suffer the fieldwork agonies so well described by Agar (1980):

> You arrive, tape recorder in hand, with a grin rigidly planted on your face. You probably realise that you have no idea how your grin is being interpreted, so you stop and nervously attempt a relaxed pose. Then you realise you have no idea how that is being interpreted. Soon you work yourself into the paralysis of the psychiatrist in the strip joint – she knows she can't react, but she knows she can't not react. It is little wonder that sometimes people hide in a hotel room and read mysteries.

In terms of how to behave, although a researcher cannot cope with every personal idiosyncrasy there are some commonsense principles of conduct for the ethnographer. These primarily involve recognising that for those in the setting, their commitment to what goes on there is their job, and the fieldworker, no matter what her personal inclinations are, must respect this. The point of fieldwork is to understand the social organisation of activities within the setting. This requires stringent attentiveness to what persons have to say and do, for the ethnographer is generally reliant on what Tennessee Williams originally termed the 'kindness of strangers.' Although this does not require an exaggerated show of interest in the (often) boring details of what people do – and organisational life is frequently boring – it does require avoiding prejudgements about what is of interest and what is not.

On top of this, however, there are choices. Discussion about the role of the fieldworker, unsurprisingly, predates ethnography-in-design. Any qualitative methods textbook will include brief sections on 'covert' versus 'overt' study; on 'participant' versus 'neutral' stances, and so on. Again, and for the most part, these matters turn out to be less than crucial in the majority of contexts, especially as design-related work is less likely to be taking place in some of the 'sensitive' arenas that sociology and anthropology love so much. They do, however, occasionally turn out to be relevant. Entry into a natural setting will inevitably mean that the fieldworker acquires a role which will be interpreted and understood by organisational members in particular ways, a role which may have effects on how forthcoming they may be, acceptability, and access.

In addition to that of researcher, one valuable role is that of the 'novice', the 'incompetent', who is licensed to ask naive, even stupid, questions and, thus, explore much of what is tacit to the experienced member. One of us, and the guilty party was Dave Randall in the ATC study, had to be told that the reason that the clock in the Operations Room was 'wrong' was that ATC works to Greenwich Mean Time, and this several months into the study. Arguably, this requires a particular kind of fieldworker: one who is comfortable with his own lack of understanding (or stupidity, depending on how you view it).

At the same time, the learning curve for the licensed incompetent is necessarily slower than it is for someone who already knows the domain, and one choice is to have as ethnographer someone who is already familiar with it. Having said that, and to make a point that is sometimes ignored, no one can be said to be wholly familiar with a domain, rather, they may be familiar with a particular job of work in that domain. This, again, has certain ramifications. The issue of articulating what is taken for granted has already been noted, for instance. In addition, however, there is a politics to all organisational life and expertise may carry with it assumptions concerning 'who knows best' especially when there are potential conflicts between one source of expertise and another. Expertise, as we have noted elsewhere (Harper et al., 2000) is 'socially distributed'. It is without question important that such assumptions be put to one side. As we have argued, one merit of the ethnomethodologically informed is that it enforces that neutrality concerning the location of relevant expertise.

A second dimension of the fieldworker's role is temporal, for a fieldworker embarking on a particular study is not the same animal as one who has become familiar with the domain. Most ethnographers would agree that there are distinct psychological phases in the conduct of a study, ranging through:

- 'Everything's really interesting.'
- 'I don't think I'll ever understand this.'
- 'Ah . . . right . . . .'
- 'This is really boring.'
- 'I've not seen that before.'

It is as well to recognise that one will go through these stages, more often than not, in that it pre-empts a loss of confidence on the part of the field-worker. An additional benefit of this stance is that subjects become aware of the fieldworker's developing expertise over a period of time and gear their responses to what the fieldworker 'knows'. One danger associated with this developing expertise is, of course, that the fieldworker may become so enculturated in the setting that she 'goes native'. Once again, our position is that adherence to ethnomethodological precepts is such that this should not happen. If our ambition is to develop as best we can the 'vulgar compe-tences' that are constitutive of the work, and to render it as best we can as uniquely adequate, then many of these problems simply disappear. The analytic rigours preclude the kinds of sympathetic/empathetic problems that bedevil standpointist ethnographies.

These issues apart, one important (although in a sense utterly trivial) aspect is that the fieldworker must gain credibility which may include, depending on the type of organisation, working the shifts, putting up with the conditions in which members have to work, and so on. In addition, a nonintrusive demeanour is important without being too self-effacing. It is also important to pay attention to dress codes and generally observe the proprieties of the setting. The vast majority of human beings are intuitively capable of working this out for themselves, but we should not forget that there may be a small number of people for whom the conviction that they know best, regardless of what their informants tell them, makes them dangerous. All this is part and parcel of what we mean when we talk about 'respecting the setting,' and there is perhaps one other feature we should mention here. The vast majority of academics have liberal and tolerant con-victions and may make the mistake of believing that their subjects will share them. We should never forget that members in the setting can often behave in ways of which we might disapprove. All three of the authors have studied settings where racist and sexist jokes, for instance, have been common-place. Our strategy, for good or ill, has been to ignore such things. Others, for good and principled reasons, may find this more difficult.

6.3.1 Focus of the Study

Ethnographic study involves choices about focus. In principle one can choose to look at an almost infinite number of things. We believe that initial ethnographic enquiry, where circumstances permit, should be done in an 'innocent' way. In other words, first time around, initial design concerns, although they might be borne in mind, should neither restrict nor prescribe too tightly. The same applies to preordained theoretical interests. Logically, if study of the domain has something to tell us, then we should let it do so. To some degree, however, as we have pointed out, this will be decided by the agenda that leads the research in question and its structure. Where research is led by a concern for the affordances of a specific new technology, as has been the case with some varieties of computer-mediated communication, it is possible that the research interest in a given domain may be narrow. Thus and for instance, it may be decided that specific problems to do with time delays, gazing and glancing, and so on constitute the analytic problem when videoconferencing is the technology in question.

For the most part, and ideally, we consider such a precipitate concern to be a mistake. Organisations are complex. One does not know, in advance of inquiry, which aspects of organisational life will turn out to be of interest and importance for the work in hand. Thus, where it may indeed be the case that visual cues of one kind or another turn out to be problematic when video-conferencing is used, this does not preclude the possibility that there are a number of other relevant matters to be investigated. These may include, in brief, matters such as the degree to which participants are familiar with each other, the kinds of knowledge they wish to share or impart, the difficulty of communicating know-how at a distance, the importance of organisational caucuses, the structure of meetings themselves (including for instance the role of the 'chair'), and the statuses of participants.

In other words, the priority is to gain a good sense of organisational life before trying to address issues of design. The latter is not irrelevant, rather the matter is one of scheduling. That is, to adequately inform design and its possibilities the ethnographer, in our view, needs to construct a portrayal of the real-world character of the work concerned in order to properly address questions about what can be supported and what cannot. In this respect it is important to effect a dialogue between the ethnographer and the designer so that, over time, the design can be gradually and informatively developed in light of a description of the complexities we have uncovered.

6.4 What to Record: Technological Support for Ethnography

These days taping interviews is almost a way of life. One of the strongest evidentiary invasions into grounded theory is the taping of interviews. The confusion is between the traditional use of the interview as complete evidence for substantiating or verifying a finding compared to grounded theory's use of interviews for conceptualization or for generation of concepts and hypotheses. When doing grounded theory there is no need for complete recording of the interview as one would want in descriptive completeness. What is not noted will, if relevant, be remembered later through associations occurring during constant comparisons. The researcher can trust this approach. Thus in frontline research by a solo researcher doing grounded theory my advice is: DO NOT TAPE INTERVIEWS. This cardinal rule is less strong for research teams.

(Glaser, 1998, p. 107)

For instance, as we played and replayed our tapes, we began to note that our analysis would follow a regular sequence. Initially, we would be able to make very little sense of a tape, especially if neither of us had been present when it was recorded. On the second or third playings, we would begin to "see" a large number of interesting features and make extensive notes. By the fourth and fifth plays, an "insight decline" seemed to arise – we found all we had heard very obvious and had little further to add. Now this obviousness was precisely what had to be broken in the second stage of the research. . . . Let us only say here that it was an obviousness that difficult to spell out in so many words. That is to say, while we knew that what was going on was obvious and felt that any other person who heard the tapes several times would come to recognise that obvious character too, we searched in vain for a way of speaking which could account for this sense of familiarity.
(Silverman and Jones, 1976)

In this section, we briefly discuss the usefulness of various technologies to support data collection. The above two quotes give some flavour of the kinds of thing that can be said both in favour of, and against, the use of various kinds of technology to support ethnographic enquiry. The value of these different technologies has at different times been both asserted and disputed and will no doubt continue to be so. Here, we assert only our neutrality in broad principle. That is, we do not believe as a matter of principle either that technology should be left at home nor do we believe (with a few exceptions) that good work cannot be done without it. We are sometimes puzzled by the assemblage of complex video equipment for the purposes of doing what seems to be straightforward analytic work and at the same time have been party to the joy of 'seeing' something through video data that one knows would otherwise have remained unseen.

We take the opportunity here to do a number of things. Firstly, to reiterate the value of some basic technologies, notably pen and paper, as data-collection tools because in the age of video it is sometimes forgotten. This is not trivial, because to assume that video does the same work as pencil and paper is to buy the same specious argument from office automation that new computer systems will see the end of paper. As has been pointed out many times, most recently by Sellen and Harper (2002), the paperless office remains a myth. So, we hope, does the paperless ethnographer.

We begin, therefore, with a few reflections on note-taking. Below is a brief extract from fieldnotes from observation at the London Air Traffic Control Centre (LATCC), taken many years ago but still useful for pedagogic purposes.

6.4.1 Routine 'Troubles'

9.16 Controller IS: 'Oh shit . . .'
Controller IS to wing: 'You got anything on a Jetset coming out of Manchester?'

185

Wing: 'Uh . . . yeah.'
[The plane has appeared on the radar but no strips have.]

9.17 ASC to Controller IS: 'Can I leave you with that [the plane referred to above] . . . the printer's just . . . disappeared up its own backside.' The controller begins to write in the flight information on a strip with only the callsign written on it, prepared by the ASC.

9.19 Printer problems continue. Wing to PH controller: 'No, it's not printed it out yet . . . just a pender is all I can offer you . . .' A pending strip is used in lieu of a live strip.

9.20 Wing to chief: 'Right . . . Shamrock strips are on their way.'

I asked what kinds of technological innovation might make the situation better. Among a series of familiar suggestions was the observation that there is no direct link between the flight information displayed on the radar and the computer database. The computer produced height, speed, and ETA from filed flight plans, not from realtime events. The consequence of this is that much of the strip information is unreliable. Wingmen tend to assume accuracy, and allocate heights without checking the info. from radar. This causes potential conflictions which in a more accurate system would be unnecessary.

Wing: 'Checking your knowledge on foreign routes here . . . where's UA 24?' skill;

Controller: 'Somewhere in France . . . no, it can't be, can it? . . . must be Belgium . . . doesn't look right, does it?'

Wing: 'Well, he seems to be going the long way round. I'll check it.' Puts strip in rack.

Wing: 'We're just checking this one . . .'

Chief: 'Looks wrong does it? Oh . . . ummmm . . . it does.'

We can make a number of observations about these notes and the analytic work being done with them for, as we persist in arguing, it is the analytic work that is important.

1. These notes are not in fact the notes that were taken at the moment that the events represented took place. They have been 'smartened up' and organised. The ethnographer has clearly left out whole passages and begun to organise the notes as 'showing something'. Nevertheless, they are more or less incomprehensible to the inexperienced reader. The importance of this cannot be overstressed, and our own experience tells us that the same problem exists in almost all domains. There is almost always a technical level of knowledge. Thus and for instance, those of us familiar with bank work can point to the seamless way in which bank employees can use a terminology relating to documentation which will be opaque to anyone who does not know the domain. Thus, ethnographic notes will contain a number of technical terms and rely on the reader having some prior knowledge of what is going on and in all

probability only the ethnographer has that knowledge, at least at the beginning. Certain basic lessons can be inferred from this immediately, including the fact that raw notes are of no value to anyone at all except the ethnographer. Their value lies in the way they are progressively organised.

2. The 'smartened-up' nature of these extracts shows that the ethnographer is making some attempt to characterise each vignette as being an 'example' of something, albeit at a preliminary level. We have here, if you like, some early indications of what he feels might be significant issues, in keeping with Glaser and Strauss' (1967) recommendations.

3. Notes can consist of many types of observation, including descriptions of, for instance, behaviour, or self-reflections, or opinion. Here, most of this is in the form of descriptions of conversation and movement. Note, however, that this extract shows none of the precision that one associates, for instance, with conversation-analytic work. Decisions have been made about the appropriate level of granularity. Observations here are not 'fine-grained' in comparison to, for instance, Heath and Luff (1992) in their video-based analysis of a London Underground control centre. No attempt has been made on our part here to do close analysis of gesture, eye movement, and aspects of turn-taking. We make this observation, not to critique what in our view is a very fine piece of ethnographic observation on Heath and Luff's part, but to point out to the inexperienced practitioner that there is no reason to presume that such fine-grain analysis is the appropriate method in all domains, or for all purposes, and also to remember that the 'stuff' captured in the field, the fieldnotes such as these, even when tidied up, are not always so fine-grained.

This is not to argue that assorted technologies have no place, for they do. Each of us, at various times has used tape recorders, videotape recorders, digital video, and a whole range of computer aids to analysis, some of which are mentioned below. Our point is not that such technologies are irrelevant and useless, but that their relevance and use will depend utterly on what purposes are required of them. Much of the time this relationship will be an analytic one. That is, it is hard to conceive of a value for video data if the analytic purpose is the kind of 'scenic' ethnography that ethnomethodologists are wont to berate. If, however, the purpose is the close analysis of coordination work, and in particular the role of glance, gesture, gaze, overhearing, and any other variety of 'economic' solutions to coordination, then the value of video is immeasurable. Similarly, of course, if the purpose is seen as conversation analytic it is more or less impossible to conceive of the analysis being done at all without the use of a tape or videotape recorder. Technology, then, is not irrelevant nor is it a solution to analytic problems. On top of this, there will be a number of quite practical issues associated with its use. These are rehearsed at length and in exemplary fashion by Jordan and Henderson (1995) and we acknowledge a debt to their work in what we have to say below, for we have borrowed extensively from their insights. At the same time, it is our own experience that has led us to confirm many of their observations.

6.5 Video

Silverman and Jones (quoted above) were using audiotape, but the point remains the same. The kind of analysis one does with audio or videotape does not spring from the material, but from the interests and 'noticings' of those who use it. Video analysis has become extremely popular for those conducting ethnographic fieldwork, and there are sound reasons for this. They include the fact that it provides a set of data which can be analysed by anyone. This means that it is both replicable and permanent. There are some very significant advantages to this:

1. It is particularly valuable when trying to get a sense of often-repeated activities, and provides for attention to detail. Such matters as eye movement, gesture, and the like are all difficult to notice and record without it.
2. It is particularly valuable in fixed or bounded locations such that a large part of what is going on can be captured in its entirety.
3. It is useful when, for one reason or another, it is difficult to get information directly from respondents. This might include where children are involved or where no one has time to stop and explain (for instance in public domains).
4. Where you do not know all the people involved in the interaction, and the presence of some of them may be transitory.
5. Where one might want to play back data to participants to the interaction to test one's worldviews against theirs.
6. Where, for whatever reason, one might want to measure events against some kind of chronology.

In sum, in some situations it is difficult to 'check' data for all the above reasons and video records provide a more or less adequate form of checking.

Nevertheless, problems can arise. Like all technologies, video can be made unreliable by the people who use it. Using video requires a familiarity with its functionalities, a familiarity which cannot be presumed. Experienced fieldworkers will, if pressed, admit to having not taken enough tapes or messing up the sound quality on occasion. Other technical matters can intrude, including domain problems. No videotaping was done in the Air Traffic Control study, for instance, for the simple reason that the (at that time bulky) machinery got in the way of a very mobile staff doing safety-critical work.

Background noise can be problematic. Sound is as important as vision, especially in contexts where the analysis of talk is seen as part of the research. We would not be the first researchers to discover, after the event, that what we imagined to be good recordings turned out to be borderline useless because we could not hear what was being said. To be clear, it is not for the most part difficult to organise matters so that direct conversation is recorded, but we should remember that often our analysis will include things overheard, said in passing, shouted from a distance, and so on.

One of the critical issues is the sheer amount of video that can be collected in even a relatively short time. A colleague of ours, researching home use of technology, recently reported that he had collected six hundred hours of videotape in a week. One should never underestimate the amount of time involved in sitting through the material. Our own recent experience of 'smart home' evaluation led to a similar conclusion. Here, using digital videorecording, the ethnographer had to find a way of viewing some eight hours per day of data. A moment's thought tells us that this simply cannot be done without regular recourse to the 'fast forward' button.

Equally, there are choices to make. Video cameras can simply be 'left' or they can be actively managed. The colleague we mention above was responsible for organising the taping of activity in twenty homes, and evidently being present for the whole of that time is impractical. Their initial solution (founded on some odd ideas about the ethics of the situation) was to hide cameras in fluffy toys! Here is as good a place as any to refer to 'informed consent'. Ethics vary with situations, but again most practitioners would agree that 'good practice' is to inform people, at least in private and work contexts, that their activities are being recorded, and seek their permission. We might also refer to a nonproblem here. It might be expected that there will be a video-awareness displayed by subjects. Our experience, shared by others we know, is that this is a very short-lasting effect, and no one need be overly concerned about it.

By far the most important consideration is the relationship between the technology and the analysis. There is a danger that focusing on video-data alone risks missing activities that are peripheral to the video 'zone' but important nonetheless. For this reason, we would make the strong claim that video never in any circumstances replaces fieldnotes, but should be used in addition to them. The sheer amount of data also presents problems of organisation and notation. Many people have attempted to provide notations which can help find and organise significant pieces of material,[43] but with limited success. There is a danger of imposing analytic categories on

---

[43]For example, Gail Jefferson's transcription notation.

the data if sticking too rigidly to pre-existing notations (this is not to say that emerging notation systems cannot be used for data collected in one domain). It may seem obvious, but some clear and mutually understood filing system is absolutely necessary. Jordan and Henderson argue for a 'content log', and suggest it be done as soon as practicable after recording. The log might include an index by tape counter and a summary listing of events.

A last point to be made is that video seems to enforce a collaborative approach to analysis. Almost everyone reports that the best analytic results are obtained when groups sit together looking at video material; it quickly becomes evident that different viewers are seeing different things. (See Silverman (ibid.) and Jordan and Henderson (ibid.).) In our view this is critically important. It has been reported often enough now, that one might state a rule:

Analysis of video has to be done by more than one person.

6.6 Tape Recording

Rather less intrusive than the video, tape recording is useful but arguably provides less rich data. In our experience it is useful in highly specific circumstances. These might be summed up as follows.

Tape recording is useful for recording long explanations, especially those of a highly technical or domain-specific kind which otherwise are difficult to follow (at least early in a study). It is equally useful for speaking into, which means the researcher can use it as a resource for quickly noting ideas. For the most part, and bearing in mind one or two caveats, it is unobtrusive. The caveats are that, at least early on in a study, people will notice, and even object to tape recording. Some would argue that awareness of the tape recorder defines the responses one is likely to get, but in our experience this ceases to be a problem in practice very quickly. Nevertheless, permission should always be sought. There are good ethical reasons for this, but there is also a practical one: subjects are surprised, distressed, angry, and so on if they discover during the course of research that you are recording material and have neglected to tell them, even when it is a genuine oversight. That is, one should never be a hostage to loss of trust. Again, and as a practical matter, tapes need transcription. This turns out to be a more serious problem with audiotape than with videotape, perhaps as a feature of bandwidth.

6.7 Asking Questions

Some purists who advocate fly-on-the-wall approaches to ethnography would argue that asking questions is an intervention in the natural domain and thus produces bias. We do not accept that view. Asking questions is an important and necessary way of gaining understanding of the domain in question. Even so, a number of practical issues arise.

Knowing what questions to ask. One of the general critiques of knowledge elicitation is that the knowledge uncovered is in part structured by the kinds of questions asked in the first place. It is certainly true that subjects will provide responses which are designed to answer the question in ways that are relevant to what they think the question is about. They will make such judgments, of course, on the basis of what they know about the person asking the questions. It means that they will leave out matters which they do not consider relevant. For this reason, asking questions early on in research should not be done with a view to getting serious answers. Although helping you get a sense of the domain in question, it is unlikely to provide you with the answers you are seeking. The point at which questioning becomes a worthwhile enterprise is the point at which you know enough about the domain that you can begin to ask questions you know to be relevant.

Discretion is important. In safety-critical domains such as ATC, it is obvious that sometimes asking a set of questions is unlikely to be welcomed at the wrong time. Equally, of course, and of particular importance in real-world arenas, it should be recognised that you 'don't frighten the horses.' That is, one should not unnecessarily produce uncertainty and fear in the people in the domain by asserting that the results of your study might, for instance, lead them to lose their jobs. This may seem obvious, but anyone who has practiced out there in the real world will attest to the extraordinary insensitivity of the occasional practitioner.

Reliance on the answers. One should not, in the context of ethnographic research, get obsessed with issues such as questionnaire design. One of the problems for tyro researchers is that they are inclined to believe that there is some 'right' way of doing things, and are inclined to read the literature with a view to finding out what it is. Doing this with the sociological literature is likely to lead one to the view that questioning is a complex matter where issues of reliability and validity are extremely important, and only to be arrived at by correct questionnaire design. Our own view is that sociological methods are overengineered for CSCW purposes. The fieldworker will learn what questions are important, how reliable the informant is, and the contingency of responses in the course of the work. Related to this is what to do with the answers. There is a tendency in both the sociological and psychological literature to produce aggregated responses, that is, statistical distributions of response. This may be valuable for some purposes, however, it contains one significant danger in the CSCW context, and that is that it may well be that the interesting problems are to be found in uncovering the significance of different responses. Again, we believe that getting a good feel for the range of different responses to particular questions is a useful exercise, more so than subjecting them to statistical analysis with a view to arriving at consistency. In this respect, the ethnomethodological injunction to treat all accounts as versions is invaluable, even if one has no sympathy with ethnomethodology. Again, the important issue is to do with the point at which one begins to favour one account over another.

191

6.8 Duration of the Study

Ethnographic material presents designers with a large amount of rich and discontinuous material among which designers have to select. For the ethnographer this issue is presented as one of completeness; when is enough, enough? In sociology and anthropology ethnographers have spent years on their fieldwork, a timescale which is excessive from the point of view of system design. Although there is no firm rule about this, there is a rule of thumb which can be useful, namely, the flattening of the field-worker's own learning curve. The fact that the social organisation of work, as with many human activities, has a routine and format to it, means that the effective ethnographer is able to grasp, within a relatively short period of time, the key aspects of the work. However, it is also vitally important to recognise that key aspects of the work may not be routine but exceptional. Knowing how work is ordinarily done is not sufficient for designers. Knowing what problems occur, how frequently, and what their significance is, how they are dealt with and with what degree of competence, can provide very useful information. Nevertheless, this poses the practical problem of how the ethnographer knows that the ethnography is 'complete.' There are no self-evident completeness rules. As a rule of thumb, however,

1. The flattening of the learning curve is an indication of adequacy, at least in terms of ordinary situations. It is clear that, in most studies, the pay-off declines as the study lengthens (which was one original justification for the quick and dirty approach).

2. Knowing what you haven't seen is a further test. For instance in the ATC research the bulk of the research took place in the winter months. Given that controllers constantly made reference to how busy it got in the summer, it pointed to a need to return to the domain. In the same research, the ethnographer never saw a disaster, but did see some 'air misses'. This provided a useful baseline for assessing exceptional events. Knowing what you haven't seen, often by letting participants describe other events to you, and reporting it to designers, can be a very useful indicator.

6.9 Tool Support for Recording Results

Although often referred to as "software for qualitative analysis", what it does is facilitate analysis. The software cannot analyse your data for you, only help.

(Fielding, 1994)

. . . no qualitative analysis package can in practise build theory, nor do analysis for the researcher.

(MacMillan and McLachlan, 1999).

There can be no doubt that software packages are, in principle, useful simply because of the enormous amount of data ethnographic work can produce. Furthermore, if ethnographic data are to be used systematically by system developers, they clearly must be structured in some way. However, regardless of the problems of storage and indexing of audio/video information, storage of such amounts of textual information in a way which allows easy access to a particular item of data is difficult. Davies (1990) reported that very few computer-based tools existed to support this process in contrast with the large number of sophisticated tools available which support traditional structured domain/requirements analysis methods. Of course, more are available now, and they are of increasing sophistication. They include Scolari Atlas-Ti™, The Ethnograph™, (Seidel and Clark, 1984; Seidel et al., 1988), and QSR International's NUDIST™ N6, which is described by its developers as 'a powerful program that allows easy access to data and extensive automation of clerical tasks . . . N6 is especially useful for those working with large amounts of data in a team environment.'[44] Dicks and Mason (1998), however, point out that such programmes can act as 'theory developers' and we are not entirely happy with this prospect. Whatever the merits or otherwise of such software, and we express no preference, it is as well to bear in mind that its proper use is to facilitate clerical, and not analytic, tasks.[45]

Our concern for these issues is that there is a danger that the technology for recording and analysing data can come to dominate the focus of the enquiry, to the extent that it can come to precede general analytic interest. It is felt by some that they '. . . impose many unwelcome constraints on the researcher, and s/he has to significantly alter the methods and techniques of analysis to fit in with a given system' (Davies, 1990, p. 35).

Indeed, discussions concerning the 'code and retrieve' mentality have prompted some considerable debate (see Coffey et al. (1996) and Lee and Fielding (1996)). Such technologies should serve analysis, not define it in our view. At the same time, many of the problems associated with ethnography and system design have to do with recording and making available both raw data and analytic results. As we have seen, the rich picture provided by ethnography is both its major virtue and its chief drawback in terms of manageability and comprehension. This becomes even more pronounced in commercial settings where there may in principle be collaboration between ethnographers across a number of fieldsites and between ethnographers and designers of many different kinds. There is, therefore, a prima facie case for some kind of tool support for ethnographic enquiry. Although we make reference to some here, it is not our purpose to compare

---

[44]See QSR International's Web site at http://www.qsr.com.au

[45]For more general discussion of the advantages and disadvantages of computer-aided ethnography, see Fielding and Lee (1991,1998), Kelle (1997), and IJSRMTP (2002), 5(3).

their merits. Rather, we are interested in how systems of this kind may be most effectively used so that results can be made available to others while avoiding some of the pitfalls we believe to be potentially present in computer support for ethnography.

Latterly, of course, the increasing sophistication of these packages has meant that what applied to text now applies equally to photographs and video. They also increasingly make use of hypermedia functionality. Regardless, we can reduce this list to certain broad functionalities:

1. More flexible storage, coding, retrieval, and analysis of greater amounts of qualitative data.
2. Consistency of presentation. In principle, everyone has access to the same data presented in the same way.

Thus, and typically, they offer a means to store extensive amounts of rich and varied material, including diagrammatic and video-based materials; a means to embed a developing conceptual framework within the data, and thus a means to search and sort through large amounts of data. What is, of course, missing from this (and any other) typology is the recognition that any such activity requires massive amounts of work, and mundane work at that. The idea of a computer system that will simply and quickly produce 'answers' to fieldworkers' queries belongs to the realm of (bad) science fiction.

By way of brief example we outline some characteristics of NUDIST™, a well-known software package of this type and highlight the analytical assumptions inherent in it. The NUDIST (NonNumerical Unstructured Data Indexing Searching and Theory-building) application offers graphical representations of hierarchical conceptual relations between coded textual data. It is designed for multi-user access, providing audit trails of retrievals and searches, can handle data on- and offline, and also supports links to quantitative data analysis packages such as SPSS. The NUDIST package is used by means of marking elements of text (of any length, from a single word to an entire document), or carrying out text-based searches to create graphically displayed hierarchical databases with links into the documents analysed, with the facility to re-enter retrievals into the indexing system indefinitely to build up more abstracted retrievals. It also allows several views on the data, by allowing multiple windows to be open, showing for example raw data and a hierarchical database. As one of the more sophisticated QDA packages, NUDIST with its audit trail aims to conserve a sense of the researcher's model of the research process and as such additionally offer some notions of project management.

It is worth noting that the processes of codification and indexing are hardly unproblematic, and for ethnomethodologists at least, there is some irony in their use. The very point of qualitative research for ethnomethodologists is to uncover how social realities are arrived at (not just simply what they are like) and the ironic feature of software support is that it can disguise the activities and processes that went into determining what the appropriate categories might be. That is, the encoded data do not provide the reader with an opportunity to assess how and why decisions concerning how to categorise were made in the first place. In a nutshell, they can produce a reified version of what might have been a contingent and tentative process. There are not, and cannot be, any fundamentally 'true' ways of analysing data, in the sense that they are necessarily better than other analytical structures; they are better or truer only in the context of what we deem to be our topic and purpose in hand. In addition, there is the grave danger that a large mass of data presented in this precodified way confers a spurious reliability or objectivity on the results so presented.

This is an important problem and bears some examination. Typically, as Padilla (1991) argues, QDA applications are used to build 'concept models' and such 'concept models' are generated from the coded information with the purpose of answering the question, 'What's the situation?'. He sees such an approach as fundamentally based upon the refinement of textual data into 'a coherent explanation of the situation,' an operation carried out by the analytic capabilities of the software package. Essentially in the QDA packages on offer a particular model of analysis that is prescribed by the formalising processes is built into their functionality, despite the calls for flexibility put forward in much of the literature. Fielding (1993) states, 'There is also a more profound concern that the existing software presumes a generic theory of qualitative analysis ... those preferring ... ethnomethodology [or] conversation analysis ... are less well served.'

Arguably, then, such QDA packages require a premature commitment to the 'generic theory of qualitative analysis' prescribed in such packages' means of organising data through codification, and the consequent constraints placed upon subsequent analytic or conceptual work. Even so, such packages could be seen as aiding the progressive refinement and specification of requirements for the designer. In our view, to perceive them in this way carries enormous dangers. Not least, there is the danger that the packages can do the analysis for the researcher, and if they do not go that far, they require data entry and codification to be of such a type that many forms of analysis are precluded: This worry is one held throughout the QDA community, as Fielding (1993) again notes, 'Indeed Seidel, the creator of one of the most popular programs, has written of his fear that researchers ... may be led into slavish adherence to conventions that are set into program assumptions.'

However, despite some early concerns that the use of QDA packages seemingly leads inexorably into grounded theory approaches – creating a 'Frankenstein's monster' alienating the researcher from his own data and producing a new orthodoxy in research – Kelle (1997) argues that many users of computer software restrict themselves to ordinary coding and retrieval rather than using any more sophisticated 'theory building'

195

functions. Such tools are primarily viewed as ways of mechanising the laborious clerical tasks associated with ethnography rather than devices for performing analysis: '... researchers are primarily guided by their research objectives and analysis strategies, and not by the software they use.'

In a similar fashion MacMillan and McLachlan (1999) question the theory-building properties of one of the most popular QDA tools commenting that any such suggestion relies on a view of theory building as simple categorization work. They argue that:

> What NUDIST does not do is build theory, but rather it encourages hierarchical links between categories, using memos and interpretations ... The main advantage of NUDIST is its ability to handle large data sets and to perform coding functions and text searches. ... But it must be stressed that NUDIST does not do the analysis, nor even play much part in it. No qualitative analysis package can in practise build theory, nor do analysis for the researcher.

And, interestingly they comment: '... It was only later, when NUDIST was abandoned (both as a tool and as a method), did the analysis really begin to take shape.'

The possibility that QDA packages might be misused is no reason to advocate that they should not be used. At various times, we have made use of software tools (Calvey et al., 1997; Hughes et al., 2000) of a similar kind, hinged on the need to find some way of making the richness of the fieldwork data available to designers and consequent issues of presentation and representation. For us, the emphasis has to be on the simple practical value of software support in communicating research to various interested parties in a way that goes beyond either the standard presentation with the inevitable glossing that is involved, or the research report and the problems of understanding that (perhaps inevitably) ensue. Such a system will have most value if it acts as a flexible information management and browsing system providing a range of facilities for representing, changing, rearranging, and referencing information (Sommerville et al., 1993).[46]

Although ethnographic studies continue to remain influential as a means of understanding the everyday aspects of work settings, the presentation of these findings remains problematic and information from an ethnographic study relatively difficult to access. The use of applications to organise and present data from ethnographic research, as well as their possible use to present user views of the application domain, may facilitate discussion across a broad development team. These kind of tools may ensure that the complex organisation of the work setting – which the system under development must support – as represented in the ethnographic record and

---

[46]See Tesch (1991) and Weitzman and Miles (1995) for a more complete discussion of the functions of tool support.

delineated in users' experiences, is made available for information, assessment, and interpretation. It thereby provides a bridge among the complexities of an ethnographic account, users' experience and knowledge, and the requirements of a system designer. Alongside the interest in tool use has been a more general focus on approaches to using representational schema to present data in a way that makes sense and is useful to designers, using such devices as 'viewpoints' (Hughes et al., 1995, 2000) or 'patterns' (Martin et al., 2001, 2003). Nevertheless, the point remains that these are all ways of presenting the data, not analysing it.

6.9.1 Summary

We pointed out at the beginning of the chapter that we felt we had no special expertise such that we would be able to advise others how to go about their studies. We stand by this, although among the authors there is a vast experience of conducting fieldwork. The main purpose in documenting the above issues is reassurance. We are of the general opinion that although there is no right way to do ethnographic research, there is definitely a wrong way. That consists of either hanging around in hotel rooms rather than at the site of the work for want of the confidence to go and do it, or 'getting it over with' by charging in, instructing your respondents as to what you are about to find out, pointing out their lack of competence to them at every available opportunity, and explaining what you know (and they don't) about their work before the first piece of observation is complete. One of the authors had the experience, years ago, of experiencing a slightly hostile response from a small group of teachers when he made an observation beginning, 'The thing about teachers is . . . .' He is older and wiser now. We remarked earlier that confidence is extremely important and we can add to that here by stating that either too little or too much is dangerous. In the end, open-mindedness, a respectful demeanour, determination, and a 'can do' mentality will overcome most of the so-called problems we discuss above. With occasional exceptions, they are scarcely problems at all.

Part 3
Analytic Issues: What Have We Got?

Common Sense and Context

7

7.1 Preamble

Thus far, we have tried to spell out some lessons concerning the role of ethnography in design, and our view concerning some the questions we posed at the outset. Others remain to be dealt with, notably those having to do with the nature and importance of fieldwork 'descriptions'. We asked at the beginning whether a 'view from nowhere' is acceptable, whether data should 'speak for themselves,' or whether concepts and theories of varying degrees of abstraction/organisation might be necessary. This clearly relates as well to the issue of what we do with these descriptions once we have them. We have been at pains to show that the commitments that each of us have shown (commitments that mean we oftentimes describe ourselves as ethnomethodologists) are not such that they need to be applied slavishly in the context of design. To reiterate, what we mean here is that ethnomethodology, and its analytic commitments, have to be understood in relation to their origins in, and difficult relationship with, their parent discipline, sociology. For ethnomethodology to make claims vis-à-vis its commitments in respect of a design-related and supposedly interdisciplinary context is something else. What we try to do here is show why some of these commitments proved attractive at the outset and that, equally, the degree to which we might choose to 'buy' them or otherwise rather depends on the job of work with which we, as ethnographers (or fieldworkers), might be tasked.

As we have seen, there are a number of competing theoretical/analytical schemes that will inevitably influence the way in which the data come to be 'seen'. In our view, and we have always tried to be consistent in this, the main danger with any analytical scheme is that its theoretical interests can determine the structure of the data from the outset. That is, the theoretical interests of sociologists, anthropologists, and psychologists can easily take precedence over the practical business at hand and can often dictate what is to be found. We remain nervous about the assumption that any particular analytic commitment can do more than sensitise the researcher towards certain kinds of issue. We feel, and most of the frameworks we have looked at allow, that analysis should evolve from the particular problems that arise from the domain in question, not least because the theoretical auspices of the work are unlikely to be of any great interest to the client. Increasingly, and moreover, ethnographic data have to relate to the human resource and process issues which may actually be the client's concern (outside purely academic research), and it is why we have attempted to highlight those relationships wherever possible.

We cannot stress too much that system design had developed a purchase on process, or the formal aspects of work with computer systems, long before the advent of HCI and CSCW, and ethnographic research cannot be defended as a superior set of techniques for understanding data structure, data flow, process boundary, and so on. In all of the perspectives we have identified it is possible to see, to varying degrees, and with different emphases, what prolonged ethnographic work can confer on our understanding of work. It is in the relationship between idealised conceptions of process and data and the lived reality of the task, work, organization, and political experience that the power of fieldwork of the ethnographic kind, is to be found. To put it another way, lengthy descriptions of organisational cultures, in and of themselves, will not provide a better solution to organisational and technical problems. Arguably, understanding how they relate to matters that system designers have always concerned themselves with, will.

In any event, we want here to show how something that looks like an ethnomethodologically informed enquiry reveals to us some of the things that we can usefully take with us into the world of design. Quixotically, the initial data we examine have nothing to do with design at all. This is a deliberate choice: we want to show what analytic orientation we might bring to the study and understanding of any ordinary interaction. We can bring this orientation with us when we set foot in specific settings such as those associated with the workplace, and we can use it regardless of what subsequent categorizing or generalizing work we might want to do with our data. Our case is useful because most of the 'facts' in question become available over a period of about three seconds (although not all), and therefore it is a manageable way of illustrating some themes.

7.2 An Illustration: The 'Three-Second' Ethnography: The Girl on the Bus

The data we examine here were arrived at serendipitously. Even the most cursory look at them reveals that they have no relationship to technical or design matters. The data are being used merely to illustrate (neatly, we believe) some analytic issues that pertain to all environments. It being the case that one of the co-authors of this book is a nondriver, he is forced to use public transport on many occasions. On one of these, the following interactional exchange was observed. The data were transcribed as soon as possible, to whit when the observer got off the bus and entered his home some fifteen minutes later:

1. 'Dave' gets on bus, which is half empty. Finds a place halfway back on the left, immediately behind a girl who is aged about 12–13 years.
2. Notices that a 40-year-old man sits next to the girl (1 sec). Dave leans forward, but says and does nothing.
3. The man says to the girl, 'Hiya, how are you?' and the girl looks away, out of the window.
4. The girl stands up and pushes past the man. He says, 'I'm sorry, I thought I knew you. . . .'
5. She says nothing and ignores him, walks towards the back of the bus where she finds an empty seat where she sits down. (3 sec).
6. Five minutes later, the man stands up to get off the bus. The girl follows him, and gets off at the same bus stop.

In many ways, this trivial piece of data is superbly adapted for ethnomethodological enquiry because it constitutes in some ways a naturally occurring example of one of Garfinkel's breaching experiments.[47] It illustrates a number of themes which consistently arise in ethnomethodological work. They include, as we show, the *processual character of interaction,* which suggests not only that what happens is organised in a sequence, but also that our understanding of it is sequentially organised as well. If nothing else, this indicates why attention to detail is important.

It also exemplifies our *contingent understanding of 'truth'* insofar as no version of what happened here is a privileged one. What ethnomethodologists sometimes call the 'problem of versions' and to which they respond with 'ethnomethodological indifference' is illustrated here by the fact that we can never be entirely sure what is going on here, but at each stage we think we have a pretty good idea.

Lastly, at every point our understanding of what is happening here, and the inferences we draw about meanings and motivations, is produced out of our assumptions concerning what typically/normally happens in ordinary social situations of this kind. We could not make sense of this situation at all, were it not for the fact that we can draw on our ordinary, commonsense knowledge of what is 'typical' in our world. It illustrates, that is, the *massive importance of commonsense understandings* in our management of social life.

---

[47]We do not recommend this as a methodological commitment. The prospect of waiting around for examples of this kind to occur is a daunting one.

It is in the light of this last point that we want to make some further observations. First, the fact that the bus is half empty is critical. We are each and every one of us familiar with ordinary social rules that suggest appropriate behaviour concerning proximity. Thus, we would not normally sit next to a stranger on a bus if we can find a seat adjacent to an unoccupied one.[48] This constitutes exactly what we have been speaking of in terms of 'rules' and their generalisation. The rule in question – that we do not normally sit next to strangers on public transport, unless no other space is available – is clearly not a rule in any causal sense, for here we see the rule broken (at least, if the two participants do, in fact, turn out to be strangers). It is a rule in the sense that it is something typically done, or normatively organised. Equally, we would as a first option choose to sit next to someone that we knew or a family member.[49] The point is we quite normally draw inferences about the behaviour of other people when we see it, even when such behaviour is of the trivial kind under discussion. Thus, we see that 'Dave' sits down next to an unoccupied seat, but even at this early stage notices the gender of the young girl in front of him and hazards a guess about her age. As we quickly see, gender and age rapidly become pertinent in this encounter.

Very quickly, a middle-aged man sits next to the young girl and greets her with, 'Hiya, how are you?' Again, we can draw immediate inferences here. The first is that this is self-evidently a greeting and the normal response to a greeting is a greeting, such as 'I'm fine, thanks . . . How are you?' (We might also note here, in passing, something that Sacks pointed out, that greetings are not questions, and thus do not require answers but reciprocal greetings in response.) When the girl, then, does not respond in this way we might ask ourselves whether we are entitled to consider her rude. Our answer, of course, is no. The kind of inference we are likely to draw at this stage is based on our background knowledge of the typical behaviour of friends and acquaintances, which has to do with the way in which they might ordinarily greet each other. The very fact that a greeting is not returned by a greeting stands as evidence that the two parties do, in fact, not know each other and thus, at this point, that we are entitled to have doubts about the middle-aged man in question. This judgement is predicated on the knowledge that when middle-aged men initiate conversation with young girls something normatively dubious may be going on, especially if the two parties do not know each other. Greetings are normally offered and accepted amongst friends

---

[48]Men can point to, so to speak, another context in which such proximity behaviour is even more pronounced.

[49]Although there can be no certainty here. The exaggerated embarrassment of teenagers when confronted with their parents in public spaces is one example when this particular preference might not be displayed.

and family, and on public occasions that demand politeness. Sitting next to a stranger on a bus is neither of these.

Immediately afterwards, as 'Dave' leans forward but says and does nothing, we can ask what inferences we might be entitled to draw about this behaviour. Our answer would be along the lines of, he is paying attention to the unusual character of this interaction, is perhaps slightly concerned about it, but as yet has no warrant for an intervention. He may well be construing it as a worrying occasion, but one where the outcome is contingent and there is no need to interfere yet, especially in the light of our knowledge of embarrassment when we misjudge situations. We could, after all, and just for a split second be entitled to view this interaction as middle-aged father with recalcitrant teenage daughter. At the point where the young girl stands up and pushes past the man, such an inference will almost certainly have to be reconsidered. An abrupt move of this kind suggests that the young girl is keen to put an end to all possibility of further interaction, perhaps on the grounds that he is disturbed or deranged, perhaps on the grounds that he is 'hitting on' her. In any normal circumstance, of course, this would be extremely impolite but here it is justified.

When, at stage 4, the man says, 'I'm sorry, I thought I knew you. . . . ', there are again certain inferences we may be entitled to draw. This could easily be an example of what Harvey Sacks called 'Doing Being Ordinary'. He has perhaps realised his behaviour can be, and has been, construed as 'odd' or inappropriate. His excuse is the excuse of someone who wishes to be seen as ordinary (i.e. not weird) and the proffering of the apology is a way of doing being ordinary. The fact that she in turn does not say something like, 'It's alright' but simply ignores him, suggests that she is rejecting his 'ordinariness' (he is still weird). The fact that she then sits some distance from him confirms that this is her understanding of the situation.

Some minutes later, we see that both individuals leave the bus at the same stop. Again, however, we can notice how vitally important the order in which they leave is. The fact that they both get off at the same bus stop, the girl following the man, suggests that maybe he knows her after all. Maybe they are neighbours and she hasn't recognised him. If, of course, he had followed her from the bus, our inferences would be dramatically different and we could easily construe this as a potentially dangerous situation and one where we might feel justified in intervening. Of such very ordinary and initially insignificant factors is our understanding of the situation in question delivered.

This example is, despite its very mundane character, a very good example of why we do fieldwork. Whether the analytic results are interesting will depend on one's own purposes, and it is most unlikely that such an analysis will have any consequences for design. Nevertheless, it does suggest some benefits that accrue from a fieldwork orientation. These are as follows.

1. The example is rich with observational detail for those who choose to notice it. Events can be thoroughly described in small time chunks, and detailed analysis of what is said and done is rewarding. As they are described, the relevance of certain features in the setting such as how full the bus is, which might otherwise be viewed as scenic, becomes apparent.

2. The events in question are sequentially organised. They have a moment-by-moment character whereby our sense of what is going on can change at each point and is, in fact, likely to as events unfold.

3. Nothing that happens is beyond our powers of explanation. We are perfectly able to account for each of the things that happens without the need for an expert to explain it to us. The reason for this is that much of what happens here is utterly familiar to us, and the point is that much of what happens everywhere will be familiar to us. When, for instance, we look at new technology in the home it seems self-evident to us that we really should start by looking at how home life looks to the people who are living it; the nature of their commonsense assumptions is likely to be hugely consequential. Nevertheless, a rigorous attention to the detail of the interaction does arguably allow us to notice things that are otherwise taken for granted. The events illustrate Garfinkel's dictum that the social world is largely 'seen but unnoticed' (1967). The events indicate very strongly the nature of our cultural knowledge, and suggest that attention to cultural knowledge in organisational settings might repay attention in the same way.

This brief excursion into an unusual event in a very commonplace location is designed to illustrate the ordinary, commonsense, inferences that ethnographers, like everyone else, must draw in order to make sense of situations. When Garfinkel suggested there was 'no time out' from this, he was pointing out this fact and arguing that some kind of situational, common-sense reasoning procedure lies behind every piece of sense-making work that we do. Importantly, this holds true whether or not we are engaged in a rigorous enquiry. This is not to say anything crass such as scientific enquiry is merely common sense, for that is to mistake the point. 'Common sense' as used here is not to be understood as a cognitive category that can describe all forms of enquiry, whatever they might be, nor a contrast category to be counterposed with science, but a gloss for the different strategies, procedures, and methods that people in their everyday lives use in an irredeemably situational way. We ignore it at our peril. Whatever else we might want to do in our enquiries, the point is that there are good grounds for thinking that this kind of commonsense, processual, professionally neutral form is a good way to start.

In what follows, we try to exemplify the analytic problem in and through discussion of a number of ethnographic settings. These are organised, largely for convenience, into two broad types of setting which we term organisational and domestic/public. The distinction is made in keeping with our data-led stance. The kinds of category that might prove useful in discussing public and domestic settings (and to some extent the practical ways in which we might assemble data) might be usefully distinguished from those typically deployed in organisational settings, although there will undoubtedly be resemblances.

This rather spurious distinction serves one other purpose: to illustrate the detail and care with which even the most apparently banal of settings can be analysed. We mention this because we want to assert a simple experiential fact, familiar to everyone who has ever done fieldwork of the kind that we have been describing. Inexperienced ethnographers are prone, in our experience, to have recourse to yet more data collection because they have not yet hit on an appropriate way of thinking about what they have. Experience teaches that no amount of data provides us with a relevant understanding of the setting.

> Going back into the field is no substitute for thinking about what the data mean. Sitting at a desk making sense of fieldnotes and other data is a much more difficult enterprise than collecting field data.

Nevertheless, the key to opening up the data is to grasp the commonsense way people doing those actions make sense of the setting in question. With these points in mind, we turn to research into organisational and work settings.

8

Organisations and Work

Organisational settings differ from the kind of social encounters described in the last chapter in one important respect: for some researchers the workplaces in question may be unfamiliar. The fieldworker comes to them as a stranger. To put it in exaggerated form, understanding workplaces may – at least in some respects – be akin to understanding other cultures and hence, the 'other'. The problem of the 'other' has been pivotal in anthropology and sociology and has created a deal of torment. Our view on it derives, as intimated in Chapter 3, from Peter Winch. Winch argued that understanding other cultures is not like understanding Martians, an almost impossible task. He claimed that, when it came down to it, other cultures are, in impor tant respects, similar to our own and hence to each other, no matter how different they may appear. Regardless of detailed differences, all cultures have foundational similarities, for if they did not it would be impossible to understand them at all.[50]

It seems to us that, in much the same way, there are features of all workplaces that can be thought of as foundational. These are things that we can reasonably assume, until we find out differently, are likely to be present in any workplace we investigate. They include what one might call the ordinary things about doing a job of work, things that are so obvious that one might take them for granted. Work normally entails labouring for regular hours or periods for example; work also typically involves going to a place for that work and, when at work, people will normally have different roles and responsibilities: some people do this; some people do that. Equally,

---

[50]Much of the discussion in the social sciences concerning the possibility of understanding another culture rests on a difference of opinion concerning whether it is literally impossible to understand another culture – a view associated with some 'relativists' – or whether it is merely difficult. If the latter, then what is mainly required is some care. We, obviously, take the latter view. A more sophisticated line of reasoning can be found in Sharrock and Anderson (1982), in which they suggest that both 'native' and researcher should be viewed as 'enquirers into culture,' that 'natives and researchers have to discover what is going on.'

some coordination of these activities may well be necessary. Of course, expectations as regards any of these particularities may be confounded in a particular workplace (some work can be done anywhere for example; some organisations don't have fixed divisions of labour), but this does not alter the point that, typically, these are the sorts of things which one imagines any workplace might have. A particular workplace may be strange, but work in general is not. So however strange a workplace might be at the outset, there should nevertheless be certain commonalities that one can orient to as one prepares for the business of fieldwork.

Our argument has been and is that fieldwork-for-design requires more than is given by any particular analytic or theoretical commitment, and cannot be reduced to any set of practical skills. It requires some combination of skills, sensibilities, and assumptions which are distinct from those found in discrete disciplinary concerns. It requires something of the commonsense orientation to be found in ethnomethodology, but may well need more than that. Practitioners also need to be versed in the methodological detail, the practical skills of collecting data through interviewing, watching, listening, transcribing, and so forth, but should not reduce ethnography to the practical. Our claim is that fieldwork-for-design entails, in particular, a combination of all these things with a training in and a sensibility for particular analytic themes and topics. Our view is that going to the field is about looking in certain ways at certain things and analysing them with particular goals in mind. In sum, it is about looking in the right way at the right things with the right intentions. This means that fieldwork will have a different hue depending upon the purposes at hand; fieldwork-for-design is not the same as, say, fieldwork as a means of undertaking cultural analysis, or fieldwork used to explore feminist arguments, or fieldwork serving theoretical needs of any kind. Each is distinct.

Getting to the relevant analytic concerns is a nontrivial matter, for it raises the themes of similarity and difference to which we have already alluded. The role of generalisation as against detail, the problem of what kind of generalisation is relevant and for what purposes, and the often neglected issue of when exactly we can safely assume that both our descriptions and our generalisations are sufficient to our needs, remain unresolved. Decisions are a product partly of training and practice, and partly the consequence of building upon and learning from prior research into the domain in question. We have been arguing that one of the distinguishing characteristics of the approach to fieldwork-for-design we have in mind is the particular cargo brought with us to a new domain or new problem. It is our view that one does not look at a new workplace as if no one has studied workplaces before, sifting through prior research to see if that research can indicate what to look for, what to focus on, and what to disregard. Although a workplace may be entirely unfamiliar to us, we can learn from others how to analyse the work practices we are likely to find there. The analysis we have in mind means something more than recognising that the work looks like work anywhere else, with such things as the foundational properties we mentioned above. There is no news in discovering that work looks like work.[51] Our view is that one needs to see that work in the imaginative light of prior 'lookings' in other settings.

8.1 Overview of the Chapter

So having done a little orienting ourselves in these opening remarks, let us now state our goal in this chapter. It is to sketch out the analytic cargo that the fieldworker may bring along with him when he ventures out into the field. We want to do so not by offering a list of what makes up this cargo, implying thereby that undertaking of fieldwork-for-design was merely a mechanical affair, achieved through the dutiful referencing of prior art. Our view is that fieldwork of the kind we have in mind succeeds when it is sensitively done, and that means through evoking and alluding, comparing and contrasting both what is seen in the here and now with what was seen and thought about in prior research. We want to convey how to be thoughtful in the field. Results in fieldwork are not solely a question of looking but are better thought of as an artful interplay among the looking and the thinking and the reflecting. For that reason, none of what we discuss below should be thought of as constituting a list.

We propose not only to outline what things might be borne in mind in the field but to say something about why some things are worth bearing in mind. Thus if this cargo can be said to consist of a set of themes, then how these can act as guides for the fieldworker can be understood in part through how these themes have evolved over the years. This in turn means understanding how they have been fought over, what the fights have been about, and what the themes have been discovered to do in the process of these disputes. This is what enables the fieldworker to deploy them sensitively in their own endeavours.

In broad outline the cargo we want to talk about is as follows. First of all, we want to remind the reader that whatever one is looking for, in the fieldwork we have in mind, one always assumes that the work in question is socially organised. This is such a basic assumption that it can almost seem a platitude. But its obviousness does not obviate its importance. Nor indeed does its obviousness obviate the need to restate what this assumption means. As we remark, for a workplace to be socially organised means more than just the fact that there is a division of labour.

---

[51]Although the reader might reflect on the fact that Winch's query was why do psychologists of various kinds make out that the world as we know it is one to be discovered, but that is another argument!

The properties of social organisation suffuse all the other thematics we then consider. The next topic we discuss has to do with concern for plans and procedures, or, if you like, planfulness. Discussion of this is most famously associated with Lucy Suchman and her book, *Plans and Situated Actions* (1987). We say a little about the explorations of plans and actions in that book as well as the debates that have ensued about what the relationship between plans and actions might be.

If rules and regulations help constitute the order of action, then artefacts provide another. The next topic we discuss is the role of artefacts in the workplace and by this we don't mind whether they are physical artefacts (bits of papers, walls, and tables) or digital objects such as a Microsoft Word document. Things come in various forms. The important point is that things are not merely the output of work, but they are also the instruments through which work gets done, whatever the work in question. And furthermore, how particular things get used in particular ways is in part always bound up with their material properties, whatever they might be: that a Microsoft Word document can be forwarded in certain way is one such property; that a paper document can be marked up with pen is another. How these sorts of things are done and why they should be an important aspect of a fieldworker's concern, although as we show, this is not just a descriptive problem: it is, as with all our themes, an analytic one.

If artefacts are part of the resources used to ensure and orient towards a particular way of organising work through time and across organisational space, the next theme has to do with the flow of work. This phrase contrasts with the mechanical fitting of processes, persons, and objects together; it is better thought of as a concern for how, in practical detail and despite daily contingency, work is concurrent and sequential, picked up and put down, interrupted or completed against a deadline, and so on. This organisation is not merely temporal and spatial, it is also a scheme of orientation. Any flow turns on different levels of awareness: an individual can orient to her work by knowing where her own work fits into the larger scheme or flow, for example.

Our last topic is with the perennial fact of life in workplaces as it is with all places, work or otherwise: with normal natural troubles. Here we explore what has been learnt over the years about the ways in which individuals in any workplace make systems work, despite contingencies and everyday problems that make getting the work done a bit more difficult than simply following the rules. Dealing with problems is thus something that is an empirical fact about workplaces, but these practical solutions, we explain, are also important resources that the fieldworker can use to reflect on the nature of skills used in any work setting.

These analytic themes are not all that one might look for, of course, merely an initial set of topics, although they are fairly comprehensive. They might be decomposed, linked, or recreated in ways of which we have not thought.

They constitute a convenient starting point and a possible route towards a destination we can only glimpse. Besides, as we have pointed out, these themes will be deployed within a larger frame of reference. This will have to do with whether the fieldwork is being done as an initial exploration, for example, or an exercise in evaluation, or to create some refinement to design ideas, and so forth. In other words, when undertaking fieldwork in an overall design process, there are different locations within that overall process and these will balance and colour how the themes themselves are deployed. Nevertheless, these themes, analytic topics, tropes, or reference points, call them what you will, are the basis of fieldwork. To wilfully misuse Winch, they are the foundational elements of our business.

8.2 Themes and Analytic Devices

'The social organisation of work' is an umbrella term. It subsumes so much that it can become vague, yet its power and importance is such that it needs proper grasping. This concept labels the fact that very little work in an organisational context is ever done in isolation. Even when the person doing the work is physically isolated, doing the work will normally involve an awareness of the work other people are doing or might do. To oversimplify, who's doing what is an important organising principle of working life.

Work is to be understood as more than merely built around a division of labour, however. The term 'socially organised' is meant to orient us to what it might mean for individuals to organise themselves in reference to others. For example, the meaning of social organisation is shown in how plans are devised and to what they are oriented. Plans are the ultimate measure of social organisation when by 'measure' we mean some indication that effort has been put into ensuring that people collaborate. Plans are not there to guide the individual; plans are there to help ensure that what an individual does is in accord with what others before have thought would be an effective way of doing things. In other words, plans are instruments for marshalling people. This does not mean that what marshalling entails is predetermined or fixed; all that is being said is that plans, planning, and planfulness have to be understood themselves as socially organisational phenomena. To put this another way: to explore the relationship between what people are planning to do and what they do in fact do is a matter suffused with social organisational properties. As we show, however, just because one assumes that this is so does not mean that it makes it easy to study. Indeed, if planfulness is illustrative of the scope of social organisation, planfulness is also a complex phenomenon in its own right.

If the meaning of plans is one of the ways social organisation shows itself, another is in the sequential and concurrent patterning of work and, along with that, what are called the 'egological' arrangements constitutive of work

213

practice. This phrase indicates to us how people determine their own courses of action, in the here-and-now, by reference to what others in the here-and-now are doing as well as what others in the past and in the future have, and will, do. Social organisation is not merely a matter of one thing at a time, but also a matter, if you like, of 'mental geography', based on knowing which others do what, when, where, why, and with what means.

This also leads one to consider the vehicle for this social organisation. What is socially organised must, by definition, take place in a world of material artefacts. Whilst we do not buy the pretensions of actor-network theory, or any other theoretical approach to materiality, the use and possible future use of artefacts will also evidently be socially organised. Artefacts have properties of one kind or another, allowing all sorts of socially organised activities to take place. Objects may be passed from person to person and can be both the subject of the work that any individual needs to do within that division of labour and a marker of where the work, whatever it might be, has reached, for example. Artefacts do many things and enable many things, all of which are bound up with social organisation. The question is how, to what ends, and with regard to what larger ecology of artefacts, they are related.

We could go on. The important thing is to note that we do not think that one should treat social organisation as a distinct topic. This contrasts with the work of human factors specialists like Vicente, mentioned much earlier in the book, where one finds a claim that one should treat social organisation as one factor to be considered in design. Our view, the view that we think comes out of the history of CSCW and its attempt to deploy fieldwork-based approaches, is that one has to assume that more or less all the activities that one might be interested in are socially organised. This does not mean that one treats social organisation as so all-encompassing that it becomes vague and useless. Rather, it is to say that it is a foundational property and thus one should orient to the way it manifests itself in whatever one looks at. As others have remarked (Hughes et al., 1992), it is how things are socially organised that is of interest, not that they are socially organised, for the latter is no kind of discovery. So, as we move on to consider the other themes, components of the (very) loose framework which we offer, we should remember that they all display the massive orderliness of organisational activity, because these are characteristic of, indeed definitive of, what it means to be an organisation.

8.3 Planning, Plans, and Procedures

We have already noted, then, that plans are important when investigating action in workplaces; any discussion of work should consider plans and planning. This is a commonplace. That this is so is probably one reason why there are no shortages of methodologies for uncovering the planful nature of work. Most of the structured design methodologies beloved of large-scale system design and the associated business process models, for instance, are examples of precisely this. But it is important to note that many of these approaches to planfulness, including the structured method ones, tend to oversimplify what plans and planfulness might mean. Suchman's book, *Plans and Situated Actions*, from nearly twenty years ago now (1987), presented a powerful critique of the user modelling and planning-based approaches to design which misunderstood, she thought, what the relationship between plans and action might be. More particularly, she suggested that 'Plans are resources for situated action but do not in any strong sense determine its course,' Her central argument was that plans do not thoroughly determine in advance and causally direct in every detail courses of action. In her view a plan is an abstract construction that needs to be applied in specific circumstances. Plans do not simply execute themselves, nor is the relationship between the plan and the action it directs a mechanical one. Plans are accomplished activities.

Her book reflected a growing number of inquiries looking at precisely this topic at that time. The book's widespread readership generated even more on this topic: indeed by the early nineties numerous empirical studies reported on the gulf between abstract idealised plans and their situated accomplishment, perhaps most noticeably in Orr's (1996) accounts of the 'war stories' of photocopier technicians. The details of all those studies aside, the basic upshot of Suchman's book was to lead researchers to rethink how plans were to be understood: not as having causal properties which determine how people do work, but as resources for action. In fact, in some respects this is not an especially new insight. As Selznick noted nearly a half a century before (1948, p. 25):

> The formal administrative design can never adequately or fully reflect the concrete organization to which it refers, for the obvious reasons that no abstract plan or pattern can ... exhaustively describe an empirical totality. At the same time, that which is not included in the abstract design ... is vitally relevant to the maintenance and development of the formal system itself.

This reflects both an observed empirical reality about organisational life – that people do not always slavishly follow the plan – and a desire to avoid underrating the skills and competencies that are required in even the most routine of tasks. Nevertheless, Suchman underlined these insights and established their importance for the newly emerged disciplines of system design. The approach to looking at work that she championed involved, as we show, reaffirming the importance of practical rationality, what Boden (1994) called 'local logics' and 'local knowledge', which are exhibited in day-to-day conduct. These practical rationalities make a mockery of idealised notions of rationality.

This perspective on plans and action had particular significance in the historical evolution of office systems, or at least in the intellectual debates surrounding their evolution and design. The office automation movement of the 1970s had taken little heed of the organisational literature as exemplified in the work of Selznick and others, and had viewed clerical work as simply routine, involving the repeated execution of planned procedures. From their view, this work was a prime candidate for automation. Typical of this research was a characterisation of offices according to the levels of routine they were said to display and descriptions of clerical work as predefined reactions to inputs (Zisman, 1977):

> Once a clerk is told about a situation, s/he can consult a predefined procedure (formally or informally) to determine what action should be taken by the organisation. The organisation does not rely on the clerk to decide what to do; instead the organisation provides a procedure which instructs the clerk how to react to the situation.

The problem that most affected office automation research of this type was the existence of 'exceptions'. Various researchers demonstrated the rich and complex nature of supposedly routine activities and the skilled, cooperative decision making and negotiation necessary to get the work done. There appeared to be, according to this research, important discrepancies between the formal office procedures that supposedly governed office work and practical actions as actually carried out by office staff. This was demonstrated by focusing upon how workers creatively solved exceptions and dealt with contingencies. These field studies showed how it was often necessary – in order to get the work done at all – to deviate from plans and improvise ad hoc procedures in the light of the exigencies of some unfolding situation (Pycock, 1999):

> The Office Automation research ran into problems because it embedded models of work in systems as if they were computer executable versions of what actually happened, of how work was actually done. The status of these models was transformed from being a resource—a resource which may provide a reference point, a grounding, a basis for discussions, a coordination mechanism and so on—into being a constraint upon how things could be done. Office automation systems have not had the impact or acceptance that was initially expected because such systems implemented an information flow that was idealised and neglected the work needed to make the "flow" possible in the first place.

What Suchman helped achieve, then, was a shift in how plans were thought about in the systems design community. In particular, she suggested a radically different sense to what 'routine' in the workplace might be, and how its analysis might be helpful for systems design. She illustrated the importance of what she called an ethnographic orientation to the status of procedural plans, an orientation which sees them as accomplished products. As Suchman (1983) noted, 'The procedural structure of organizational activities is the product of the orderly work of the office, rather than a reflection of some enduring structure that stands behind the work.'

The work of Suchman then illustrated how important it was to consider the 'fit' of procedural models with the ways in which work was actually done. Studies of this sort uncovered the fact that office systems had been 'automating a fiction'. They found that systems had never worked as described in idealised versions; in contrast it was people who construct the processes in question in the doing of those processes. Their everyday judgements, the ways they interpreted rules and requirements, their improvising standard procedures, was what 'gets the work done'. It is thus artfulness, according to this literature, that makes work routine and planned rather than procedure.

Plans and CSCW

This shift in understanding led to a greater awareness of the issues facing those hoping to model one particular kind of office work, namely co-operative work. It was at this time, the 1980s, that CSCW began to emerge. A concern for understanding the apparent failure of automation in offices naturally led to studies of many other contexts in which co-operative work existed and where automation was thought to offer a route to improvement, such as in air traffic control (a domain mentioned at several points earlier on in the book). Here, an emphasis on supporting co-operative work with resources other than automated ones came to be influential. Many researchers began to develop their own inquiries in other domains too, all in light of the view that the ad hoc, the impromptu, needed to be better understood. As Schmidt (1997, insert added) writes:

> In a way CSCW can be said to have been born with these concerns [i.e. the tension between plans and actions]. The office automation movement had already given way to disillusionment, and artificial intelligence was increasingly being confronted with unfulfilled promises. At the same time, a number of critical studies had demonstrated that the problems were deep rooted: office procedures were of a different nature than presumed by the protagonists of office automation. The general conclusion of these studies were that such constructs, instead of determining action causally, serve as "maps" which responsible and competent actors may consult to accomplish their work. Thus, Lucy Suchman's radical critique of cognitive science . . . and the "situated action" perspective she proposed [as an alternative] has played a significant role in defining the CSCW agenda and has become a shared frame of reference to many, perhaps most, of us.

By the late nineties, however, what was being taken from Suchman and others in her vein was becoming contentious. It was being taken to extreme.

One reading of this sort we might term celebratory. In particular, it celebrated the contingent, the unexpected, and the exceptional. According to this view, 'ethnographic fieldwork' should only emphasise (celebrate) the contingent, the unexpected, and the exceptional. It should emphasise the high degree of skill and competence that workers demonstrate in ad hoc ways. But this came at the expense of concern for the formal, the organisationally standard and routine. This view limited the empirical scope of fieldwork. It thus got criticised extensively, for obvious reasons.

This view also inhibited the practical ways of doing fieldwork effectively, and the reasons for this are perhaps worth mentioning. In most circumstances it is unlikely a fieldworker will be able to recognise the exceptional, the ad hoc, the unexpected unless they can already recognise the routine in the first place. One of the easiest ways of recognising routines is to read manuals and other sets of instructions, guidelines, rulebooks, and so on. Yet some took Suchman as saying that one ought to disregard these resources in fieldwork: they were, these researchers believed, fictions. But many other researchers, less enamoured of Suchman, pointed out that good fieldwork requires appreciating the formal before one can appreciate the informal. This is not to say that they thought that 'plans' (whatever they might be) had to be reported in any detail but that knowing what the plans were, they argued, was important in being able to see the work for 'what it is'. They came to the view, one that is now generally held, that the celebratory reading of Suchman's work not only limited empirically what was done in fieldwork, but potentially stunted fieldwork even before it started. The reason was this: one cannot get to see the contingent and the ad hoc unless one already knows the formal.

A Distance Between Plans and Action

The miscasting of research that these odd readings of Suchman engendered should not distract attention from the plain fact that, in workplaces, plans are important. Nor should they distract attention from the fact that action, too, especially the unplanned, is important. The relationship between them is important as well. But beyond what is especially salient in fieldwork-for-design is the extent to which the distance between plans and actions matters and for whom it matters. These differences are sometimes startling, sometimes unexpected, but often extremely important when thinking about how design might effect change. Subtlety is required and one way one can convey this subtlety is to use the following extract from our own fieldwork in a bank to show how plans, rules, and proper procedures are oriented to as socially organised and as essentially social affairs that are not to be understood as things to be contrasted with the informal. Plans are things oriented to in various ways.

In this case, someone who was called a 'Business Manager's Assistant' was assembling the necessary information for assessing whether a loan (or an overdraft) was something that the bank wanted to provide. She had at hand the customer file and the computer record, but she encountered difficulties in making a decision about whether a loan 'fit' what one might call the plans or the rules embedded in the parameters for using a software package. Basically, the problem was that to agree a loan required that the request be done on a computer application, and this had been designed on the basis of various (perfectly reasonable) assumptions about what would be already known about the requesting client. These assumptions did not fit in this case.

> I did that this morning; it was one we had slight problems with because we only GAPP accounts (i.e. see if a loan is acceptable) with facilities (i.e. already agreed loan limits) in excess of £20,000 but I came to put it on the machine, and (the client has already) actually got a business card limit of £5000 and (there have been) negotiations (to extend that limit). ... Those two facilities (i.e. the business card limit and negotiations for a larger limit on that card) can't actually key into the GAPP machine, so I have to check with (managers elsewhere and higher up) to make sure I still have to GAPP it (i.e. put it through the process). ... It still needs a GAPP grade.

This shows that following the plan can involve more than can be specified by a literal interpretation of the plan (as in 'just do this' and 'just do that'). The example does not show that plans are irrelevant or worked at in an ad hoc way. What the example shows is that this individual was trying to figure out how to work in accordance with the plans, not merely to work around them. It shows too that doing so involves some kind of social process of definition, agreement, and accountability.

In short, plans, then, don't spell out everything in minute detail, nor are they fabricated without some persons doing particular jobs in particular places in mind. The example is suggestive of how plans are most often designed around the assumption that the users of them will be familiar with the circumstances in which those plans are to be followed or, as in this case, worked through. The muddle about GAPPing and overdrafts here had a solution; there was, in the plans, a route to figure it out. These plans were designed on the assumption that users are sufficiently trained in the tasks involved to get them done according to plan, and this meant given the normal, routine, practical circumstances in which they are to be used and this would sometimes entail getting permission, asking someone above, and so on.

In sum, fieldworkers should not be fooled by plans, nor should they ignore them. Plans are part of work and thus part of what needs to be understood when looking at work. Having said that, and to reiterate, the important issue for design is the degree to which the gap between plan and execution matters in practice: assessing how often and at what monetary and temporal cost these gaps occur is an important topic. After all, there may be remedies to the gap, solutions that make abiding by the rules easier to do. Indeed, as the application of technology becomes more entwined with the complexities of organisational working, so the challenges facing systems designers as regards these sorts of matters increase. Suchman's original insights, along with the results of a series of observations (our own included) in a whole range of workplaces, confirm the fact that planned activities are always subject to various worldly contingencies. Unless these are understood the success of systems can be brought into doubt. The added value of the fieldwork we have in mind lies, then, in recognising how the implementation of a plan is bound up with issues concerning Boden's (aforementioned) 'local logics' of day-to-day affairs. In the case of the bank assistant mentioned above, this is done in the knowledge that the assistant herself may be required to account for a decision, or make a case in ways that can be seen and understood as manifestly complying with organisational objectives and rules, despite the fact that in the case in question 'things didn't quite fit.'

The Power of Formal Procedures

So, plans and planfulness and what they might mean have both a historical and current importance in CSCW, one which fieldworkers ought to bear in mind. But, if truth be told, just what is at stake remains controversial. In what is, perhaps, best seen as an extension and exploration of Suchman's work, Schmidt (1997) suggests that the role of 'formal constructs' in cooperative work—plans being an exemplar of these—remains misunderstood and that few CSCW researchers have attempted to adequately address this issue:

> The prevalent understanding in CSCW of the status of formal constructs in cooperative work is problematic. The empirical evidence for the received understanding is not as robust as we may have believed and there is evidence from other studies that indicates that formal constructs are not always as feeble and ephemeral as we may have taken for granted.

Schmidt (1997) points to the success of various workflow technologies to suggest that

> The role of formal constructs is more differentiated than generally taken for granted. They not only serve as "maps" but also as "scripts" and that ... Instead of merely observing in case study after case study that procedures are impoverished abstractions when confronted with the multifarious and contingent nature of practical action, it is necessary to investigate precisely how they stipulate the articulation of cooperative work, how they are interpreted and used, designed and adapted by competent actors "who have to live with them from day to day."

Schmidt also points to some of the methodological issues that arise from ascribing what he calls excessive ceremonial status to constructs such as plans. He suggests that much of the debate surrounding Suchman's book implies that members of the organisational settings take formal constructs literally, as if plans for instance are supposed to be exhaustive specifications for doing work. Schmidt agrees that there should be continued detailed empirical investigation (although he did not want to endorse case study after case study, as we just saw in the quote above). But he also suggests that there may be differences in the use of formal constructs both between small and large-scale settings and between routine and nonroutine work activities and settings. This, Schmidt suggests, limits the extent to which we can generalize about plans and situated action. Certainly, we might note how plans often include fail-safe devices to cope with situations where things are not going to plan by specifying arrangements for adaptation of the plan to exceptions, unforeseen circumstances, and even for extensive revision. The plan may also incorporate mechanisms to oversee its own implementation and enforce its requirements. A feature of plans and procedures is that they develop and are modified; they unfold in realtime. What the plan means, what interdependencies there are, only become clear as the courses of action specified in the plan unfold, creating additional workloads in terms of coordination and the awareness of work.

Put very simply, the ethnographer would do well to pay attention to the gap between plans, procedures, and processes and the way things are actually done. This would include awareness of the influence of time constraints and knowledge constraints on how things get done: relations with customers, dealing with exceptional cases, the unfolding nature of planning, sensitivity to participants' view of good and bad ways of getting things done, the role of organisational 'language in the formulation and management of planning, issues of relevance and moral implicature, and so on (for instance as they pertain to help systems; see Randall et al. (1996)).

8.4 Artefacts

If there has been extensive debate about what plans might be then so too has there been extensive debate about artefacts in the workplace. Indeed, these debates go well beyond the limits of CSCW. Much of the competition between the candidate approaches to sociological and anthropological ethnography, for example, can be encapsulated as a set of competing claims about the materiality of the world. Hence, activity theory makes much of the way tools mediate activity; distributed cognition stresses the representational qualities of different objects; actor-network theory treats both human beings and objects as logically equivalent actants in the construction of systems. Regardless of the differences between different camps, these debates attest to the recognition that the materiality of the world, its 'thingi-ness' if you like, has a powerful role in the organisation of the world.

This concern has led to inquiries of the most diverse kind, but also ones that, although apparently distant from CSCW, have natural resonance with it. Yates, for example (1989), an organisational historian, described how in the late Victorian era memos, files, standard forms, and the like evolved to solve problems of 'distributed coordination', as organisations became larger and the problems of management and control correspondingly increased. According to her, these kinds of bureaucratic artefacts specifically evolved so as to func-tion in distributed organisations. Only with them could coordination of a cer-tain, document-centred type, occur. A particular step change in distributed organisations was enabled by the vertical filing cabinet, she argues, because it allowed easy storage and ready access to much more information than had been possible before. It allowed organisations to spread across distance without the burden of having to increase the number of bureaucratic centres.

Whatever one thinks of Yates's work, the point is that artefacts, things, have had a role in distributed systems since long before that term was used to label computer-based systems. Yates's work stands as testament to exten-sive inquiries. That the insight is old should not lead the contemporary fieldworker to avoid benefiting from the insight or ignoring it, however. Indeed, just as with social organisation, the fieldworker should assume that materiality is important and aim to explore how aspects of materiality affect the work in question.

At least two broad dimensions of effect have been shown to be important. The first is often labelled 'ecological', and refers not simply to any one arte-fact or object in work, but the bundles of artefacts in particular spaces that are constitutive of work as elegantly organised places. The second dimension has to do with how various subsets of objects and spaces act as mechanisms for mediation for needs to be done in a workplace. This is sometimes termed 'coordination through artefacts'.

Beyond this, a concern with artefacts can provide a tool for organising fieldwork. In particular, a fieldworker can use the lifecycle of certain types of artefacts as a guiding mechanism for organising her fieldwork; it can also help in analysis. This is particularly so when the artefacts in question are information carriers, embodied in one form or another (such as in a flight progress strip). We deal with the first two, both empirical, then the third, more programmatic, in turn.

Artefacts and Ecologies in the Workplace

Ethnographers in anthropology and sociology very quickly acquire the habit of drawing diagrams or taking photographs of 'where things are'. This has the not inconsiderable benefit of helping with their memory and offering them an easy way to show others what a setting is like. How they explore the spatial arrangements of things, whatever the things in question might be, is driven by the particular concerns that the ethnographers have: if it is in the religious beliefs of a culture, it might be in how the arrangement of artefacts reflects and guides understanding of the heavens above for example; if it is in the hierarchical structure of a society, for example, then artefacts are examined for how they betray the mechanisms of power. These are entirely legitimate concerns, but not necessarily the ones that pertain to design.

The ways that ecology relates is somewhat subtle, but once understood is enormously productive as a resource for design insight. Numerous researchers in CSCW and cognate disciplines have noted how, for example, the spatial organisation of workspaces turns out to be consequential for how work is possible. The office automation literature, for instance, is replete with spatial metaphors of one kind or another and this reflects this awareness. And, as we say in the introduction to this book, researchers in the human factors and the contextual inquiry traditions recognise that artefacts are an important topic of inquiry.

The question is, however, just how and in what ways. It seems to us that the fieldwork-for-design take on problems of the spatial organisation of those things (whatever they might be) has a particular nuance. It has been developed or at least explored not only by ourselves but perhaps more famously by Heath et al. (1996) and by Dourish (1995), amongst many others. The nuance is this (even if it does not appear a particularly radical form of observation). The ecological arrangement of things in a workplace does two things: it allows work to be done (and thus comes before work, if you will) and is part of how work gets done and is mediated (it is part of the work itself). One can put this another way. The first has to do with how things are arranged so that people can focus; the second is on what they focus. The difference here is subtle but important. The two aspects can also easily be confused: the how can be mistaken for the what and vice versa.

Without wanting to list the examples of such confusions in prior research, the important point is to realise that fieldworkers need to organise their concerns for artefacts in light of these two dimensions. They need to sketch some aspects of the spatial distribution of artefacts, for example, before focusing in detail on how some of those artefacts have special roles. In other words, some of their descriptions of the spatial ecology of a workplace are, if you like, necessary preambles to subsequent more detailed descriptions. A descriptive preamble does not mean an exhaustive description of the environment: this is not necessary or illuminating, but it does mean some kind of detailed descriptions indicative of how things in space (in a particular space, we should say) need to be organised in order that the work with particular things (such as documents) can be done.

223

Examples of the kinds of descriptions appropriate here can be illustrated by how a fieldworker might examine a desk and the artefacts on and around it. A desk can be many things: a symbol of status or a repository for orna- ment; for design, the concern is what does the particular ecological arrange- ment of things do for work. It is perhaps unsurprising that there have been numerous studies of desks and the things on them in CSCW and related areas (for a review see Sellen and Harper (2002)). We don't propose to review this literature with quite the concern we showed the literature on plans and planfulness and instead want to summarise what we think are the key things to learn from it. First of all, it should be obvious that a desk is at once the 'scenic locale' of work (where work is done) and the receptacle for some of the specific things that are oriented to in work. It is a place where both of the properties of thinginess we have mentioned are at play.

One might note, further, that there is a purposeful arrangement to the things that one finds there. Typically, one might expect to find that the most commonly used artefacts are those kept to hand: a description of what this means might therefore be appropriate. This is sometimes described in terms of an 'economy rule', that is to say as reflecting an economy of action oriented to by users (see Lee and Watson (1993)). Although seemingly obvi- ous, such an insight can be powerful. It takes attention away from the pre- sumption that the functions of computer systems on the desk top are all-encompassing, for example; it helps the fieldworker recognise that much work goes on around the computer (rather than within it). This work is undertaken through myriad often very simple artefacts, many of which have unique properties. It will lead the fieldworker to ask, for instance, questions about Post-it notes, taped-up messages, notepads, certain kinds of documentation and the annotations they might contain, all of which are economically kept at hand, that is, put in places where they can be seen easily, picked up readily, and referred to in a moment.

Why they are arranged this way might give the fieldworker initial insight into many things. For example it might help him understand the ubiquity and use of paper in the setting in question, something that is often worth- while. Paper is just one type of material tool that one finds on or around a desk; paper has many forms too: not just sheets and Post-it notes, but books and manuals; all these can come in paper form. But there will be other types of tools too: phones and calculators, and much else beside.

A significant feature of this way of looking is to distance the analysis from the kind of logical modelling that can tend to oversimplify. That is, a focus on the spatial arrangement of things, on their ecological patternings has the merit, or at least the distinctive quality, of recognising that different arte- facts can have different qualities dependent upon the way other artefacts are used in that place. This approach leads one away from the over-simple assumption that the medium of an artefact (that it is paper, for example) has universal properties that apply in all places and all times, rather than having properties whose salience is melded by the affordances of other artefacts and the process(es) of which the artefacts in question are a part. It is all too easy to slip into that manner of thinking that holds that there might be an observable and simple essence (or a model) underneath it all.

The spatial patterning itself can be brought to bear through the use of photographs, diagrams, and text, just as with nondesign-oriented ethnographies. Even the messiest of work desks – familiar to many academics – disguises some kind of order. There is always an ecological arrangement of sorts.

As one colleague said,

> I know . . . I'm messy aren't I? I work on the "If it's been there more than a year, its safe to throw it out" principle. But actually I can usually find things I need. Anything I really need to look at is just there (points to lower right-hand corner). . . . If I leave stuff there I know I have to deal with it. . . . All that stuff over there (points to left-hand side of desk) . . . well, if something crops up, I have to search through 'til I find it . . . but it hardly ever happens.

Beyond the Desk

Of course, some kinds of artefact are, so to speak, bolted into place and beyond the control of the individual who might use them. This does not invalidate the notion that these things, some fixed and some movable, are part of an ecology. The structure of this ecology will, in addition to this, have various forms. For example, the ecology may reflect a particular process, and thus a description of it can help map out or provide initial sketches of the process(es) in question. This is especially true where processes are tightly coupled through the sequential arrangement of physical artefacts, because rough descriptions of 'typical' processes are easy to find in the physical layout, and suffice to orient the fieldworker to what goes on. The account of the organisation of the piles on the desk, above, is indicative of how these piles reflect the binding of a particular ecology to a particular process (what needs to be done now, what can be put aside, what can be forgotten, and so on), for example.

If one of the benefits of having a concern with the ecological arrangements of a work domain is that it can encourage a recognition of diversity and complexity (and can thus avoid the misleading reductiveness often associated with certain types of logical modelling), a second benefit is that it helps orient the fieldworker to the possibility that small detailed ways in which artefacts are used can be important. Without an awareness of this possibility these details can be easily overlooked.

In our early work on the banks and building societies, for example, we noticed the arrays of Post-it notes, pasted documents on walls, and sets of drawers in which different materials were variously kept without being sure at first what these artefacts were doing. Whatever it was, it did not appear so important to work that the work might not be done without them; but then on the other hand they seemed important enough to be there so as to be a prerequisite for work. Questioning practitioners about the reasons for the arrangement of these things led to answers with the flavour of, 'Well, you can see the stuff you need straightaway, can't you?' or, 'Well, the reason I carry it around with me is that its organised so I can use it. . . . I put the stuff in there and I know exactly where it is. . . .'

As we reflected on this, we began to see that small details can often be important in understanding both larger processes and elements within processes, in being able to distinguish between the ways things enable work and the way they are sometimes the vehicle of work. So we began to examine and pay attention to how documents were frequently annotated, and this prompted further investigation into the typical kinds of information these annotations carried (and which included both informal customer information and, vitally, information about who was doing the annotating, allowing what was called 'bias discounting', although we won't say anything about that now). We began to see more clearly the importance of having information at a glance, and we saw how this could sometimes be a need that other techniques for mediating information failed to satisfy. The need for at-a-glance ability turned out to be why help screens and other information resources were seldom used in the bank, for example (see Randall et al. (1996)). This issue also had implications for question/answer forms of information searching.

Above all, our concern with details led us to recognise that clearly defined and standardised work processes did not, in this setting, guarantee standardised work. We were astonished to see one bank operative, being very evidently unproductive in a branch of the bank, appearing to fail because they had not created the necessary ecology of information that let him do the work. The work in question required, amongst other things, knowing, at a glance, where the forms where and who knew how to fill in any particular form, and so on, all of which was just the kind of information suffused on the Post-it notes and other artefacts in the ecology of the bank that this individual did not have. In short, he was 'failing' because he had not built the ecology necessary for his work.

Artefacts, Coordination, Paperwork

Given the central role of coordination within cooperative activities, the identification of the features of work that promote coordination is clearly important. Computer-based tools are obviously important here. But noncomputational ones are crucial too, and are highlighted through reference to the idea of the ecological. If we have pointed towards this with the everyday example of desks and the things on and around them, let us now turn

to explore the equally prosaic but typically more complex and organisationally salient ecological properties of what is often called paperwork. 'Paperwork' is a term that covers many things; not merely a label for bureaucratic burdens nor yet only a term for paper, any document can constitute paperwork.

An ecological concern can help the fieldworker recognise and come to understand the importance of paperwork in workplaces, an importance which is indeed sometimes viewed as a burden by workers themselves but which also offers them benefits (sometimes), although just what these may be may not seem to clear to the fieldworker when he or she first starts to look at paperwork. The reasons for this are to do with the fact that paperwork – or if you prefer, documents and records – is often glosses of what the work is and often disguises what work has been undertaken in its production. Documents, files, forms, memos, and so forth are at once the material that lets work be done and the material through which work is done. They are in many ways the most central ecological artefacts of organisational action.

Paperwork is then something that the fieldworker has to attend to very carefully. Key to grasping its role is to understand the relationship between it and the organisation in question, and this means both the organisation as it is manifest in the physical arrangement of things 'there and then,' and in the relationship of documents to the organisation through time and space. If a fieldworker can get to know what a record represents he will have got to know the work that produced it and what the paperwork means within this activity in question, and within this organisation. What documents mean, what they refer to, and what they might indicate, have everything to do with their place within an organisational setting: a fieldworker can get to understand this by looking ecologically at paperwork. In this view, paperwork is an organisational object that represents and displays organisational activities. As we say, it might be complained about, lamented even, but here, perhaps almost more than anywhere else, the fieldworker can get to grips with what the organisation is in terms of the things, the artefacts, that constitute it.

Over the years, many researchers have explored this. Paperwork is thus often the title of a major element in a fieldwork work treatise. Indeed, so commonplace is this that one even reads puns about the size of the paperwork burden being dealt with in any study and hence claims about the importance of the research itself. This levity should not disguise the commonly recognised importance of paperwork, however. As the body of research on paperwork has built up, so insights about paperwork have become more solidified and clear; indeed, now they can be presented as a list, as we do below. This list shows that however mundane and dull a piece of paper or a Microsoft Outlook Schedule Plus memo might appear to be, paperwork is a treasure for research.

Paperwork is:

- Integral to the socially organised patterns of work
- Representative of organisational objects and actions
- A sediment of an organisation's activities, inquired into and used for accountability
- The 'shared material' of organisations
- Politically important as reflected in regulated access which in turn describes the hierarchical order of organisations
- Has a procedural implicativeness in it (as in a form implies what is next and what has gone before)

To understand paperwork therefore means to understand the local because all the above are achievable only if one knows how, when, and in what ways a document fits a particular organisational setting. Lists such as these are not always entirely easy to grasp, at least at first reading, so let us illustrate how a fieldworker might orient to paperwork as a tool for his own analytical work. What this list is saying is that, as a form, for example, passes through any organisation, it can gather additions of various kinds that make plain who has handled it and what action has been taken as a result. In some cases this history can provide a stratified trace of the activities of the organisation. Members of an organisation can and often do routinely interrogate the form to see if the work has been done properly by those with rights to do so. It is not just auditors who do this, but almost anyone within the organisation trying to see whereabouts the work is.

The point here, however, is that so too can the fieldworker: indeed he can test his own understanding of the setting by asking himself whether he can read the history of a form. Once he has done this the fieldworker can then begin the task of examining how forms provide a trace of organisational work and thus come to be tools for co-ordinating tasks across divisions of labour. This is because the work visible on a form makes the divisions of labour visible or, if you prefer, socially available. The fieldworker will also come to see how such ready availability of information (concerning where the organisation is) also facilitates a certain degree of flexibility on the part of the members of the organisation, allowing them to respond to myriad contingencies. In other words, as a 'mechanism of interaction' (Schmidt 1993) paperwork acts to facilitate the coordination of work.

Now, in reading the above one might be led into thinking that forms exist alone or by themselves. Of course they don't. By way of ending this section let us note that documents fit in ways that are bound up with their ecological location. This entails meshing and modal transformations as in when a form is moved from paper to digital and back again (Anderson et al., 1989; see also Harper et al. (2001)). It's all paperwork, but the documents in question are

of different kinds, doing different things in different ways for people with different jobs. That is why paperwork is important to the fieldworker.

Artefacts and Information Lifecycles

If the ecological arrangement of artefacts and the ways in which artefacts enable coordination is central to design fieldwork, then artefacts have been seen to also provide a route to help organise the mechanics of fieldwork. They do so in ways that can generate resources for comparison and analysis beyond what is possible with a strict concern with ecology and co-ordination, at least as we have just explored these themes. Now this methodological topic is somewhat different to the primary one of this chapter, analytic orientation. But these preceding discussions of artefacts make this extended aside worthwhile, and certainly easier to comprehend than if we noted this elsewhere in the book.

In particular, over the years one tried and tested way of defining a programme of fieldwork is on the basis of what is called the 'lifecycle of artefacts' (Harper, 1998; also Harper et al. (1996)). As it happens, in most organisations, the thing in question is information and its various embodiments. Thus the term 'information lifecycle' is more often used. This term points towards the fact that information is marshalled, is worked up, reviewed, circulated, used, stored, and then forgotten about. Information within organisations has, if you will, a birth, a life, and a death. Furthermore, during its life, information will exist, as suggested above, in various modalities, including in documents of one kind or another, databases, and even marks on an object going through a production line, or the shape of an object itself. Whatever its form, one way a researcher can get around an organisation is by following the lifecycle of the key information in that organisation.

To some degree at least, all organisations can be seen as having an information lifecycle. Thus, studies of air traffic control (which the authors have been involved in) were organised around the same idea. That is to say that the key features of this organisation and hence the organisation of its study were mapped out by use of the device of following the information lifecycle. To explain, when entering the operations room at London Air Traffic Control Centre, the tyro ethnographer can have little sense of how flight progress strips play an important part in the work. One might, in much the way we speak of it above, have a vague idea of what goes on but one can be confident that any understanding will be superficial and wanting. But one can learn a great deal, and quickly, simply by planning the early stages of the fieldwork around the lifecycle of the information used by controllers, namely information used on such things as the paper flight progress strips. Doing this will lead the fieldworker to learn about where that information comes from, where it goes, and what uses it gets put to throughout.

229

The important features of information lifecycles are the junctures in the work, the way in which information is organised to be used at each stage in question, and the rhythms of work activity that result. To emphasise the point, this focus allows comparisons to be made, and hence both generalisations to be made and differences to be identified. Thus and for instance, to refer to air traffic control again, in civilian ATC the important stage occurs when the controllers are using the strips. The activities here are complex and subtle, and this reflects the overall organisation of the airways and the relationship between pilots and controllers. In a phrase, because the civilian airspace system is flexible, the controlling is complex.

In contrast, in military control the juncture in the cycle when controllers actually use strips is one that causes few problems. Controlling in military operations is, to put it bluntly, rather facile. Controllers rarely have any difficulties undertaking this part of their work; it is relaxed and unproblematic. This is because of the character of the relationship between the pilots and the controllers and the different flight procedures in operation. Military controllers have to bring military pilots together, and it is the pilots who solve all collision difficulties. However, military control does have its problems, but these occur at another juncture. This juncture is when the rostering of staff occurs. For in military Ops, there can be very little prediction of what the workload will be: air exercises will be undertaken at short notice reflecting such things as the weather and the need for the practice of emergency operations. As a result, it is difficult to determine how many staff should be on duty at any one time. Often military control finds it has staff idle; a few hours later it may have too few staff on duty. Their problem, the problem of military ATC, is being able to predict what work will arrive and when.

These examples help demonstrate the claim that reference to the information lifecycle can enable the fieldworker to map out fundamental differences in the organisation of two (or more) work settings which might at first glance seem quite similar. The differences might turn out to be in the information lifecycle and in the emphases and rhythms that result. It may appear to be the same information that flows through an organisation, but careful examination of its life may show how each is different. Furthermore, this way of organising fieldwork can enable the researcher to determine matters that are relevant to any specific locus of work within that lifecycle.

If one wants to design systems to support work, one needs to bear in mind these factors, amongst others. An interface for the use of electronic flight progress strips in civilian ATC needs to be designed in recognition of the fact that the relationship between the controller and the pilots, controller and controller, and the patterns of airspace procedure they are part of is extremely important. In contrast, an interface for Military ATC would demand little in terms of subtlety or thoughtfulness. What would be harder to design is a work schedule.

8.5 The Flow of Work

If these discussions have dealt with how objects in a place are important topics of a study, then the next set of themes has to do with matters that can be, at times, well removed from the embodied: they have to do with what it is (or how it is) people reflect upon and orient to, when at work. This topic is all about the reasoning procedures people use when doing a job. In effect, we are referring to intuitions concerning what people are attending to when they are trying to do their work, in particular with the flow of work. The flow of work can be thought of as the temporal, and more specifically, the sequential and concurrent organisation of work activities. So far so simple, but as before, the way we want to consider it is in part through a contrast with more directive and idealised conceptions. The conceptions we have in mind this time are related to what is often called workflow. In our mind, where workflow contains an element of how work ought to be organised, an analysis of the flow of work concerns how it is actually organised. It seems to us, and indeed the literature affirms this, that design fieldwork should concern itself with the realities of the flow of work and rather less with workflow.

That there is a difference between the realities of work and the ideal of work is of course a commonplace. We saw that human factors researchers undertake fieldwork precisely to discover what this difference might be; we saw too that contextual inquiry urges consideration of contingency, flexibility, and so on; and as we saw in the research and debates that Lucy Suchman's book (ibid.) engendered, there can be many muddles and confusions to analytically exploring plans and actions. Although there is no news in saying that what is done does not quite fit how things ought to be done, it seems to be something that researchers seem to want to keep recasting and restating in new ways.[52] Indeed, one might say that a peculiar property of the debates that result is their repetitive nature: one would sometimes think that every time a fieldworker goes into the field she has to discover for herself that things are not quite what they seem in the formal plans and charts. Perhaps one of the reasons for this dullness of mind is that researchers are not always fully aware of the subtle ways in which the distance between the ideal and the actual manifests itself, and the ways in which it should be investigated. If, as we saw, the relationship between plans and action is complex and can certainly not be encapsulated by one single maxim, then so too is the distance between the flow of work and the formal descriptions of that work; it is complex, subtle, and diverse.

---

[52]See, for instance, the special edition of the journal *CSCW* on the Co-ordinator, a workflow tool designed to allow flexibility but which was critiqued for not doing so (Harper, 1995, pp. 43–46.); as too are debates about the particular role of workflow technologies, where it is often said that they fail or succeed to the extent to which they either support or inhibit workarounds or flexibility (see for example Dourish (1995)).

Nevertheless this relationship is traceable as long as the researchers orient to certain thematics and so make themselves sensible to specific topics. The topics themselves have to do with matters that are, as we say, peculiarly minded in the sense that they are largely about how individuals orient their own actions to the actions of others and how they deploy skills in light of what they think others' skills might be at any moment in time. These matters are themselves bound up with locations, with time, and with places. The topics have to do with what we earlier called the mental geography of the workplace (although as we say we do not want to imply any warrant for psychological claims in this term). In any event, this focus on the flow of work provides for attention to such matters as interruptions, good and bad practices, seeking help, making mistakes, and so on.

Awareness of Work

The first of these has to do with 'awareness of work'. This refers to the way in which work tasks are made available to others, in the sense of being visible, traceable, and noticeable; basically it is a label for the various ways people in a workplace can see what is going on. This visibility, typically called 'accountability' in the ethnomethodological literature, plays a fundamental role in the real-world, realtime social organisation of work, whatever that work might be. Moreover, the various ways in which awareness is developed, the ways in which work is made public and available to others, are not separate from the work itself, but are essential ingredients in doing the work.

We should perhaps point out here that 'awareness of work' is intended to be a rather more specific usage than 'awareness' per se. As has been pointed out (Schmidt, 2002), the term 'awareness' is open to any number of different meanings and can carry with it an assortment of intellectual baggage. Our usage has much to do with the sense in which Heath et al. (2002, p. 346) use the term when they speak of a 'phenomenal domain . . . a domain which directs our attention to a complex body of socially organised practice and reasoning.' So, for example, the layout of different offices and, within them, the layout of individual workspaces, permits the development of an ecology of awareness. Properties of this ecology may be as simple as the fact that people are co-located, and doing much the same things, or who are performing 'stuff that needs to be done together' because of their interdependency. This results in co-workers being able to ask for advice from others nearby just when it is needed, for example, and it allows the updating of colleagues as one is passing. Co-proximity allows 'gangs of workers' to deal with emergencies, when all hands are needed,, and more. In other words, awareness of work can often be informal, often intermittent, and support events that are facilitated by appropriate spatial layouts of work areas.

Similarly, the visible state of desks, where someone is in their 'heap of stuff', where they have got to in their pile of paperwork, furnishes to others information about what the person is doing and to where that person has got. All this allows measures of how busy they are, how slow they are, and even if they are struggling. Such information lets others update themselves on the state of all of their work (i.e. the team's), how it is going, whether 'we are behind,' 'on top of it,' and so on. The point about such properties is that they represent arrangements which are used in the day-to-day doing of work.

Awareness and Modal Transformation

These arrangements have various particular properties. If we have just sketched out how people are aware of each other's activities by dint of being near, then another way in which awareness is achieved is through the modal transformation of information that people share. This has a clear relationship to the previously considered notion of 'information lifecycles' but emphasises the specific organisation of information at a particular point or locus within this cycle.

One illustration of this is the way in which information may be extracted from different computer and other records and reconfigured when put to different purposes. What the various transformations do in this case is facilitate coordination through appropriate representations of the basic information. This is a process that is deeply involved in coordination, by making the work available to others in a form on which they work, that is, representing the work within the work so that others can do theirs. In many cases, these transformations serve to routinise work by using standard procedures and standard formats for representing the tasks done and the tasks to do.

So, one of the properties of formatting is the way in which it can proceduralise representation and, through this, represent the work to others for particular purposes. The format functions as a set of instructions in both information creation and its use. Different computer records and paper forms are, in this way, designed to collect standard information, to make the information comparable, and to control the information that is provided.[53]

Despite the obvious benefits of standardised processes and formats, the format does not always, in itself, convey an adequate sense of the work,

---

[53]In this respect the use of formats and so on are solutions to what one might think of as the administrator's problem of the assembly of information in organisations identified by Garfinkel (1967). The problem here is what information is needed and what is its 'value'. That is, it has to do with such things as the worth of collecting the information with reference to the effort involved in its collection, an issue highlighted in the earlier section on decision making.

however. Sometimes more is needed: local knowledge, for example, skills developed over time to help make sense of documents that, as it were, don't speak for themselves: in this way what documents afford is sometimes more than what they can embody (Anderson and Sharrock, 1993).

Awareness of Work and the Sense of Organisation

> I wouldn't say to the customer, "I've got to go to *the Bank* (to get a decision), because *I'm* the Bank."

A further sense of awareness is seldom mentioned in the literature, but is, it seems to us, nevertheless important, as attested to in the above quote. It has to do with the 'sense of the organisation'.

We have just been arguing that workers orient to the routine character of the work and its setting by noting how they look at the piles on other people's desks and so on. We have noted too that workplaces are organised so that events are seen for the order they have. Activities within an organisation are performed in ways which ensure their recognisability, their visibility as the actions that they are, as exemplifying organisational routines. In a wider and more general sense, though, what we are trying to get to at this point is that workers are normally well aware of their work as part of some larger institution and that their work activities are the work of and represent the organisation. The very characterisation of them as, for instance, bank workers, or as people with specific job titles, calls them into play as people who are organisationally positioned and people who have organisationally prescribed responsibilities and tasks.

At the same time, there are limits to this awareness and recognising them can be extremely useful in fieldwork. Our bank studies threw up a number of examples of the problem of new or tyro staff who manifested their lack of particular kinds of awareness, not knowing who to approach for information or help, for example, or not knowing how various procedures were locally accomplished, and not knowing, worst of all, how they might embody the bank (as per the quote above).

If there is then this larger sense of organisation, between this and the awareness enabled by working together, there is a sense of how the larger organisation works, across distance and time, whatever the organisation as a whole might be. In our studies of banks, problems of coordination that we observed sometimes had to do with the fact that groups of workers in one location had little or no knowledge of the practices of other groups elsewhere. This was exemplified in something as trivial as organizing the passing of information and work to another workplace and not recognising that this coincides with their lunch break, and then complaining about a lack of response.

Linked to this is the notion of the egological organisation of a working division of labour we discuss below. As an encountered phenomenon, the

division of labour becomes not so much a smooth, highly integrated, and planned framework but a weave of activities that can and often do fragment into diverse tasks and jobs. That is, immersion in a division of labour on a day-to-day basis is experienced as a stream of differentiated and discrete tasks to be done, of forms to be completed, of accounts to be prepared and with which to be dealt. Individual performance within a working division of labour is consequently bounded by horizons of relevance which formulate concerns relevant to the tasks to be accomplished. This can be manifested in some very simple ways, as with casual questions to colleagues, where that awareness is constituted in knowing that there is someone else who might be able to resolve your problem.

As we show, this deceptively simple idea contains in it some serious consequences for design, insofar as it relates to the speed, elegance, and simplicity with which problems can be solved (or not, as the case may be). It can be exemplified by some rather more oblique considerations, as in the fact that in many areas of work it is important to let other people know where you're up to, and this is certainly true of financial services as it is of other work settings too. The contingencies of working life mean that, for instance, customers may make enquiries to people other than those who are dealing with their case. This leads to a fairly common practice in work which involves annotating files, forms, and the like so as to indicate for other potential users of information what has been done and what remains to be done, as with:

> The survey shows a lot of problems. We need to get in touch with Mr ... and tell him about the damp. He may not wish to proceed.

This simple fact of working life (i.e. making it clear where the work has reached), however, is still arguably not taken seriously enough by systems designers (although flagging work done is a feature of some more recent CSCW systems). It is, equally, not something that the design of many work-flow tools would suggest has been taken seriously either. Perhaps this is one reason why fieldworkers persist in reporting as new the finding that how work is done does not reflect how it ought to be done. As we noted, how-ever, the key for the fieldworker is not to discover this so much as to map out the distance between the ought and the actual. The fact that work is often picked up and put down, often by more than one person, is some-thing that might need investigating; that necessary artefacts have to be kept handy as visible signs both that there are things that need comple-tion, for example, is also something that might be examined, that work can often only be completed with the assistance and knowledge of others, are all important resources that ensure how work ought to be done and at least ori-ented to, if not achieved. These and more are always going to be important when thinking of workflow technologies.

The Egological

One of the most obvious problems that workflow type technologies have is that they cannot be designed to encompass the delicate web of mutual understanding that coheres a work team. The tasks performed by any one individual form an interdependent part of larger sequences of tasks done by others within a workgroup and a workflow may only support some of these. Yet, one of the features of such divisions of labour is that particular tasks are, most often, performed by individuals. There is then a balance between what is 'mine' and what is of 'others' concern, a balance that is flexible, changing with the vagaries of daily routine but robust enough to be accountable. After all, knowing what is one's own task and what is another's is an important way in which one can judge and have one's managers judge whether one has done a good job.

The importance of this balance is such that it is reflected in being given its own name in the ethnomethodological literature. The orientation is called 'the egological principle of organisation' by Anderson et al. (1989), although it is less often used in the CSCW literature. Nevertheless it is worth using here because what is meant by it is now a regular component of claims made in CSCW, even if the term egological seems to be avoided itself. Anderson et al. (1989, p. 161) note: 'From the point of view of an actor in a division of labour, working through the endless stream, getting things done, means doing-what-I-do and passing tasks on to others so they can do what they do.'

What this label draws attention to is that, from the point of view of a person within a division of labour, the practical accomplishment of the work requires learning about and knowing how to use those artefacts, files, documents, and systems that are relevant not only to oneself but others too.

For the fieldworker, the difficulty in analysis is to capture the balance between what is shared and what is individual, between what one might call the fragmented and the individualised, the interdependent and the cohered, without ending up describing a division of labour that does not 'fit' together. Anderson et al. use words like 'consociation', and 'gearing into' the social world of work to point towards the subtleties that are required. As they write (Anderson et al., 1989, pp. 159–160), 'to move . . . to the exploration of how activities in a division of labour are encountered and perceived by those working within it . . . what becomes prominent at the mundane level is not integration but the fragmentation of activities and task performance.'

The 'egological principle' is then a complex aspect of working life. It is not merely the ability to 'just do things'; it is an ability to do this by an awareness that 'these are the things that I do given that those people over there do that.' The detailed understanding that 'this is my work,' that 'these are the processes that I accomplish before handing on to someone else'

enables workers to do many things, from the most vital to the most prosaic. For example, it can let them quickly evaluate an interruption. The phone call, shout, or personal approach can be seen as either 'their problem' or 'not their problem but someone else's problem.' Although interruptions may seem minor, interruptions can play an important part in what Gasser (1986) called 'articulation work'–the meshing of particular work processes and tasks to produce some finished 'product'.

One way the fieldworker can unpack the egological is to examine work according to the questions participants might ask themselves as they do it, notably, 'What must I do next ?' Such questions specifically draw attention to the way in which work may be interrupted, the things may be picked up and put down, the way that work may be left incomplete as more pressing matters have to be dealt with, and so on.

Our studies of the financial sector, for instance, raised the issue of what customer services might mean from the perspective of the individual working within a larger division of labour and did so in a way that is quite different from, let us say, business process approaches which do not consider the egological. Take a cashier at a bank counter: the concerns that dominate his decision making are the length of the queue and what might be the problem that the next customer brings with her. The queue must be kept flowing, because customers who have to wait become dissatisfied, but at the same time each individual customer must have his query dealt with to his satisfaction, whatever it might be. This may seem, on the face of it, obvious and straightforward but this is less so once observation makes the sheer range of queries apparent. Customers introduce a very high level of unpredictability into the flow of work. The cashier needs to know what he can deal with and what he can't, and if he can't, what ought to be done to help the customer. Sending a customer to someone else to solve the problem keeps the queue moving but it is not a case of handing jobs over to anyone. It is handed over to someone who can answer the customer's query.

It is not just bank cashiers where the egological orientation to the fitting of the next customer to the workflow is an issue. In a study of museum work, for instance, we noted how curators took turns at answering telephone queries. Of interest here was the fact that they had to be attentive to the nature of the query (and therefore often had to do clarification work in order to formulate the question), who was asking (thus and for instance, requests from television reporters, academics, and casual enquirers might all have to be dealt with differently), and they had to figure out how to go about finding out the answer which raised the issue of 'knowing who knows' – a form of organisational knowledge that is still too seldom dealt with. (However, see Groth and Bowers (2001), and Larsson (2005).) Furthermore, and for a variety of reasons, not every query could be dealt with 'here and now'. Queries were sometimes so unusual that no procedure existed for dealing with them, so time consuming that to follow them to their conclusion could mean an ever-lengthening queue, or the information available was not adequate to provide a solution. Sometimes saying no was the best thing to do. One might note too the importance of 'demeanour work' in these situations, insofar as part of what goes on has to do with convincing customers that everything that reasonably can be done, has been done, and finding ways to send the customer away satisfied, perhaps with a telephone or postal answer. The egological is not just a matter of work then, but of showing that work is being done.

In a roundabout way we are saying that observation in the field needs to concern itself with what this customer wants here and now, and rather less with, say, what the computer system is structured to do, because it is the former which determines what the worker will be required to do next, not the latter. This has more than a little significance for design: consider the user interface. If one finds, as indeed one does all too often in customer-facing work, that the information available on screens is not pertinent to solving customers' problems, then there are almost certainly lessons for how to respecify what information is available onscreen.

The answer to this is not to model how the worker would prefer to navigate through information without reference to the vagaries of the customer-driven request, it is to focus on those vagaries as the basis of information layout and design. It is understanding the character of interruption that is important. And, one should note that oftentimes the interruptions do not just affect what the worker will need to do to satisfy the customer, but often affect what the worker was doing that had no reference to the customer. Even bank cashiers have work that is not customer-facing. Yet that work is often interrupted by customers. This work has to be picked up and put down as customers appear. One solution that cashiers often turn to as a case in point is to get their colleagues to pick up their work as and when they are free to do so. Thus what started off as being tasks that 'I do' can end up being tasks that 'others are doing'; what was meant to be a division of labour can sometimes dissolve into 'all do anything and everything' every time a customer comes along and asks, 'Can you help me?' In other words, the egological can sometimes appear to dissolve in a moment. The paradox for the fieldworker interested in design is to figure out why, when, and how.

Skills and Expertises

Charles Perrow was one of the first organisational theorists to produce a conception of technology that had to do with its use in practice rather than its hypothetical performance. Books such as *Normal Accidents* (Perrow, 1984) and *Complex Organizations* (Perrow, 1972) provided a basis for the ethnographic turn in the early years of CSCW. The perceived value of ethnographic methods, and the sociological focus implied by them, was that

they were thought, rightly, to encourage analysis of work in terms of outcomes, outcomes of the intersection of the social and the technical, of how the social is embedded in making the technical 'work', and vice versa. From the outset, CSCW was concerned to avoid viewing process outcomes as wholly a product of the functionalities of the technology. The skills which allow system functionalities to be realised were thought to be worth investigating in their own right. At the same time, skills were recognised as having limits, and these too were thought worthy of examination. Limits in training, the complexity and rarity of problems, were recognised, from the outset of CSCW, as potential resources for designing better technical support fir human–computer interaction.

Skill, of course, is only relevant if it is employed in pursuit of objectives which are consistent with those of the official organisation. There is little point, therefore, for the fieldworker to merely describe skills, because what is important is whether those skills are necessary to efficient and effective practice. Thus, a major analytic focus of fieldwork for design is the deployment of skill, and particularly how skills relate to the business objectives of the organisation. This in turn relates to the effective deployment of technology within that context. That is, decisions about appropriate technology must relate to the value of the skills that are used. Nevertheless, and it is an important point, understanding the limits of skill vis-à-vis technology is only possible if one wants to have adequate descriptions of the skills in play in the first place. Those descriptions may not otherwise be available to decision makers.

Skill is obviously dependent on the specific work context, and it is difficult, not to say impossible, to generalise about the skills that are likely to be found in a given domain. Nevertheless, certain pointers are available in the literature which can be used to orient the fieldworker towards aspects of skill which otherwise do tend to remain invisible.

A study of breast screening conducted by Hartswood et al. (2000a,b, 2003) exemplifies this well. Here, the authors make use of the concept of 'professional vision' (Goodwin, 1994). Professional vision has to do with what being a competent practitioner entails. It invokes in particular the ability to distinguish between 'normal' and 'abnormal', 'territories of normal appearance' and territories of 'incongruity' (Sacks, 1972). Examples from their data include the following accounts of how experts read mammograms in such a fashion that they can see more than is visible to the untrained eye and, in this instance, more than is visible to a computer-aided detection system (see also Driessen (1999)):

I'm having trouble seeing the calc it's picked up there ... (pointing) ... I can only think it's an artefact on the film (a thin line at the edge of the film).

I'm surprised the computer didn't pick that up ... my eye went to it straight away.

> This lady's got lots of little blobs everywhere ... but they're not very interesting and I'm going to let her go.
>
> ... just making sure there's nothing the other side (using fingers) ... and there is ... a bit of chalk but its harmless.

As Clarke et al. explain, these experts are able to spot abnormalities within the films they read. Thus the positioning of an object in a particular area of the breast renders it more suspicious than if it had been elsewhere. At the same time they note that certain areas within the mammogram are regarded as more difficult than others to interpret and professionals particularly orient to them in their examinations. The social distribution of expertise again becomes evident, as these professionals also frequently express the opinion that one or other of their colleagues is better at 'spotting' some cancers than others.

Professional vision also crops up in a study of a steel mill (Clarke et al., 2003). In this case, it involved some kind of comparison between what the computer said and what an operator's experience and skill said was the case. This was most obvious where the operator overrode a computer scheduler in some way. So, for example, it was common for the most experienced operators to go into manual for the last few passes of putting slabs of metal through the machinery. This was because their experience had taught them that '... the computer pisses about [i.e. gets it wrong] (when the speed its low) ... does 4–5 passes ... that's what causes turn-up,' and 'because it says 45 the computer tries to do it in 3–4 passes when you can do it in 2.... It's to do with the pacing of the mill ... we're rolling plates quicker than the computer thinks we are.'

Local Knowledge

The professional knowledge of readers of mammograms and the know-how of operators in a steel mill are both forms of local knowledge. The concept has its roots in the idea of tacit knowledge which itself has a relatively long history in the social and human sciences. Michael Polyani (1966) is usually credited with the notion. Local knowledge is a concern that has been developed by ethnomethodological enquiry and has entailed studies of how knowledge is bound to the specifics of particular workplaces. Both concepts have something to do with the kind of distinction, made by Ryle (1963) originally between 'know-how' and 'know what'. A focus on this distinction serves to remind us that not all knowledge is procedural or propositional. Knowledge, as more recent writings increasingly show (see Ackerman et al. (2003)), can be seen as embodied, as difficult or impossible to articulate, and as sometimes taking a radically different form to that which is anticipated in the orthodox knowledge management literature.

Uncovering this local knowledge, whether it be know-how or know-what, embodied or articulated, is then an obvious focus for fieldwork. Once again, it contrasts with process-oriented methods such as BPR, which are of course based on approaches to standardisation. There ought to be no surprise in this, because standardisation has been an objective since the time of Frederick Taylor. However, there is, of course, a rather important issue at stake in that it may well turn out to be the case that there are limits to how far standardisation can be successfully implemented in situations where local knowledge is key to the effective completion of work. Indeed, our own observations have shown that, for instance, even in environments where standard business processes are in operation, local differences almost inevitably arise, which have to do with the distribution of resources and, more importantly, local knowledge.

In other words, where it may be presumed that it is the processes that are producing efficiency, it may be that it is only in conjunction with local knowledge that tasks can be efficiently performed. This is not an argument against standardisation, but against the simple presumption that it is standardisation alone that produces business rewards. Local knowledge can, of course, take an almost infinite number of forms but would certainly include knowledge of local aspects of the business operation, local aspects of the environment, and local knowledge of the distribution of knowledge and skill through the organisation (knowing who knows).

Some of this knowledge is often in semi-codified forms, and thus one feature that one can legitimately prescribe as being of interest to the fieldworker is attention to the local organisation of knowledge resources. Thus, the existence of 'bibles' is well known to fieldworkers: files, books, or what have you, in which individuals keep large amounts of information that is relevant to their work and not readily obtainable elsewhere. Bibles are very useful resources for an awareness of the information that workers find useful but their existence is not always recognised by the organisation. As one bank operative put it:

> ...carry these mortgage bibles around ... and other policies ... then there's products and handy info like the thing that's on your crib sheets ... marketing initiatives and competitions. All this could be on the screen. You could have your frauds, like your dodgy solicitors and accountants, telephone lists and other useful info, but we want it all organised so you'll use it.

Observations of this kind raise important issues for knowledge use and retrieval, for they imply that 'at-handedness' is important even in nonsafety- and nontime-critical environments. There is an important issue having to do with the formulation of questions, as mentioned above. It certainly seemed to us at the time that having things 'organised so that you'll use it' had to do with the personal structuring of information resources such that problems of indexing, understanding titles, formulating questions in an appropriate way, and so on disappeared. It does, of course, raise the issue of how and whether databases can usefully be structured so as to provide this kind of information without increasing rather than decreasing the overhead of use (see Randall et al. (1996)).

Equally, it is a feature of local knowledge that some people have more of it than others, and it is often worth investigating how certain individuals are commonly recognised as local experts to be used collaboratively, or contrastively how relevant knowledge can emerge out of a set of different and distributed knowledge deployed at a problem (see Normark and Randall (2005)). We have referred to this as the social distribution of expertise and it carries a clear implication not always recognised by fieldworkers of organisations, particularly of the 'celebratory' kind (i.e. those who took Suchman's work as emphasising the merits of the informal). This has to do with the self-evident fact that ways of working can implicate people doing things well or badly. Now, we would never seek to defend a variety of fieldworkers who aimed at identifying who did their work badly (or well) but it is quite another thing to identify what it means to do something well or badly. This has an obvious relationship to the notion of skills and expertise that we have discussed.

The existence of local knowledge, and its differential distribution across the organisation, has potential consequences for policy decisions which relate to human resources issues. For instance, one of the issues that is commonly discussed in many management strata today is that of devolved decision making. Human relations credos often advocate the devolution or dispersal of decision-making capacity to localities, but the extent of local knowledge is clearly relevant to this, in that if decision making were devolved to individuals who were not party to local knowledge, nor had a means to access it, problems might arise. On the other hand, the value of devolution is held to lie in considerable economies of reduced time and less duplication of effort. If devolution were a strategy to be adopted, it would suggest the nature and distribution of local knowledge might become a requirement for a distributed knowledge base. A flavour of the complexities involved in this is given by the following comments from operatives involved in mortgage processing work.

> You always come across these that you've never heard of before. You always go to the expert ... that's what you've heard all through your career.

> We're supposed to send all mortgage enquiries to the advisors ... we shouldn't have to ... there's some we can handle.

> A lot of time and emotional energy is spent on berating people who get things wrong ... you know, like leaving out codes on forms, miscalculating premiums, incomplete Miras forms and suchlike ... we don't always have the time.

> There's no permanent staff who really know their job inside out ... we've too many people doing a bit of everything ... with this one, the client has been sitting there for days waiting for the valuer because the instructions got sent to the wrong address.

Skill, 'Fit', and Organisational Change

This concern with skill is still uncovering interesting and unexpected aspects of technology use and so one cannot conclude on what has been learnt in the CSCW corpus: it is evolving. For example, we made brief reference above to issues of temporality, rhythm, and so on, and here we might elaborate a little on how research from well before the emergence of CSCW is infusing some new topics and dimensions for the exploration of skill that are still current even as we write.

For instance, Mumford's (1963) study into the temporal regularity produced by the clock and Zerubavel's (1985) thoughtful inquires into temporal rhythms, have recently come into prominence as various contemporary researchers have tried to explore the problem of how skills and their deployment are organised with reference to time, and the problem of how, through time, organisations change and skills evolve (see for instance Reddy and Dourish (2002)).

Taking the first: skills through time, the relevance of rhythms in everyday working life has begun to help researchers account for the way work might be driven by available time, something that is too often overlooked but which we have attempted to point towards above. We might think of these 'rhythms' as having various kinds of temporality. There is 'timeliness', i.e. getting things done so as to deal with immediate time constraints. Another is 'orientation to future information needs' which has to do with how people orient what they are doing now to what future expectations might be. These can be anything from a concern for the prospect of being busy to a concern for what information needs others will have in the future.

How skills change through time is more perplexing. It is, nevertheless, central to any inquiry into working life. It has to do not simply with time, but with how what one might call the generational use of knowledge and know-how might shift over fairly long periods of time. Technology is obviously likely to be important in giving momentum to such changes. Change is ever-present in organisations of course; the issue here is one of scale. If in our bank studies we were party to a gradual shift in the distribution of skill and know-how, the pace of such change was, it has to be said, rather modest, although the potential was sufficiently great as to warrant our own and other investigations. More generally, changes can take years to take effect, as Davenport (1994) notes. The important point is that the impact of technology may not always be immediately apparent, but neither may the impact of skill deployment on the effectiveness of the system. This has a relevance to notions of adaptability in business, inasmuch as all changes in business processes are intended to allow organisations to adapt to changes in the environment readily and flexibly. The way in which changes unravel over time is subtle. Consider this extract of a senior manager in an engineering firm:

> We've been particularly worried recently about the use of spreadsheets … in our company everyone uses spreadsheets for analysis and forecasting … but

we're getting mistakes . . . for instance, in one case two spreadsheets were merged and the people who did it obviously didn't understand the functions . . . the really worrying thing is that the data got all the way to me before it was noticed. . . . I looked at the data and I knew it was wrong. . . . It's not as if I know anything about spreadsheets, but I do know the business . . . and I've got all these figures and I knew they were wrong . . . we think that there's a process where the people who set the spreadsheets up have left or retired and new appointees are just assuming it all works fine without checking. It's as though they have this faith in systems, perhaps because they haven't lived through all the problems there were when the new systems get put in place.

Furthermore, the relationship between skill and technology will not always be readily apparent, even to the trained observer, because long-term changes in the environment can impinge on the relationship. Research in an insurance company to which we were party in an advisory capacity showed that apparently stable relationships can deteriorate as a result of unanticipated changes outside the organisation:

The [expert] system I suppose has worked fine for the people who use it, although there are many that don't. You must have heard people talk about the problems there are with it, but for those that rely on it, it produces useful [insurance] quotes. However . . . some of the older underwriters . . . it is mainly the older ones . . . have always said, "These people may know about computers, but they don't know anything about insurance." And just recently, the last five months or so, I'm beginning to think they're right, because what we've seen is a shift in the market. The market's gone "soft" and the machine's throwing up quotes way above the going rate. It's losing us business because some of the people who've always used the machine are relying on the quotes it gives. An insurer would have a "nose" for it, would know he's got to come down or he'll lose the business.

As stated, we can make no serious claim as to how precisely one might address these issues of time and temporal rhythm. We have some of our own data and have presented some others'; but really the topic is one that has yet to be thoroughly researched and thought through in CSCW. Nevertheless, we should see it as part of fieldwork-for-design ambitions, perhaps. That is, far from the 'snapshot' work that in some views characterises fieldwork, their orientation should include recognition of the way things change.

8.6 Normal Natural Troubles

Fieldwork-for-design would be a very narrow – one might say a conservative – procedure if it did not find new ways of reporting on problems in work. By conservative we mean here that a feature of problems at work is

their diversity, and there can be no certitude that prior ways of uncovering and listing them will succeed in new work domains. Thus a conservative approach to fieldwork may leave new problems undiscovered. The problem with problems, so to speak, is that they are rarely the same. Consequently, ways of looking for them can rarely be the same either: one needs to be radical.

Yet the issue for fieldwork is not to conjure infinite numbers of ways of capturing and listing problems, as if all that were needed was a catalogue. As with all of the concerns of the fieldworker, the issue at heart is one of a sensibility, sensibility in this case to both the fact that in workplaces problems are often listable things, but problems are also a question of orientation: people assume that work, whatever it is, will be full of problems. The question is, how do they deal with them, how do they solve them, and what is, if you like, the 'work' they put in to fixing them. Now, bound up with this particular topic, the one of the worker's sensibility, is a further distinction that needs to be made clear, a distinction of an analytical kind. One possible approach to the work of problems could be to see how individuals maintain motivation or good morale. This is a classic human relations type of topic (although as it happens an enduringly unsolved one!). Now, although motivation is clearly pertinent to our own interest, the focus we advocate when thinking about problems has a different hue. In our case, the goal is to explore the ways in which technology and problems of work are interwoven and whether the design of either the technology or the process or attendant on that, the skills, know-how, and so on can be redesigned.

Although it is easy enough to state this it is, alas, not so easy to study it. It is often difficult to recognise whether procedures or technology are doing the job for which they are intended. In their desire to get the job done, people often disguise the inadequacies of technology and procedures they have at hand by working around them. Their skills often compensate for inadequacies of procedure or technology, without anyone outside the immediate work environment being aware of this. And if it is sometimes difficult to find problems, sometimes it is difficult to see anything else but problems. In some instances, the fieldworker will come across what can only be called 'headless chicken' behaviours, behaviours that entail a great deal of running around because something has gone wrong but which seem to have little effect.

In between these two opposites, the invisible and the all too visible, there is of course a great deal of ground. Examination of it is made even harder by the fact that perceptions of this ground, particularly from afar, say from the view of managers in the centre of an organisation or even system administrators in technical support, may be quite contrary. What to the workers in question are obvious instances of workarounds for failing technologies, to managers in the centre may be thought of as work practices enabled by successful technology; what to system administrators may seem to be technologies that never fail might in fact be technologies that are never used. We ourselves, singly and severally, have encountered more than one information system which was deemed a success by some in a given context when investigation showed that others thought the system in question a failure because it was hardly ever used. Part of the task of the fieldworker is to help provide evidence for the arbitration of these sorts of views, although obviously one would expect the evidence to produce more than points of view. We would like to imagine that design is more than just a atter of opinion.

Still to get to what this 'more than' might be, we now want to say a little about the nature of the kinds of problems that one will find people dealing with in any and all workplaces. We want also to give a hint as to what the sensibility of the worker to work will be, a sensibility we want the fieldworker to understand as one that entails treating problems as natural, normal, and routine. As should be clear, what the problems of work are and how they are dealt with are not the same and should not be confused. One can refer to Winch again, whom we first mentioned at the outset of this chapter. He noted that there were certain basic facts of life that made life, whereever it was conducted, comprehensible. Nevertheless, life has its particularities, and this gives life is diversity. So too does this apply to the workplace and the problems of work: work, wherever it is, involves dealing with troubles; it's the stuff of work which makes all work more or less familiar to us. One should not be surprised to find this. But one cannot necessarily predict beforehand what the troubles might be. These are not just different in different workplaces, either; they change day by day, week by week.

So, let us convey a sense of the troubles and sensibilities for them by illustrating the nature of the problems (the problems themselves if you will) and the orientation that results. A fieldworker needs to grasp both to be able to explore in an imaginative and thoughtful way how design interventions might alter them.

'Here's Another One'

In prior examples we have mentioned the work of a steel mill. Steel mills, like all workplaces, have problems of their own, problems which are routine and ordinary, the kinds of problems that workers within the mill will view as 'the stuff they deal with.' There is no news in the dealing with some problems. This does not mean these problems are best not thought of as problems. They are, but they are just mundane.

Clarke et al. (ibid.) provide a simple checklist of the kinds of 'troubles' with which steel mill workers have to deal. They label these problems as having to do with 'dependability', with how dependable are the slabs of steel that the mill produces. Dependability here means a variety of things. In particular, it means:

- 'Cobbles' or 'turn-up' of the part rolled slab that makes it difficult, and sometimes impossible, to manipulate the slab through the mill
- Badly shaped slabs coming into the mill that produce 'fishtails' or other defects in the finished slab
- Slab defects produced by the furnace, for example, 'thermic shock' requiring the mill operator to make adjustments in how the slab is rolled that may mean the final rolled plate will not yield all the ordered plates
- Various kinds of marking on the slab produced by difficulties in rolling that may influence the quality of the final plate
- A variety of computer problems related to the identification, measurement, and sequencing of the slabs

One might say of these problems that they are essential to the task itself: these are the very reason why the workers are there; this is what they work at. When you roll steel (as in this case), cobbles and fishtails occasionally show themselves. It is the point of the work to sort them out. It is in this sense they are normal natural troubles.

In turn, having recognised certain kinds of problem, it is possible to elaborate what consequences such problems have in the large. In the case of the steel mill, the problem that ensues with these dependability issues has to do with scheduling. Slabs which are odd in the above ways make scheduling of slab production through the entire process of steel milling difficult. These normal problems make particular problems and, as it happens in the steel mill, these particular problems relate to the computer systems used to control the scheduling of steel slab movements through the mill.

For whatever reason (we need not go into it here) these systems do not allow the kinds of flexibility that the vagaries of normal troublesome steel production produces. Workers within the steel mill that Clarke et al. studied found this perplexing because, for them, the fact that steel slabs do have these problems is, as we say, a natural fact, one that anyone who took the business of working a steel mill seriously would know. Yet they found that the computer scheduling system appeared to have been designed without understanding of this fact. As one highly experienced operator wryly remarked about 'them' (i.e. those who had designed the system): '... for them to design scheduling ... is a bit like me trying to design a plane because I've flown in one.'

For the fieldworker, the question is not simply to list such complaints, of course; it is to examine and describe how the individuals in question deal with the problems. Here we are thinking of how steel workers need to work around the scheduling system, for example, and what skills are used in the decision making about this. We are thinking too of the consequences that working around the scheduling system have on the management of the steel mill as a whole. In other words, having mapped out the ordinary routine character of the problems that work entails dealing with, the fieldworker needs also to map out the skills, the local knowledge, the tools, and techniques (often artefactual and dependent on spatial ecologies as we have explained) that enable normal natural solutions to be normal problems. Hence, in this steel mill the operators were aware that different slab qualities were liable to various defects, such as 'fishtails', and so they adjusted their work accordingly.

Exactly what is 'accordingly', is the question that results for fieldworkers. They need to concern themselves with what might be the measures of accordingly or more commonly what is called 'appropriateness'. In the case of the steel mill, it turned out that the answers had to do with how scheduling and pacing were not only about any one point in the steel production process, but how the entire mill was organised around a process. Ways of dealing with problems were selected in terms of how they solved the problem there and then and yet did not create problems down the line. The solutions were, then, 'egological' insofar as individual controllers would attend to solving what was 'their problem with this fishtail,' and what was 'ecological', in terms of other problems with the fishtail slab down the line.

> If I send that at 49 … it's going to shoot up (turn up in the Finishing Mill) … it's 233 quality which is the worst one for turn-up … you need a minimum of 3 metres in length … because if you get less than that there's a good chance it could turn-up in the Finishing Mill.

> Instead of finishing at 35 I'll drive it down and put a bit more length on it … less chance of it turning-up then.

Thus it is that realtime real-world work often involves the utilisation of local knowledge and local logics, commonly interpreted as cutting corners or bending the rules, to support the overall objectives of the plan. Doing the job 'properly' can often entail, then, doing it 'wrongly': a paradox that the fieldworker must understand. In the mill this was perhaps most obvious when things began to go wrong and operators were faced with slabs 'turning up' and the steel hand saying, 'Here's another one' (Clarke et al., 2003).

Normal Troubles and the Avoidance of Errors

One recurring feature of fieldwork-for-design has been its interest in how errors are made and from which they are recovered. Thus, in a succession of studies, insight has brought out the collaborative nature of recovery from error. We have identified this feature, for instance, in our own air traffic control studies where one of the fundamental differences between fieldwork-based research undertaken in this domain and, say, psychological, lab-based studies of the same was the way in which the former focused on who noticed what mistakes were being made and who noticed what skills

were required to rectify them whilst the latter approach, the psychological one, focused on how those mistakes were made in the first place. The first is about the examination of an orientation to the dealing with error, the second to the source of error.

In the steel mill example we considered, errors stubbornly confronted the mill worker come what may. Sometimes steel slabs fishtail. But here we want to look at how errors, or if you prefer, oddities such as fishtails, are avoided beforehand. If the steel mill provided a good example of the stuff of problems, police forces can provide a good example of quite a different kind of problem, of how one of the properties of work is to prevent errors happening even as one sees them emerging. Police forces provide a particularly helpful example because their error avoidance procedures directly relate to the design of database systems, which have rather general characteristics, whereas scheduling of steel mill production can seem rather arcane.

More particularly, during studies of the design, introduction, and use of new technologies in a U.K. police force, we examined the fate of laptops introduced to facilitate prompt crime reporting. These laptops were given to all police officers so that they could enter data about a crime as soon as it was reported, and this was most often at the scene of the crime. The ostensive purpose behind the introductions seemed plausible enough: to enable the force as a whole to have the most accurate and up-to-date data about crimes and so be able to more effectively manage its crime-fighting activities.

What we found, however, was that in practice, the impact of the introduction of the new devices was not as expected. Instead of the crime report data being more accurate, it became the reverse. The crime reports entered into the system were found to be 'rather rough', omitting important facts, and containing inaccuracies. Auditing of the crime reports also showed that many were continuously revised and modified for some time after they were originally entered. In combination, these errors and revisions gave an embarrassing impression to the world outside the force. It implied the officers were often unable to categorise or comprehensively report crime. Reporting crime was thought to be the basis of their work, rather than one of its more complex arts. If they could not even do this, one could imagine commentators saying the likelihood that the force could stop crime or even catch criminals was low. In sum, the fate of the laptops had the politically disastrous consequence of making the force seem incompetent.

Yet what the fate of the laptops and more generally the electronic reporting system of which they were a part revealed was not the incompetence of the reporting skills of police officers, but rather the fact that accurate crime reporting needed to be done artfully so as to avoid problems. Crime reporting was a process which by its very nature unfolded over time; the new system did not allow this and resulted in errors appearing.

More particularly, crime reporting involves the following stages. First it involves meeting with a victim, during which some initial data gathering can be done. The crucial point to bear in mind, though, is that dependent upon the amount of data gathered or even available at that time, police officers may have to revisit the victim. The reason for this is not only because victims are not always in a fit state to give all the required facts; it is also sometimes the case that the facts aren't always available.

Some aspects of crime don't always show themselves straight away: consider how long it takes to determine what has been stolen in a house burglary, for example. It is not always clear that a burglary is a burglary. Even when someone reports that the door is smashed down, it sometimes remains unclear whether the incident was 'breaking and entry' or a 'burglary'. It is only a burglary when something it taken and it may take some time for a victim to discover whether that something is missing. As another example, oftentimes cars go missing and are reported stolen, for it only to be discovered later on that someone had 'borrowed' it during a domestic dispute. In other words, it is a normal natural problem with crime reports that they aren't always completable straight away, and that a crime might turn out to be something different from what it was first thought. New evidence might be discovered; time will give objectivity. The new system, apparently sensible in its design and in the expectations behind it, was then inimical to the nature of the problems that are endemic in crime reporting, and to the ways in which police officers had hitherto dealt with those problems. Prior to its introduction, they had treated crime reports as things that were 'worked up,' gradually corrected before they were filled. Now, realtime data entry made the reports look wrong and the police officers incapable of even basic bureaucratic activity (form filling).

In light of this, it should then come as no surprise that what we found police officers beginning to do as we undertook our study was to delay entering crime reports into the electronic database until they were happy with their completeness and accuracy. They avoided making errors by reverting back to their original paper forms. The paper forms acted essentially as temporary holding devices used to make sure that information was not shared with others or subjected to audit until it was ready. This was not so much to ensure that it reflected well on the reporting officer, as much as it was to ensure that the crime-reporting system contained accurate data.

The particular lessons we should take from the fate of electronic systems in police work is not that, say, paper is the ideal answer to technological failures. Indeed, the fact that, in the force just described, the officers ended up having to create both paper and electronic versions of crime reports (paper during the interviews with victims, electronic versions later on) is indicative of how paper is not a medium that provides all that is needed. After all, the electronic versions of the crime reports were made accessible throughout the force, whereas if they remained on paper such access would have been

impossible. No medium necessarily provides the perfect solution. Our main point, the one we want to draw from this example is that whatever the work, the nature of the problems routinely dealt with needs to be understood. In police work, one finds an example of where the stuff they deal with is pregnant with possible problems and they orient to that stuff in such a fashion as to mitigate those problems even before they arise. In police work, like all work, problems are indeed normal affairs. But they are made normal by being treated in particular ways. And these particular ways are this: by treating those problems as normal, as routine, and as workable. The systems in this case were designed without recourse to this commonplace.

8.6.1 Conclusion

This has been a long chapter, covering a great deal of ground. We have ended up considering how work entails dealing with events and affairs which have problemlike features but which get dealt with, 'worked at' if you prefer, in such a fashion that their solution seems ordinary and mundane. Problems at work are normal for work.

Part of the way in which troubles are managed is not only through the minded behaviours of individuals in the workplace but through the material properties of the setting. The physical attributes of paper documents can be used to demonstrate who has used it when and for what ends; the placement of a slab of metal is an all too visible declaration of the scheduling process in a steel mill. The ways in which things get used in the workplace can result in these things coming to hold a place that almost speaks for itself: 'Come pick me up,' one can (almost) hear them say. That things then can come to be actors in the theatre of the workplace is not meant to be a dramatic exaggeration, though, a claim, if you like, to support some radical ontology. This is simply a fact of working life.

We got to that argument, just as we got to that one about troubles at work, by recognising that workplaces are first and foremost socially organised affairs, places in which the term 'division of labour' barely suffices to convey its richness, complexity, and scope. CSCW ostensibly started out as an enterprise seeking to define collaborative systems. These were thought distinct from individual systems. But as CSCW developed it became clear that even the desktop PC supported collaborative work, long before it was networked, and that new tools were needed not just for the collaborative work alone, but for the tasks of understanding any and all work. CSCW came to realise soon after its inception, that work, in all places, is essentially collaborative, although collaborative computer tools were not always a prerequisite of that work. And so it was that CSCW came to fieldwork as a way of capturing these collaborative essences of work, and this meant fieldwork that had traditionally focused on collaboration and social properties: namely of the ethnographic kind.

251

This gets us back to the beginning of the chapter and the goal of the book: to answer what this fieldwork, of an ethnographic kind, might be or more precisely what it has become so many years after CSCW researchers first turned to this way of doing business. We argued at the outset of this chapter that fieldwork can help design better systems, whether those systems be ones that run on PCs, over networks, or in the massive environments of steel mills, but only if that fieldwork entails more than looking. We have wanted to explain that it entails looking at social organisation, at planfulness, at arte-facts, and the ecologies in which they exist; it entails looking for and explor-ing how individuals arrange their activities egologically and in terms of sequences and flows of tasks. We suggested that looking with these topics and orientations in mind consists of a sensibility, an analytical state of mind that makes fieldwork more than a technique for seeing; to paraphrase our-selves, it's a way of seeing particular things in particular ways with particu-lar questions and concerns. This does not mean that workplaces become unfamiliar to the fieldworker.

Our opening gambit in the chapter was to note that Peter Winch com-mented on how human endeavour, in all its variety, has something grossly similar about it wherever it is and whatever it entails. Here we have explored what we suggest are the basic facts of any and all workplaces, facts that are not so much to be listed and classified as ones that are part of a geography of workplaces. The fieldworker needs tools to navigate around these facts intelligently. How people in workplaces deal with troubles, how they worry about what is their own responsibility and what is others', how they deploy the things around them to help in their work, and how they share and demonstrate skills and know-how and competence; all this and more is the stuff of work. Although a fieldworker may come to a workplace unfamiliar with how all this stuff is fitted together in some particular way, that it is the stuff one will find should come as no surprise.

That it is what work is made of should not intimidate them into reporting it as a surprise. It's only work. But that it is only work does not mean that what it might become, how it might be done differently, is unexciting to investigate or consider. Work is mundane, routine; it is in its essence a daily affair, some-thing that workers themselves want to get away from once it's been done. But it can be looked at with imagination, through comparison and insight, in ways that can enable other ways of doing work to be envisaged. This would be the deployment of what we have called, at various points, an ethnographic imagination, alluding to the phrase that anthropologists and sociologists use to distinguish mere description from something more.

Imaginative insights cannot be predetermined nor can they be guaran-teed when any fieldworker commences his or her endeavours. But what we have done in this chapter is explore some of the tropes that might be a basis for that imagination to work, combining ways of seeing with ways of thinking, and building always on the work of others. It is on their backs that ways of looking at the present can be made more profitable, that enable fieldworkers to direct their line of sight to issues and topics that are likely to hold promise and potential, and to avoid looking at those which are likely to be less fruitful. It will enable them to at least orient to the kind of work they will need to do when they look at the work of others. Fieldwork-for-design is a job too.

Into the Home

9

Throughout this book we have, naturally, been focused on work for the simple reason that it remains CSCW's main topic. But if our thesis about the relationship between analytic themes and domains holds true, then it would also be the case that for nonwork domains there should also be a set of themes to which the fieldworker can turn. Here, we venture into domestic life mainly because we have each of us researched in this area. Nevertheless the basic idea – that themes and domains might be usefully (but only approximately) grouped – can be evidenced here as well as anywhere. There are of course lots of other places that one might want to deploy fieldwork-for-design: they include public spaces, for example, where one might want to design new experiences in settings as diverse as large public squares or within the much more limited spaces of retail outlets. There are, too, the semi-private domains of nursing homes and halfway houses; places that are as it were half way between work and home. And then there is the home itself, the most private place of all.

The home, needless to say, is at once a place, a social zone associated with the use and deployment of particular technologies (washing machines, TVs, video game consoles, and so on), and a locale, a domain for a type of social activity, for family life and all that entails. What family life is, what is done at home, is broad indeed. Home is not just about home, for example; it is a place of work too, not just in the need for housework, but in the sense that much work from work is done at home. Although it is certainly doubtful whether more people work at home than say, in the 1950s or before it is certainly true that the Internet and home-based PCs are allowing people to work at home more flexibly, as and when they wish, in all sorts of ways. Work at home might be occasional, but it is not infrequent or rare. Home is then a place where a great deal of 'work' gets done.

We want to focus on home life (family, work, technology) not because we think CSCW researchers ought to be turning some of their attention to the home and the family as a new domain of inquiry, but because doing so will let us explore and, we hope, confirm some of our theses about the need for analytic acumen; for themes and tropes which help to orient fieldworkers for design, and for the claim, in broad terms, that the kind of fieldwork-for-design we advocate is a particular and distinctive kind of practice. This domain of inquiry has only just begun to reach the status of having a substantive, albeit not complete, body of ideas and practices that can be relied upon in the context of design. We show that it is, still, in some part, new territory. This is not to say that little research has been undertaken because over the years a great deal has been done, but it is still inchoate and inconclusive. It is, nevertheless, substantial enough to indicate the degree to which prior analytic and theoretical commitments can lead us to deal with a 'new' domain, like the home, in precisely the same way as we dealt with the 'old' ones, like workplace settings. Genuine fieldwork-for-design requires us to move on from self-imposed limitations.

We approach this domain not entirely innocently: our own research endeavours led us into this topic. Some years ago, for example, we were commissioned by the European mobile phone network operator, Orange, to study their 'Orange@Home' project. Here we were asked to study how people 'lived in' and experienced a smart home and what design implications this experience might have for new products and services. Soon thereafter we were involved in further projects, this time for other operators, and sometimes for the commercial companies by which we were then employed. This led to studies of different possible forms of interactive technologies in domestic environments, and one particular theme was with new forms of messaging, much of it following on initial studies of paper mail in the home (Harper and Shatwell, 2002). Various prototypes were produced in this period (e.g. Textboard, O'Hara et al. (2005)) and this research continues (e.g. Taylor et al., 2006).

Whatever the specifics of our history these endeavours led us to the sociological and psychological literature on the family and the home (for an overview, see Harper (2003)) and the many studies that have, since that time, appeared on design for the home. Our reflections on this literature, and experienced in our own work, we use this chapter to start identifying the themes we thought, and think, would build the analytical acumen we need in our fieldwork endeavours. It could almost go without saying that such themes take time and repeated effort to work up and develop and our efforts were simply those of various initial attempts. But our own explorations of them, our appropriation of ideas from other disciplines, what we were trying to do in the development of these ideas, all this and the insights we gleaned from others' work, we turn into the gist of this chapter. Our goal is to present at least an initial sketch of the analytic themes we think can help ensure that fieldwork in this setting is more than merely hanging around or a 'looking to a vague purpose': these themes can provide a basis for looking at certain things in certain ways with certain issues in mind. This helps us restate the claim of this book: that fieldwork-for-design is not

just a commonsense task (although founded on common sense): it is about analytic purpose.

9.1 Overview

The structure of this chapter takes the following form. First, we sketch some of the arguments that we ourselves reviewed when we began researching on this area. It is historical, although it will lead us to contemporary topics and issues. We then start exploring, conceptually, what might be meant by the terms, 'home', the 'domestic setting', and 'family'. We found (bearing in mind that we were working for commercial clients who demanded some early direction) that these terms and others were often used interchangeably, producing more confusion than illumination. Our clients, understandably, wanted to know what the topics of our investigation would look like. Clarity cannot be a bad thing, although difficult to achieve sometimes, and we needed, we felt, to be clear about the intersections of space, time, practical purpose, and emotional, moral, and symbolic life which affect our understanding of the family.

This led us to think in terms of some early 'enablers and inhibitors,' drawn partly from our review of a disparate literature and partly from our earliest research in the smart home. They reflected our instinct that the term 'family' disguises a set of behaviours which are sometimes oriented to the family group and sometimes not; sometimes inward-facing and sometimes outward-facing; sometimes entailing narrow conceptions of the 'family' and sometimes something much wider; and where well-known concepts such as 'ease of use', 'robustness', 'reliability', and 'overhead' may or may not apply.

In turn, and as our research progressed, we discovered some of these themes were indeed important. Nevertheless, and as we progressively discovered, the behaviours, relationships, rights and responsibilities, routines, and disruptions were not always so easily captured and perhaps needed a slightly broader-brush treatment. We also learnt about the degree to which our work-related tropes were or were not relevant to the home. One theme that became evident very quickly was the difficulty of separating the physical and the social. These matters are to do with geography and morality. Hence we can use the sociological term 'moral order' to label a concern for the ways in which families organise themselves and their use of home space in ways that are suffused with codes of what is good, bad, thoughtful, negligent, sensitive, and crude. Although workplaces have morality too, we argue that when it comes to studies of home and families, the nature and inflection of the moral order is distinct, and warrants special attention in fieldwork.

Following on from this we then discuss the importance of artefacts for families and in home settings. Artefacts are, like moralities, important in

257

work settings just as they are at home, but just how they play out, just what role they have, is somewhat distinct. If, at work, artefacts are essentially informational devices of various kinds, at home they are informational devices too but they are also what one might call coders of morality or, if you prefer, devices that help the household learn and orient to certain ways of living. Most importantly they are displays of aesthetic value, homes being made special in part by how artefacts within them are arranged and used to ornament bare walls, bedside cabinets, mantelpieces, noticeboards, fridge doors, and much else beside. Artefacts make a home; artefacts at work merely support how to do that work.

This leads us on, naturally, to 'tailorability', to the ways in which artefacts, processes, and technologies of various sorts get rearranged and altered to fit local needs and circumstances. This, too, is a theme deployed in work settings but here needs to be altered to have an emphasis on aesthetic elements. The question is not merely how do users make things look nice but how members of households make things fit when they have practical tasks to finish, jobs to do. It's this fitting that is the issue, bundling up matters of style with function, moral orders, and practical realities, with costs at the expense of desires.

This leads us on to the point that homes are not simply centres of leisure, opposed as it were to all that constitutes work, but in themselves require industry and labour of sorts, as we noted in our preamble. Thus a next theme we propose is important has to do with the flow of work, a term we have already used. Here we emphasise the need to look at how households organise themselves to ensure that tasks get done, and that these tasks relate to both the practical management of paying bills and running the infrastructure of a home, as well as things to do with what is traditionally thought of as housework, where ideas about cleanliness, tidiness, what one might grandly call order, are paramount: the trick for the fieldworker, however, is to realise that work at home, and the typical used nomenclature for it, housework, is actually a label for activities that are not an analogue for the work done at work. Housework is not merely about the work of tidying, for example; it's about who tidies, when, and how. As we show, it's about a moral change as much as any physical one. This is not something that should be excluded from the scope of fieldwork, however. We argue it is something to which sensitivity to will ensure a better understanding of the requirements for tools that help in housework and other activities that have similar 'soft' properties, such as domestic medicine, ideas, health and fitness, and so on.

If housework is often about keeping things clean, then fieldwork-for-design needs to bear in mind also that households are places in which sensuality and the body are important. If, at work, lunch and coffee are merely the backdrop to the task at hand, feeding, cleaning, sleeping, and even sex are all central to what the home is about. This does not mean that the

fieldworker should seek to examine every detail of the sensual – daft as well as unacceptable – it is to alert the fieldworker to how sensual matters are important for home settings: information use, for example, is to be understood and designed for not in terms of speed but in terms of pleasure. The sensual is not always matter of pleasantness either. Consider the difference between one's work colleagues being locked out when the security systems fail at work and the reaction to one's children being locked out at home. One may produce fury, the other fear, both one could say sensual experiences of sorts, but different in character and in the design implications.

This then leads us on to the theme that has to do with what is achieved by some of the events we have just listed. If there are the daily processes of cleaning and feeding, then there are also those much more occasional and irregular events that somehow, despite their infrequency, seem more important than anything else: we are alluding to such things as marriages, retirements, graduations, births, christenings, even deaths too, and the funerals that ensue. These events, some admittedly rare, are bound up with how families are at times local arrangements, a set of people who share a particular space, and at other times, 'occasioned' by special events, a larger entity spread across distance, filial bond, legal association, and affection. This is the extended family, if the use of an old-fashioned term can be forgiven, and our concern here is not to say that the size or scope of family ought to be an analytic theme, so much as patterns and forms and consequences of what we would like to call social connectivity. Here we suggest that the fieldworker inquire into how families attend to matters of connection between themselves and those spread across time and geography. Family, in this view, is indeed something that is mostly about the home but what the home is thought to be is in part measured and created by family elsewhere.

Achieving the right balance between the sensual and the moral, between the practical and the desirable creates, unsurprisingly, normal troubles for households. So, just as we think one ought to look at normal troubles in the workplace, so too do we think that this is a right concern for the home setting: this is the last of the themes we propose. Amongst the issues we think are encapsulated here are not so much the systems failures that affect work but the failures of families to behave in sought for and desired patterns that we have in mind, patterns here meaning things like the daily routines that ensure that the right child is cleaned and fed and delivered to the right school at the right time, the rhythms of special events, ones that happen on a weekly basis, like Sunday lunch, and those which are more infrequent although regular like birthdays and Christmases and summer holidays. In all these different doings, getting things done in the right way takes organization; it takes work, particularly given the daily grind of misunderstandings, changing requirements, and constraints on money, time, and effort. The trouble with family life is the trouble it affords.

9.2 Background: Prior Research on Home Life and Families

For many corporations and academic research departments, the home has been the last frontier for digital technologies for some years. It is the place in which they have been investing much research effort, the place where they have been hoping for some time great changes will happen (presumably as a result of their research efforts). One of the issues that has perplexed the many researchers involved over the years has been why, given that the Internet brought PCs to more or less every home (at least in theory), the home itself has remained resistant to all that the PC might afford. They see a paradox: the technology in question is there, in the right place (the home), but is not used for all it could be.

Now one could of course doubt this particular view, but it is more or less an assumption, an initial premise that has been a persistent basis of research in this area. We can use it to help explain some of the many arguments and research questions one finds dealt with over the years. For example, one early and influential debate had to do with the question of how much effort there had been put into interactive systems design for home settings before the Internet revolution occurred. The question was asked whether this has been sufficient to ensure high levels of take-up when that revolution happened.

A well-known study of this topic by the research organisation Interval (Hindus, 1999) noted that there had been little effort and thus expressed no surprise at the failure of PCs to have as much impact on home life as they did in, say, the office. From Hindus's point of view, what was perplexing was not the failure of computers at home; it was that, in contrast, a great deal of research had been undertaken historically into what one might call the ergonomics of home activities, into the design of kitchens, for example, and into the so-called white goods that fill them up, such as washing machines and stoves and so on, and yet none of this seemed to have been leveraged by computer systems designers. The issue for Hindus and others was that once research on the home turned to computing, all of a sudden the research seemed to dry up. This led to the further suggestion that all the claims about great efforts being put into understanding the domain by the computer were egregious. She commented that this might have to do, in large part, with the fact that most technologies for the home are viewed as gendered products, or, more particularly, technologies for women and thus worthy of less attention than other, more masculine technologies and that research (or the lack of it) may well have been structured by that fact.[54]

Whether Hindus was right about the gendering is, of course, somewhat open to debate. It could be, for example, that the home has simply been a place that designers of interactive systems had failed to understand was

---

[54]For a more general discussion of this possibility, see Banta (1995).

different, and that they had naively assumed that their prior research would easily apply to the new setting. Or it might have been that their choice of prior topics might have had their own merits which had little or nothing to do with gender. In our case, for example, long before we were led to think about design for the home, we were focusing on the problem of information use and knowledge work; these seemed ambitious topics to us because we thought that work would change in radical and exciting ways it if became a matter of knowledge use rather than, say, a question of manufacture. Gender had nothing to do with our motives. Nor did we think research would carry over to the home. We knew that our research goals resulted in us learning a great deal but nothing that would show benefits there: after all, how much knowledge work gets done at home, as against in the office?

In any event, it was not at all clear why the levels of research on the home had been low, nor was it clear why prior understandings from outside the system design world had not been carried over into this new domain. But nevertheless, once the topic had been marked out, it began to get a lot more attention. Oddly, at first anyway, the issues of concern were not related to the interaction itself but to matters that were external to that interaction. Topics in this vein included things such as the aesthetics of PCs and the implications of those aesthetics for the home. The question here, basically, was where to put PCs so that they become ornaments rather than ugly intrusions (see Venkatesh, op. cit.). Another question asked who in particular took on some of the 'management tasks' that PCs imposed upon users (see Frohlich and Kraut (2003)). This question was addressing the problem of who would become the systems administrator when PCs went home. Shadowing some of Hindus's claims, much of this research found that it was males, particularly teenage males, who adopted this role. Not only would they maintain the PCs, but they would upgrade them, even, in some cases, set up timesharing systems with their parents and siblings, ensuring, of course, that they (i.e. the teenage male) got the most access.

All of these sorts of questions turned around the view that if these external matters could be solved then issues of interaction design would be easier to deal with (and indeed might vanish altogether). Gradually, however, research began to move towards exploration of what people did with the interactive functions of their PC, and rather less with these external matters. Again, it was still not concerned with how to improve interaction design, being more focused on what impact use of the PC might have, given usability of PCs. There was the famous HomeNet study, for example, an examination of how access to and use of the Internet at home affected social relationships between distributed family members (Kraut et al., 1996). This study suggested that those who were high users of the Internet on their home PC were likely to find the quality of their personal and family lives would diminish. These findings obviously caused much concern, it being thought hitherto that PC-based communications would bring people together, not isolate them.

In any event, the HomeNet study was treated as a one-off, and essentially a study of behaviours that were going through periods of adjustment. Subsequent research did not help clear matters up, however. It might have been a period of transition, but it turned out to be right that some of the transitional behaviours persisted. Some research found that the 'wired homestead' was becoming a place of more isolation and loneliness rather than less; according to other research it was bringing spatially distributed families together in new ways (for an overview see Turow and Kavanaugh (2003)). These particular debates echoed long-term concerns about the shift in community relations effected by capitalism, by railways, by telegraphs, even by such mundane technologies as the vertical filing cabinet (as we discussed in the previous chapter; see Yates (1989)). These debates became manifold, with numerous commentators across a range of disciplines. Key players included, for instance, Wellman, from sociology (see for example, Wellman (1998,2000a,b), Kraut from social psychology (see Kraut et al. (2005)), and from the systems and CSCW research domain, and even ourselves (Harper, 2003).

Gradually, however, these debates broke down into various particular areas, and here at last issues to do with interaction design came to the fore. We don't need to review all these different views but some are worth mentioning. The so-called appliance argument emerged which holds that one of the reasons why computer-enabled technologies had failed in the home is that they offer so many applications that each individual application becomes almost impossible to comprehend.[55] What is needed instead, it was suggested, are devices and applications that are unbundled from each other so as to enable easier modes of use. In essence, the argument holds that the home should have lots of different computational devices, each designed with one or two or a set of related applications in mind, rather than to provide the home with a single device, a 'converged device' with all applications on it.

In contrast to this, there were various convergence-type approaches, ones that held more or less the opposite view. Research here particularly focused on ways of converging broadcast entertainment with the function of the Internet-enabled PC; Microsoft's Media PC is one recent technology that follows on this line of reasoning. This combines both a handheld remote control for navigating through broadcast content, and a keyboard with mouse for Internet services. Whatever the user wishes to do, he or she will use the same machine and screen. Curiously, although there is now a range of such integrated devices in the marketplace, there is little academic and scientific research published on their success or usability. If the appliance argument seems to accrete many academic followers, the same cannot be

---

[55]For a well-known introduction to this read Norman (2002).

said for the convergence view. Standing in between these two opposites have been various researchers who have sought to identify just what role technologies of the convergence kind might have, even if it is not to offer complete convergence.[56]

Beyond the appliance argument on the one hand, and the converged device approach, there has appeared a range of different research projects. They have become almost too numerous to mention. There have been many projects investigating computer-based tools that enable families to invigorate their social bonds, for instance. In some instances, these propose appliancelike solutions and in others more converged PC-type approaches. The applications range from calendaring (Plaisant et al., 2003; Neustaedter and Brush, 2006), technologies for intimacy (Vetere et al., 2005), and Web-based family portals (Venkatesh et al., 2005). As discussions and reports on these attempts have appeared, so there has been shift towards what is called emotional design, where the claim is made that part of the design requirements of technologies in home settings is that they offer not just speed of use but pleasurable experiences. According to this view, good design appeals to the heart as well as the mind (see Jordan (2000), also Norman (2004)). This approach has, in turn, led to studies that attempt to design devices that evoke entirely new reactions, such as the RCA's tilting table (Gaver, 2002). It has led also to exploration of lifestyle and the implications of different lifestyle choices on form, factor, and function (see Philip's HomeLab project[57]).

Whilst these endeavours have been underway, other, more technical activities have been developing which have sought to build the seamless infrastructures that will, in the view of the proponents, transform home settings. The goal here has been to create something like ubiquitous or pervasive computing environments, ones that allow the users to do anything at any place. These attempts have been largely prototypes, to date. They have led to some curious spinoffs, however, such as smart homes that are able to monitor every movement and action of the occupants. Georgia Tech has built one (Abowd et al., 2003), and the Media Lab another. These smart homes have been built not as illustrations of what homes of the future might do, but as short-term projects designed to enable learning what people do in the home. These projects assume that understanding what these doings are is difficult. These ubicomp-type applications are, then, tools for gathering data, for doing, if you like, fieldwork, in this case by machines rather than say, ethnographers.

In sum, there are, now, a number of concerns and topics driving major programmes of research into the home and family life. Despite all the years of effort since Hindus first scolded the computer world, most are driven by

---

[56]See for example O'Brien and Rodden (1997), also O'Brien et al. (1999), and Brow (2006).

[57]http://www.research.philips.com/technologies/misc/homelab/index.html

the same conviction that applied when she first wrote that the home remains 'undiscovered' or at least somehow inadequately served by computational devices. Our own view on this research is that much of it has achieved a great deal in terms of exploring and defining modes of interaction that might succeed in the home but much is still to be learnt. We think also that some of the research, particularly on smart homes, attests to a different set of problems. In our view, this research serves to remind us how little is known about the home (or what goes on inside) and attests to a lack of clarity about how to look. We would say that it is not lack of expertise or interest that is the issue; it is confusion. For example, the efforts by some to use smart home technologies to track behaviour are testament in our mind not to the wise evolution of technology, but to the naivete of those conducting this research. Understanding the home, knowing what goes on inside is not difficult; the question is what activities should one look at for design purposes.

9.3 Conceptual Distinctions: Family, Domestic Space: Geography or Morality?

This leads us on to the first set of thematic issues we think are turning out to be important when one approaches the task of fieldwork in home settings. It's about coming to terms with what one might be looking at, and what, on that basis, one would expect to see and learn. Part of the issue turns out to be not so much the deliberate naivete of those mentioned above, but the bundles of assumptions and agendas one finds when the home purports to be a topic of inquiry. It turns out that this term is a label for a number of things.

When a technology company such as Orange explained to us that they were interested in technologies for the home and that they wanted to investigate this by building a smart home in which people could live (and it would be us who did the watching), we had assumed that it was the home itself that was the research topic. What we found, however, was that they had in mind not technologies that would support anyone in home settings; what they had in mind were technologies that would support a particular type of group of people. It wasn't bachelors nor was it spinsters (to coin some old-fashioned but nevertheless parallel terms), nor was it homes shared by friends. What Orange had in mind were families: mums and dads and several kids. In short, research into the home turned out to be research into more than simply a place; it turned out to be about a particular type of social grouping.

Now why would this matter? It might sound as if we were making a big deal over minor conceptual distinctions: after all, it is not uncommon for people to use the term 'home' when they mean the people who live in a home; equally it is not unusual for people to use the term 'family life' when referring to the places in which families exist. It does matter, however. For what type of group exists in a space is fundamental to the organisation and character of that space: who lives where is crucial to what 'where' is.[58]

'Who', in this case, means the particular social organisation of the group in question. Now to say that something is socially organised is not to claim that it is not organised in other ways as well, but it is to draw attention to certain properties of the ways things are done in that place. As an aside, whatever the salient properties of this social organisation, that a setting is socially organised should not be a finding but an assumption in field-work-for-design: one should not go to a home, for instance, and discover that certain people have more power than others, nor should we note that the organisation of a home results in the objects that one finds therein having socially endowed meaning: of course these things hold true. The issue is in what ways and, given that, what implications this has for other more particular issues. The question is not whether the home is socially organised, but what about its social organisation makes it a home. The trouble is that there are many types of social organisation in the home: as we have alluded to above, a spinster's or a bachelor's home is not like a retired couple's; none of these types of homes are at all like households with teenagers.

One can prove this point by exploring the differences that different groupings create in relation to the likely practical realities of using almost any type of tool in different places and with different social orders. Given our own concerns, a computational version of a diary and scheduling tool will do. One of the most common such applications is Microsoft's Outlook. How successful would Outlook be in the home? It depends, we now explain, on what kind of social organisation, what kind of grouping of persons or individuals who occupy a place called home, one has in mind.

So, to begin, one can readily accept that most homes with busy parents and children might find a scheduling tool useful. Such a computational tool might ease some of the practical difficulties of knowing who is where and when, and could help in planning the logistics of feeding and so forth. But before we consider how other types of families might use Outlook let's pause for a moment and think about the different roles Outlook would have at work. Doing so can highlight some issues. At work one might say that an entry into an Outlook calendar is a commitment to an action, a statement, if you like, that the owner of the application will, indeed, turn up at some meeting at some specified time. Outlook at work is a testament to organisational commitment; in contrast a failure to abide by an Outlook appointment represents an unwillingness, to be blunt, to abide by those commitments.

---

[58]This is something that is occasionally made plain in the CSCW literature, in papers such as Harrison and Dourish (1996). The inverse of this, the possibility that some places are not lived in by anyone at all, has created its own sociology, the sociology of the 'third place'. See Auge (1995).

Now let us return to the home. Think of what an Outlook entry in a home calendar might be. It is not likely to be quite the same as a work entry. A home entry might be 'See Aunty Maeve next Wednesday night at 7 PM.' Now, the trouble here is that in the home setting, there are so many other factors impinging upon the achievement of tasks that such a statement on a calendar does not have the same status as a diary entry written on a work version. At home one might say that such a statement is a hope, a wish list, an expression of the possibility that 'If everything is alright then we might as a family get to see Aunty Maeve.' At work, it is a command. Why this difference? Why would an entry on Outlook be more of a statement of hope in the home, and more of a statement of action at work? It is because of the relationship the various types of individuals have with one another in the home. In some groupings, one set of members may have an expressly willful relationship to another set of members, for example. The set we have in mind is teenagers and their relationship with their parents.[59] Thus one can all too easily imagine a parent marking down on Outlook the hope that everyone will come and see Aunty Maeve but one can as easily imagine the surly responses and recalcitrance of teenagers to this proposition: 'Oh no, she is so boring,' one can hear them say, or 'I don't want to. I want to go out with my friends!' with obvious results in terms of the negotiation of rights and obligations.

The issue is that the particular pattern of social relationships in homes can significantly affect the role of devices such as scheduling and diary tools. Parent/teenagers comprise only one set of relationships that might create these peculiarities. There is too what one might call the paradoxes of life stage, again a social matter, and how this will affect the use of a calendar tool. Whereas teenagers may actively resist contributing to a calendaring tool, young children may be encouraged to participate for reasons which have little to do with calendaring. They may be encouraged to fill out things on the diary so as to help them to learn to write, to give them encouragement through drawing attention to their activities, to make them feel important and valued, and much else beside. Yet, although they are encouraged to do this, all the things that they might produce as a result of these

---

[59] Again, this was forcefully brought home to us when we spoke (separately) to parents and teenagers about mobile phone use. Compare the following two extracts when a mother and daughter speak about their mobile phone use:

Mother: 'I bought C. her phone when she was 15, because I wanted to know where she was. It was great for a while, very reassuring to me. Then, in fairly short order, I found that her phone was switched off later in the evening, usually when she was out later than I wanted her to be. I started ringing her friends to find out where she was.'

C.: 'The thing I like most about my mobile is, well, the sense of intimacy it gives me. I always ring my boyfriend last thing at night and talk to him. . . .It's like he's here with me and my parents don't know. . . .'

encouragements, all the things they might enter onto an Outlook calendaring tool, can and most probably will be disregarded as parental priorities intervene. This has nothing to do with the affordances of the technology, and everything to do with the social positions of family members, or 'users'. Those who are children are treated as such.

Now, it will be the case that the particular roles that children, teenagers, and parents have in any particular household will vary; we are not saying that all households behave in this way. What we are trying to show is that social organisation is clearly an important factor in understanding how devices get used and hence, also, how one might go about understanding criteria that would produce better-designed devices. The issue is, given any particular social organisation, how does that organisation show itself in any particular place. And this in turn leads to the question of what aspects of the social organisation in question pertain to design.

9.4 Our Initial Topics

If the first stages of our research travels in the home space entailed us voyaging around the tacit concepts that underscored those who funded projects such as Orange@home, we, nevertheless had our own initial set of admittedly rather prosaic assumptions or tropes that we deployed once the fieldwork began. It is worth mentioning these now as a way of helping to orient the reader to the more comprehensive thematics that we developed and that we turn to again after this section In particular our early concepts were as follows.

9.4.1 Individual Versus Collaborative Activity and the Issue of Personalisation

Our initial suspicion was that some activities in the home would be more or less 'collective' whilst others would be more 'individual'. This, it seemed to us, had a direct bearing on the way in which technologies might be designed for family use.

9.4.2 Connectivity/Information Use

Many of the new technologies have been predicated on a contrasting view of 'use'. Where some have felt that the need for information would be paramount in the market for new technology, others have looked to support human connectivity. This has been the broad difference between the Personal Digital Assistant and mobile communications devices such as the mobile phone and the focus of much debate around convergence. We felt it might prove interesting to assess the relative information and connectivity issues in the home. In particular, there might, we thought, be issues of control of information. As we discovered, some of these turned on conceptions of privacy and monitoring. Bandwidth issues, we thought, might be equally important.

9.4.3 Ease of Use/Usability/Overhead

In an organisational context, where time is, at least sometimes, of the essence, 'overhead' can be extremely important. Our early investigations, in a context where a task might be less important and thus time taken might not seem to be significant, suggested that people were in fact subject to the same irritations that they experience with technology at work. We were definitely interested in the kinds of complaint about the technology that they voiced.

9.4.4 Usefulness/Fitness for Purpose

If the above can be thought of, broadly, as usability issues, we were also concerned with the idea of usefulness. If it is true that family life is not always as task-oriented as work life, then it may turn out to be the case both that usefulness is hard to distinguish and that whether technologies are deemed to be useful may depend on a set of moral and symbolic perspectives as much as practical ones. As we quickly saw, and for anyone who might doubt this, the moral rights and responsibilities of teenagers, for instance, turn out to be deeply relevant to the deployment of location-based functionalities.

9.4.5 Location

The existing literature pointed to the way in which certain locations in the household are arguably more important than others (see e.g. Mateas et al. (1996)), and focused on the role of the kitchen in family life. We wanted to see whether the location of particular new technologies was equally important.

9.4.6 Trust/Reliability

Trust or as it is often termed now, 'dependability', is also a well-known issue in organisational contexts, especially in safety-critical environments. Again, it seemed interesting to us to see whether it had a similar importance in the domestic context.

9.5 Thematics: The Moral Order

As we undertook our research at the Orange@home and as we pursued various subsequent projects so this initial checklist became fleshed out to produce a rather more nuanced view of things to look at and ways to look in the home. The basis of this was a more subtle view of social organisation in the home and all that implies.

In terms of themes, the phrase social organisation is too broad to be helpful in guiding just how a fieldworker looks. But another more commonly used term in sociology is, we came to realise, more detailed, and more evocative and appropriate for the home: it is the term 'moral order'. All places have a moral order, not just homes, but it seems to us that this term has greater utility when it comes to studies of the home than elsewhere. This is because the 'stuff' that makes up the moral order is, we came to learn, manifestly more to do with what is ordinarily called moral matters than elsewhere, where rights and responsibilities are more regularly negotiated because of the relative absence of the formalities of the workplace. After all, although we might well speak of rules and regulations in the home, it is unlikely for the most part that they will be either codified or enforced in quite the same way. Equally, and *pace* Hochschild's work on 'emotional labour', there are few aspects of the workplace that entail emotional commitments in quite the way that the home does.

The term draws attention, also, to how a home is constituted, in part, through what the term 'home' conjures in the ideas and hopes of its members: they think of the home not as a place that they are forced to go to, like work, but as a place they go 'home to'; in other words as a place which is symbolically laden. We came to learn then, that fieldworkers need to be attentive to the specialness of the home, and how it is achieved. It seems to us that this trope, the moral order, does help fieldworkers in home settings ensure that they can capture something of this specialness in their analysis. We can exemplify this using examples from our own work. In our smart home study, the use of two technologies in particular could be understood directly in these terms. Thus, where we had earlier thought simply in terms of robustness and reliability, the degree to which this mattered when children were involved, was striking.

This was nowhere more evident than with the locking and security features. Again, it should be stressed that the general principle of security systems of this kind was very warmly received by respondents in this study, as in, 'I really liked it. I felt very secure. I think its very good to be able to check up that you've locked all the doors and windows from afar . . .', but unreliability became an issue to such a degree that a sense of 'lack of control' arose from systems that were supposed to increase the degree of control: 'I felt that there was a real risk that people would get locked out. In fact, while I was there the kids got locked out in the garden because there are no door handles on the outside of the patio doors in the kitchen.'

Similarly, 'We went out once and I locked up, and E. needed a wee . . . so we were outside waiting, and she's only 5 . . . and after a while, I went back in to see where she was, and the locking system had failed and she couldn't reach the door handle. She was stuck. At the time it was funny, but it could have been more serious. Afterwards, I was thinking, 'What if we hadn't been there?'

We learnt then, quite paradoxically, that the elaboration of control can result in a sense of lack of control.[60] And, in turn, this sense is associated with strong feelings about the responsibilities of parents for their children.

This same negotiation of rights and responsibilities was found in family use of a music system in the house. It seems strange, so many years later, to see that at that time, a music system which played everywhere, and where there was a hierarchy of control built in, was regarded as state-of-the-art. Such systems, it turns out, require more than command structures which allow different individuals access to different menus in such a way that their musical preferences are available, their preferred volume settings, and so on. They also need a sensitivity to the history of control, covering such matters as who last used the device, when, and what for. It raises, amongst other things, the vexed issue of entitlement: who has a right to override other commands, and who has not. It was, in fact, clear in this context that the house's music system, although broadly popular, underestimated the passion of the music buffs and their desire to be in complete control of that to which they listen. Arguments about volume, type of music, frequency of use, and the like were reported gleefully. This collaborative aspect of control led us, in turn, to think about approaches to personalisation, as discussed later.

9.6 Artefacts

If the control of locks and music systems pointed towards social organisational matters, then so too did the role of other artefacts in the home. That artefacts exist in the home as well as the workplace is a rather trivial observation. In work settings we saw that this concern focuses on the properties of artefacts that afford certain types of interactions: how a placement of a whiteboard or a noticeboard can affect how individuals monitor each other's work, and so forth. In the home there are similar (though not identical) ways in which artefacts are salient (for a review see Taylor and Swann (2004)).

Even before we began our research we imagined that, just as at work, at home artefacts and their properties support practical organisation. Paper

---

[60]This sense of lack of control was evident in ergonomic matters as well, reflecting the need for attention to particular categories of user: 'Little kids can't reach the control panels, and they need lights to do things like sit on the potty. The cleaner, Mary, had to borrow specs to read what the control panels said' (general laughter from a rather middle-aged group of people).

mail is one example of this and one project that we undertook soon after Orange@home was into the physical properties of paper mail. Long before the emergence of the PC paper mail was thought of as a dying form of expression, the expectation being that it would be replaced by fax, but it persists even today long after the Internet, let alone fax, has reached most homes. For a variety of reasons, paper mail is a highly effective form of business-to-consumer messaging. We don't need to explore all the reasons for this, but we can list some artefactual properties of paper mail that have value in home life as a way of illustrating the kinds of sensitivities a fieldworker needs to have regarding artefacts in general.

We can approach this by saying that we are trying to convey how a field-worker should look and see and analyse. Thus one could reasonably claim that, crudely speaking, anyone could see that paper mail arrives on a door-mat, is eventually picked up by someone and is, then, dealt with by someone in a household. This much is obvious. The trick, so to speak, is to link these mere facts to social organisation, to the moral order we have just explored. If one does this, then, if one looks carefully, one will find that paper mail gets put in particular places, by particular persons, for particular reasons.

A bill will be placed on the kitchen table not simply because the table is a convenient place, but because putting it there will result in that letter being dealt with at an appropriate time and in an appropriate way. How so? In the sense that a paper bill is not merely a message, it can also become, in the way it is used and placed, an embodiment of tasks to do. Where a bill is put and why it is put somewhere is likely to be bound up with what one might call the arrangement of 'domestic to-do' lists. Thus, if a bill is on the table then that can mean something needs to be done with it. It might not be simply that a cheque is made and an envelope addressed: a bill might have been put in that particular place, the kitchen, because that is the place most likely to get everyone in the house to notice it. This in turn might lead to a conversation about the bill, its size, who is responsible for it, and so forth.

In short, we find that putting a bill somewhere can be – most often is – bound up with who, within the household, does what with what, who pays for those doings, and how those payings are the result of what kind of bar-gainings, all of which come at a cost. Ironically, money may be the least expensive commodity in a household. In other words our research shows that the physical properties of paper mail, its affordances, are those that support how members of households do things together (see Harper et al. (2002, 2003)). It's not just that the thinginess of mail means that can be bumped into by one person in particular; it turns out this thinginess facili-tates the social organisation of the home and its particular moral order.

Discovering this relationship is not the end goal of design-oriented studies of home life. It's a step on the way. If we began to see when we initially intro-duced the term social organisation what implications there might be for the role of an calendaring tool in different kinds of households, and this in turn implied certain sorts of design possibilities (ones that we chose, admittedly, not to discuss) then the relationship of artefacts and moral order should provide a basis for design insight too. Thus early research taught us that there might be a relationship between space and behaviour and that this relationship may be something that needs to be borne in mind in design. It might matter hugely where some piece of information gets put and displayed.

Even as we write, there are beginning to appear numerous research papers reporting on what messaging to place and more especially what a particular place might be (for an overview see O'Hara et al. (2005)). One of the obvious examples, and reported on by various commentators, is that of the use of images in the home, and notably the use of photographs (see Frohlich et al. (2002)). Put simply, looking at pictures is something that is typically done as an ensemble. Families will review recent experiences, will share them with other kin or with friends, and will use images as a focus for recall and talk about these experiences. A significant element in the popularity of this form, then, is the way that digital images can be conveniently meshed with ordinary family concerns to record their history; and relive recent events and significant occasions of family life. The popularity of Netmeetings can very much be seen in these terms:

> Net meeting would be a popular option with us. With the speed of the access here, and the *bandwidth*, that would be fantastic. Actually, the image quality isn't that important to us. I can tell enough. We can still see [our niece] growing up. Through Net meetings, our friendship networks have actually grown, like my sister now knows some of my other friends and will talk to them even when we're not logged on. With MSN you can send files more or less immediately, so you can look at photos and stuff like that.

9.6.1 Personalisation

At the same time, other technologies may turn out not to be collaboratively used as much as we might assume. The rhythms of family life are, for the most part, unlike the rhythms of work. In the Orange@home we noted how, for instance, young children often 'check out' their siblings and their parents, whilst older siblings engage in avoidance behaviour. We were reminded, then, that families are not always, in a behavioural sense, units. Neither are they collections of individuals who happen to live in the same location. They can be understood as individuals who orient to their family membership at specific times and in specific ways. Our data showed how family members both avoided other family members and sought their company, could be engaged in activities that entailed them being alone, and otherwise acted collaboratively.

The point is, of course, to distinguish which is which, and when. It is important because it pertains to, along with issues of control, the problem of personalisation and point solutions. It is a critical issue for the desirability

of personal point solutions in the household. In the near future, however, other forms of personalisation will become more salient. The likely reason for this is the spread of networked devices through the home, just as the network has become the default in workplaces. The prospect of most computer-related devices in the home operating from one central server opens up a whole range of possibilities, of which the personalisation of the interface is one. If we take as an example the kitchen, we can see that different screen sizes may be appropriate in different locations. (Information screens near the fridge and/or cooker will not need to be large; around the kitchen table, they may well be bigger.)

Given the problems of control, which were referred to above in terms of overhead, reliability, and so on, the use of information resources will depend on how quickly and easily information can be input, used, and retrieved at various locations, which will in turn depend on dedicated menu structures/local interfaces. To give an obvious example, the use of lists in kitchens, and a variety of technologies suggested for use in association with the list (e.g. bar coding, automatic food ordering, prompts for suitable meals, and so on) will depend in part on the elegance and immediacy of the design solution in question.

Thus, the kind of personalisation the smart home will deliver will deal with the issues of control observed in the bathroom, and which are captured by these sentiments: 'Why can't you . . . why can't you specify a temperature for each person, and an amount to fill it up. That would be great, wouldn't it? I could just input [the name of son] and he'd get a lukewarm bath, which is what he likes. Me, I like it scalding.'

Such an arrangement would obviate almost all complaints about lack of control in the bathroom, and indeed elsewhere. We might call this personalisation by profile. Nevertheless, this kind of personalisation is also fraught with difficulty. We have seen how problems arise with the control of security, entertainment, and other systems in the home.

Another kind of personalisation issue is that of personalisation by activity. Thus, when kitchen equipment and the possibility of electronic support for shopping, cooking, and the like was discussed at the Orange@home, few family members showed any interest. When they did, it was surprising how little they wanted. There was some support for keeping electronic lists using stylus entry on a wall-screen, along with prompts (presumably from the fridge and/or the cupboards) indicating that certain goods were running short. One mother, when asked if recipes on a screen would be useful, said, 'not really . . . mind you, if they were connected up to the oven and the microwave, so they automatically went through the right heating sequences and the like . . . that'd be good. . . .' What this indicated to us was that we needed a much better sense of what the activities in question, such as shopping or cooking, actually were before we could decide on the usefulness of technologies to support them.

Lastly, and most profoundly, the issue of personalisation depends on the degree of local social connectivity observed, and this affects personalisation by location above all. The expected move away from the PC in the home will have to be accompanied by some careful consideration concerning which kinds of both device and application will turn out to be appropriate in which location. We are not the first to observe that the PC is inappropriate as a bedroom-based resource for young people to engage in educational work for the simple reason that educational work turns out to be typically collaborative. Given that parents are often busy with other activities when demands are made of their time, consideration must be given to the appropriate kinds of control surface for the kitchen. It is also relevant to patterns of entertainment use, for the location and type of entertainment systems will depend very much on the nature of family life.

Again, returning to our own experiences, several parents expressed their anxiety about the way in which their children were more isolated/spent more time watching TV and so on. Increased personalisation of technology for children may well exacerbate that situation. Moreover, and something that needs appreciably more research, is how personalised devices can be provided in such a way that more casual visitors to the home (guests; wider family members) can also use them.

9.6.2 Tailorability and Aesthetics

In another respect, the way one needs to explore artefacts in the home takes us well away from some aspects of work into features which are much more expressly and uniquely to do with home. The theme we talk about here is aesthetic tailorability. Home is constituted in the arrangement of things that one finds therein. The rub, though, is that these things bind sentiment and practical tasks in various relationships. We have just explored practical tasks with our discussion of artefacts, but homes are ornamented in ways that are quite distinct from work, and the ornament is designed to say something about the occupants, their hopes, and their lives: artefacts then are not merely practical devices; they are aesthetic too. This aesthetic entails a kind of patterning, a way of arranging physical space in particular ways to help give that atmosphere that distinguishes home from elsewhere, and which in turn leads to the home being special. Thus it is that when the door to home is opened, and an individual crosses that threshold, more than a physical shift in location occurs, a transformation in the moral space of that individual has occurred as well: they have to 'come inside'; and are thus (it is hoped) safe, clean, secure, able to rest, and let their hair down.

This might entail a seldom remarked upon kind of flexibility. Being able to alter aspects of interactive systems, being able to make them fit into local practices and contexts, is certainly one of the key requirements of any and all systems. Tailorability in the home, as opposed to the workplace, may mean appreciably more than designing for practical or task-oriented concerns. Home is different from work not simply in the absence of 'work' (housework notwithstanding for the moment) but in how things and processes in the home get tailored in particular ways to make each and every home in varying degrees unique. As we have said, this is a crucial property of home life: its specialness (Taylor and Swann, 2005; see also Tolmie et al. (2002)). Now one should not go so far as to say that each and every householder makes a point of tailoring things in his home so as to be different from everyone else; putting things in particular places is not always so systematic nor intentional. But nevertheless where things are put is one of the ways that people give their home identity, their identity (see O'Brien et al. (op cit., 1997, 1999)). Of course, this entails design considerations which are at least to some degree different to those we are normally concerned with in the HCI/CSCW environment. One of the problems of projects like the Orange@home was that this tailorability was specifically prohibited; it was designed by a professional. The home was not 'just anyone's'; it was the designer's idea of a home (and one that the designer didn't live in).

9.6.3 The Flow of Domestic Work

If the Orange@home environment was peculiar in this vital sense, it was peculiar in the following regard too: in terms of housework and how it's done, its rhythms, properties, and consequences. But housework is not a domestic analogue of work. If, in the workplace, the nature of work itself is oriented to the production of some kind of stuff, some kind of output, and if, most often, if not always, there is not much debate about what that stuff might be, then in home settings the stuff that is the nature and output of housework is much more difficult to define. We have seen there is a moral order in the home, that this order is at once related to social hierarchies – what mum or dad does and what the kids can do – and to the use of objects and things, but we have not seen or commented on how all this is all assembled, made into a successful amalgam.

The issue here is partly to do with the fact that what is entailed when making a home special is variable and there are no simple rules or metrics to judge success or failure. Indeed, one might go further and say that there can be no objective rulings here because housework is not as it were solely about tidying up, although it is clearly sometimes to do with that. It is, more importantly, also if not more so about tidying up in the right ways as opposed to the wrong ways. This is a roundabout way of saying that housework is as much a moral matter as a physical one, as much about cleanliness as about the moral rightness of 'order'. This has implications for how we understand what housework entails, how it is done, by whom it is done, and indeed for design too.

'Housework' here covers a multitude of behaviours. We could, for instance, be referring to the ordinary business of cleaning; to the business of cooking, or even to that of shopping. Again, the point we want to make here is that rationalistic pictures of work are of even less relevance in the domestic environment. Housework may be done for a gamut of reasons (and the desire to avoid feelings of 'shame' when one has visitors is only one). Martin, a feminist sociologist, argues in 'Mother Wouldn't Like It' (1984, pp. 19–36) that housework has curious overtones. This is because it is not simply about tidying up; it is also sometimes about other things too. She notes that many mothers (or whoever takes on responsibility for housework) order things in the house as only they see fit. Oftentimes they do so in ways that are impenetrable to everyone else. Although these individuals may account for how they do this ordering as a move from dirty to clean, what this ordering really consists of, Martin claims, is a change in moral status: the clean things are those objects which have been tidied up by Mum; the dirty things are those which have not. Crucially this may have little to do with any real measures of cleanliness or filth. In this respect, then, Martin argues that housework is about ritual transformations, about the changing of things that have what she calls 'profane status', and which are 'dirty', into those 'clean things' that are sacred. For Martin, housework is in part the exercise of magical transformations of things.[61] As children discover, when they seek to help, there are quite specific ways to do housework of whatever kind.

Now we are not saying we need to completely reconsider what the home might be as a site of particular action. Rather, it is to say that when one looks at the work done within the home, one should be sensitive to how the consequences of that work might be more than the objective transformation of something or other. It is sometimes moral work, as we have seen. It most certainly has the character of interruptable work, as our observations about the behaviour of children would suggest. Most significantly, the work done may have a significance beyond the immediate accomplishment of the task. In other words, the fieldworker needs to pay particular attention to the relevancies that are entailed in the work in question. Hence, it matters who does it, it can matter when it is done, and it often matters too how it is done even though in different houses all the particulars of each of these may alter. All of this means that the fieldworker must recognise that criteria for design, as regards what possibilities of change are enabled by new design, have to support and reflect the ways in which the peculiar doings of the home function.

---

[61]The origin of a concern for this derives in large part from Durkheim (2001) although it had its most insightful interpretation in the work of Douglas (2002).

One should be able to see – if one has been persuaded by the above – that what might look like simply the accomplishment of a task might entail any number of other factors. A brief rehearsal of shopping behaviour as 'housework' (with obvious ramifications for Internet shopping, for instance) throws this into sharp relief. Firstly, shopping can, for some, be a social experience, viz:

> 'I usually meet up with friends for coffee at the end of it, cos I always shop on a Saturday morning …' or, 'I take the kids with me cos I have to … but its a very valuable learning experience for them and as they get older, well, actually I like having them with me now. …' or, 'I love shopping – I absolutely love it. Even food shopping, I go every day. … Well, at least two or three times a week as well as the weekly shop.'

Equally, it may be done in a variety of different ways:

> Well, we're both rather different. I like supermarket shopping, but Liz doesn't. We both go, and it's a matter of I wander round with the trolley picking up the staples, while she looks at clothes, plants, and what have you. I find that as I go round, I plan the meals for the forthcoming week. I see items and think, 'Oh, we haven't had a Chinese for a while, I think I'll do a beef in oyster sauce.'[62]

Furthermore, it can be replete with all the emotional, moral, and symbolic resonance to which we have referred. Buying food is a matter of buying for the family. It can carry implications of thriftiness: 'I usually buy Special Offers. I like the three for two type of offer, and although you can find some of them on the Website, you can't find all of them.'[63]

It may entail navigational routines:

> OK, I always know where I'm going … I pick up the staples … see, here's the fruit and veg. … I always buy grapes (picks up packet of grapes and places them in trolley) … then bananas … and apples … the grapes and bananas I put in my cereal. … OK, its meat next … we need smoked bacon … we use quite a lot of smoked bacon in our cooking, or pancetta, or something like it … its over there … don't think I'll be buying any fresh meat … we've got stacks in the freezer. …'

The way housework flows, then, can be roughly bundled as a set of relevancies. In our chosen example of doing the shopping, they include product relevancies such as the business of shopping by eye rather than weight, shopping for freshness, and being attentive to sell-by dates. Other relevancies included what we might call, 'categorisation problems', and which have something to do with the navigational issues mentioned above.

---

[62]These particular data are taken from a research project at the Digital World Research Centre, University of Surrey, and were collected by John Strain.

[63]Her husband, however, who had admitted he avoids shopping at all costs, said, 'I'd use it all the time.'

One woman in our data referenced the ease of finding things when the layout of the supermarket is known, and pointed to the relative overhead online, giving as an example, 'S [her husband] . . . likes Mars Bars and I buy packs of them, but I always buy the same pack in the supermarket . . . it took me ages to find the same pack on the Net. I tried 'Sweets', 'Chocolate', 'Bars of Chocolate', 'Children's sweets' – about 15 different categories – to find the size packet I usually buy.' As we observed above, many people navigate through the physical spaces of the supermarket on the basis of a familiarity built over many visits. One consequence of this, of course, is that they seldom have to refer to items by name, and even more rarely do they have to give precise descriptions. Ironically, making sense of precise description is exactly what they are required to do when shopping online as the above examples illustrate.

Furthermore, a range of other factors crop up when people discuss policy on buying individual foodstuffs, including issues of health, where an assortment of allergies and conditions, for instance, often afflict children. They include E-numbers, potential allergies, and other concerns with diet and health, such as sugar, salt, and fat content. In another instance, we observed the following. 'OK, yoghurts . . . we eat a lot of yoghurt . . . hang on, where's the low-fat stuff? . . .' D: 'Oh, you buy low-fat things, do you?' 'Yeah . . . cos I'm on a diet . . . it's not really a health issue for me, it's just that my arse seems to get bigger and bigger [laughs]. I do like to check how many calories there are in things . . . it's good for B. [husband] too . . . though he doesn't give a toss. . . .' These brief extracts show yet another consideration that appears to matter at least to some shoppers, and which we might call 'lifestyle relevancies'.

The flow of domestic work, then, has a rather different character to the flow of work in an organisation largely because the relevancies that determine that flow are quite distinctive. Tasks are overlaid with a set of considerations one would not typically expect to feature largely in the workplace. What we might naively consider to be chores are not only chores. They carry with them a gamut of expectations, carry a moral and symbolic weight, and entail a kind of attentiveness or awareness that is quite distinct from the workplace. To put it simply, housework is not merely a labour, but is, to a degree, a labour of love.

9.6.4 Sensualities: The Body and the Home

It should be clear by now that families, homes, households, are more than just, say, information economies; they are more, too, than hierarchical systems and economic units. They are bound by ideas of a moral unity, didactic purpose (where kids are taught to be clean, respectful, and the rest), and they are temporally organised, with differences in what happens in the morning and what happens in the evening, with what happens at weekends and what happens at special times such as birthdays and Christmas. This domain of inquiry consists of an intersection, a matrix of practices, beliefs, places, memories, and plans. Bodily matters are simply a further complexity in this matrix. The body in this context is best thought of in terms of entitlements. Its management is much more than a consideration of bodily function. It might include matters such as who has the right to demand presence or absence. It is manifested in such matters as who can monitor whom, and in what circumstances. It has ramifications in terms of, for instance, information-seeking and information-giving behaviour. Issues of health are one way in which we can understand this.

Technologies to support healthy lifestyles were a feature of the Orange @home. Some, such as sophisticated baby-monitoring equipment, were universally applauded by the families we studied, because they were technologies that provided an ongoing reassurance, afforded the kinds of checking up we have already mentioned. In a similar vein, respondents spoke to us about their own information-seeking behaviour in respect of health concerns:

> I had a contraceptive injection and I browsed the Net and had a look: there were thousands of women who had the same side effects as me. It was brilliant to be reassured. I did a search on the name of the drug, and found it posted on a bulletin board. My doctor never said anything about side effects like emotional and hormone problems. I could talk to other women who felt the same way as me in a chat room.

Now this is unremarkable in and of itself. The way in which people have used the WWW as a resource for managing health and other issues is well known. Nevertheless, the two examples we have given both entail clear and obvious rights over the body. Parents have a right to monitor young children; women have a right to monitor their own health. Results were strikingly different, however, when others asserted a right. Thus and for instance, monitoring of bodily matters from the outside, and by health professionals was, in those we researched, almost universally unpopular. Partly this was because it involved a regimen imposed by others:

> We started off using it but it dwindled away. For a start, we're not as fit as we thought we were. I'm not a hypochondriac so I didn't really need the help. We didn't get any feedback from them in any case – perhaps that should be reassuring – the nurse was very thorough when she came round – if you actually had some condition it would be very good. The nurse suggested we did it every day, but we didn't. Just occasionally. It wasn't really for us.

More important, family members were reluctant to cede rights over their bodies to outsiders. As one mother said, 'It's good. I like the idea of checking blood pressure, cholesterol, etc. but only for my own consumption – not outsiders.'

279

We proffer this only as a brief example, and it was a very minor part of the work we did in this context. Nevertheless, it does indicate that specific rights and responsibilities concerning the body – sensual matters, as we are calling them – can be important in family life. We are alluding to a tension between information use, on the one hand, and sensual experiences, such as touch and comfort. There may be much wider things to consider.

We can, for instance, toy with what relationship might emerge between bodily matters, physical presence, and the home in the future. In other words a little futurology might help us understand the present. It seems perfectly reasonable, in this line of thought, to assume that in the future, just as now, members of some households will find themselves physically separated from one another. One might find too, that this is not always the case with occasional periods when the families in question can be, as it were, entirely together in one place. One would probably agree too that whatever family life will, in fact, become, some kind of mix of these two extremes will be the norm: families will sometimes find themselves apart, sometimes together, sometimes work at home, and sometimes work away. In light of these possibilities, what might one say about bodily issues such as eating and washing? Will it be the case that, say, those individuals who are forced by dint of work and school to be separated from other members of their family, therefore are not able to be a 'real' family because they cannot unite bodily in an actual place, the 'home'? Will this only be the case when they are apart and that, when they come together again, will they suddenly be able to re-emerge as a family? If this ever happened, or did not happen for years, would they cease to be a family in between times? In short, without being able to bundle bodily and spatial matters in time, will aggregations of individuals not be families through time? If so, what will become of the home?

What we have found in our research is that the body, the spatial, and the temporal are bundled with other aspects of family life but in elusive ways. Physical co-proximity makes a home and a family: but not always. After all, tokens of the physical may sometimes stand instead of real contact: hence the intention of 'being there' for a special dinner can be satisfied by the expression of a willingness and desire, even though in some circumstances that desire cannot be acted upon. Consider as another example how it is, for some families, that every meal of the week can be eaten outside the home just as long as the aforementioned Sunday lunch is eaten together, whilst for other families being together over dinner is something they attempt every day. In short, it is neither the case that bodily matters are always linked to a particular place, nor is it the case that when they are linked it is always in ways that one might call 'real': sometimes it is merely the willingness, the attempt to do something (to be physically present say), that is a measure, of sorts, that this aggregation of persons is a family, a household. Put another way, these physical, sensual, aspects are bound closely up with the symbolic importance of events for family members.

The moral of all this is that when one starts looking at what goes on in a household it is not first and foremost whether something is done that should be documented as the measure of family, because some doings are sometimes important for certain types of times and certain types of places, but not always. To be sure, couples might like to celebrate their marriage in their conjugal bed, for example, but because they don't doesn't mean that they cease to be married. It is more important, in other words, to see how matters that might seem purely related to the body – such as sexuality as just mentioned but also washing, eating, and so forth – are as much ideas about how things ought to be done as realities of action. The body, just like anything else in the household, is to be understood as a repository of hope as well as an embodiment of action.

This has lots of implications for fieldwork: it means that observation of acts is not the same as analysis of the social setting. As we have just noted, a couple might like to have sex in their marriage bed but, from the field-worker's point of view it does not matter whether or even how often they manage this. Although ethnographers famously, 'like to watch,' this is not what we have in mind. Our point is to show that the home setting is certainly bound up with matters that have to do with the sensual, but that these need to be understood within a larger compass of meaning. Thus when one starts to look and analyse, one should not seek to reduce some of the observable bodily processes into behaviours that are, for example, essential to the home or inimical to it. Nor, if one starts to conjure future possibilities, should one seek to reduce sensual properties to literal analogues: for whatever bodily matters are at issue they need to be understood within a larger frame of intentions and meaning.

What is the significance of this? It turns out that little attention has been given to this difference in the past, and thus interactive systems designers have thought that the way of making people at home become as avid users of their technologies as people at work was to adjust the interface (of the PC, primarily) to suit the somewhat different physical circumstances of the home. Thus icons needed to be designed to be read from afar, from a couch rather than from a chair placed close to a screen; navigation on the Web should be available with a TV handheld rather than a mouse. But these efforts have missed the point: when someone sits on a couch and turns the TV on, she is not seeking a different way of using multimedia content. Our engagement with the issue of sensuality aims at demonstrating that something quite different, at least part of the time, is going on at home. The purposes people engage in, and the significance of their activities, may be characterized by things as simple as managing bodily fatigue after a day at work, unwinding with a drink and a soap opera after hours of mental effort. Concentration and effort, in the context of the home, may be precisely the last thing that family members have in mind. For the fieldworker, his or her 'task', then, is not to describe the mechanical differences in circumstances

281

of technology use, but to characterise the purposes that lie behind those mechanics. It is to capture and convey why people throw themselves down on a couch and gaze (apparently) mindlessly at a soap opera; it is to explore too how they arrange their domestic affairs so that they can put off till tomorrow what they could do today.

9.6.5 Social Connectivity

A further distinguishing characteristic of family and the domestic setting is that its rhythms are hourly, daily, and weekly, but they are also seasonal and periodic. What 'family' is now, at any particular moment in time, may well remain pretty much what family is, most of the time. Yet, at other times, particular events occur that suddenly change who is thought to be in a family, who has rights because of that membership, and what needs to be done as a consequence of that membership. We are thinking here of the following issue. When we studied families living in the Orange@home setting, we pointed out that it would be worthwhile considering how the smart home could help support special times, such as when cousins and aunties visit, and special events such as Christmas. This was difficult to do because the occupants were only allowed to stay short periods of time, and in any event contractual difficulties made such arrangements impossible. Nevertheless, it might lead one to think about what anthropological ethnographers say is the sine qua non of their trade: infinite amounts of time. This resource is needed, claim, so that every event, minor, major, occasional, or regular, can be observed as it occurs 'naturally'. But we are not arguing for this. We did not then nor do we believe now that observing homes and domestic life requires any particular length of time. The issue here is that one of the characteristics of family is how, at certain times, what family means, even who is in a family, expands greatly.

This is one the most conspicuous ways in which home is different from work. At work, the population remains pretty stable across time, bar gradual shifts in size (up and down) and in movements of personnel through promotion and boredom. In families, meanwhile, some individuals will not be heard of for years, (and indeed may be so remote that some members of the family may have never heard of them), when all of a sudden they turn up and demand rights, rights as a member of the family. They do so most often not over Sunday lunch (although we can all recollect as a child awkward affairs when strangers turned up that one's parents called 'Uncle so and so'). They do so when the family, here invoked as a system of rights suffused across almost infinite distances, legal, filial, and geographic, get together. Such events as maybe marriages and funerals, and in between these all-encompassing life-shifting occasions there are other events with somehow less consequential titles: engagements, graduations, christenings, and even some birthdays that warrant especial attention (it used to be 21 but these days it seems to be more likely 40, 50, even 80). Whatever the reason, whatever event that becomes the pretext, the family gets together.

The point is not that one can list all of these events: each and every family has is own take on what they are and why they are held, but it is this very difference, the fact that families do, all, in their own way, have a take that makes these events a defining characteristic of this domain. But thereby it also becomes a problem for research. Family life is, most of the time, about practical doings, about getting kids up and out the door, about remembering to pay the bills by ensuring that the same bills are put in the right place to bump into at the right time. Families are built on the layering of objects in a set of rooms called home so that all in the family feel cosy and loved and relaxed when they are in those rooms. But all of this is, also, at times, affected by a much larger set of relationships and bonds that are constitutive of what being family might be. Then, somehow the rooms need to expand; then, somehow, another plate has to be set on the table.

The point about this is, of course, that domestic living entails a great deal more than parent(s) and children taking part in the daily round. It involves a set of moral and ritual obligations as well. These obligations may be occasional but they are nevertheless powerful, as many adults will attest when they reflect on their practice of ringing their own parents once a week or thereabouts. Keeping this business going, keeping in touch with those one has no natural relationship with (natural here meaning daily, practical, or routine connection) is something that takes work. It may take the form of sending annual tributes in the form of Christmas cards, phoning Mum or of maintaining and drawing attention to the family blog. Again, the purpose and content of these, and indeed other communications, may be sentimental but they are also potentially fraught with tension: rights entail responsibilities in the family; responsibilities of politeness, caring, attention, and so on. Forgetting to send a birthday card can, in some cases, become a big deal.

These then are the ways one keeps in touch. The maintenance of family history in this way is purposeful, emotionally rich, and sometimes tense. If one decides to have a good old-fashioned marriage one needs to recollect not only who is owed an invitation by dint of having invited one's own family to one of their marriages in the distant past, but also who has a right to say no, they can't come. And just as one worries about making sure the right people are invited to the big events, the marriages and funerals and so forth, one has to make sure that sufficient contact has been made in between these events to elicit the sought-for response when the big event is about to occur: the aforementioned Christmas cards might be enough for some, a monthly phone call for others, but not for all. Thus family requires attending to how to sustain these others, these people who can't be dealt with like the rest. Techniques vary of course, and this in turn, creates new problems.

In much the same way, we can extend these comments about the wider family into comments about visitors in general. If the home has boundaries, these boundaries are frequently crossed by others. Sometimes, the visitor at our threshold may be a friend, someone who drops in unannounced, sometimes it might be a visit from Jehovah's Witnesses, and sometimes (perhaps most important) a delivery. The household, in other words, is connected in a whole variety of ways to the world outside.

All of this is meant to highlight the often peculiar character of families when they are conceived of as much more than a household, as an aggregation of persons who occupy a home on a daily basis. This has potential ramifications for technology in more than one way. Firstly, and most obviously, we cannot assume that the technologies we design for the home will only ever be used by members of the household. The home, as it were, is an interface with the outside world. Cleaners, tradesmen, relatives, and family friends, as well as the friends of our children will visit and stay for some period of time. They too, in some circumstances, may need to interact with the technology. We will, as family members, want to circumscribe what those interactions might be.

Thus, in the Orange@home, we noted the way in which 'netmeetings' and related technologies were popular. At that time, instant messaging had not become so popular amongst the young. We can point out an interesting feature of both, however, which is that bandwidth considerations were not paramount. Relations with wider kin, in the families we studied, were not a matter of immediate interactional consequence, but more to do with maintaining family histories, that is, maintaining contact. Our respondents talked about wanting to know how much someone had grown, how they were doing at school, and the state of health of third parties.

Among teenage peer groups, we have observed in a similar way, their endless enthusiasm for chat; a willingness to send each other poor quality photographs which capture, 'what we're up to', and their broad indifference to technologies requiring more bandwidth, such as video (at least at the moment). Issues of connectivity are, then, primarily social issues. Our task as ethnographers is to understand what family members are 'up to' when they connect with each other at a distance. What are the occasions, what is the symbolic importance, and what emotional work is being done, when family members connect?

9.6.6 Normal Troubles

One hardly needs, now, to elaborate what troubles all of this affords. If at work, there is the need to get things done by close of business, at home, within the family, the work never ceases and if it does albeit for a moment

appear to, it is only a mistake, a pause before the onslaught brought about by an envelope containing another invite. People go home to seek peace and quiet and what they find are hassles and obligations and errands. But this is home life; this is what it is made up of and what it is like. And it is because of the variable and complex nature that the work entailed in making family come to be whatever it is the family want to be that normal troubles ensue. Family is not something that one retires to; it's a place one has to work at to keep alive. Family is a responsibility that needs tending.

All families have ways of making do, of compromising between that 'event' ('Can't we miss it just this once?') so as to do that 'job' ('It's been worrying me . . .'). Families try to avoid some things that need doing, but may recognize the need to find excuses that seem real and don't create a burden of obligation and debt owed in the future. Many of these tricks of the family trade can be supported in different ways by technologies, computational and otherwise. For the fieldworker the task is not to take too literally the claims that members of family might make about how well they do things as a family; nor is it to be too cynical about the sham that some aspects of every family might be seen to be: it is to see and understand and describe how families work their way around different points in the spectrum of their existence so that, despite everything, all the stresses and strains, failures to turn up or return invites, the dirtiness and disorder, and the disagreements about who should do what and when, that nevertheless the people in question can reasonably assert, 'We are a family.'

These tools will need to help people 'do' family in the here and now. One would expect that they enable family to be something in the future, too. That future will, of course, be different from how it is now, but the fieldworker should recognise that although members of families might want, for themselves, a different future, in practice, that future will probably end up being pretty much like the past: populated with uncles and aunts and cousins and events that no one claims to want to see, but which nevertheless are wholeheartedly invited, met, chatted to, and sat down beside when the possibility of seeing becomes too real to deny. The ritual character of family life is, put simply, extremely earnest and important.

Equally, the existence of a threshold deserves consideration. How we deal with a variety of visitors with a range of businesses to conduct – what happens when we are not there, when visitors are unwanted, of getting breakdowns dealt with and attended to, of having repairs to the roof done, and so on – are as much as the world of work, issues of the home. Hence issues which seem outwardly central to CSCW, issues to do with coordination, collaboration, division of labour, and so on, turn out to be salient in the home too. Above all, normal natural troubles occur as much in our home life as they do elsewhere. In real life, the postman may ring only once, and we may well be in the bath.

9.7 Conclusion

At the outset we listed some of the ways that family and home, space and morality, and the physical and the ideational are tied together. A woman in a set of rooms may be a mother and a set of rooms, a home, by dint of the mother being there. We provided, later on, examples related to technology, space, and morality and discussed how it is that when computer systems fail and lock the doors this means one thing at work, another at home. The home and the family, that is, are analytically distinct from the work environment.

Yet, in truth, they are all too often practically linked. The extent of our arguments about these and many other examples may suggest that knowing all of this and hence being able to do the kind of fieldwork we have in mind is hard, a fear that we have alluded to in previous sections. We do not think so. It does require analytic work. Much of the literature on the subject of ethnography-for-design has suggested that the analytic work in question is either (in the case of the more theoretical approaches) given at the outset by the theory or (in the case of more ethnomethodological stances) merely a question of understanding or inhabiting the context in which the people in question (the 'subjects') find themselves. We are not wholly happy with either, for in CSCW the analytic work may be about a particular purpose with particular tools in mind and may require commitments up to which purists simply cannot live. We started off this chapter with the claim that home life and all it might mean – a constellation of associated terms and labels for a mixture of things – is an area that has come to be a major focus of attention and into which we, like many others, have put a lot of work of our own. Our analytic devices (like any others) only make sense (outside the hermetic world of sociology) in terms of the practical purposes to which they might be put, and we make no great claims for the kinds of analysis we have subjected our own data to both in the case of domestic life and the world of work. Successful fieldwork for design, nevertheless, is precisely for design. Our own work, concerned with the evaluation of existing technologies, led us to think in terms of the moral order, artefacts, aesthetic tailorability, social connectivity, and so on because these encapsulated the uses we saw technology being put to, or the problems it engendered.

We would not expect everyone engaged in similar research to agree with us about the relevance of these conepts. Like all concepts, we treat them as ultimately disposable. Nevertheless, we do believe that thinking of home and family as something that entails orientations above and beyond task accomplishment, and just as importantly, something that is characterized by stuff which is not necessarily immediately visible in specific interactions, is valuable. We carry 'family' with us, but the way in which we deal with family matters is clearly occasioned. Family life has a rhythm all of its own, and is characterized by desires and demands that are not always well understood. The real issue for the fieldworker is to ascertain how and where, in any household or set of households he or she is looking at, the 'work' that

is undertaken needs to be allowed to continue because it has an emotional or a symbolic resonance, where it might be assisted, and where we might dispose of it entirely. Labours of love have many forms.

Similarly, the point with social connectivity is not that families are Byzantine constructions that also orient in a wide variety of ways to outsiders; it is that the nature of family life is such that these constructions (about insiders and outsiders) can at times be irrelevant and at other times all too real. How this shift occurs, the ways that family individuals navigate their way through the maze of possibilities, dead-ends, and expectations that is family at large is not something that in itself can be modelled or rendered like some database; it is better thought of as a set of orientations, a way of proceeding with regard to possible connections, possible events, and possible accountabilities. Computational technologies should support the richness of these orientations; they should not try and fix them. To date, few researchers have managed to divine ways of doing this. Somewhat more have succeeded in understanding the extraordinary fluidity of family life but very few have managed to convey, at the same time, its apparent concreteness.

The management of these orientations, regardless of the role of computational tools or otherwise, requires dedication and persistence; these are but the routines and burdens of daily, weekly, monthly, and perennial family life. In solving these puzzles in whatever way they can, members of families, irrespective of their particular role, gender, or skill, are seeking to ensure the vitality of a particular kind of family, which is another term for a particular way of binding space, bodies, and morals. Family life, in this sense, is nothing if not political. In offering solutions to some of these problems the fieldworker for design is thus offering her own vision (her own political view) of the organisation of the family, a vision that, is ultimately a view from 'somewhere'. Families are nothing if not measures of good and bad, appropriate and inappropriate, tender and cruel, and loving and cold. The fieldworker is not exempt from these judgements.

Our reasons for dealing with work and family settings separately have in part been to do with the puzzle of 'similarity and difference' and how we organise ethnographic knowledge so that it might prove useful. Work settings have characteristics which can, if we so choose, be described in some generic ways. Particular tropes can be used which may orient us to the kinds of thing we might find. They should never obscure the differences we find. The home and the family are different enough (using the kind of common-sense judgement we have already pointed out is a necessary precursor to all our work) that maybe a different set of tropes is required. This chapter has sought to explore what these differences might be. As Alfred Korzybski (1931) apparently first said, 'The map is not the territory.' There cannot be a map that can guide every choice, and we really need a good grasp of the territory in which we find ourselves. This does not make maps useless, and they become especially useful when used in conjunction with a compass. What we are offering is precisely such a navigational aid.

Conclusion: Not the Last Word

10

We began this book by arguing that the turn to ethnography in design arose from a recognition that something had gone wrong in the design process. The failure – if that's what it is – had and has something to do with complexity. Not only are the technologies themselves more complex, so are the circumstances of their deployment. We first realized this during the Lancaster Air Traffic Control study[64] (see for example Bentley et al. (1992)), where it quickly became apparent that the design problem was a great deal more difficult than we had realised up until that point. Firstly, it seemed that relying on some classic methods of eliciting information was problematic. The observation that, 'If you ask twelve different air traffic controllers for an opinion, you'll get thirteen different answers,' was commonplace and so there was an obvious issue to do with the amount of trust and reliability we invested in the accounts we were being given. Secondly, the longer we spent in the environment, the more it became clear that there were many different interests in play: professional, managerial, and technical. Indeed, differences of opinion as regards the appropriateness of technology for future work practices between these stakeholders led to more than a little tension. It became increasingly clear that no group had particular confidence in the shape of the future of Air Traffic Control (see Twidale et al. (1994)). It took us a great deal of time to get some understanding of this highly technical domain, and even after the project was finished we were aware that we still had not got to grips with many aspects of the work. The problem we had then, understanding the situated practices of people at work, both individually and collaboratively, in a complex organisational environment, has not gone away.

We also suggested that recognizing a new problematic was not the same as solving the problems it contains, and we set up five basic questions we felt needed to be answered in some way. The answers to these questions

---

[64]For two of us, this was our first exposure to CSCW-related work.

are hard to find. Many problems remain. Nevertheless, and in the way that practitioners learn in the process of doing, we learnt a great deal about the business of doing ethnography. We continue to learn. In any event, we can at least by now outline our view of the possible answers.

10.1 The Relationship Between Ethnography and Fieldwork

We tried to show that there is a rough continuum along which various approaches to fieldwork can be placed. At one end is a view we associate mainly with anthropology and sociology and which we can view as being the 'ethnographic' end. It is a professional view. Substantial training in method, allied to a sophisticated conceptual grasp, is, in this view, a prerequisite of 'good' ethnography. At the other end is a more 'scientific' approach that sees fieldwork as providing the kind of data that other methods cannot find, and which sees the important problems as having to do with the way in which these new data have to be integrated with generalising theory.

All through, we have adopted a third view. In our view, the professional demands of ethnography are exaggerated, and a large part of what is required of us is common sense allied to determination. We are equally suspicious of the kinds of conceptual apparatus with which sociologists and anthropologists come to the table. We say this because doing HCI or CSCW is not the same thing as doing sociology or anthropology. Whatever the concerns of these disciplines may be, there is, we feel, no reason to presume they should remain the same in interdisciplinary work.

At the same time, we are equally negative about the way in which fieldwork is viewed, more or less unproblematically, as an alternative method, and which sees the status of theory as all-important. We have tried to show that the degree to which theories in HCI and CSCW are likely to prove valuable has to do with the purposes we set for them. Most of what is termed 'theory' in CSCW (in particular) is, in fact, not theory at all in any strong sense. The conceptual frameworks concerned (for that is what they are) seldom if ever provide a determinate or causal connection between concepts, and never provide precise outcomes. They are usually rather loose attempts to guide practitioners in useful directions. Their value in respect of ethnography cannot be determined by disciplinary interests and cannot be guaranteed in advance of the investigation of context. The latter is a given of ethnography, as opposed to fieldwork.

Ethnography is always about asking the initial question, 'What kind of problem have we got?' before beginning to provide solutions to the problems we identify. In other words, ethnography is in no way associated with hypothesis testing in any strict sense. Our 'third way' is very much predicated on the position that the initial questions cannot be answered merely by reference to sociological, psychological, or anthropological interests.

The relevance of questions will only become apparent as the research progresses, and only in relation to the design interests we try to accommodate.

10.2 Ethnographic Descriptions and the 'View from Nowhere'

We said at the outset that one problem for ethnography has to do with the nature of its descriptions. Most practitioners, by now, will be familiar with another continuum, which has at one end a concern for very detailed descriptions of the kind associated with ethnomethodology and conversation analysis, and at the other with the so-called 'scenic' descriptions which are sometimes associated with particular generalising theoretical interests. Again, we have tried to be insistent that the measure of an ethnography's quality does not necessarily lie in the amount of detail it provides or even in the degree to which it captures the subtlety of interactions. These things matter only in respect of their relevance to the technical and organisational problems that are being addressed. Their merits or otherwise (in the contexts which interest us) have nothing to do with how closely they follow, for instance, ethnomethodological injunctions or conversation analytic tropes.

Our 'third way' is founded on the development of an interdisciplinary sensibility. This sensibility owes something to the disciplinary training and knowledge associated with the social sciences, because they, at their best, provide us with a training in 'attentiveness'. It nevertheless refuses to accept social scientific definitions of the problematic. At the same time, and not to put too fine a point on it, by definition this sensibility refuses the notion that designers 'know best' about the problems for which they are designing (what has historically been thought of as the 'requirements' issue). It is reasonable to assume, however, that they know more than anyone else about the feasibility of solutions.

An interdisciplinary sensitivity requires us to take design seriously, understanding how designers go about solving their problems, identifying candidate solutions, and applying their technical knowledge to them. None of this constitutes an appeal to the ludicrous notion of the 'universal' man or woman. It is an appeal, rather, to an ethnographic approach which is 'design relevant' but not 'design laden'. Max Weber argued, in the early part of the twentieth century, that sociology could and should be 'value relevant' but not 'value laden.' It is often forgotten that one of the bases for his position was his profound cynicism about the ability of sociologists to say anything much at all in the way of generalisation, and in particular about the future. His reasons for arguing this way had to do with his initial assumption that the real world is simply too complicated for any strong predictive statements to be of value. We think this is right. No group – not social scientists, not designers, not managers, or cost accountants – has a privileged picture. Our best guesses, the process of satisficing, will be arrived at through listening carefully to each other.

291

It is for these reasons that we have tried to steer a path through the entirely valid concern for contextuality that stems from ethnomethodology and situated action, but on the other hand, the recognition that relevant and timely generalisation is necessary to the design process. Design, in the end, should be attentive to both similarity and difference. Its problems have a great deal to do with figuring out which similarities and which differences are the relevant ones. We undertook, therefore, to show how some modest tropes, concepts, illuminating devices, whatever you want to call them, can inform us in terms of our search for design relevance. They cannot, however, dictate the shape and purpose of our enquiries. The tropes we have used at various times are emphatically not a typology, simply because their relevance and use are utterly contingent.

10.3 Doing Fieldwork: The Minor Nature of Methodological Problems

We make no apology for seeming a little disrespectful about method. It has long been an aspect of ethnomethodological work that inasmuch as it treats much professional work as being inevitably tethered in common sense, problems of method are not viewed as terribly important (see also Feyerabend (1975)). To be clear, there are of course choices to be made. Our disdain is for the illusion that these choices require a high level of professional expertise. At root, what any ethnographer (ethnomethodological or otherwise) seeks to do is establish what questions she deems relevant to her research and what the best ways might be of getting robust and reliable answers to those questions.

Having said that, a great deal has been remarked in recent years about particular problems of knowledge elicitation in different circumstances. It has been suggested, for instance, that certain environments such as the 'virtual organization,' where distributed and mediated collaboration has become the norm, require special methods. A similar argument has been produced about mediated forms of communication and collaboration regardless of organisational context, hence, studies of e-mail, multiplayer games, blogging, and so on are sometimes held to require methods which subsume under the heading of 'virtual ethnography'.

10.3.1 Virtual Ethnography

The idea that the development of some new technology has been accompanied by some new social arrangements, and thus may enforce a new kind of ethnography – sometimes called 'virtual' ethnography (see Hine (2000)) – has gone largely unchallenged. Such claims are sometimes accompanied by the suggestion that this 'new' kind of ethnography is confronted with particular kinds of problem, and requires a particular kind of procedural and analytic solutions. They can lead, in our view, to some mistaken assumptions concerning social networks, communities, and what have you, predicated on a casual assumption that something radically new is taking place and thus radically new methods might be needed. We are less than convinced by these arguments and, in this short digression, want to suggest why some issues are rather less important than they might at first appear to be, because they are essentially mundane and can be solved practically. Let's take the following examples to show this.

1. Technologies for communicating at a distance are hardly new. An ethnographer of communication amongst some tribe, should such a figure have ever existed, would have been confronted with the problem of figuring out what two different groups at each end of the communication process (to whit two bonfires and two blankets) were up to. We certainly should remember that some of the earliest conversation analytic work was about opening sequences on the telephone.

2. Observing and investigating individuals sitting at computer terminals is not entirely new either (all of the authors have being doing this kind of thing for at least ten years). Such observations fit nicely with the standard ethnomethodological interest in the processual character of things and require no special insights. Indeed, one could argue that it is the fetishisation of interaction (as opposed to our insistence that 'work done' is the appropriate category) that leads to remote, or computer-mediated, communication being seen as a special problem at all.

3. Virtual ethnographies require particular kinds of technological support. This seems to us to be broadly true, though hardly a new thing. Our own studies of domestic life, for instance (see Harper and Shatwell (2002)) entailed some complex use of digital video in a (largely forlorn) attempt to capture simultaneous activities in different locations in the home. We did, in fact, begin to think about the way in which families come together and separate largely because fast-forwarding the video brought the balletic nature of family interactions, their rhythms, if you will, to our attention. Equally, it seems that some forms of data will increasingly be available as 'logs' of one kind or another and the collection of this kind of data might involve various kinds of technological support in much the way that making sense of a telephone conversation is a great deal easier when you can record both ends of the conversation.

Nevertheless, virtual ethnographies are just ethnographies. The argument that something new is going on, methodologically and substantively, seems to us to be based precisely on the sociological privileging of method that we have discussed earlier. These methods, we want to insist, are not much more than common sense or wisdom based on accumulated experience. They entail no uniquely difficult data-collection problems. Nor, more important, do they demonstrate any particularly interesting analytic problems.

10.3.2 Sensitive Settings

Nevertheless, our imaginations can inform our practices. If, as we insist, ethnography is characterized by its analytic interests rather than any claim to method, we can afford to be catholic in our choice of method. Thus and for instance, there are some domains where the continued presence of the ethnographer turns out to be problematic or where the ordinary business of finding out might be especially difficult for one reason or another. One such, for instance, turned out for Cheverst et al. (2001a, 2003) to be the study of a centre for psychiatric patients. Studying the routine activities of people suffering from acute schizophrenia or paranoia through direct observational techniques may well trigger debilitating episodes and relapses, for example. In such situations, there are very good grounds for an imaginative use of methods to gather data. Various methods which can be collected under the rubric of 'self-reporting' can be associated with this. At various times, subjects have been encouraged to use diaries, carry with them recording devices, or respond to stimuli of various kinds. An example of the latter is the 'cultural probe', probably first used in this context by Gaver (1999, 2001, 2002, 2004). His interest in this emanated from an interest in domestic environments and from the conviction that such environments could best be understood as ludic. He suggests, 'They may seem whimsical, but it would be a mistake to dismiss them on that ground: for unless we start to respect the full range of values that make us human, the technologies we build are likely to be dull and uninteresting at best, and de-humanising at worst.'

In effect, cultural probes refer to some fairly ordinary methods for eliciting responses. They might include, for instance, diaries, photographs, disposable cameras, Post-it notes, and so on. Such methods have, of course, been used on innumerable occasions over the years in anthropological work. What makes the notion of a cultural probe a little different, in our understanding, is the way these artefacts and others are packaged, and accompanied by instructions. Hence, Cheverst et al. (2003, p. 67),

> These items are cultural probes – but don't worry – they're just a way for us to find out more about you, your everyday life, what you think and feel. We'd like you to use them to tell us about yourself – and below are a few ideas you might want to think about. Ignore these if you like – nothing is compulsory – do as much or as little as you like. We hope its fun. I'll come back to collect them in about a week.

Now, Blythe et al. were using this device and what they term 'technology biographies' to investigate domestic settings. We make no comment about the degree to which such adjuncts to looking and talking might be useful in the domestic setting (see Hutchinson et al. (2003)), but there would be good reasons, we feel, for thinking they might be useful in other contexts. For Cheverst et al. (2003) (ibid.; see also Crabtree et al. (2003)), the probes consisted of items such as a set of postcards, a map of the local area, a disposable camera, a voice-activated Dictaphone, a visitors' book, various paper-based items such as Post-it notes, and a photo album. They were handed out, according to the authors, 'much like a birthday or Christmas present.' Put simply, probes of this kind allow members to do some of the ethnographic work of recording data in situations where ethnographers might find it difficult to do any sustained observation.

However, whatever the restrictions of method we might encounter, the ethnographic task is primarily analytic. We need to ask what analytic benefit such an approach may have. It is claimed here that the results of the probes are valuable inasmuch as they reveal abiding concerns, that is, the kinds of problem and preoccupation that seem to be common in care settings. In this case, they have much to do with safety and security, and with the management of medication. It is at least plausibly the case that the ordinary business of looking and asking may not lead us to the same analytic conclusions. Perhaps this is a function of the 'snapshot' orientation to be found in (quick and dirty) ethnography sometimes, or the particular difficulties entailed with unreliable interviewees who might be more reliable when they have more control over the data collection process. Regardless, there can be no doubt that the move into sensitive settings has prompted heightened awareness of the need for sensitivity in data collection, and has led to the adoption of the techniques we briefly describe here. We certainly would not want to be negative about them; in our view they represent imaginative approaches to some problems of data collection, analysis, and evaluation.

10.3.3 Scope and Ambition: Who Are the Appropriate Subjects of an Enquiry?

A key theme of our discourse has been the problem of relating settings to design problems. In the past, as we suggested, when ethnographic enquiries were limited to control-room settings or specific problems of computer-mediated communication, this rather simple and obvious relationship between a known setting and a specific technology drove, we think, much of the argument about the relationship between ethnography and design. In particular, it led to the dominance of the 'implications for design' mentality. This somewhat simplistic view is increasingly challenged (see e.g. Dourish

(2006)) perhaps because the remit of ethnographic enquiry is larger and more complex today. It may include, for instance, work in complex organisational settings, where one might find, for instance, a wide range of professional skills, competencies, relevant rules and procedures, parallel hierarchies, and so on. Medical work would be an example of this.

Sometimes, we might be engaged in studies which encompass more than one organisation, as with coordination work across supply chains. We might be embarking on studies which are supposed to relate to applications for vaguely understood and barely existing applications to run on technologies such as 3G telephony, and so on. That is, we might be in a situation where not only is an application searching for a use, it might even be searching for a domain in which it might be used. This kind of problem raises a whole set of issues which relate to the size, scope, and intensity of any given enquiry, along with the degree of comparison required, evaluative function, critical function, and so on. It ought to be apparent that such matters as the level of detail required of ethnographic enquiry also depend on the kind of relationship it has with a proposed design space. It is surprising to find that, apart from Hughes et al.'s seminal paper on 'Moving Out of the Control Room' (which we discussed earlier), little has been said on this subject.

We have tried in this book, at least in outline, to suggest at least the axes along which the relationship between ethnography and design may vary. There are two observations in particular that we want to make at this juncture concerning the ways in which standard assumptions may break down. Firstly, we want to argue that ethnographic practices in HCI and CSCW have been singularly unambitious. (We should admit here that this complaint applies every bit as much to ethnomethodological work as any other.) There are good reasons for this, having to do with the ease of getting grant monies for dealing with small contained problems as opposed to a grander, more speculative set of objectives. Nevertheless, ethnographers should be doing more to encourage the investigation of large and complex domains. As, for instance, the so-called virtual organisation becomes a little more real than it hitherto has been, so ethnography's remit will radically change. The virtual organisation implies a range of cross-organisational collaborations, distributed across time and space, and probably carrying with it huge problems of communication and concurrency. Very few studies have been done at all which deal with the range of organisational, technical, and cultural practices and knowledge that will be germane to these complex commercial environments. Moreover, we may be forced to think less about the requirements for individual technologies and more about the integration of a whole range of technologies.

Secondly, the fact of mobile technology will dramatically alter our remit, for it implies that our attention will shift towards the public setting. Arguably, this is an area that remains significantly underresearched.

10.3.4 Public Settings: Mobility

Public settings arguably produce a different set of problems. Where work or domestic life is founded on a relatively close, permanent set of ties, public life is characterised by temporary, brief, sometimes anonymous encounters. Moreover, mobility is relatively unconstrained and hence following people about may well prove more difficult. There have, we should say, been a limited number of rather Goffmanesque studies of, for instance, navigation, scheduling, and map-reading (see e.g. Brown and Chalmers (2003) and Randall (2002)) and a few studies of mobile working as well (see for instance Fagrell (2003)), but as yet the best explored aspects of mobility have been those surrounding mobile phone use. In the face of new mobile technologies, research into public settings is also likely to become increasingly common. This may well be another example of a context where the use of support technologies such as video comes into its own.

More importantly, this is a very good example, we feel, of the contingent relationship between ethnography and design. At a minimum it can be argued that there is a fault line here, one where research is predicated either on the view that information needs will drive the mobile device market or on the view that social connectivity will drive it. Of course, this relates to a number of research questions, not least such matters as the role of online communities, the relevance of social networks, the behavioural patterns of teenagers, and so on.

The point is that, at the moment, we know very little at all about what information or connectivity needs might in fact drive the market in the near future, and equally little about whether the holy grail of convergence is realizable. What we do want to suggest is that the room for what we have called 'scoping' ethnographies in this area is immense. It is likely that, in a situation where we have only the sketchiest of information about what the technological possibilities might be even in the near future, ethnographies can provide a great deal of knowledge about shifting contexts, but knowledge which is not geared towards specific design problems. That is, some innocence as to the nature of the matter to be investigated is likely to be a positive virtue.

If we think about ethnographic work to support, for instance, tourism, then our first problem, of course, is 'What tourists, where?' Our answers to the question are likely to have a significant effect on our chosen methods. Brown and Chalmers (ibid.), for instance, used daylong observation, video diaries, and video recordings of tourists in public to investigate tourism in the city. Randall used what has been termed, 'occasional' ethnography, the serendipitous collection of occasionally relevant conversation, perspicuous examples, and so on to collect relevant data. Whether these methods would be appropriate for investigating, say, information-gathering behaviour by foreign tourists preparing for travel on an unfamiliar rail network is an open question (one of the authors has cause to regret not knowing what the Danish word for 'cancelled' is). Similarly, it might seem intuitively obvious that the right place to look if we are interested in the affordances and constraints of, say, online shopping behaviour is instances of online shopping. It turns out, in our experience, that this may not be the case. Regardless, there are huge and as yet only partially realized opportunities for ethnographic work in the developing context of mobility and more particularly in public spaces, whether in the shopping malls pertinent to the last example, or any place through which people come and go, performing whatever it is that public behaviour might be.

10.4 Summary: Analysis and the Design Process

Any number of sins have been committed by commentators who want to discuss the relationship between ethnographic data and the subsequent design process. A moment's thought tells us that it is absurd to hold ethnography to account for any design decision. Such decisions are contingent, and may well be out of the hands of the people who might normally be thought of as the designers (as the history of the Xerox Corporation has shown).

In other words, even beginning to get to grips with this issue requires us to confront some intractable problems. They include whether fieldwork is a sole individual's (or small group's) unique task within a complex division of labour where others do the design work. If so, how data are represented to others and equally crucially, when they are of major importance. How, for instance, are design insights based on fieldwork data agreed, tested, and iterated? Do they need to be?

We have argued that the answers to these kinds of question are themselves contextual: there are no general solutions to the problem of relating ethnographic enquiry to design. It will depend on the many and varied possible uses to which ethnography can be put, the kinds of design team in which the data are to be examined and used, the scale of the project in question, the relationship of ethnography to other methodologies which might be in use, and so on. Part of this has to do with what is usually held to be a (somewhat vexed) problem of representation. We argue that it may be helpful to think of it in other ways. In other words, we feel there is a tendency to think of the problem of representation as being a product of incommensurability between different kinds of research paradigm. Although there may be some truth in this, it may be more useful to treat these problems as more prosaic: problems of timeliness and relevance.

Ethnography of whatever ilk must be adequate to interdisciplinary tasks. Now, of course, this in turn begs the question of how this 'adequacy' might be assessed and evaluated: this relates in fact to the question of the peer review process that Marcus (1998) mentions. Oddly enough, although he claimed that there is a need to make questions of evidence more central to ethnographic enterprise in anthropology he made no suggestion as to how this was to be done. At this point in our argument, we hope it is becoming clear that we do have a view on this. Indeed, if one were to glance at the CSCW literature and other, related, disciplines one would see that there is an emerging 'body politic', a set of tools and assumptions that are beginning to be used to evaluate and comment on matters of empirical adequacy, scope, relevance, tractability, and so on. Key to these things, what Marcus calls the '*mis-en-scène*' of a discipline (and this is the last trope we use) are the following assumptions and views about fieldwork-for-design.

First, we do believe and hope to have begun to persuade the reader that, when it comes to fieldwork-for-design, there is a need for researchers to be ethnographic in their approach. This has to do with being familiar with what to look for in terms of themes, topics, and issues, and in knowing how to explain or explicate aspects of the observed setting around these themes and topics.

Second, the kind of ethnographic fieldwork we have in mind is based, to some degree, on knowledge of prior design-oriented fieldwork. We do not contend that this equates to the years of training in prior studies that anthropologists and sociologists undergo, but we do say that enough needs to be undertaken to produce an analytic sensibility for fieldwork-in-design.

Third, we have shown, quite conclusively we hope, that when fieldwork-for-design is undertaken, the evidence it produces is of a particular kind. The way the fieldworkers in design look, what they look for, what they capture, all this and more, is wrapped up with their design motivation. There is, then, no inevitable separation between data and design, although they may be quite distinct at various points in the process.

Fourth, one further consequence of this view on data is that the kind of materials produced enable or help create a space for design thinking. Although the long written monograph is only one of these, others include graphical representations of the work in question, arranged through the themes and topics already mentioned: Beyer and Holtzblatt's (1998) affinity analysis and its use of Post-it notes is a case in point. Another is to undertake design workshops where the fieldworker or fieldwork team proffers examples, 'stories' about how they do the work, and even begin the process of 'patterning' these examples in some way, as Crabtree suggests. There are needless to say other ways too.

Fifth, we have wanted to suggest that design-oriented fieldwork can be undertaken by teams or that at least it should be thought of as essentially a collaborative affair. This requires its own tools and processes, and part of the motivation for these is to enable evaluation and testing of fieldwork understanding in ways that avoids the many pitfalls of the solitary ethnographer approach. So when we say collaborative we don't mean that fieldwork has to be undertaken by teams, but we do mean that the evidence produced should be part of an overall process of team-based activities. These include collaborative evaluation and review and collaborative design thinking and much more besides. As one colleague said to us on the occasion of a discussion about ethnography, 'There's no shortage of ethnographers. The shortage is in ethnographers who know anything about design.' This does not equate, however, to a view that every member of a research team can do every job. It is, rather, an appeal to the organisation for genuine collaboration.

Sixth, it should also be clear from what we have seen that design-oriented fieldwork requires an iterative and dynamic approach to the role and position of fieldwork in the overall process. Fieldwork-in-design needs to be suffused with concerns from other stages in the overall process and though fieldwork may be mostly undertaken at the early stages of the process, it may be returned to later on as design iterations are made available for testing and evaluation.

This then is what we think fieldwork-in-design requires. It entails a hybrid of skills and tools from the ethnographic and from what we have called the fieldwork tradition; it involves the use of a set of empirical interests, conceptual tools, sensitivity to interdisciplinary concerns, and it requires a dynamic and flexible approach to its role in a design process. And finally, it requires a particular view about evidence, its evaluation and its use, and about the role of evidence generated by other disciplinary-specific approaches to fieldwork. CSCW is unique we believe, not because the technologies it has and will produce are special, but because it needs to do its business in a particular way. This book has attempted to explain why that is so.

Bibliography

Abowd, G., Edwards, K., and Grinter, B., 2003, Smart homes or homes that are smart? *SIGCHI Bull. Suppl. Interact.* 2003:13.

Ackermann, M., Pipek, V., and Wulf, V. (Eds.), 2003, *Sharing Expertise: Beyond Knowledge Management*, MIT Press, Cambridge, MA.

Ackroyd, S. and Hughes, J.A., 1992, *Data Collection in Context*, 2nd edn., Longmans, London.

Adams, R.N. and Preiss, J.J. (Eds.), 1960, *Human Organization Research: Field Relations and Techniques*, Dorsey Press, Homewood, IL.

Agar, M., 1980, *The Professional Stranger: An Informal Introduction to Ethnography*, Academic Press, New York.

Agre, P., 1995, Accountability and discipline: A comment on Suchman and Winograd, *Comput. Support. Coop. Work*, 3(1), 31–35.

Akrich, M., 1992, The de-scription of technical objects. In: W. Bijker and J. Law (Eds.), *Shaping Technology, Building Society: Studies in Sociotechnical Change*. MIT Press, Cambridge, MA, pp. 205–224.

Akrich, M. and Latour, B., 1997, A summary of a convenient vocabulary for the semiotics of human and nonhuman assemblies, In W.E. Bijker and J. Law (Eds.), *Shaping Technology/Building Society: Studies in Sociotechnical Change*, The MIT Press, Cambridge, MA, pp. 259–264.

Alexander, C., 1977, *The Timeless Way of Building*, Oxford University Press, Oxford, UK.

Alexander, C., 1979, *A Pattern Language: Towns, Building, Construction*, Oxford University Press, Oxford, UK.

Amsterdamska, O., 1990, Surely you are joking, Monsieur Latour!, *Sci. Technol. Human Values*, 15: 495–504.

Anderson, J.M., 1988, The integration of HCI principles in structured system design methods. In: *Conference Proceedings MIlcomp '88, Military Computers, Graphics, and Software*, 27–29 Sept., London.

Anderson, R. and Sharrock, W., 1993, Can organisations afford knowledge, *CSCW: Int. J.* 1(3): 143–61.

Anderson, R.J., Hughes, J.A., and Sharrock, W.W., 1989, *Working for Profit; The Social Organisation of Calculation in an Entrepreneurial Firm*, Avebury, Aldershot, UK.

Anderson, R.J., 1994, Representations and requirements: The value of ethnography in system design, *Hum.–Comput. Interact.* 9: 151–182.

Artman, H. and Waern, Y., 1999, Distributed cognition in an emergency co-ordination center. Fördelade kunskapsprocesser i ledningscentraler vid nödsituationer: koordination och situationsmedvetenhet. H. Artman. Linköping, Tema Kommunikation, Linköping, Sweden, pp. 183–199.

Asad, T., 1986, The concept of cultural translation in British social anthropology. In J. Clifford and G. Marcus, *Writing Culture*, University of California Press, Berkeley, pp. 141–164.

Auge, M., 1995, *Non-Place: An Introduction to an Anthropology of Supermodernity*, (Trans. J. Howe), Verso, London.

Bannon, L., 1991, From human factors to human actors: The role of psychology and human–computer interaction studies in system design. In Greenbaum J. and Kyng M. (Eds.), *Design at Work: Cooperative Design of Computer Systems*, Lawrence Erlbaum, Hillsdale, NJ, pp. 25–44.

Bannon, L., 2000, Situating workplace studies within the human–computer interaction field. In P. Luff, J. Hindmarsh , and C. Heath, *Workplace Studies*, CUP, pp. 230–241.

Bannon, L. and Bødker, S., 1991, Beyond the interface: Encountering artifacts in use. In: J. Carroll (Ed.), *Designing Interaction: Psychology at the Human–Computer Interface*, Cambridge University Press, Cambridge, UK, pp. 227–253.

Bannon, L. and Kuutti, K., 1991, Some confusions at the interface; Re-conceptualising the interface problem. In: M.I. and W. Nurminen, and G. Weir (Eds.), *Human Jobs and Computer Interfaces*, Amsterdam, North Holland, pp. 3–19.

Bansler, J., 1989, System development in Scandinavia: Three theoretical schools, *Scandinavian J. Inf. Syst.* 1.

Banta, M., 1995, *Taylored Lives: Narrative Productions in the Age of Taylor, Veblen, and Ford*, University of Chicago Press, Chicago.

Bardram, J., 1997, Plans as situated action: An activity theory approach to workflow systems. In: J. Hughes et al., *Proceedings of the 5th European Conference on CSCW*, Kluwer, Dordrecht.

Barley, N., 1983, *The Innocent Anthropologist: Notes From a Mud Hut*, London, British Museum Publications.

Barlow, J. and Gann, D., 1998, A changing sense of place: Are integrated IT systems reshaping the home?, paper presented to the Technological Futures, Urban Futures Conference, Durham, 23–24 April.

Barnes, B. and Bloor, B., 1982, Relativism, rationalism, and the sociology of knowledge. In: M. Hollis and S. Lukes (Eds.), *Rationality and Relativism*, Oxford University Press, Oxford, UK.

Barthelmess, P. and Anderson, K.M., 2002, A view of software development environments based on activity theory, *CSCW: J. Collab. Comput.* 11(1–2): 13–37.

Barth, J., 1991, *The Last Voyage of Somebody the Sailor*, Mariner, Boston.

Becker, H., 1967, Whose side are we on? *Social Probl.* 14: 239–247.

Bellamy, R.K., 1996, Designing educational technology: Computer mediated change. In: B.A. Nardi (Ed.), *Context and Consciousness: Activity and Human–Compuer Interaction*, MIT Press, Cambridge, MA and London, pp. 124–146.

Benson, D. and Hughes, J.A., 1991, Method: evidence and inference. In: G. Button, (Ed.), *Ethnomethodology and the Human Sciences*, Cambridge University Press, Cambridge, UK, pp. 109–136.

Benson, D. and Hughes, J.A., 1984, *The Perspective of Ethnomethodology*, Longman, Harlow, UK.

Bentley, R., Hughes, J., Randall, D., Rodden, T., Sawyer, P., Shapiro, D., and Sommerville, I., 1992, Ethnographically informed systems design for air traffic control. In: J. Turner and R. Kraut (Eds.), *Proceedings of CSCW '92*, October 31–November 4, Toronto, ACM Press, New York, pp. 123–129.

Bentley, R. and Randall, D., 1994, Tutorial Notes, Conference on Computer Supported Cooperative Work (CSCW 04), Toronto, Canada.

Berg, C., 1994, A gendered socio-technical construction: The smart house. In: C. Cockburn and R. Furst-Dilic (Eds.), *Bringing Technology Home: Gender and Technology in a Changing Europe*, Oxford University Press, Buckingham.

Bermann, T. and Thorenson, K., 1988, Can networks make an organization? In: *Proceedings of the Conference on Computer-Supported Cooperative Work '88*, Portland, Oregon, September 26–28, ACM Press, New York, pp. 153–166.

Berndtsson, J. and Normark, M., 1999, The coordinative functions of flight strips: Air traffic control revisited. In: *Proceedings of the International ACM SIGGROUP Conference on Supporting Group Work*, Phoenix, AZ.

Beyer, H. and Holzblatt, K., 1998, *Contextual Design: Defining Customer-Centered Systems*, Morgan Kaufmann, San Francisco.

Bijker, W.E., Hughes, T.P., and Pinch, T., 1987, *The Social Construction of Technological Systems*, MIT Press, Cambridge, MA.

Bittner, E., 1965, The concept of organisation, *Social Res.* 23: 239–255.

Bittner, E., 1973, Objectivity and realism in sociology, in G. Psathas, *Phenomenological Sociology*, Englewood Cliffs, Prentice Hall.

Bjerknes, G. and Bratteteig, T., 1987, Florence in wonderland. In: G. Bjerknes, P. Ehn, and M. Kyng, *Computers and Democracy: A Scandinavian Challenge*, Gower Press, Brookfield, VT. Bjerknes, G. and Bratteteig, T., 1988, The memoirs of two survivors: Or the evaluation of a computer system for cooperative work. In: *Proceedings of the Conference on Computer-Supported Cooperative Work (CSCW '88)*, Portland, Oregon, Sept. 26–28, ACM Press, New York, pp. 167–177.

Bjerknes, G., Ehn, P., and Kyng, M. (Eds.), 1987, *Computers and Democracy: A Scandinavian Challenge*, Gower Press, Brookfield, VT.

Blomberg, J., 2000, Co-constructing the relevance of work practice for CSCW design: A case study of translation and mediation, Occasional papers from the Work Practice Laboratory, University of Karlskrona, Sweden.

Blomberg, J.L. and Henderson, A., 1990, Reflections on participatory design: Lessons from the Trillium experience. In: *Proceedings of CHI '90 Conference on Human Factors in Computing Systems*, ACM Press, New York, pp. 353–359.

Blomberg, J. and Kensing, F., 1998, Participatory design: Issues and concerns, *CSCW: J. Collab. Comput.* 7(3–4): 167–185.

Bloomfield, B. and Vurdubakis, T., 1997, Paper traces: Inscribing organisation and information technology. In: B. Bloomfield, R. Coombs, D. Knights, and D. Littler (Eds.), *Information Technology and Organizations: Strategies, Networks and Integration*, (Eds.) Oxford University Press, Oxford, UK, pp. 85–111.

Bloomfield, B.P, Coombs, R., Cooper, D.J., and Rea, D., 1992, Machines and manoeuvres: Responsibility accounting and the construction of hospital information systems, *Account. Manage. Inf. Technol.* 2: 197–219.

Blumer, H., 1940, The problem of the concept in social psychology, *Amer. J. Sociol.* 45(5): 707–719.

Blumer, H., 1954, What is Wrong with Social Theory? *American Sociological Review*, 19(1): 3–10.

Blumer, H., 1956, Sociological analysis and the "variable", *American Sociological Review*, 21(6): 683–690.

Blumer, H., 1969, *Symbolic Interactionism: Perspective and Method*, Prentice-Hall, Englewood Cliffs, NJ.

Blythe, M. and Monk, A., 2002, Notes towards an ethnography of domestic technology. In: *Proceedings of DIS 2002*, ACM Press, New York, pp. 271–288.

Blythin, S., Hughes, J., O'Brien, J., Rodden, T., and Rouncefield, M., 1997, Designing with ethnography: A presentation framework for design. In: *Proceedings of Designing Interactive Systems '97*, Amsterdam, ACM Press, New York.

Boden, D., 1994, *The Business of Talk: Organisations in Action*, Polity Press, Cambridge, UK.

Bødker, S., 1989, A human activity approach to user interfaces, *Human–Computer Interaction*, 4(3): 171–195.

Bødker, S., 1991, *Through the Interface: A Human Activity Approach to User Interface Design*, Lawrence Erlbaum, Hillsdale, NJ.

Bødker, S. and Gronbaek, K., 1991, Cooperative prototyping: Users and designers in mutual activity, *International Journal of Man Machine Studies*, 34(3): 453–478, March (special edition on CSCW & Groupware).

Bødker, S., Ehn, P., Knudsen, J., Kyng, M., and Madsen, K., 1988, Computer support for cooperative design. In: *Proceedings of the Conference on Computer-Supported Cooperative Work (CSCW '88)*, Portland, Oregon, September 26–28, ACM Press, New York, pp. 377–394.

Boehm, B.W., 1981, *Software Engineering Economics*, Prentice-Hall, Englewood Cliffs, NJ.

Bose, C., Bereano, P., and Malloy, M., 1984, Household technology and the social construction of housework, *Technology and Culture*, 25: 53–82.

Bowers, J.M. and Martin, D., 1999, Informing collaborative information visualisation through an ethnography of ambulance control. In: S. Bødker, M. Kyng, and K. Schmidt (Eds.), *ECSW '99 Proceedings of the Sixth Conference on Computer Supported Cooperative Work*, pp. 309–330.

Braudel, F., 1975, *Capitalism and Material Life: 1400–1800*, Harper Colophon, New York.

Braverman, H., 1974, *Labour and Monopoly Capital: The Degradation of Work in the Twentieth Century*, Monthly Review Press, New York.

Brewer, J.D., 1994, The ethnographic critique of ethnography: Sectarianism in the RUC, *Sociology*, 28(1, Feb.): 231–244.

Brewer, J.D., 2000, *Ethnography (Understanding Social Research)*, Open University Press, Milton Keyes, UK.

303

Brooks, F.P., 1975, *The Mythical Man Month*, Addison-Wesley, Reading, MA.

Brooks, F.P., 1987, No silver bullet: Essence and accidents of software engineering, *IEEE Computer*, 20(4): 10–21.

Brow, B.B., 2006, The television will be revolutionised: Effects of PVRs and filesharing on television watching. In: *Proceedings of CHI '96*, Montreal, ACM Press, New York.

Brown, B. and Chalmers, M., 2003, Tourism and mobile technology. In: *Proceedings of ECSCW '03, 2003*, Kluwer, Amsterdam.

Brown, J.S. and Newman, S.E., 1985, Issues in cognitive and social ergonomics: From our house to Bauhaus, *Human-Computer Interaction*, 1(4): 359–391.

Bryman, A., 1988, *Quantity and Quality in Social Research*, Unwin Hyman, London.

Burgess, R. (Ed.), 1982, *Field Research: A Sourcebook and Field Manual*, Allen & Unwin, London.

Burke, K., 1935, *Permanence and Change: An Anatomy of Purpose*, New Republic Press, New York.

Burke, K., 1945, *A Grammar of Motives*, University of California Press, Berkeley.

Burke, K., 1973, *The Nature of Art Under Capitalism, The Philosophy of Literary Form*, 3rd revised ed., University of California Press, Berkeley, pp. 314–322.

Button, G., 1990, Going up a blind alley. In: P. Luff, N. Gilbert, and D. Frohlich (Eds.), *Computers and Conversation*, Academic Press, London, pp. 67–91.

Button, G. (Ed.), 1991, *Ethnomethodology and the Human Sciences*, Cambridge University Press, Cambridge, UK.

Button, G., 1993, The curious case of vanishing technology. In: G. Button (Ed.), *Technology in Working Order: Studies of Work, Interaction and Technology*, Routledge: London, pp. 10–28.

Button, G., 1995, What's wrong with speech act theory, *Computer Supported Cooperative Work: An International Journal*, 3(1): 39–42.

Button, G. , 1997, A Review of Ed Hutchins' 'Cognition in the Wild', Unpublished manuscript of a talk.

Button, G. and Dourish, P., 1996, Technomethodology: Paradoxes and possibilities. In: *Proceedings of CHI '96*, Vancouver, BC, 19–26. ACM Press, New York.

Button, G. and Dourish, P., 1998, On technomethodology: Foundational relationships between ethnomethodology and system design, *Hum. Comput. Interact.* 13(4): 395–432.

Button, G. and King, V., 1992, Hanging around is not the point, paper presented to workshop on Workshop on 'Ethnography in Design', *CSCW '92*, Toronto.

Button, G. and Sharrock, W., 1997, The production of order and the order of production. In: J. Hughes et al. (Eds.), *Proceedings of ECSCW '97*, Kluwer, Dordrecht.

Button, G., Coulter, J., Lee, J., and Sharrock, W., 1996, *Computers, Minds and Conduct*, Polity Press, London.

Callon, M., 1986a, The sociology of an actor-network. In: M. Callon, J. Law, and A. Rip, (Eds.) *Mapping the Dynamics of Science and Technology*, Macmillan, London.

Callon, M., 1986b, Some elements of a sociology of translation: Domestication of the scallops and the fishermen of Saint Brieuc Bay. In: J. Law (Ed.), *Power, Action and Belief: A New Sociology of Knowledge? Sociological Review Monograph*. Routledge and Kegan Paul. London, 32: 196–233.

Callon, M., 1997, After the individual in society: Lessons on collectivity from science, technology and society, *Canadian Journal of Sociology*, 22(2), pp. 165–182.

Calvey, D., Hughes, J., O'Brien, J., Rodden, T., and Rouncefield, M., 1997, On becoming a DNP user: Ethnography and support for design. In: *Proceedings of IRIS20*, Oslo.

Chalmers, M., 2003, Awareness, representation and interpretation, *CSCW: The Journal of Collaborative Computing*, 11: 389–409.

Checkland, P., 1981, *Systems Thinking, Systems Practice*, Wiley, London.

Checkland, P. and Scholes, J. 1989, *Soft Systems Methodology in Action*, Wiley, London.

Cheverst, K., Clarke, G., Dewsbury, T., Hemmings, and Rouncefield, M., 2002, When geography matters: Location awareness and community care. In: R. Harper (Ed.), The Social Shaping of Mobile Futures, *Proceedings of the Third Wireless World Conference*, Digital World Research Centre, University of Surrey, pp. 69–83.

Cheverst, K., Clarke, K., Dewsbury, G., Rouncefield, M., Sommerville, I., Blythe, M., Baxter, G., and Wright, P., 2003, Gathering requirements for inclusive design. In: *Proceedings of 2nd BCS HCI Workshop on Culture and HCI: Bridging Cultural and Digital Divides*, K. Gunter, A. Smith, and T. French (Eds.), University of Greenwich, pp. 65–71.

Cheverst, K., Cobb, S., Hemmings, T., Kember. S., Mitchell, K., Phillips, P., Procter, R., Rodden, T., and Rouncefield, M., 2001a, Design with care, *Journal of New Technology in the Human Services*, 14(1/2): 39–47.

Cheverst, K., Fitton, D., and Dix, A., 2003, Exploring the evolution of office door displays. In: K. O'Hara, M. Perry, E. Churchill, and D. Russell, (Eds.), *Public, Community and Situated Displays: Social and Interact ional Aspects of Shared Display Technologies*, Kluwer, Dordrecht.

Clarke, K., Hartswood, M., Procter, R., Rouncefield, M., and Slack, R., 2002, Minus nine beds: Some practical problems of integrating and interpreting information technology in a hospital trust. In: J. Bryant, *Proceedings of the BCS Conference on Healthcare Computing*, Harrogate, March 18–20, 2002.

Clarke, K., Hughes, J., Martin, D., Rouncefield, M., Sommerville, I., Gurr, C., Hartswood, M., Procter, R., Slack, R., and Voss, A., 2003, Dependable red hot action. In: K. Kuutti, E. Karsten, P. Dourish, G. Fitzpatrick, and K. Schmidt (Eds.), *Proceedings of ECSCW '03*, Helsinki, Finland, Kluwer Academic, Dordrecht, pp. 61–80.

Clifford, J., 1988, *The Predicament of Culture: 20th Century Ethnography, Literature and Art*, Harvard University Press.

Clifford, J. and Marcus, G. (Eds.), 1986, *Writing Culture: The Poetics and Politics of Ethnography*, University of California Press, Berkeley.

Cockburn, C., 1997, Domestic technologies: Cinderella and the engineers, *Womens Studies International Forum*, 20(3): 361–371.

Coffee, A., Atkinson, P., and Holbrook, B., 1996, Qualitative Data Analysis: Technologies and Representations, *Sociological Research Online*, 1: 1.

Cole, M., 1984, The zone of proximal development: Where culture and cognition create each other. In: J. Wertsch (Ed.), *Culture, Communication, and Cognition: A Vygotskian Perspective*, Cambridge University Press, Cambridge, UK.

Cote, J.E., 1994, *Adolescent Storm and Stress: An Evaluation of the Mead–Freeman Controversy*, Lawrence Erlbaum, Hillsdale, NJ.

Cowan, R.S., 1983, *More Work for Mother: The Ironies of Household Technology from the Open Hearth to the Microwave*, Basic Books, New York.

Crabtree, A., 1998, Ethnography in participatory design. In: R. Chatfield, S. Kuhn, and M. Muller (Eds.), *Proceedings of PDC '98*, Seattle, WA, Computer Professionals for Social Responsibility, pp. 98–105.

Crabtree, A., 2003, *Designing Collaborative Systems*, Springer, New York.

Crabtree, A. and Hemmings, T., 2003, SPAM on the Menu: The practical use of remote messaging in community care. In: *Proceedings of CUU 2003 ACM Conference on Universal Usability*.

Crabtree, A., Hemmings, T., Rodden, T., and Mariani, J., 2003a, Informing the development of calendar systems for domestic use. In: K. Kuutti, E. Karsten, P. Dourish, G. Fitzpatrick, and K. Schmidt (Eds.), *Proceedings of ECSCW '03*, Helsinki, Finland, Kluwer Academic, Dordrecht, pp. 139–158.

Crabtree, A., Hemmings, T., Rodden, T., Cheverst, K., Clarke, K., Dewsbury, G., Hughes, J., and Rouncefield, M., 2003b, Designing with care: Adapting cultural probes to inform design in sensitive settings. In: *Proceedings of the Australian Computer–Human Interaction Special Interest Group [OzCHI '03]*, 26–28 November at the University of Queensland, Brisbane, Australia.

Dant, T. and Francis, D., 1998, Planning in organisations: Rational control or contingent activity? *Sociological Research Online*, 3(2), 1998.

Dartington, T., Miller, E.J., and Gwynne, G.V., 1981, *A Life Together: The Distribution of Attitudes around the Disabled*, Tavistock, London.

Davenport, T., 1994, *Process Innovation: Reengineering Work Through Information Technology*, Harvard Business School Press, Cambridge, MA.

Davenport, T. and Short, J.E., 1990, The new industrial engineering: Information technology and business process redesign, *Sloan Manage. Rev.* (Summer), Harvard Business School Press, Boston.

Davies, J.R., 1990, A methodology for the design of computerised qualitative research Tools., *Interact. Comput.* 2(1): 33–58.

De Keyser, V., 1991, Work analysis in French language ergonomics: Origins and current research trends. *Ergonomics*, 34: 653–669.

Dicks, B. and Mason, B., 1998, Hypermedia and ethnography: Reflections on the construction of a research approach, *Sociol. Res. Online*, 3(3).

Dingwall, R., 1981, The ethnomethodological movement, In: G. Payne, R. Dingwall, J. Payne, and M. Carter, (Eds.), *Sociology & Social Research*, Croom Helm, London, pp. 124–138.

Douglas, M., 2002, *Purity and Danger: An Analysis of the Concepts of Pollution and Taboo,* (originally published 1966), Routledge, London.

Dourish, P., 1995, Space is the place. Position paper at *European conference on Computer Supported Cooperative Work.*

Dourish, P., 1995, Developing a reflective model of collaborative systems. *ACM Trans. Comput. Hum. Interact.*, 2(1): 40–63.

Dourish, P., 2001, *Where the Action Is: The Foundations of Embodied Interaction*, MIT Press, Cambridge, MA.

Dourish, P., 2006, Implications for design. In: *Proceedings of CHI '06*, Montreal, ACM Press, New York.

Draper, S.W. and Norman, D.A., 1985, Software engineering for user interfaces., *Softw. Eng.*, 11(3): 252–258.

Drew, P. and Heritage, J. (Eds.), 1992, *Talk at Work*, Cambridge University Press, Cambridge, UK.

Driessen, J. 1999, Worldly interpretations of a suspicious story, *Ethnograph. Stud.*, 1(2).

Durkheim, E. 2001, *The Elementary Forms of Religious Life*, C. Cosman, Trans., originally published 1912, Oxford Paperbacks, Oxford, UK.

Edles, L., 2002, *Cultural Sociology in Practice*, Blackwell, Oxford, UK.

Ehn, P., 1988, *Work-Oriented Design of Computer Artifacts*, Arbetslivscentrum, Stockholm, 1988.

Ehn, P., 1993, Scandinavian design; On participation and skill. In: D. Schuler and A. Namioka (Eds.), *Participatory Design – Principles and Practice*, Erlbaum, Hillsdale, NJ.

Emerson, R., 1981, Observational Field Work, *Ann. Rev. Sociol.*, 7: 351–378.

Emery, F.E. and Thorsrud, E., 1976, *Democracy at Work*, Martinus Nijhof, Leiden.

Emery, F.E. and Trist, E.L., 1960, Socio-technical systems. In: C.W. Churchman and M. Verhulst (Eds.), *Management Science, Models and Techniques*, vol. 2, Pergamon, Elmsford, NY.

Engeström, Y., 1987, *Learning by Expanding: An Activity-Theoretical Approach to Developmental Research*, Orienta-Konsultit Oy, Helsinki.

Engeström, Y., 1990, *Learning, Working, and Imagining: Twelve Studies in Activity Theory*, Orienta-Konsultit, Helsinki.

Engestrom, Y. and Escalante, V., 1996, Mundane tool or object of affection?: The rise and fall of the postal buddy. In: B. Nardi (Ed.), *Context and Consciousness*, MIT Press, Cambridge, MA.

Fagrell, H., 2003, Newsmate: Providing timely knowledge to mobile and distributed journalists. In: M. Ackermann, V. Pipek, and V. Wulf (Eds.), *Sharing Expertise: Beyond Knowledge Management*, MIT Press, Cambridge, MA.

Feldman, M. and March, J., 1981, Information in organisations as signal and symbol, *Admin. Sci. Quart.*, 26: 171–186.

Feyerabend, P., 1975, *Against Method*, New Left, London.

Fielding, N., 1993, Qualitative data analysis with a computer: recent updates, *Soc. Res. Update*, (1), University of Surrey.

Fielding, N., 1994, Ethnography. In: N. Gilbert (Ed.), *Research in Social Life*, Sage, London.

Fielding, N. and Lee, R., (Eds.). 1991, *Using Computers in Qualitative Research*, Sage, London.

Fielding, N.G. and Lee, R.M., 1998, *Computer Analysis and Qualitative Research*, Sage, Thousand Oaks, CA.

Filstead, W.J. (Ed.), 1970, *Qualitative Methodology: Firsthand Involvement with the Social World*, Markham, Chicago.

Fish, S., 1994, Being interdisciplinary is so very hard to do. In: S. Fish, *There's No Such Thing As Free Speech and a Good Thing Too*, Oxford, Oxford University Press, Oxford, UK, pp. 231–242, originally in *Profession*, 1989, pp. 15–22.

Fitzpatrick, G., 2003, *The Locales Framework: Understanding and Designing for Wicked Problems*, Kluwer Academic, Amsterdam.

Fitzpatrick, G., Kaplan, S., and Mansfield, T., 1996, Physical spaces, virtual places and social worlds: A study of work in the virtual. In: M. Ackermann (Ed.), *Proceedings of CSCW '96*, Cambridge, MA, ACM Press, New York.

Fodor, J., 1989, Why should the mind be modular? In: A. George (Ed.), *Reflections on Chomsky*, Blackwell, Oxford, UK, pp. 1–21.

Fraser, J., 1993, *The Golden Bough: A Study in Religion and Magic*, Wordsworth, Ware, Herts. UK (abridged version, first published in 1922).

Freeman, D., 1999, *The Fateful Hoaxing of Margaret Mead*, Westview, Boulder, CO.

Frohlich, D. and Kraut, R., 2003, The social context of home computing. In: Harper (Ed.), *Inside the Smart Home*, Springer, Godalming. pp. 127–162.

Frohlich, D. and Luff, P., 1990, Applying the technology of conversation to the technology for conversation. In: P. Luff, N. Gilbert, and D. Frohlich, (Eds.), *Computers and Conversation*, Academic Press, London, pp. 187–221.

Frohlich, D., Chilton, K., and Drew, P., 1997, Remote homeplace communications: What is it like and how can we support it? In: H. Thimbleby, B. O'Conal, and P. Thomas (Eds.), *Proceedings of People and Computers 12*, pp. 38–41.

Frohlich, D.M. and Luff, P., 1989, Conversational resources for situated action. In: *Proceedings of ACM CHI '89 Conference on Human Factors in Computing Systems*, pp. 253–258.

Frohlich, D.M., Kuchinsky, A., Pering, C., Don, A., and Ariss, S., 2002, Requirements for photoware, *Proceedings of CSCW '02*, November 16–20; New Orleans, ACM Press, New York.

Garfinkel, H., 1963, A Conception of, and experiments with, trust as a condition of stable concerted actions, in O.J. Harvey (ed.), *Motivation and Social Interaction*, New York, Ronald press, pp. 187–238.

Garfinkel, H., 1967, *Studies in Ethnomethodology*, Polity Press, London.

Garfinkel, H. (Ed.), 1986, *Ethnomethodological Studies of Work*, Routledge and Kegan Paul, London.

Garfinkel, H. and Weider, L., 1992, Evidence for locally produced, naturally accountable phenomena of order, logic, reason, meaning, method, etc. In: G. Watson and R. Seiler (Eds.), *Text in Context: Contributions to Ethnomethodology*, London, Sage, pp. 175–206.

Gasser, L., 1986, The integration of computing and routine work, *ACM Trans. Office Syst.* 4(3): 205–225.

Gaver, B., Dunne, T., and Pacenti, E., 1999, Cultural probes. *Interactions*, vol 6, no 1. p. 21–29.

Gaver, B., 2002, Provocative awareness, *CSCW: J. Collab. Comput.*, 11: 475–493.

Gaver, W., 2001, Designing for ludic aspects of everyday life, *ERCIM News*, No. 47. www.ercim.org/publication/Ercim_News/enw47/gaver.html

Gaver, W., Boucher, A., Pennington, S., and Walker, B., 2004, Cultural probes and the value of uncertainty. *Interactions*, vol 11, no 5, p. 53–56.

Geertz, C., 1973, *The Interpretation of Cultures*, Basic, New York.

Gibson, J.J., 1977, The theory of affordances. In: R.E. Shaw and J. Bransford (Eds.), *Perceiving, Acting, and Knowing*, Lawrence Erlbaum, Hillsdale, NJ.

Gibson, J.J., 1979, *The Ecological Approach to Visual Perception*, Houghton Mifflin, Boston.

Giddens, A., 1984, *The Constitution of Society*, University of California Press, Berkeley.

Gilbert, N., Woofitt, R., and Fraser, N., 1990, Organising computer talk. In: P. Luff, N. Gilbert, and D. Frohlich, (Eds.), *Computers and Conversation*, Academic Press, London, pp. 235–259.

Gilbreth, L.M., 1927, *The Home-Maker and Her Job*, Appleton, New York.

Glaser, B., 1998, *Doing Grounded Theory: Issues and Discussions*, Sociology Press, Mill Valley, CA.

Glaser, B.G. and Strauss, A.L., 1965, *Awareness of Dying*, Aldine, Chicago.

Glaser, B.G. and Strauss, A.L., 1967, *The Discovery of Grounded Theory: Strategies For Qualitative Research*, Aldine, Chicago.

Glaser, B.G. and Strauss, A.L., 1968, *Time for Dying*, Aldine, Chicago.

Goffman, E., 1968, *Asylums*, Penguin, Harmondsworth.

Goffman, E., 1969, *The Presentation of Self in Everyday Life*, Penguin, Harmondsworth.

Goguen, J., 1993, Social issues in requirements engineering. In *Proceedings of RE 93: International Symposium on Requirements Engineering*, January 4–6, IEEE Press, San Diego.

Gold, R., 1958, Roles in sociological field investigation. *Social Forces*, 36: 217–223.

Goodwin, C., 1994, Professional vision, *Amer. Anthropol.* 96: 606–633.

Goodwin, C. and Goodwin, M., 1993. Formulating planes: Seeing as a situated activity. In: Y. Engeström and D. Middleton (Eds.), *Communication and Cognition at Work*, Cambridge University Press, Cambridge, UK.

Gould, L., Walker, A., Crane, L., and Lidz, C., 1974, *Connections: Notes From The Heroin World*, Yale University Press, New Haven, CT.

Goulding, C., 2002, *Grounded Theory: A Practical Guide for Management*, Business and Market Researchers, London.

Greenbaum, J., 1988, In search of cooperation: An historical analysis of work organization and management strategies. In: *Proceedings of the Conference on Computer-Supported Cooperative Work* (CSCW '88), Portland, OR, September 26–28, ACM Press, New York, pp. 102–114.

Greenbaum, J., 1996, Back to Labor: Returning to labour process discussions in the study of work. In: *Proceedings of CSCW '96*, Boston, ACM Press, New York.

Greenbaum, J. and Kyng, M. (Eds.), 1991, *Design at Work: Cooperative Design of Computer Systems*, Lawrence Erlbaum, Hillsdale, NJ.

Grinter, R.E., 1997, Doing software development: Occasions for automation and formalisation. In: J. Hughes, W. Prinz, T. Rodden, and K. Schmidt (Eds.), *Proceedings of ECSCW '97*, Lancaster, Kluwer, Amsterdam.

Grinter, R.E. and Palen, L., 2002, Instant messaging in teen life, *Proceedings of CSCW '02*, November 16–20; New Orleans, ACM Press, New York.

Groenbaek, K., Kyng, M., and Mogensen, P., 1997, Toward a cooperative experimental system developmental approach. In: M. Kyng and L. Matthiesen, (Eds.), *Computers and Design in Context*, MIT Press, Cambridge, MA, pp. 201–238.

Groth, K. and Bowers, J., 2001, On knowing who knows: Situating organizational knowledge in CSCW. In: *Proceedings of ECSCW '01*, Kluwer, Dordrecht.

Grudin, J., 1988, Why CSCW applications fail: Problems in the design and evaluation of organizational interfaces. In: *Proceedings of ACM CSCW'88 Conference on Computer-Supported Cooperative Work*, ACM Press, New York.

Grudin, J., 1990, The computer reaches out: The historical continuity of interface design. In: *Proceedings of ACM CHI'90 Conference on Human Factors in Computing Systems*, pp. 261–268.

Grudin, J. 1991, CSCW: The convergence of two disciplines. In: *ACM SIGCHI Conference on Human Factors in Computing Systems*, New Orleans, April 28–May 2, ACM Press, New York, pp. 91–98.

Habenstein, R. (Ed.), 1970, *Pathways to Data*, Aldine, Chicago.

Hackman, J.R., 1987, The design of effective work teams. In: J.W. Lorsch (Ed.), *Handbook of Organizational Behaviour*, Prentice-Hall, Englewood, NJ, pp. 315–342.

Hackman, J.R. and Oldham, G.R., 1975, Development of the job diagnostic survey, *J. Appl. Psychol.* 60(2): 159–170.

Hales, M., 1993, User participation in design – What it can deliver, what it can't and what this means for management. In: P. Quintas (Ed.), *Social Dimensions of Systems Engineering*, Ellis Horwood, New York.

Halverson, C., 1995, Air traffic control: Inside the cognitive workplace, unpublished doctoral thesis, University of California, San Diego.

Halverson, C., 2002, Activity theory and distributed cognition: Or what does CSCW need to do with theories, *CSCW: J. Collab. Comput.*, 11(1–2): 243–267.

Hammer, A. and Champy, J., 1993, *Re-engineering the Corporation: A Manifesto for Business Revolution*, Nicholas Brealey, London.

Hammer, M., 1990, Re-engineering work: Don't automate, obliterate, *Harvard Bus. Rev.*, (July/August).

Hammersley, M., 1989, *Herbert Blumer and the Chicago Tradition*, Routledge, London.

Hammersley, M., 1990, What's wrong with ethnography? The myth of theoretical description, *Sociology*, 24: 597–615.

Hammersley, M., 1992, *What's Wrong With Ethnography?* London. Routledge.

Hammersley, M. and Atkinson, P., 1983, *Ethnography: Principles in Practice*, Tavistock, London.

Hansson, C., Dittrich, Y., and Randall, D., 2004, Agile processes: Enhancing user participation for small providers of off-the-shelf software. In: *Software Engineering '04*, Munich.

Harding, S., 1986, *The Science Question in Feminism*, Cornell University Press, Ithaca, NY.

Harding, S. (Ed.), 1987, *Feminism and Methodology*, Indiana University Press, Bloomington.

Harding, S., 1991, *Whose Science, Whose Knowledge? Thinking From Women's Lives*, Cornell University Press, Ithaca, NY.

Harding, S. and Merrill, H., (Eds.), 1983, *Discovering Reality: Feminist Perspectives on Epistemology, Metaphysics, Methodology, and Philosophy of Science*, Reidel, Dordrecht.

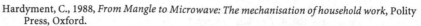

Hardyment, C., 1988, *From Mangle to Microwave: The mechanisation of household work*, Polity Press, Oxford.

Harper, R., 1991, The computer game: Detectives, suspects and technology, British J. Criminol. 31(3): 292–307.

Harper, R., 1995, Radicalism, beliefs and hidden agendas, *CSCW: Int. J.*, 3(1): 43–46.

Harper, R., 1996, Why people do and don't wear active badges: A case study, *CSCW: Int. J.*, 4: 297–318.

Harper, R., 1998, *Inside the IMF: An Ethnography of Documents, Technology and Organizational Action*, Academic Press, London.

Harper, R., 2000a, Getting to grips with information: Using ethnographic case materials to aid the design of document technologies, *Inf. Des. J.*, 9:(2–3): 195–206.

Harper, R., 2000b, The organisation in ethnography: A discussion of ethnographic fieldwork programs in CSCW, *CSCW: Int. J.*, 9: 239–264.

Harper, R., (Ed.), 2003, *Inside the Smart Home: Interdisciplinary Perspectives on the Design and Shaping of Domestic Computing*, Springer Verlag, Godalming and Heidelburg.

Harper, R. and Shatwell, B., 2002, Paper-mail in the home of the 21st century: An analysis of the future of paper-mail and implications for the design of electronic alternatives, *J. Interact. Market*, 3(4): 311–323.

Harper, R., Evergeti, V., Hamill, L., and Shatwell, B., 2003, The social organisation of communication in the home of the 21st century: An analysis of the future of paper-mail and implications for the design of electronic alternatives, *J. Cogn. Technol. Work*, 5: 5–22.

Harper, R., O'Hara, K., and Sellen, A.J., 1996, Documents in action: A case study of anaesthetists at Papworth Hospital, Rank Xerox and Papworth Hospital Trust.

Harper, R., Procter, R., Randall, D., and Rouncefield, M., 2001, 'Safety in nunbers': Calculation and document re-use in knowledge work. In: S. Ellis, T. Rodden, and I. Zigurs, (Eds.), *Proceedings of Group '01*, Boulder, CO, ACM Press, New York, pp. 242–251.

Harper, R., Randall, D., and Rouncefield, M., 2000, *Organisational Change and Retail Finance: An Ethnographic Perspective*, Routledge, London.

Harper, R., Taylor, A., and Palen, L., 2005, *The Inside Text: Social and Design Perspectives on SMS*, Springer, Godalming.

Harrington, H.J., 1991, *Business Process Improvement*, McGraw-Hill, New York.

Harrison, S. and Dourish, P., 1996, Re-Place-ing Space: The roles of place and space in collaborative systems: In: *Proceedings of CSCW '96*, ACM Press, New York, pp. 67–83.

Hartson, H.R. and Smith, E.C., 1991, Rapid prototyping in human–computer interface development., *Interact. Comput.*, 3(1): 51–91.

Hartswood, M. and Procter, R., 2000a, Managing errors in a computer-aided clinical decision-making task. In: C. Johnson (Ed.), Special issue on Human Error and Clinical Systems, *J. Topics Health Inf. Manage.*, 20(4): 38–54.

Hartswood, M. and Procter, R., 2000b. Designing for breakdowns and repairs in collaborative work settings. In: B. Fields, and P. Wright (Eds.) Special issue on Understanding Work and Designing Artefacts, *Int. J. Hum. Comput. Stud.*, 53 (May).

Hartswood, M., Procter, R., Rouncefield, M., Slack, R., Soutter, J., and Voss, A., 2003, 'Repairing' the machine: A case study of evaluating computer-aided detection tools in breast screening. In: K. Kuutti, E. Karsten, G. Fitzpatrick, P. Dourish, and K. Schmidt (Eds.), *Proceedings of the Eighth Conference on Computer Supported Cooperative Work*, Helsinki, Finland, Kluwer, Dordrecht, pp. 375–394.

Heath, C. and Luff, P., 1991, Collaborative activity and technological design: Task coordination in London Underground control rooms. In: L. Bannon, M. Robinson, and K. Schmidt (Eds.), *ECSCW '91. Proceedings of the Second European Conference on Computer-Supported Cooperative Work*, Amsterdam, 24–27 September, Kluwer Academic, Dordrecht, pp. 65–80.

Heath, C. and Luff, P., 1992, Collaboration and control: Crisis management and multimedia technology in London Underground control rooms, *CSCW: Int. J.*, 1(1–2): 69–94.

Heath, C. and Luff, P., 1996, Documents and professional practice: "Bad" organizational reasons for "good" clinical records. In: M. Ackerman (Ed.), *Proceedings of CSCW '96*, Boston, ACM Press, New York.

Heath, C., Hindmarsh, J. and Luff, P., 2000, *Workplace Studies: Recovering Work Practice and Informing System Design*, Cambridge University Press, Cambridge, UK.

Heath, C., Sanchez Svensson, M., Hindmarsh, J., Luff, P. and Von Lehn, D., 2002, Configuring awareness, *CSCW: J. Collab. Comput.* 11(3–4).

Hemmings, T., Clarke, K., Francis, D., Marr, L., and Randall, D., 2001, Situated knowledge and virtual education. In: I. Hutchby and J. Moran-Ellis (Eds.), *Children, Technology and Culture: The Impacts of Technologies in Children's Everyday Lives*, Routledge, London.

Hemmings, T., Crabtree, A., Rodden, T., Clarke, K., and Rouncefield, M., 2002, Probing the probes: domestic probes and the design process. In: S. Bagnara, S. Pozzi, A. Rizzo, and P. Wright (Eds.), *Proceedings of the Eleventh European Conference on Cognitive Ergonomics*, Rome, September, Instituto Di Scienze E Tecnologie Della Cocnizione Coniglio Nazionale Delle Ricerche, pp. 187–193.

Heninger, K.L., 1980, Specifying software requirements for complex systems. New techniques and their applications, *IEEE Trans. Software Eng.*, SE-6(1): 2–13.

Hepso, V., 1997, The social construction and visualisation of a new Norwegian offshore Installation. In: J. Hughes et al. (Eds.), *Proceedings of ESCW '97*, Kluwer, Amsterdam.

Heritage, J., 1984, *Garfinkel and Ethnomethodology*, Polity Press, London.

Herzberg, F., 1966, *Work and the Nature of Man*, World, Cleveland.

Hesse-Biber, S., Dupuis, P., and Scott Kinder, T., 1991, HyperRESEARCH: A computer program for the analysis of qualitative data with an emphasis on hypothesis testing and multimedia analysis, *Qualitat. Sociol.* 14(3).

Hester, S. and Francis, D., 1999, Ethnomethodology, conversational analysis and 'institutional talk', *Text*, 20(3): 391–413.

Hiltzick, M., 1999, *Dealers of Lightning: Xerox Parc and the Dawn of the Computer Age*, HarperCollins, New York.

Hindmarsh, J., Fraser, M., Heath, C., Benford, S., and Greenhalgh, C., 1998, Fragmented interaction: Establishing mutual orientation in virtual environments. In: *Proceedings of Computer Supported Collaborative Work 1998*, Seattle WA, ACM Press, New York.

Hindus, D., 1999, The importance of homes in technology research. In: N. Streitz, J. Siegel, V. Hartkopf, and S. Konomi (Eds.), *Cooperative Buildings - Integrating Information, Organizations, and Architecture, Proceedings of the Second International Workshop on Cooperative Buildings (CoBuild '99)*, Pittsburgh, October 1–2, *LN CS* 1670. Springer, Heidelberg, pp. 199–207.

Hine, C., 2000, *Virtual Ethnography*, Sage, London.

Hochschild, A.R., 1983, *The Managed Heart: The Commercialization of Human Feeling*, University of California Press, Berkeley.

Hofstede, G., 1980, Motivation, leadership and organization: Do American theories apply abroad? *Org. Dynamics*, (Summer), pp. 42–63.

Hofstede, G., 1986, Cultural differences in teaching and learning, *Int. J. Intercult. Relations*, 10(3): 301–320.

Hofstede, G., 1991, *Culture and Organisations*, Harper Collins, New York.

Hughes, J., King, V., Rodden, T., and Anderson, H., 1994, Moving out of the control room: Ethnography in system design. In: *Proceedings of the ACM Conference on Computer Supported Cooperative Work, Chapel Hill, NC*, ACM Press, New York, pp. 429–438.

Hughes, J., Martin, D., Rouncefield, M., Sommerville, I., Hartswood, M., Procter, R., Slack, R., and Voss, A., 2003, Dependable red hot action. In: K. Kuutti, E. Karsten, G. Fitzpatrick, P. Dourish, and K. Schmidt (Eds.), *Proceedings of ECSCW '03*, Kluwer, Dordrecht.

Hughes, J., O'Brien, J., Rouncefield, M., Rodden, T., and Rouncefield, M., 2000, Ethnography, communication and support for design. In: C. Heath and P. Luff (Eds.), *Workplace Studies: Recovering Work Practice and Informing System Design*, Cambridge University Press, Cambridge, UK, pp. 187–214.

Hughes, J., O'Brien, J., Rouncefield, M., Rodden, T., and Sommerville, I., 1995, Presenting ethnography in the requirements process, *Proceedings of RE '95*, IEEE Press, Washington, DC.

Hughes, J.A. and King, V., 1993, Paperwork, Department of Sociology, Lancaster University, UK.

Hughes, J.A., Randall, D., and Shapiro, D., 1992, Faltering from ethnography to design. In: J. Turner and R. Kraut (Eds.), *Proceedings of CSCW '92 Conference on Computer-Supported Cooperative Work*, ACM Press, New York, pp. 115–122.

Hughes, J.A. Randall, D., and Shapiro, D., 1993, Designing with ethnography: Making work visible, *Interact. Comput.*, 5(2): 239–253.

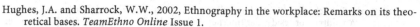

Hughes, J.A. and Sharrock, W.W., 2002, Ethnography in the workplace: Remarks on its theoretical bases. *TeamEthno Online* Issue 1.

Hutchins, E., 1995, *Cognition in the Wild*, MIT Press, Boston.

Hutchinson, H., McKay, W., Westerlund, B., Bederson, B., Druin, A., Plaisant, C., Beaudouin-Lafon, M., Conversy, S., Evans, H., Hansen, H., Roussel, N., Eiderback, B., Lindquist, S., and Sundblad, Y., 2003, Technology probes: Inspiring design for and with families. In: *Proceedings of CHI '03*, Ft. Lauderdale, FL.

International Journal of Social Research Methodology Theory & Practice, 2002, 5(3, July–Sep), A Special Issue on Methodological Issues and Practices in Using QSR NVivo and NUD*IST.

Jacobson, I., Ericcson, M., and Jacobson, A., 1994, *The Object Advantage: Business Process Re-engineering with Object Technology*, Addison-Wesley, Wokingham, UK.

Jenkins, D., 1978, The West German humanization of work programme: A preliminary assessment, *WRU Occasional Paper No. 7*.

Johnson, J., Ehn, P., Grudin, J., Nardi, B., Thoresen, K., and Suchman, L., 1990, Participatory design of computer systems. In: *Proceedings of CHI '90*, ACM Press, New York, pp. 141–144.

Jordan, B. and Henderson, A., 1992, Interaction analysis: Foundations and practice, Rank Xerox Technical Report SPL–94 –059.

Jordan, B. and Henderson, A., 1995, Interaction analysis: Foundations and practice, *J. Learn. Sci.*, 4(1).

Jordan, P.W., 2000, *Designing Pleasurable Products: An Introduction to the New Human Factors*, Taylor & Francis, London.

Juhlin, O. and Weilenmann, A., 2001, Decentralizing the control room: Mobile work and institutional order. In: *Proceedings of ECSCW '01*, Bonn, Germany, Kluwer Academic Press, Dordrecht.

Junker, B., 1960, *Field Work*. University of Chicago Press, Chicago.

Kaptelinin, V., 1994, Activity theory: Implications for human computer interaction. In: M.D. Brouwer-Janse and T.L. Harrington (Eds.), *Human Machine Communication for Educational Systems Design*, Springer, Berlin, pp. 5–15.

Kaptilinen, V., 1996a, Activity theory: Implications for human–computer interaction, in B. Nardi (1996a) (op. cit.), pp. 101–116.

Kaptilinen, V., 1996b, Computer-mediated activity: Functional organs in social and developmental contexts, in B. Nardi (1996a) (op. cit.), pp. 45–68.

Karasti, H., 2001, Bridging work practice and system design: Integrating systemic analysis, appreciative intervention and practitioner participation, *CSCW: J. Collab. Comput.* 10(2): 211–246.

Kelle, U., 1997, Theory building in qualitative research and computer programs for the management of textual data, *Sociol. Res. Online*, 2(2).

Kensing, F., Simonsen, J., and Bodker, K., 1998a, Participatory design at a radio station, *CSCW: J. Collab. Comput.* 7(3–4): 243–271.

Kensing, F., Simonsen, J., and Bødker, K., 1998b, MUST – A method for participatory design, *Hum. Comput. Interact.* 13: 2.

Kidd, C.D., Abowd, G.D., Atkeson, C.G., Essa, I.A., MacIntyre, B., Mynatt, E., and Starner, T.E., 1999, The aware home: A living laboratory for ubiquitous computing research. In: N. Streiz, S. Konomi, and H.-J. Burkhardt (Eds.), *Cooperative Buildings - Integrating Information, Organization and Architecture, Proceedings of CoBuild '98*, LNCS 1370, Springer, New York, pp. 190–197.

Klein, H.K. and Myers, M.D., 1999, A set of principles for conducting and evaluating interpretive field studies in information systems, *MIS Quart.*, Special Issue on Intensive Research 23(1): 67–93.

Korzybski, A., 1931, A non-Aristotelian system and its necessity for rigour in mathematics and physics, paper presented to the American Mathematical Society, December 28, 1931. Reprinted in *Sci. Sanity*, 1933, pp. 747–761.

Kotonya, G. and Sommerville, I., 1992, Viewpoints for requirements definition, *Softw. Eng. J.*, 7(6): 375–387.

Kraemer, K.L. and Pinsonneault, A., 1990, Technology and groups: Assessments of the empirical research., In J. Galegher, R.E. Kraut, and C. Egido (Eds.), *Intellectual Teamwork: Social Foundations of Cooperative Work*, Lawrence Erlbaum, Hillsdale, NJ, pp. 373–404.

Kraut, R., Brynin, M., and Kiesler, S. (Eds.), 2005, *Domesticating Information Technologies*, Oxford University Press, Oxford, UK.

311

Kraut, R., Scherlis, W., Mukhopadhyay, T., Manning, J., and Keisler, S., 1996, HomeNet: A fieldtrial of residential Internet services. In: *Proceedings of CHI '96*, ACM Press, New York, pp. 284–291.

Kuhn, T., 1970, *The Structure of Scientific Revolutions*, 2nd edn., University of Chicago Press, Chicago.

Kuutti, K., 1991, The concept of activity as a basic unit for CSCW research. In L.J. Bannon, M. Robinson, and K. Schmidt (Eds.), *Proceedings of the Second ECSCW Conference*, Kluwer, Amsterdam, pp. 249–264.

Kuutti, K., 1994, Information systems, cooperative work and active subjects: The activity – theoretical perspective, Research Papers Series A23, University of Oulu Printing Centre.

Kuutti, K., 1996, Activity theory as a potential framework for human–computer interaction research. In: B. Nardi, *Context and Consciousness*, MIT Press, Cambridge, MA, pp. 17–44.

Kuutti, K., and Arvonen, T., 1992, Identifying CSCW applications by means of activity theory concepts: A case example. In: J. Turner and R. Kraut (Eds.), *Sharing Perspectives, Proceedings of the ACM 1992 Conference on Computer-Supported Cooperative Work (CSCW '92)*, ACM Press, New York, pp. 233–240.

Kyng, M. and Mathiassen, L., 1975, A "new systems development": Trade union and research activities. In: Sandberg (1975), pp. 54–74.

Lakatos, I., 1970, Falsification and the methodology of scientific research programmes. In: I. Lakatos and M. Musgrave (Eds.), *Criticism and the Growth of Knowledge*, Cambridge University Press, Cambridge, UK.

Larsson, A., 2005, unpublished PhD. Thesis, Dep't of Engineering, Lulea Technical University, Sweden.

Laslett, P., 1972, Mean household size in England since the 16th century, In: P. Laslett, *Household and family in Past Times*, Cambridge University Press, Cambridge, UK.

Latour, B., 1987, *Science in Action: How to Follow Scientists and Engineers Through Society*, Harvard University Press, Cambridge, MA.

Latour, B., 1996, *Aramis, or the Love of Technology*, MIT Press, Cambridge, MA.

Latour, B., 1999, On recalling ANT. In: J. Law and J. Hassard (Eds.), *Actor Network Theory and After*. Blackwell, Oxford, UK, pp. 15–25.

Latour, B. and Woolgar, S., 1986, *Laboratory Life: The Construction of Scientific Facts*, 2nd edn., Princeton University Press, Princeton, NJ.

Laursen, D., Please reply! The replying norm in adolescent SMS communication. In: R. Harper, A. Taylor, and L. Palen (Eds.), *The Inside Text: Social and Design Perspectives on SMS*, Springer, Berlin.

Lave, J. and Wenger, E., 1991, *Situated Learning: Legitimate Peripheral Participation*, Cambridge University Press, Cambridge, UK.

Law, J., 1991, (Ed.), *A Sociology of Monsters? Essays on Power, Technology and Domination*. Routledge, London.

Law, J., 1992a, Notes on the theory of the actor-network: Ordering, strategy and heterogeneity, *Syst. Pract.* 5: 379–393.

Law, J., 1992b, The Olympus 320 engine: A case study in design, development, and organisational control. *Technol. Cult.* 33: 409–440.

Law, J., 1994, *Organizing Modernity*, Blackwell, Oxford.

Law, J., 1997, Traduction/Trahison: Notes on ANT, Department of Sociology, Lancaster University.

Law, J., 1999, After ANT: Topology, naming and complexity. In J. Law and J. Hassard (Eds.) *Actor Network Theory and After*. Blackwell and the *Sociol. Rev.* Oxford and Keele, 1–14.

Law, J. and Hassard, J., (Eds.), 1999, *Actor Network Theory and After*, Blackwell, Oxford, UK.

Lee, J. and Watson, R., 1993, Social interaction in urban public space – Final Report Plan Urbain Project, Manchester University.

Lee, R.M. and Fielding, N., 1996, Qualitative data analysis: Representations of a technology: A comment on Coffey, Holbrook and Atkinson, *Sociol. Res. Online*, 1(4).

Leont'ev, A.N., 1974, The problem of activity in psychology, *Sov. Psychol.* 13(2):4–33 and reprinted, 1981, in: J.V. Wertsch (Ed.), *The Concept of Activity in Soviet Psychology*, M.E. Sharpe, Armonk, NY.

Leont'ev, A.N., 1981, *Problems of the Development of Mind*, Progress, Moscow.

Locke, K.D., 2000, *Grounded Theory in Management Research* (SAGE Series in Management Research), London, Sage.

Lofland, L., 1976, *Doing Social Life: The Qualitative Study of Human Interaction in Natural Settings*, Wiley, New York.

Lyas, C., 1999, *Peter Winch*, Acumen, Teddington, UK.

Lynch, M., 1993, *Scientific practice and ordinary action: Ethnomethodology and social studies of science*, Cambridge University Press, Cambridge, UK.

MacKenzie, D. and Wajcman, J. (Eds.), 1985, *The Social Shaping of Technology*, Open University Press, Milton Keynes, UK.

MacMillan, K. and McLachlan, S., 1999, Theory-building with Nud.Ist: Using computer assisted qualitative analysis in a media case study, *Sociol. Res. Online*, 4(2).

Malinowski, B., 1922, *Argonauts of the Western Pacific; An Account of Native Enterprise and Adventure in the Archipelagoes of Melanesian New Guinea*, reprinted 1984, Waveland Press, Long Grove, IL.

Malinowski, B., 1929, *The Sexual Life of Savages in North-Western Melanesia; An Ethnographic Account of Courtship, Marriage and Family Life Among the Natives of the Trobriand Islands*, Halcyon House, New York.

Malinowski, B., 1935, *Coral Gardens and Their Magic; A Study of the Methods of Tilling the Soil and of Agricultural Rites in the Trobriand Islands*, Woodstock GA. American Book.

Malinowski, B., 1967, *A Diary in the Strict Sense of the Term*, Routledge and Kegan Paul, London, reprinted 1989, Stanford University Press, Stanford, CA.

Malone, T., 1995, Commentary on Suchman article and Winograd response. *CSCW: Int. J.*, 3(1): 37–38.

Marcus, G., 1998, *Ethnography Through Thick and Thin*, Princeton University Press, Princeton, NJ.

Marcus, G. and Fischer, M., 1986, *Anthropology as Cultural Critique*, University of Chicago Press, Chicago.

Markus, M. and Connolly, T., 1990, Why CSCW applications fail: Problems in the adoption of interdependent work tools. In: *Proceedings of Conference on Computer-Supported Cooperative Work (CSCW '90)*, ACM Press, New York.

Marr, L., Francis, D., and Randall, D., 1999, 'The Soccer Game' as journalistic work: Managing the production of stories about a football club. In: P. Jalbert (Ed.), *Media Studies: Ethnomethodological Approaches*, University Press of America, New York, pp. 111–133.

Martin, B., 1984, Mother wouldn't like it!: Housework as magic, *Theor. Cult. Soc.* 2(2): 19–36.

Martin, D. and Bowers, J., 1999, Informing collaborative information visualisation through an ethnography of ambulance control. In: S. Bodker, M. Kyng, and K. Schmidt (Eds.), *Proceedings of the Sixth European Conference on Computer Supported Cooperative Work*, Copenhagen, Denmark, Kluwer, Amsterdam.

Martin, D., Bowers, J., and Wastell, D., 1997, The interactional affordances of technology: An ethnography of human–computer interaction in an ambulance control center. In: *People and Computers XII, Proceedings of HCI '97*, Springer-Verlag, London.

Martin, D., Rodden, T., Rouncefield, M., and Sommerville, I., and Viller, S., 2001, Finding patterns in the fieldwork. In: *Proceedings of ECSCW '01*, Kluwer, Bonn, pp. 39–58.

Martin, D., Rouncefield, M., and Sommerville, I., 2003, Informing the RE process with patterns of cooperative interaction, *Int. Arab J. Inf. Technol.*, 1(1).

Mateas, M., Salvador, T., Scholtz, J., and Sorensen, D., 1996, Engineering ethnography in the home. In: *Proceedings of CHI 96*, ACM Press, New York.

Matza, D., 1969, *Becoming Deviant*, Prentice-Hall, Englewood Cliffs, NJ.

May, T. 2000, Reflexivity in social life and sociological practice: A rejoinder to roger slack, *Sociol. Res. Online*, 5(1).

McCall, G.J. and Simmons, J.L. (Eds.), 1969, *Issues in Participant Observation: A Text and Reader*, Addison-Wesley, Reading, MA.

McRobbie, A. (Ed.), 1991, *Feminism and Youth Culture*, MacMillan, London.

Mead, M., 1973, *Coming of Age in Samoa: A Psychological Study of Primitive Youth for Western Civilization*, American Museum of Natural History, New York.

Michael, M., 1998, Co(a)gency and the car: Attributing agency in the case of the 'road rage', In: B. Brenna, J. Law, and I. Moser (Eds.) *Machines, Agency and Desire*. TMV, University of Oslo, pp. 125–141.

Middleton, D. and Engestrom, Y., 1995, *Cognition and Communication at Work*, Cambridge University Press, London.

Miller, E.J. and Gwynne, G.V., 1972, *A Life Apart: Pilot Study of Residential Institutions for the Physically Handicapped and the Young Chronic Sick (Soc. Sci. Pbs.)*, Tavistock, London.

Miner, H., 1956, Body ritual among the Nacirema, *Am. Anthropol.* **58**: 503–507.

Monteiro, E., 2000, Actor–network theory. In: C. Ciborra (Ed.), *From Control to Drift*, Oxford University Press, Oxford, pp. 71–83.

Monteiro, E., Actor network theory and cultural aspects of interpretive studies. Available at http://www.idi.ntnu.no/~ericm/LSE.draft.htm

Monteiro, E. and Hanseth, O., 1996, Social shaping of information infrastructure: On being specific about the technology. In: W. Orlikowski, G. Walsham, M.R Jones, and J. DeGross (Eds.), *Information Technology and Changes in Organisational Work*, Chapman and Hall, London.

Mort, M., 2003, *Building the Trident Network: A Study of the Enrollment of People, Knowledge and Machines*. MIT Press. Cambridge, MA.

Mozer, M.C., 1998, The neural network house: An environment that adapts to its inhabitants. In: M. Coen (Ed), *Proceedings of the American Association for Artificial Intelligence Spring Symposium*, AAAI Press, Menlo Park, CA, pp. 100–114.

Mumford, E., 1983, *Designing Human Systems*, Manchester Business School, UK.

Mumford, L., 1963, *Technics and Civilization*, Harcourt Brace, New York.

Murray, S., 1990, On Boasians and Margaret Mead: Reply to Freeman, *Curr. Anthropol.* **32**: 448–452.

Nardi, B., 1996b, Studying context: A comparison of activity theory, situated action models, and distributed cognition. In: B.A. Nardi (Ed.), *Context and Consciousness: Activity and Human–Computer Interaction*, MIT Press, Cambridge, MA and London.

Nardi, B. and Redmiles, D., 2002, Special Issue on Activity Theory and the Practice of Design, *CSCW: J. Collab. Comput.* **11**(1–2).

Nardi, B., Whittaker, S., and Shwartz, H., 2002, NetWORKers and their activity in intensional networks. In: B. Nardi and D. Redmiles (Eds.), Special Issue on Activity Theory and the Practice of Design, *CSCW: J. Collab. Comput.* **11**(1–2).

Nardi, B.A. (Ed.), 1996a, *Context and Consciousness: Activity and Human–Computer Interaction*, MIT Press, Cambridge, MA and London.

Nardi, B.A., 1996c, Activity theory and human computer interaction. In: B.A. Nardi, (Ed.), *Context and Consciousness: Activity and Human–Computer Interaction*, MIT Press, Cambridge, MA and London.

Nardi, B.A. and Miller, J.R., 1990, An ethnographic study of distributed problem solving in spreadsheet development. In: *Proceedings of CSCW '90 Conference on Computer-Supported Cooperative Work*, ACM Press, New York, pp. 197–208.

Neustaedter, C. and Brush, A., 2006, LINC-ing the family: The participatory design of a linkable family calendar. In: *Proceedings of CHI '06*, Montreal, ACM Press, New York.

Nielson, J.F. and Relsted, N.J., 1993, The new agenda for user participation: Reconsidering the old Scandinavian perspective. In: *Proceedings of the Sixteenth IRIS Conference*, Copenhagen.

Noblit, G.W. and Hare, R.D., 1988, *Meta-Ethnography: Synthesizing Qualitative Studies*, Sage, Newbury Park, CA.

Norman, D.A., 2002, *The Invisible Computer*, Basic, New York.

Norman, D.A., 2004, *Emotional Design: Why We Love (or Hate) Everyday Things*, Basic, New York.

Normark, M. and Randall, D., 2005, Local expertise at an emergency call centre. In: *Proceedings of ECSCW '05*, 18–22 September, Paris, Springer, New York.

O'Brien, B., 1992, *Demands and Decisions*, Prentice-Hall, Englewood Cliffs, NJ.

O'Brien, J., 1999, Informing CSCW systems design; Theory, practice and the paradigm of 'the workaday world', Unpublished PhD thesis – Departments of Sociology and Computing, Lancaster University.

O'Brien, J. and Rodden, T., 1997, Interactive systems in domestic environments. In: *Proceedings of DIS '97*, ACM Press, Amsterdam, NL, pp. 247–259.

O'Brien, J., Hughes, J., Ackerman, M., and Hindus, M., 1996, Workshop on extending CSCW into domestic environments. In: *Proceedings of CSCW '96*, November 1996, p. 1.

O'Brien, J., Rodden, T., Rouncefield, M., and Hughes, J., 1999, At home with the technology: An ethnographic study of a set-top-box trial, *ACM Trans. Comput. Hum. Interact.* **6**(3, Sept.): 232–308.

O'Hara, K. and Sellen, A.J., 1997, A comparison of reading on-line and paper documents. In: *Proceedings of CHI '97*, Atlanta, GA, ACM Press, New York, pp. 335–342.

O'Hara, K., Harper, R., Unger, A., Wilkes, J., Sharpe, B., and Jansen, M., 2005, TextBoard: from text-to-person to text-to-home. In: *Proceedings of CHI 2005*, April 02–07, ACM Press, New York, pp. 1705–1708.

Oliver, M., 1992, Changing the social relations of research production? *Disability Handicap Soc.*, 7(2).

Orlikoski, W., 1992, Learning from notes: Organizational issues in groupware implementation. In: *Proceedings of ACM '92 Conference on Computer Supported Cooperative Work*, Toronto.

Orr, J.E., 1996, *Talking About Machines: An Ethnography of a Modern Job*, ILR Press, Ithaca, NY.

Padilla, R., 1991, Using computers to develop concept models of social situations, *Qualitat. Sociol.*, 14(3).

Park, R., 1952, *Human Communities: The City and Human Ecology*, Free Press, Glencoe, IL.

Park, R. and Burgess, E., 1921, *Introduction to the Science of Sociology*, University of Chicago Press, Chicago.

Park, R., Burgess, E., and McKenzie, R., 1925, *The City*, University of Chicago Press, Chicago.

Parsons, T., 1937, *The Structure of Social Action*, Free Press, New York.

Patching, D., 1990, *Practical Soft Systems Analysis*, Pitman, Guildford, UK.

Peppard, J. (Ed.), 1993, *IT Strategy for Business*, Pitman, Guildford, UK.

Perrow, C., 1972, *Complex Organizations: A Critical Essay*, Scott, Foresman, Glenview, IL.

Perrow, C., 1984, *Normal Accidents: Living with High-Risk Technologies*, Basic, New York.

Peters, T. and Waterman, R.H., 1982, *In Search of Excellence*, Harper and Row, New York.

Petersson, M., Randall, D., and Helgeson, B., 2002, Ambiguities, awareness and economy: A study of emergency services work. In: *Proceedings of CSCW '02*, New Orleans, LA, ACM Press, New York, pp. 286–295.

Piercy, M., 1980, *Vida*, Penguin, Harmondsworth, UK.

Pinker, S., 1997, *How The Mind Works*, Allen Lane the Penguin Press, Harmondsworth, UK.

Pinker, S., 2002, *The Blank Slate: Denying Human Nature in Modern Life*, Allen Lane, London.

Plaisant, C., Bederson, B., Clamage, A., Hutchinson, H., and Guimbretière, F., 2003, Shared family calendars: Promoting symmetry and accessibility, *Tech Rep HCIL-2003-38*, University of Maryland.

Plowman, L., Rogers, Y., and Ramage, M., 1995, What are workplace studies for ? In: *Proceedings of ECSCW '95*, Stockholm, Kluwer Academic, Dordrecht.

Polanyi, M., 1966, *The Tacit Dimension*, Doubleday, New York.

Pollner, M., 1974, Mundane Reasoning, *Philos. Social Sci.*, 4: 35–54.

Pomerantz, A., 1984, Agreeing and disagreeing with assessments: Some features of preferred/ dispreferred turn shapes. In: J.M. Atkinson and J. Heritage (Eds.), *Structures of Social Actions: Studies in Conversation Analysis*, Cambridge University Press, Cambridge, UK.

Pontecorvo, C. and Burge, B. (Eds.), *Discourse, Tools and Reasoning: Essays on Situated Cognition*, Springer-Verlag, Berlin, pp. 41–62.

Popper, K., 1968, *The Logic of Scientific Discovery*, Hutchinson, London.

Procter, R.N. and Williams, R.A., 1992, HCI: Whose problem is it anyway? In: *Proceeding of the Fifth IFIP WG2.7 Working Conference on Engineering for Human-Computer Interaction*, Ellivuori, Finland, 10–14 August, Elsevier Science, Amsterdam.

Pycock, J., 1999, *Designing Systems: Studies of Design Practice*, Unpublished PhD, Manchester University.

Raeithel, A., 1992, Activity theory as a foundation for design. In: C. Floyd, H. Züllighoven, R. Budde, and R. Keil-Slawik (Eds.), *Software Development and Reality Construction*, Springer, Berlin, pp. 391–415.

Randall, D., 1995, A comment on Lucy Suchman's 'Do Categories Have Politics?' CSCW, 3(1): 47–50.

Randall, D., 2002, Home is where the heart is: A sociological view of location. In: R. Harper (Ed.), *Proceedings of the Third International Conference: Social Shaping of Mobile Futures*, University of Surrey.

Randall, D. and Hughes, J.A., 1995, CSCW, sociology, and working with customers. In: P. Thomas (Ed.), *The Social and Interactional Dimensions of Human–Computer Interfaces*, Cambridge University Press, Cambridge, UK, pp. 142–160.

Randall, D., Harper, R., and Rouncefield, M., 2005, Fieldwork and ethnography: A perspective from CSCW. In: *Proceedings of the First International Ethnographic Praxis in Industry and Commerce (Epic) Conference*, Redmond, WA, pp. 81–99.

Randall, D., Hughes, J., and Rouncefield, M., 1995b, Chalk and cheese: BPR and ethnomethodologically informed ethnography. In: *Proceedings of ECSCW '95*, Stockholm.

Randall, D., Hughes, J., and Shapiro, D., 1993, Systems development – The fourth dimension: Perspectives on the social organization of work. In: P. Quintas (Ed.), *Social Dimensions of Systems Engineering: People, Processes, Policies and Software Development*, Ellis Horwood, Hemel Hempstead, UK, pp. 197–214.

Randall, D., Marr, L., and Rouncefield, M., 2001, *Ethnography, Ethnomethodology and Interaction Analysis, Ethnographic Studies*, vol. 6, November, Manchester Metropolitan University, Manchester.

Randall, D., O'Brien, J., Rouncefield, M., and Hughes, J.A., 1996, Organzational memory and CSCW: supporting the 'Mavis' phenomenon. In: *Proceedings of the Sixth Australian Conference on HCI (OzCHI '96)*.

Randall, D., Twidale, M., and Bentley, R., 1997, Dealing with uncertainty – Perspectives on the evaluation process. In: P. Thomas (Ed.), *CSCW Requirements and Evaluation*. Springer. London.

Rasmussen, J., 1988, Human error mechanisms in complex work environments, *Reliability Eng. Syst. Safety*, **22**: 155–167.

Reddy, M. and Dourish, P., 2002, A finger on the pulse: Temporal rhythms and information seeking in medical work. In: *Proceedings of CSCW '02*, New Orleans, ACM Press, New York.

Richards, T.J. and Richards, L., 1991, The NUDIST System, *Qualitat. Sociol.*, **14**: 289–306.

Richards, L. and Richards, T.J., 1994a, From filing cabinet to computer. In: A. Bryman and R.G. Burgess (Eds.), *Analyzing Qualitative Data*, Sage, London.

Richards, T.J. and Richards, L., 1994b, Using computers in qualitative analysis. In: N. Denzin and Y. Lincoln (Eds.), *Handbook of Qualitative Research*, Sage, Berkeley, CA, pp. 445–462.

Rittel, H. and Webber, M., 1973, Dilemnas in a general theory of planning, *Policy Sci.* **4**: 155–169.

Rivett, P., 1983, A world in which nothing ever happens twice, *J. Oper. Res. Soc.* **34** (8): 677–683.

Robertson, T., 1998, Shoppers and tailors: Participative practices in small Australian design companies, *CSCW: J. Collab. Comput.* 7(3–4): 205–221.

Rogers, Y., Integrating CSCW in evolving organizations. In: *Proceedings of CSCW '94*, ACM Press, New York, pp. 67–78.

Rosenhan, D.L., 1973, Being sane in insane places. *Science*, **179**: 250–258.

Rouncefield, M., Hughes, J., O'Brien, J., and Rodden, T., 2000, Designing for the home, *Pers. Technol.* Special Issue on Home Life, vol 4, pp. 76–94.

Rouncefield, M., Hughes, J., Rodden, T., and Viller, S., 1994, Working with 'constant interruption': CSCW and the small office. In: R. Futura and C. Neuwirth (Eds.), *Proceedings of CSCW '94*, ACM Press, New York.

Ruhleder, K. and Jordan, B., 1999, Meaning making across remote sites: How delays in transmission affect interaction. In: S. Bodker, M. Kyng, and K. Schmidt (Eds.), *Proceedings of the Sixth European Conference on Computer Supported Co-operative Work*, 12–16 September, Copenhagen, Kluwer Academic, Dordrecht.

Ryle, G., 1963, *The Concept of Mind*, Penguin, Harmondsworth, UK.

Sacks, H., 1972, Notes on the police assessment of moral character. In: D. Sudnow (Ed.), *Studies in Social Interaction*, Free Press, New York, pp. 280–293.

Sacks, H., 1984a, Notes on methodology. In: J.M. Atkinson and J. Heritage (Eds.), *Structures of Social Actions: Studies in Conversation Analysis*, Cambridge University Press, Cambridge, UK.

Sacks, H., 1984b, On doing "Being Ordinary". In: J.M. Atkinson and J. Heritage (Eds.), *Structures of Social Actions: Studies in Conversation Analysis*, Cambridge University Press, Cambridge, UK.

Sacks, H., 1992, *Lectures in Conversation*, G. Jefferson (Ed.), Blackwell, Oxford, UK.

Sacks, H., Schegloff, E.A., and Jefferson, G., 1978, A simplest systematics for the organization of turn-raking for conversation. In: J.N. Schenken, (Ed.), *Studies in the Organization of Conversational Interaction*, Academic Press, New York.

Said, E., 1978, *Orientalism*, Pantheon, New York.

Salaman, R., 1949, *The History and Social Influence of the Potato*, Cambridge University Press, Cambridge, UK.

Salvendy, G. (Ed.), 1987, *The Handbook of Human Factors*, John Wiley, New York/Chichester.

Sandberg, O., 1975, Harmony and conflict perspectives in system development work (Harmoni – och konfliktperspektiv i systemutvecklingsarbetet). In: *The Aarhus Conference*, Arbejdsformer i systemudviklingpp, pp. 237–265.

Sanne, J., 1999, *Creating Safety in Air Traffic Control*, Arkiv, Lund, Sweden.

Sayer, A., 1992, *Method in Social Science: A Realist Approach*, Routledge, London.

Schegloff, E., 1972, Notes on a conversational practice: Formulating place. In: D. Sudnow (Ed.), *Studies in Social Interaction*, New York, Free Press, pp. 75–119.

Schegloff, E. and Sacks, H., 1973, Opening up closings, *Semiotica*, 8(4): 289–327.

Schegloff, E., Jefferson, G., and Sacks, H., 1977, The preference for self correction in the organization of repair for conversation, *Language*, 53: 361–382.

Schein, E.H., 1985, *Organizational Culture and Leadership*, Jossey-Bass, San Francisco.

Schensul, S. and Schensul, J., 1999, *Essential Ethnographic Methods Observations, Interviews, and Questionnaires: Observations, Interviews, and Questionnaires (The Ethnographer's Toolkit)*, Sage, London.

Schensul, J., LeCompte, M.D., Nastasi, B.K., and Borgatti, S.P., 1999, *Enhanced Ethnographic Methods: Audiovisual Techniques, Focused Group Interviews, and Elicitation Techniques (The Ethnographer's Toolkit)*, Sage, London.

Schlager, M.S., Means, B., and Roth, C., 1990, Cognitive task analysis for the real (-time) world. In: *Proceedings of the Human Factors Society 34th Annual General meeting*, Human Factors Society, Santa Monica, CA, pp. 1309–1313.

Schmidt, K., 1991, Riding a tiger, or computer supported cooperative work. In: *Proceedings of the Second European Conference on CSCW*, Dordrecht, Kluwer.

Schmidt, K., 1993, Initial notes on mechanisms of interaction. COMIC Working Paper, Riso-3-1. Riso National Laboratory.

Schmidt, K., 1997, Of maps and scripts: The status of formal constructs in cooperative work. In: *Proceedings of GROUP 1997*, ACM Press, New York.

Schmidt, K., 2002, The problem with 'awareness': Introductory remarks on 'awareness in CSCW', *CSCW: J. Collab. Comput.* 11(3–4): 285–298.

Schmidt, K. and Bannon, L., 1992, Taking CSCW seriously: Supporting articulation work, *CSCW: Int. J.*, 1(1–2): 7–40.

Schmidt, K., Heath, C., and Rodden, T. (Eds.), 2002, *CSCW: J. Collab. Comput.*, Special Issue on Awareness in CSCW, 11(3–4).

Schutz, A., 1970, *Reflections on the Problem of Relevance*, Yale University Press, New Haven, CT.

Schutz, A., 1972, *The Phenomenology of the Social World*, Heinemann, London.

Schutz, A., 1972, Subjectivity and typification: A note on method in the social sciences, *Philosophy of the Social Sciences*, 2: 167–176.

Searle, J., 1995, *The Construction of Social Reality*, Allen Lane, Penguin Press, London and New York.

Seidel, J. and Clark, J., 1984, The ethnograph: A computer program for the analysis of qualitative data. *Qualitat. Sociol.*, 7 (1/2).

Seidel, J., Kjolseth, R., and Seymour, E., 1988, *The Ethnograph: A User's Guide*, Qualis Research Associates, Littleton, CO.

Sellen, A.J. and Harper, R., 2002, *The Myth of the Paperless Office*. Cambridge, Mass. MIT Press.

Selznick, P., 1948, Foundations of the theory of organization, *Amer. Sociol. Rev.*, 13: 25–35.

Shakespeare, T., 1993, Disabled people's self-organisation: A new social movement? *Disability, Handicap Soc.*, 8(3): 24 –264.

Shapiro, D., 1994, The limits of ethnography: Combining social sciences for CSCW. In: *Proceedings of CSCW '94*, Chapel Hill, NC, ACM Press, New York.

Shapiro, D., Hughes, J.A., Randall, D., and Harper, R., 1994, Visual re-representation of database information: The flight data strip in air traffic control. In: M. Tauber, D.E. Mahling, and F. Arefi (Eds.), *Cognitive Aspects of Visual Languages and Visual Interfaces*, Elsevier, The Hague.

Sharrock, W., 1995, Issues in ethnography: Ethnomethodology and constructionism, *COMIC document*, MAN-2-4.

Sharrock, W. and Anderson, R., 1982, The demise of the native, *Hum. Stud.* 15: 2.

Sharrock, W. and Anderson, R., 1991, Epistemology: professional scepticism, In: G. Button (Ed.), *Ethnomethodology and the Human Sciences*, Routledge, London.

Sharrock, W. and Randall, D., 2004, Ethnography, Ethnomethodology and the problem of generalization in design, *European Journal of Information Systems*, 13(3): 186–194.

Shaw, C.R., 1930, *The Jack Roller. A Delinquent Boy's Own Story*, University of Chicago Press, Chicago, London.

Shaw, C.R., 1931, *The Natural History of a Delinquent Career*, Albert Saifer, Philadelphia.

Schegloff, E.A., Jefferson, G., and Sacks, H., 1977, The preference for self-correction in the organization of repair in conversation. In: G. Psathas (Ed.), *Interactional Competence*, University Press of America, Washington DC.

Silverman, D., 1985, *Qualitative Methodology & Sociology*, Gower, Aldershot, UK.

Silverman, D., 2000, *Doing Qualitative Research: A Practical Handbook*, Sage, London.

Silverman, D., 2001, *Interpreting Qualitative Data: Methods for Analysing Talk, Text and Interaction*, Sage, London.

Silverman, D. and Jones, S., 1976, *Organizational Work*, Collier Macmillan, London.

Simonsen, J. and Kensing, F., 1997, Using ethnography in contextual design, *Commun. ACM*, 40(7): 82–88.

Slack, R., 2000, Reflexivity of sociological practice? A Reply to May, *Sociolog. Res. Online*, 5.

Solheim, I., 2002, Talk, silence and the study of situated action, *Proceedings of CSCL 2002*, Boulder, CO.

Sommerville, I., 1992, *Software Engineering*, 4th edn., Addison-Wesley, New York.

Sommerville, I., Rodden, T., Sawyer, P., Twidale, M., and Bentley, R., 1993, Incorporating ethnographic data into the systems requirement process. In: *Proceedings of RE 93: International Symposium on Requirements Engineering*, January 4–6, IEEE Press, San Diego, pp. 165–174.

Spasser, M.A., 2002, Realist activity theory for digital library evaluation: Conceptual framework and case study, *CSCW: Int. J.*, 11(1/2): 81–110. Also available at: *http://www.ics.uci.edu/~redmiles/activity/final -issue/Spasser/Spasser.doc*

Stanley, L., 1990, Doing ethnography, writing ethnography: A Comment on Hammersley, *Sociology*, 24: 617–627.

Star, S.L., 1991. Power, technologies and the phenomenology of convention: On being allergic to onions. In: J. Law (Ed.), *A Sociology of Monsters*, Routledge, London, pp. 26–56.

Sterelny, K., 1990, *The Representational Theory of Mind: An Introduction*, Blackwell, Oxford, UK.

Strauss, A. and Corbin, J., 1990, *Basics of Qualitative Research: Techniques and Procedures for Developing Grounded Theory*, Sage, London.

Suchman, L., 1983, Office procedures as a practical activity: Models of work and system design, *Trans. Office Automat. Syst.* 1(4): 320–328.

Suchman, L., 1988, Designing with the user, review of computers and democracy: A Scandinavian challenge. In: G. Bjerknes, P. Ehn, and M. Kyng (Eds.), *TOOIS*, 6(2): 173–183.

Suchman, L., 1993, Centers of coordination: A case and some themes. In: R. Säljö, C. Pontecorvo, and B. Burge (Eds.), *Discourse, Tools and Reasoning: Essays on Situated Cognition*, Springer-Verlag, Berlin, pp. 41–62.

Suchman, L., 1994, Do categories have politics? *J. CSCW*, 2(3).

Suchman, L., 1995, Making work visible, Special Issue of *CACM*, 38(9): 56–64.

Suchman, L., 2000, Making a case: Knowledge and 'routine' in document production. In: C. Heath, J. Hindmarsh, and P. Luff, (Eds.), *Workplace Studies: Recovering Work Practice and Informing System Design*, Cambridge University Press, Cambridge, UK.

Suchman, L., Beeman, W., Pear, M., Trigg, R., Fox, B., and Smolensky, P., 1987, Social science and system design: Interdisciplinary collaborations. In: *Proceedings of ACM CHI+GI'87 Conference on Human Factors in Computing Systems and Graphics Interface*, pp. 121–123.

Suchman, L.A., 1987, *Plans and Situated Actions: The Problem of Human-Computer Communication*, Cambridge University Press, New York.

Tallerico, M., 1991, Application of qualitative analysis software: A view from the field *Qualitati. Sociol.* 14(3).

Tang, J.C., 1991, Findings from observational studies of collaborative work, *Int. J. Man Mach. Stud.* (Special edition on CSCW & groupware), 34(2): 143–160, Republished in Greenberg, 1991.

Taylor A. and Swann. L , 2004, List making in the home. In: *Proceedings of CHI '04*, ACM Press, New York.

Taylor, A., Harper, R., Swann, L., Izadi, S., Sellen, A., Perry, M., 2006, Homes that make us smart, *J. Pers. Technol.*, Springer, Godalming.

Taylor, A.S. and Swan, L., 2005, Artful systems in the home. In: *Proceedings of CHI '05*, ACM Press, New York.

Ten Have, P., 1999, *Doing Conversation Analysis: A Practical Guide*, Sage, London.

Tesch, R., 1991, Software for qualitative researchers. In: R. Lee and N. Fielding (Eds.), *Using Computers in Qualitative Research*. Sage, London.

Thomas, W.I. and Znaniecki, F., 1927, *The Polish Peasant in Europe and America* (2nd edn.) Alfred A. Knopf, New York (originally published in 5 vols. Richard G. Badger, Boston, 1918–1920) (Vol. I and II originally published by the University of Chicago Press, 1918). Reprinted 1958, 2 vols., Dover, New York.

Thompson, H., 1966, *Hells Angels: The Strange and Terrible Saga of the Outlaw Motorcycle Gangs*, New York, Random House.

Thompson, P., 1989, *The Nature of Work: An Introduction to Debates on the Labour Process* (2nd edn.), Macmillan, London.

Tolmie, P., Pycock, J., Diggins, T., Maclean, A., and Karsenty, A., 2002, Unremarkable computing, in: *Proceedings of CHI '02*, ACM Press, New York, pp. 399–406.

Trist, E.L. and Bamforth, K.W., 1951, Some social and psychological consequences of the long-wall method of coal getting, *Hum. Relations* 4:3–38 and in D.S. Pugh (Ed.), 1990, *Organization Theory*, Penguin, New York.

Turow, J. and Kavanaugh, A., 2003, *The Wired Homestead*, MIT Press, Boston, MA.

Twidale, M., Randall, D., and Bentley, R., 1994, Situated evaluation for cooperative systems. In: *Proceedings of CSCW '94*, Chapel Hill, NC, ACM Press, New York.

Twidale, M., Rodden, T., and Sommerville I., 1993, The Designers Notepad: Supporting and understanding cooperative designers. In: *Proceedings of ECSCW '93*, Milan, September 13–17, 1993, Kluwer Academic Press, Dordrecht.

Vanek, J., 1978, Household technology and social status, *Technology and Culture*, 19: 361–375.

Venkatesh, A., 1996, Computers and other interactive technologies for the home, *Commun. ACM*, 39(12, December).

Venkatesh, A., 2005, The tech enabled networked home: An analysis of current trends and future promise. In: W. Dutton, B. Kahin, et al. (Eds.), *Transforming Enterprise*, MIT Press, Cambridge, MA.

Venkatesh, A., Chen, S., and Gonzalez, V., 2005, Designing the family portal for home networking. In: R. Kraut, M. Brynin, and S. Kiesler (Eds.), *Domesticating Information Technologies*, Oxford University Press, Oxford, UK.

Venkatesh, A., Kruse E., and Shih, C., 2003, The networked home: an analysis of current developments and future trends, *Cogn. Technol. Work*, 5(1):23–32.

Vetere, F., Gibbs, M., Kjeldskov, J., Howard, S., Mueller, F., Pedell, S, Mecoles, K., and Bunyan, M., 2005, Mediating intimacy: Designing technologies to support strong-tie relationships. In: *Proceedings of CHI '05*, ACM Press, New York.

Vicente, K., 1999, *Cognitive Work Analysis*, Erlbaum, Hillsdale, NJ.

Viller, S. and Sommerville, I., 1997, Coherence: social analysis for software engineers, Lancaster University.

Vygotsky, L.S., 1978, *Mind and Society*, Harvard University Press, Cambridge, MA.

Vygotsky, L.S., 1982, *Thought and Language*, Cambridge, MA: MIT Press.

Wajcman, J., 1991, *Feminism confronts Technology*, Cambridge: Polity Press.

Walker, B.L., 1993. Computer analysis of qualitative data: A comparison of three packages. *Qualitative Health Res.* 3(1): 91–111.

Walsham, G., 1997, Actor-network theory and IS research: Current status and future prospects. In: A. Lee, A.J. Liebenau, and J. DeGross (Eds.), *Information Systems and Qualitative Research*, Chapman and Hall, London.

Watts, J.C., Woods, D.D., Corban, J.M., and Pattersson, E.S., 1996, Voice loops as cooperative aids in space shuttle mission control. In: *Proceedings of the Conference on Computer Supported Cooperative Work* (CSCW '96), M.S. Ackerman, Cambridge, MA, ACM Press, New York, pp. 48–56.

Wax, R.H., 1971, *Doing Fieldwork: Warnings and Advice*, University of Chicago Press, Chicago.

Weber, M., 1947, *The Theory of Social and Economic Organisation*, New York: The Free Press.

Weitzman, E. and Miles, M.B., 1995, *Computer Programs for Qualitative Analysis: A Software Sourcebook*, Sage. London.

Wellman, B., 1998, A computer network is a social network, *SIGGROUP Bull.*, 19(3, December):41–45.

Wellman, B., 2000a, Designing the Internet for a networked society: Little boxes, glocalisation, and networked individualism, *Commun. ACM* (May).

319

Wellman, B., 2000b, Changing Connectivity: A future history of Y2.03K, *Sociological Research Online*, vol 4, no 4.

Wertsch J., 1981, The concept of activity in Soviet psychology: An introduction. In: J. Wertsch (Ed.), *The Concept of Activity in Soviet Psychology*, M.E. Sharpe, Armonk, NY.

Whalen, J., 1995. Expert systems versus systems for experts: Computer-aided dispatch as a support system in real-world environments. In: P.J. Thomas, *The Social and Interactional Dimensions of Human–Computer Interfaces*, Cambridge University Press, Cambridge, UK.

Wiener, E. and Nagel, D., 1988, *Human Factors in Aviation*, Academic Press, San Diego.

Williams, M., 2000, *Science and Social Science: An Introduction*, Routledge, London.

Williams, R. and Edge, D., 1996, The social shaping of technology, *Res. Policy*, 25: 856–899.

Williamson, B., 1989, Review article: Sentiment and social change, *Sociol. Rev.*, 37(4).

Wilson, N.A.B., 1973, *On the Quality of Working Life*, Manpower Papers No.7, HMSO.

Winch, P., 1958, *The Idea of a Social Science*, Routledge and Kegan Paul, London.

Winch, P., 1972, *Ethics and Action*, Routledge and Kegan Paul, London.

Winograd, T. and Flores, F., 1986, *Understanding Computers and Cognition*, Ablex, Norwood, NJ.

Woolgar, S., 1987, Reconstructing man and machine: A note on sociological critiques of cognitivism. In: W.E. Bijker, T.P. Hughes, and T. Pinch, *The Social Construction of Technological Systems*, MIT Press, Cambridge, MA.

Woolgar, S., 1988, *Science: The Very Idea*, London, Routledge.

Woolgar, S. and Ashmore, M., 1988, *Knowledge and Reflexivity*, London. Sage.

Work in America, 1973, Report of a Special Taskforce to the Secretary of Health, Education and Welfare, MIT Press, Boston.

Yates, J., 1989, *Control through Communication: The Rise of System in American Management*, John Hopkins University Press, Baltimore.

Zerubavel, E. 1985, *Hidden Rhythms: Schedules and calendars in social life*. Berkeley. University of California Press.

Zisman, M.D., 1977, Representation, Specification and Automation of Office Procedures. Report from the Dept. of Decision Science, The Wharton School, University of Pennsylvania.

Author Index

Subject Index

A

Activity theory, 16, 61, 89–99
  activities and actions in, 92
  application of, 94–96
  approach to cognition, 95
  as conceptual tool, 91–92
  construction of context, 93–94
  elements of, 91, 93
  features of , 93–94
  and human computer interface (HCI), 90
  origin of, 89
  principles of learning technology, 95
Actor-Network theory (ANT), 16, 94,
    104–109
  design in terms of, 108
  development of network, 107
  elements, 106
  purpose and background, 105–106
  stages, 108
Actors, 106–107
Ad nauseam, 36
Affinity analysis, 30
Air Traffic Control study, 177
American sociology, 62
Analysis *vs.* Synthesis, 141
Anthropological tradition and fieldwork, 17
Antianthropology, 17
Appliance argument, 262–263
Artefacts as informational devices, 258
Artifact, kinds of, 225
Artificial intelligence, 217
Artefacts and ecologies in workplace,
    222–225
Artefacts in social organisation
  coordination and paperwork,
    226–228
  information lifecycles, 229–230
Artefacts, in home, 270–284
Automation in offices, apparent
    failure of, 217

B

Baby-monitoring equipment, 279
Behaviourism, 89
Behaviouristic model of human conduct, 24
Beyer and Holtzblatt's exposition, 29
Bias discounting, 226
Bureaucratic artifacts, 222
Business-led strategies, 2
Byzantine constructions, 287

C

Categorisation problems, 277
Central ecological artifacts, 227
Central server, 273
Chicago School, 23, 61, 146, 169
Cultural activity, 34
Culture, 29, 99–102
  conceptions of, 100
  'situatedness', 101
  physical artifacts, 102
  media usage, 103
Cognitive ergonomics and tradition,
    16, 22
Cognitive ethnography, 103
Cognitive work analysis, 19–22
  'artifact task cycle', 20
  complex sociotechnical systems, 19
  functions of, 22
  'intrinsic work constraints.', 21
  implications for, 20
  prototyping in, 21
Cognitivism, 36
Collaborative systems designing, 35–39
  coherence model, 38
  fieldwork-based investigations of, 35
  viewpoints analysis, 38
Common sense, 201
  'Three-Second' ethnography, 202
Communication, in ethnography, 293
Complex organisational settings, work in, 8

Out of print titles

Mark Sharples (Ed.)
Computer Supported Collaborative Writing
3-540-19782-6

Dan Diaper and Colston Sanger
CSCW in Practice
3-540-19784-2

Steve Easterbrook (Ed.)
CSCW: Cooperation or Conflict?
3-540-19755-9

John H. Connolly and
Ernest A. Edmonds (Eds)
CSCW and Artificial Intelligence
3-540-19816-4

Duska Rosenberg and
Chris Hutchison (Eds)
Design Issues in CSCW
3-540-19810-5

Peter Thomas (Ed.)
CSCW Requirements and Evaluation
3-540-19963-2

Peter Lloyd and Roger Whitehead (Eds)
Transforming Organisations Through
Groupware: Lotus Notes in Action
3-540-19961-6

John H. Connolly and Lyn Pemberton (Eds)
Linguistic Concepts and Methods in CSCW
3-540-19984-5

Alan Dix and Russell Beale (Eds)
Remote Cooperation
3-540-76035-0

Stefan Kirn and Gregory O'Hare (Eds)
Cooperative Knowledge Processing
3-540-19951-9

Reza Hazemi, Stephen Hailes
and Steve Wilbur (Eds)
The Digital University: Reinventing the
Academy
1-85233-090-2

Mary Lou Maher, Simeon J. Simoff and
Anna Cicognani
Understanding Virtual Design Studios
1-85233-154-2